Lecture Notes in Computer Science 7048

Commenced Publication in 1973
Founding and Former Series Editors:
Gerhard Goos, Juris Hartmanis, and Jan van Leeuwen

T0223391

Howard Leung   Elvira Popescu   Yiwei Cao
Rynson W.H. Lau   Wolfgang Nejdl (Eds.)

Advances in Web-Based Learning – ICWL 2011

10th International Conference
Hong Kong, China, December 8-10, 2011
Proceedings

 Springer

Volume Editors

Howard Leung
City University of Hong Kong
Kowloon Tong, Hong Kong, China
E-mail: howard@cityu.edu.hk

Elvira Popescu
University of Craiova
Software Engineering Department
200585, Craiova, Romania
E-mail: popescu_elvira@software.ucv.ro

Yiwei Cao
RWTH Aachen University, Informatik 5
52056 Aachen, Germany
E-mail: cao@dbis.rwth-aachen.de

Rynson W.H. Lau
City University of Hong Kong
Kowloon Tong, Hong Kong, China
E-mail: rynson@cs.cityu.edu.hk

Wolfgang Nejdl
Institut für Verteilte Systeme
Wissensbasierte Systeme (KBS)
30167 Hannover, Germany
E-mail: nejdl@kbs.uni-hannover.de

ISSN 0302-9743   e-ISSN 1611-3349
ISBN 978-3-642-25812-1   e-ISBN 978-3-642-25813-8
DOI 10.1007/978-3-642-25813-8
Springer Heidelberg Dordrecht London New York

Library of Congress Control Number: Applied for

CR Subject Classification (1998): H.4, H.3, I.2.6, H.5, K.3, D.2, I.2, J.1

LNCS Sublibrary: SL 3 – Information Systems and Application, incl. Internet/Web
and HCI

Typesetting: Camera-ready by author, data conversion by Scientific Publishing Services, Chennai, India

Printed on acid-free paper

Springer is part of Springer Science+Business Media (www.springer.com)

Preface

The first ICWL conference was held in Hong Kong in 2002. This year marked the 10th anniversary of our ICWL conference which was organized back in Hong Kong. ICWL has been held in Asia, Europe and Australia and aims to unite especially the Web-based learning communities of Europe and Asia-Pacific. Hong Kong (meaning "Fragrant Harbor" in Chinese) is an international city with a rich history embracing multi-culture from the West and the East. It stands for speedy development of economics and science of high quality.

This year we received around 100 papers for the main conference and the associated workshops. Based on the review comments and relevancy, we accepted a total of 27 full papers plus 9 short papers for the LNCS proceedings. The authors of these accepted papers came from five different continents resulting in a remarkable international diversity. More than half of the accepted papers were from Europe. This was the first time that we adopted the double blind review system which is a common practice in top-tier conferences. We would like to thank all the reviewers for providing valuable comments that aided significantly in the paper selection process. Authors of the best papers presented in this conference will be invited to submit extended versions of their papers for further review and possible publication in *IEEE Transactions on Learning Technologies* and *World Wide Web*.

We would like to thank the entire conference Organizing Committee for their hard work in putting the conference together. In particular, we would like to give a special thanks to our Registration Chair, Jiying (Jean) Wang, Local Arrangements Chair, Hao Yuan, and Sponsorship Chair, Hong Va Leong, for their very important support. Our Workshop Co-chairs, Dickson Chiu and Maggie Wang, liaised with different scholars to organize several workshops that were co-located with ICWL 2011. Furthermore, we would like to thank our Steering Committee representative, Qing Li, for his continuous reminding of various important issues.

We would like to thank all the authors of the submitted papers, whether accepted or not, for their contributions in maintaining a high-quality conference. We count on all your continual support in the future in making significant contributions to the Web-based learning community.

December 2011

Howard Leung
Elvira Popescu
Yiwei Cao
Rynson W.H. Lau
Wolfgang Nejdl

Organization

Organizing Committee

Conference Co-chairs

Rynson W.H. Lau   City University of Hong Kong
Wolfgang Nejdl   University of Hannover, Germany

Program Co-chairs

Howard Leung   City University of Hong Kong
Elvira Popescu   University of Craiova, Romania
Yiwei Cao   RWTH Aachen University, Germany

Workshop Co-chairs

Dickson Chiu   Dickson Computer Systems, Hong Kong
Maggie Wang   The University of Hong Kong

Tutorial Chair

Wenyin Liu   City University of Hong Kong

Sponsorship Chair

Hong Va Leong   The Hong Kong Polytechnic University

Registration Chair

Jiying Wang   City University of Hong Kong

Conference Secretary

Ping Huang   City University of Hong Kong

Local Arrangements Chair

Hao Yuan   City University of Hong Kong

Publicity Co-chairs

Frederick Li   University of Durham, UK
Hua Wang   University of Southern Queensland, Australia
Lizhe Wang   Indiana University, USA

Web and Media Chair

Edmond Ho   Hong Kong Baptist University, Hong Kong

Steering Committee Representatives

Qing Li	City University of Hong Kong
Timothy Shih	National Central University, Taiwan

International Programme Committee

Isabel Azevedo	Polytechnic of Porto, Portugal
Costin Badica	University of Craiova, Romania
Stephane Bressan	National University of Singapore, Singapore
Liz Burd	University of Durham, UK
Wing Kwong Chan	City University of Hong Kong
Dan Chen	University of Birmingham, UK
Wei Chen	Beijing Institute of Technology, China
Chi Yin Chow	City University of Hong Kong
Ulrike Cress	Knowledge Media Research Center, Germany
Dumitru Dan Burdescu	University of Craiova, Romania
Pieter De Vries	Delft University of Technology, The Netherlands
Giuliana Dettori	Institute for Educational Technology (ITD-CNR), Italy
Wanchun Dou	Nanjing University, China
Erik Duval	Katholieke Universiteit Leuven, Belgium
Sandy El Helou	EPFL, Switzerland
Baltasar Fernández-Manjón	Universidad Complutense de Madrid, Spain
Denis Gillet	EPFL, Switzerland
Carlo Giovannella	University of Rome Tor Vergata, Italy
Sabine Graf	Athabasca University, Canada
Christian Guetl	Technical University of Graz, Austria
Eelco Herder	L3S Research Center in Hannover, Germany
Edward Ho	The Hong Kong Polytechnic University, Hong Kong
Maria Grazia Ierardi	IMATI-CNR, Italy
Malinka Ivanova	TU Sofia, Bulgaria
Vana Kamtsiou	Brunel University, UK
Ioannis Kazanidis	Technological Educational Institute of Kavala, Greece
Michael Kickmeier-Rust	Graz University of Technology, Austria
Ralf Klamma	RWTH Aachen University, Germany
Tomaž Klobucar	Jožef Stefan Institute, Slovenia
Jun Kong	North Dakota State University, USA
Milos Kravcik	RWTH Aachen University, Germany
Barbara Kump	Graz University of Technology, Austria

Table of Contents

Computer Supported Cooperative Learning and Serious Gaming

Web 2.0 and Social Learning

Competence Development and Professional Training

Learner Modeling and Assessment

E-Learning Applications, Platforms, Tools, and Infrastructure

Learning Resource Management and Recommendation

Strategies Used by Students on a Massively Multiplayer Online Mathematics Game

Roberto Araya[1], Abelino Jiménez[1], Manuel Bahamondez[1], Pablo Dartnell[1,2],
Jorge Soto-Andrade[1], Pablo González[1], and Patricio Calfucura[1]

[1] Centro de Investigación Avanzada en Educación, Universidad de Chile,
Periodista José Carrasco Tapia 75, Santiago, Chile
[2] Centro de Modelamiento Matemático, Universidad de Chile,
Blanco Encalada 2120, 7° Piso, Santiago, Chile
robertoaraya@automind.cl

Abstract. We analyze the logs of an online mathematics game tournament, played simultaneously by thousands of students. Nearly 10,000 students, coming from 356 schools from all regions in Chile, registered to the fourth tournament instance. The children play in teams of 12 students from the same class, and send their personal bets to a central server every 2 minutes. Each competition lasts about one clock hour and takes place within school hours. Students are pre-registered and trained by their school teacher. The teacher is responsible for reviewing curriculum contents useful for improving performance at the game and coaches students participating in trial tournaments taking place a few weeks before the national tournament. All bets are recorded in a database that enables us to analyze later the sequence of bets made by each student. Using cluster analysis with this information, we have identified three types of players, each with a well-defined strategy.

Keywords: on-line tournaments, learning, data mining, algebra, statistics.

1   Introduction

One of the biggest problems in education concerns students affective states, as great motivation is needed to exercise and practice constantly to be able to master the concepts and procedures taught at school. However, the classroom is, for many, too flat and uniform. In particular, mathematics classes are usually the least attractive [15]. Normally, teachers and parents try to have students study with extrinsic motivations, either long-term, such as several years later they would succeed in getting a good job, or short-term, such as after completing the proposed tasks the student may play. A great challenge in education is to design intrinsically motivating academic activities.

A natural strategy is to use games, since this is a learning mechanism used not only by humans but also by other mammals, birds and even reptiles [7]. For example, rough-and-tumble play that prepares animals for fighting and hunting, social games

H. Leung et al. (Eds.): ICWL 2011, LNCS 7048, pp. 1–10, 2011.

like playing with dolls to prepare for social interaction and games with rules like soccer and chess. At least in some mammals, distinct neural systems for the generation of rough-and-tumble play have already been identified [16]. Since ancient times people have realized the great educational value of play. Plato wrote, "... teach your children not in a compulsory way but by game playing, and you will be able to better tell the natural abilities of each one." However, determining exactly how games help in this context has turned out not to be an easy task. One approach in game playing research has been to study its adaptive value. That is, considering that young animals spend much energy as well as a big fraction of their time playing, which in humans is about 10% of energy and time [5], it is necessary to identify the benefits and determine if they compensate the costs. There is some consensus in that game is an inborn mechanism allowing young animals to prepare for adult life, to hunt, mate, interact with others, lead, work in teams, behave appropriately in social hierarchies, etc. According to Bjorklund [5], games also teach how to learn, how to generate solutions to new problems, and provide a means for discovery. Also games make learning easier, more enjoyable and more flexible.

In the human case it is important to distinguish games without rules versus games with rules [18]. The former are very similar to those played by other mammals: rough-and-tumble play, fake fighting, etc. These games are the most popular among preschoolers. Games with rules are the most frequently played at school, mainly by older students. These are sport games like soccer and basketball, and board games like checkers and chess. In the 60's the New Game Movement arose, proposing the use of multi-player games in schools to promote intra-team collaboration as well as inter-team competition [23]. This movement has published several books, promoted tournaments, and it has had a major impact on school playground games and physical education games.

With mathematics and science games we pursue two goals. On one hand there is the affect goal: to motivate students to approach mathematics and science, to see them as attractive, and perceive them as something they can do and enjoy. One of the most popular strategies is to employ videogames to induce a state of pleasure called "flow" [9], in which an enjoyable state of great effortless attention arises [19]. On the other hand we have the cognitive goal: to help student players understand contents that are biologically secondary [13-14]. These are very different from biologically primary contents, which are really basic and are learned by everybody even without any explicit instruction. Examples of biologically primary contents are speaking, walking, number sense, geometry of shapes, sense of risk, etc. Learning biologically secondary contents is the real educational challenge: learning fractions, algebra [4], natural selection, inertia, laws of motion, etc.

A well-designed game is a powerful metaphor [8]. It is an activity that maps abstract biologically secondary concepts into a biologically primary activity. For instance, chess is a metaphor for a battle. In this paper we analyze Magical Surprises, a mathematical game aimed at guessing what is inside given opaque boxes. This game is a metaphor for pattern recognition and statistical concepts [1-2].

2   Massively Multi-player Online Game

Computer based games in science and mathematics available on the market are primarily single-player or very-few-player ones. This entails that they do not take advantage of online networking opportunities that could provide a strong motivation based on the appeal of a massively multiplayer game, like many of the recent highly popular commercial games. Playing single-player or few-player games does not allow for a sense of identity or of global community to arise. In this work we report on the use of an online massively multi-player game, where thousands of students from different regions of the country simultaneously and synchronously participate in tournaments. According to game designer Chris Crawford [8], the massively multiplayer game "is one of the most interesting ideas that emerge from the introduction of the computer in game playing."

The most common massively multiplayer games are RPGs (Role playing games). A comprehensive literature review [26] and an Internet search show absence of this type of game designed especially for science education. There are, however, studies of the educational impact of popular massively multiplayer games designed with exclusively commercial goals. For example, [10] analyzes the impact of the games Everquest and Second Life played by 36 university students in the classroom. In [6], the impact of these games on military training, particularly in decision-making, leadership and conflict resolution, was studied. The Institute for Advanced Research in Human Sciences and Technology (HSTAR) of Stanford has recently begun to investigate the potential of massive multiplayer games commercially available to support the teaching of mathematics for elementary and middle school students [11-12]. Another exception is NASA [20-21], which through the NASA Learning Technologies Project is developing Moonbase Alpha, a massively multiplayer online game recently released to the educational system. Since the game still is not finished and released, we do not know its design or contents. There are also no studies yet of its impact on learning. Today, followers of the New Game Movement [17] propose to extend the movement into the digital age with massive multiplayer online games, drawing lessons from physical games that have been successful.

3   Mathematics and Science Online Games National Tournaments

Here we report on the implementation of the National Tournaments of mathematics and science online games in Chile. Similar competitions in the country are the Mathematical and Scientific Olympic Games. But, unlike the tournaments, Olympic Games do not use information and communication technologies and are intended only for very talented students. In an internet survey we found only one type of tournament involving online games. These are the DimensionM [27] tournaments, an educational game with a 3D engine. Two teams compete in a gym, each of about 15 students selected from one school. Taking advantage of the highly appealing 3D engine, students drive vehicles or virtual agents and every so often they must answer mathematical questions in order to go on playing. These tournaments are not massively multiplayer games, because there are just two small teams playing, all located in the same gym, and most of the students participate by just cheering and supporting the teams. That is, only the viewers and supporters are massive in number, as in a basketball or soccer championship.

This paper reports the result of a three year effort implementing tournaments involving massively multiplayer games to support mathematical contents in statistics and algebra with students from third to tenth grade, and at present, games with physics and biology contents also. Semester after semester participation has been strongly increasing including thousands of students from all regions of the country. In each tournament, students of the same grade play the same game online, simultaneously and synchronously. Every two minutes a round closes, and all students must submit their bets during these two minutes lapses. The game schedule is defined through pairs of grade levels: third and fourth graders play at 09:00, fifth and sixth play at 10:30, seventh and eighth grade play at 12:00 and the ninth and tenth graders play at 13:30 hrs. The game is played in a 12x1 mode, in which one computer is assigned to a team of 12 students, with a team representative entering the personal bet of each member. Games are so designed to optimize computing resources and to let many students play even in schools with small labs, few computers and very narrow bandwidth (the computer must be connected to the internet with only a minimal bandwidth). To run the game, each team of 12 students uses one computer only, which must have a permanent Internet connection, Windows or Linux operating system, Java 1.6, a 1024x768 resolution video card and at least 512 MB of RAM.

Our massively multiplayer online mathematics games share several friendly features. For instance, we have developed a registration system where teachers register their schools and teams online, there is a national ranking system by region and county, an automatic system for generating certificates, an empathetic intelligent system that recognizes and acknowledges good moves from each team or student in a team, giving encouragement to those who might not be winning. Since it is impossible to offer in situ training to teachers and students from all over the country, we have developed a web video and an online training strategy with teams playing synchronously. First, students and teachers get acquainted with the game by reading instructions and watching videos available on the web. Then, on two occasions, approximately 40 and then 20 days before the tournament, an online synchronous game is played. On these occasions, a live web transmission is broadcasted where a trainer comments on the game and the strategies, and makes suggestions to the different teams. At the same time teams receive, via chat, on line answers to their questions and also appropriate personalized feedback. Besides that, the game is open in the internet for teams to practice at any time. We analyze here the data of the final of the third tournament that took place on October 23, 2009 and where 3432 students participated from the nearly 10 thousands students registered.

4   Game Description

In this paper we report the results of the game Magical Surprises, originally designed and implemented in 1995 [1], but now adapted to a web version. In this game, each member must try to find a pattern. On each round, a box appears, in different sizes and colors, containing a card with 12 cells, one for each team member.   Each player must bet on the color (white or black) of his/her cell. Once the time is over (about 2 minutes) the box opens displaying its contents. If the student succeeds he gets 2 points, if he does not, then he loses a point. The Magical Surprises version used in the third and fourth tournament has two additional variants: first, each player can bet "gray", meaning "I don't know" and earning one point. Moreover, each player can also bet following a rule. For example,

```
IF
length + 2.5 x width > 3
THEN
cell color = white
ELSE
cell color = black.
```

If applying the rule to the current box data predicts the right color for his cell, then the player earns 4 points. If the rule predicts the wrong color for the slot, then he loses 4 points. So, betting following a rule is appealing but also more risky because the loss is higher. The team's accumulated points are displayed immediately in a ranking with several tabs: national ranking, county ranking, level ranking and students ranking within the team.

Each student decisions in the course of the game and associated team response times are registered to be subsequently analyzed. The game server tracks all the bets, "White", "Black", "Gray" or an explicit rule. This way we can estimate not only whether the student seems to have discovered a pattern, but also if he/she can describe this pattern explicitly in algebraic language. This type of betting allows us to tell explicit versus implicit pattern discovery. Our register allows us to investigate cognitive aspects such as student strategy selection [25] in different rounds and its evolution as the game progresses. For example, in [3], an analysis of strategies used on a previous version of Magic Surprises in the second tournament is reported.

5   Learning

As the game progress, the students begin to hit the right cell colors. From round 10 onwards, students are hitting significantly above random guessing. The games have different degrees of difficulty depending on the level. For Level 1, intended for 3[d] and 4th grade students, Magic Surprises was loaded with two variables describing externally the boxes. One is the (three valued) *color* variable and the other is the dimension variable *length*, which is always a whole number. Moreover, patterns are defined by a single variable. For example, in one cell when the external box *color* is red, then the chosen cell is black. On another cell the pattern could be: when the *length* of the box is less than 5 cm then the chosen cell is white. Since there are 12 cells and each student of the team is in charge of one cell, then the type of pattern can be different for different students and difficulty can be vary. However, for all teams, the difficulty of cell 1 is identical, the difficulty of cell 2 is identical, etc. In all other levels, 4 variables were used: *color, height, width* and *length* of the boxes. This expands the number of possible patterns. Moreover, variables were decimal or fraction valued. Additionally, at higher levels, patterns were introduced that were defined by two variables. For example, when the *length* of the box is at least twice the *width*, the chosen cell is white.

A quick analysis shows how the score achieved varies in a statistically significant way with respect to some monitored variables. As shown in Table 1, student performance depends on *type of school* (except for level 1). Moreover, for levels 3 and 4), *grade, age, gender, cell* and *type of school* impact the game score in a statistically significant way. We also notice that for each level (which comprises two grades), *grade* has an impact on the score of success.

Table 1. p-values of the hypotheses that for different levels, the average performance on the game for different grade, age, gender, cell, and school type do not affect performance

LEVEL	GRADE	AGE	GENDER	CELL	TYPE OF SCHOOL
(3rd & 4th)	0,000	0,000	0,467	0,853	0,148
(5th & 6th)	0,007	0,569	0,201	0,11	0,000
(7th & 8th)	0,000	0,035	0,049	0,016	0,000
(9th & 10th)	0,002	0,033	0,000	0,000	0,000

6   Types or Clusters of Players

From the stored information that contains the bet of each student in each round, we tried to find types or clusters of players, i.e. to determine whether there are clearly defined ways to play according to which we could classify all students. For this we considered several basic variables that record performance and type of bets made:

- *Number of bets "gray" from round 1 onwards*
- *Number of bets "gray" from round 7 onwards*
- *Number of bets "gray" from round 15 onwards*
- *Number of hits from round 1 onwards*
- *Number of hits from round 7 onwards*
- *Number of hits from round 15 onwards*
- *Number of bets using a rule from round 1 onwards*
- *Number of bets using a rule from round 7 onwards*
- *Number of bets using a rule from round 15 onwards*
- *Hits using rule from round 1 onwards*
- *Hits using rule from round 7 onwards*
- *Number of hits using rule from round   15 onwards*
- *Number of hits before the first rule was used*
- *Number of errors before the first rule was used*
- *Number of bets "gray" before the first rule used.*

With these variables we used the **Two-Step algorithm** to search for clusters using SPSS 15.0 software. This proposal is similar to [28], searching for clusters or groupings of individuals in ways that ensure statistically optimal grouping. This analysis is different from that undertaken in [3], which was based on determining the frequency of pre-defined strategies by the researchers. Three clusters were found:

— "White-Blackists", who bet white or black most of the time.
— "Grayists" who primarily bet "gray."
— "Rulists" that from a given round onwards bet following rules.

In level 1 (3d and 4th graders), "white-blackists" dominate. This cluster decreases for older students, but remains always the largest. In Level 2 (5th and 6th graders) the "rulist" cluster appears, which indicates that the students are using algebraic language. At level 4 (9th and 10th graders), about 20% of students are "rulists" already.

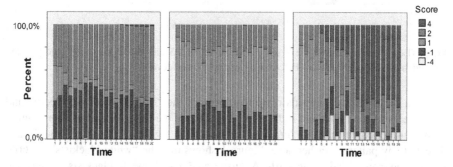

Fig. 1. (Left) White-blackist cluster for level 2, consisting of students betting black or white. (Center) Grayist Cluster for level 2 of conservative students who take no risk. (Right) Cluster of students belonging to level 3 who play following a rule that explicitly defines a pattern. Score 4: student bets and hits following a rule; score 2: student bets white or black and hits; score 1: student bets gray; score -1: student bets black or white and does not hit, score −2: student uses a rule but does not hit.

As seen in Figure 1, white-blackists bet mainly white or black, although in the first two rounds we found roughly one third of "gray" bets. Success rate stabilizes to 60% after round 10, which indicates a level of learning above the random hitting. Later, two sub clusters are analyzed within this cluster: those who detect the right pattern and those who do not.

The grayist cluster is the conservative cluster, consisting of students that do not take risks. From round 4 onwards they bet gray about 60% of the time. These students play without showing discovery of a pattern.

The "rulist" cluster starts by playing gray, but already in round 8 they are betting following a rule about 20% of the time, and from round 13 onwards they bet following a rule over 80% of the time, making very few mistakes. These students have learned the pattern and know how to make it explicit using algebraic language.

In figure 2 we can see that "rulists" appear more frequently in paid private schools, then in subsidized private schools and hardly in municipal schools. There is also a gender bias. There are more "whiteblackists" among girls, and there are more "grayists" and "rulists" among boys.

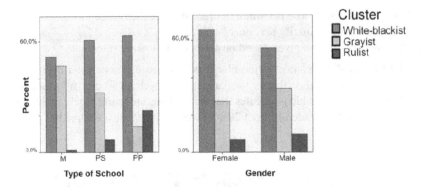

Fig. 2. (Left) Percentages by type of school (M municipal, PS subsidized private, PP paid private), for students of all levels. (Right) Percentage by gender for all levels.

From the 8th round onwards more than 50% of the "rulists" predict correctly, and from the 11th round, they are right more than 80% of the time. Moreover, from Figure 1 we can conclude that the "grayists" do not show evidence that they would have detected any pattern. Furthermore, Figure 1 shows that the "white-blackists" hit 60% of the time from round 12 onwards. A cluster analysis of "white-blackists" shows two subclusters: those who are detecting a pattern and therefore play better than random and those who are not. The first subcluster represents 42.3% of the "white-blackists" and the second, consisting of "random bettors", 57.7% of them. Interestingly, those who detect patterns and hit better than random are concentrated in the lowest level: 3d and 4th grade. This can be explained because many of the older students in higher levels who detect a pattern make it explicit by giving a rule, and so they do not appear in the cluster of "white-blackists".

7   Conclusions

We have performed data mining on the extensive data logs from the Chilean national tournaments. Thousands of students play online simultaneously in a big tournament with hundreds of teams from about 400 schools. Data recorded by each student in the different rounds allow us to have some estimates whether students are in fact able to detect patterns. Since the required data analysis techniques to detect patterns on the game are not directly taught in schools, we presume that the on line web material, videos, training sessions and trial tournaments have made possible that teachers and students learn to apply their mathematical knowledge to pattern discovery problems.

Additionally, from the betting information registered, three distinct types of groupings or clusters of players appear. The "rulist" cluster is the most interesting one, because it entails a greater understanding of the detected patterns. These students are characterized by betting with an algebraic rule. We note that in general when they use rules they guess right, which means not only that they use algebraic language, but that they build mathematical models. Indeed they are building models and writing mini computer programs that bet for them. It remains to investigate situations in which although students still respond poorly, there is some evidence that they are learning and this soon will be noticeable in their responses. This evidence would come from successes in the near future

The use of the more advanced strategy is more frequent on private schools with students of higher socio economic status and with higher performance on the national standard assessments. The subsidized private school students have the second proportion of "rulist". They also have better performance on the national assessments than the public schools, but lower performance than the paid private schools. Therefore, there is an agreement between the use of more advanced strategies and the results of the national mathematics assessments. There is also a gender difference: higher proportion of males than females use the more advanced strategy. This fact agrees with an important gender bias on math performance in the country. Teachers have not been formally interviewed to know the impact on their students, but there has been an increasing interest on the tournaments throughout the years since the first tournament with 600 students. This year the first Latin-American tournament has been run with participants from different countries www.torneoslatinoamericanos.org. The data will allow us to explore the differences across countries as well.

Acknowledgements. Conicyt Project CIE-05 Center for Advanced Research on Education, Centro de Modelamiento Matemático U. de Chile and Fondef Grant D06I1023.

References

1. Araya, R.: Inteligencia Matemática. Editorial Universitaria, Santiago (2000)
2. Araya, R.: Guess What Is Inside This Box: Look At These Opened Boxes For Clues. In: Proceedings of the Fifth Congress of the European Society for Research in Mathematics Education Larnaca, Cyprus 22-26, pp. 101–110 (2007)
3. Araya, R., Bahamondez, M., Jiménez, A., Calfucura, P., Dartnell, P., Soto-Andrade, J., Lacourly, N.: Estimación de Estrategias de Juego de Estudiantes en Torneo Masivo de Estadística. In: MATECOMPU 2009 La Enseñanza de la Matemática y la Computación, Matanzas, Cuba (2009)
4. Araya, R., Calfucura, P., Jiménez, A., Aguirre, C., Palavicino, M., Lacourly, N., Soto-Andrade, J., Dartnell, P.: The Effect of Analogies on Learning to Solve Algebraic Equations. Pedagogies: An International Journal 5(3), 216–232 (2010); Special Issue The teaching of Algebra
5. Bonk, C., Dennen, V.: Massive Multiplayer Online Gaming: A Research Framework for Military Training and Education (2005),
http://www.adlnet.gov/SiteCollectionDocuments/archive/GameRe
port_Bonk_final.pdf

6. Burghardt, G.: The Genesis of Animal play. MIT Press (2005)
7. Crawford, C.: On Game Design. New Riders (2003)
8. Csikzentmihalyi, M., Abuhhamdeh, S., Nakamura, J.: Flow. In: Elliot, A.J., Dweck, C. (eds.) Handbook of Competence and Motivation, Guilford (2005)
9. Delwiche, A.: Massively multiplayer online games (MMOs) in the new media classroom. Educational Technology & Society 9(3), 160–172 (2006)
10. Devlin, K.: Learning Mathematics in a Commercially Successful "Massively Multiplayer Online" Game. In: 2010 American Association for the Advancement of Science (AAAS) Annual Meeting (2010),
    http://aaas.confex.com/aaas/2010/webprogram/Paper1103.html,
    http://news.stanford.edu/news/2010/february15/
    devlin-aaas-mathematics-021910.html
11. Devlin, K.: Mathematics Education for a New Era: Video Games as a Medium for Learning. A.K. Peters, Ltd. (2011)
12. Geary: The Origin of Mind. Evolution of Brain, Cognition, and General Intelligence. American Psychology Association (2005)
13. Geary: Educating the Evolved Mind: Conceptual Foundations for an Evolutionary Educational Psychology. Information Age Publishing (2007)
14. Hektner, J., Schmidt, J., Csikzentmihalyi, M.: Experience Sampling Method. Measuring the Quality of Everyday Life. Sage (2007)
15. Panksepp, J.: Affective Neuroscience. Oxford University Press (1998)
16. Pearce, C., Fullerton, T., Fron, J., Morie, J.F.: Sustainable Play: Toward a New Games Movement for the Digital Age. Games and Culture 2(3), 261–278 (2007),
    http://www.lcc.gatech.edu/~cpearce3/PearcePubs/
    DACSustainablePlay.pdf
17. Pellegrini, A.: The Role of Play in Human Development. Oxford University Press (2009)
18. Moller, A., Meier, B., Wall, R.: Developing an Experimental Induction of Flow: Effortless Action in the Lab. In: Buya, B. (ed.) Effortless Attention: A New Perspective in the Cognitive Science of Attention and Action. MIT Press (2010)
19. Nasa, Nasa MMO Game (2009), http://ipp.gsfc.nasa.gov/mmo/
20. Nasa, Development of a NASA-Based Massively Multiplayer Online Learning Game (2008), http://www.spaceref.com/news/viewsr.html?pid=26717
21. National Mathematics Advisory Panel, The Final Report. U.S. Department of Education (2008)
22. Salem, K., Zimmermann, E.: Rules of Play: Game Design Fundamentals. MIT Press (2004)
23. Siegler, R.: Emerging Minds. The Process of Change in Children´s Thinking. Oxford University Press (1996)
24. Siegler, R.S., Araya, R.: A computational model of conscious and unconscious strategy discovery. In: Kail, R.V. (ed.) Advances in Child Development and Behavior, vol. 33, pp. 1–42. Elsevier, Oxford (2005)
25. Steinkuehler, C.: Massively multiplayer online games & education: an outline of research. In: Proceedings of the 8th International Conference on Computer Supported Collaborative Learning (2007), http://portal.acm.org/citation.cfm?id=1599726
26. Tabula Digita DimensionM, Tabula Digita Video Games Add Up Fast: One Million Dimensionm Games Played By Math Students (2010),
    http://cache.dimensionm.com/qa/newspdfs/1%20Million%20Games%
    20NR%20FINAL.pdf, http://www.dimensionu.com/math/
27. van der Maas, H., Straatemeier, M.: How to detect cognitive strategies: commentary on Differentiation and integration: guiding principles for analyzing cognitive change. Developmental Science (2008)

Learning Programming Languages through Corrective Feedback and Concept Visualisation

Christopher Watson[1], Frederick W.B. Li[1], and Rynson W.H. Lau[2]

[1] School of Engineering and Computing Sciences, University of Durham, United Kingdom
[2] Department of Computer Science, City University of Hong Kong, Hong Kong
{christopher.watson, frederick.li}@durham.ac.uk,
rynson@cs.cityu.edu.hk

Abstract. In this paper we address common issues faced by students in programming courses by combining implicit and explicit feedback measures to provide real-time assistance in coding tasks. We also introduce our concept visualisation technique, which aims to visually convey programming concepts and information on the execution state to students. The mapping between game content construction actions and actual source code forms an implicit example-based learning environment, allowing programming concepts to be more clearly conveyed than in conventional integrated development environment (IDE) or static lecture materials. An experimental evaluation of a prototype system suggests the potential of this approach for programming education by scoring highly in terms of both user satisfaction and potential pedagogical capability.

Keywords: Programming Education, Corrective Feedback, Concept Visualization.

1 Introduction

Learning to program is a fundamental skill required to obtain a Computer Science degree throughout the world. However, each year many students find the process of learning a programming language to be a difficult and even unpleasant task [4,11,17]. Several reasons have been put forward to explain this. Some are attributed to the individual traits of students. For example, they may lack problem solving, logical reasoning or mathematical ability. They may lack a learning preference for the subject material or perceive the course to be too difficult based on reputation [2, 4]. Others may become impatient with the lack of immediate results despite only applying little syntax [2] or struggle with the social stereotype of being perceived as a "nerd" [11].

Additional reasons are associated with the quality of the teaching process. For example, the use of traditional static lecture materials generally fails to convey programming dynamics to students. Instructors may focus upon teaching the syntax and semantics of a language rather than relevant problem solving techniques. Furthermore, a traditional one size fits all approach neglects the individual student's characteristics such as learning style and ability, making it very easy for less able students to rapidly fall behind the rest of a cohort [11].

H. Leung et al. (Eds.): ICWL 2011, LNCS 7048, pp. 11–20, 2011.
© Springer-Verlag Berlin Heidelberg 2011

Although there are many varying theories concerning why introductory programming courses are perceived to be difficult, the majority of literature tends to share a common sense of panic about their perceived high dropout rates [11, 16]. This is perhaps justified considering that a recent survey of 63 international institutions found that on average 33% of students fail an introductory programming course [4]. The question is how to address this problem. One-to-one tutoring has been demonstrated to be one of the most effective pedagogical approaches [6] but it is practically unfeasible to use this method at university level, especially for larger cohorts. A more suitable method could be to increase the pedagogical effectiveness of existing instruction by using adaptive e-learning systems [19] to provide individualized guidance and feedback to a student. Another approach could be to try and increase the student's motivation to learn programming through the use of a more stimulating and less intimidating learning tool than a conventional IDE.

In this paper, we address common issues faced by students in programming courses by combining implicit and explicit feedback measures to provide real-time assistance in coding tasks. We also introduce our concept visualisation technique, which aims to convey programming concepts and constraints to students more clearly than in conventional IDE or static lecture materials. The mapping between game content construction actions and actual source code forms an implicit example-based learning environment.

The remainder of this paper is organised as follows. Section 2 summarises existing approaches to improve the effectiveness of programming instruction. Section 3 presents our method and implementation. Section 4 discusses findings of a user evaluation. Section 5 concludes the paper.

2   Related Work

Throughout the years, numerous techniques have been used to make the teaching of introductory programming skills to novices more effective by adopting a simplified learning environment. General methods include simplifying the language (e.g., BASIC) or reducing the need to type syntax by allowing program construction using visual objects (e.g., Scratch) [17]. Whilst visual and block-based programming languages, such as Scratch or Alice, have shown some success in teaching basic programming concepts, a student is still required to eventually scale-up to a more complex language and the use of these introductory tools does not imply this will automatically follow. In fact, it could be argued that removing a language's syntax defeats the point of learning a programming language to start with [2].

Another approach to make the learning process more effective is to teach programming using computer games. The ability of games to teach problem solving skills through a repeated cycle of expertise [10] makes them ideally suited to programming education, as students are required to develop a hierarchy of skills through repeatedly extending their existing problem solving techniques and knowledge of syntax [16]. Game usage can be divided into two main categories. The first approach attempts to convey programming concepts visually through a set of turtle-based challenges [2, 5]. However, these systems are generally restricted in terms of feedback provided and their teaching capability limited to function calling. Adaption to learner characteristics is even rarer and an outdated appearance means their appeal is rapidly diminishing with the current generation of students [5]. The second approach uses the constructivist technique of game development as the main teaching tool. Although this approach has shown notable success in terms of both learning performance and student satisfaction [3, 18], it is still likely that novices will encounter the usual issues of IDE complexity, vague compiler messages and no visualisation of state and syntax execution until a basic game structure is completed.

Appropriate feedback is among the major influences on learning achievement [12]. Usually in introductory programming courses, students are provided with instant knowledge of result feedback [20] on syntax correctness from a compiler. Instant feedback offers several advantages to students. For example, it focuses the learner's attention on relevant information, ensuring that the important information is perceived consciously and processed in working memory [24]. However, many novices can struggle to act upon standard compiler messages, which can be too general [21] or not accurately describe the fault in their code (Table 1).

Several systems have been developed over recent years to address the need for further guidance. Although functionalities provided vary from system to system, most share several common limitations. The range of exercises are usually limited to either completing missing lines in a skeleton program [14, 25], satisfying an input-output program specification [8, 28] or computing the value of a variable after code execution [1, 13]. Correctness is usually verified using case tests and then feedback is generated. Feedback is usually limited consisting of a set of test cases on which the students code has passed and failed [1, 13-14], possibly based on the ratio of fails and passes [8] and accompanied with instructor comments on specific test cases based on constraint violation [28]. More detailed BRT feedback [20] was provided by the JITS system, which included an algorithm to correct student syntax mistakes [25]. A final limitation is that concepts are presented in an un-stimulating environment with no visualization of code execution. Considering that many errors which novice's make can be attributed to an inadequate understanding of program state [9] visually been able to monitor an effect of code execution could enhance the learning experience.

3 Our Method

We believe that a more effective method of teaching programming concepts can be obtained by merging the reasoning capabilities of adaptive learning systems with a highly motivational visual-based environment. Previous research has suggested that combined environments of this nature can be pedagogically effective [27]. Yet examples of such systems for programming education are rare. To support novices in developing an understanding of syntax and program logic, we perform source code analysis to provide implicit, explicit and program logic level feedback. We then combine our feedback mechanisms with a game content construction front end to provide concept visualisation allowing programming concepts and the execution state to be conveyed in a clearer manner than through static course material or IDE.

3.1   Scene Modelling and Code Assessment

To disseminate content to students we use a set of *learning scenes*. We currently model a *learning scene LS* by using a set of properties $\{n, m, k, s, r, x\}$ including:

- A tuple of n concepts $\{C_1, C_2 ..., C_n\}$ enumerates the concepts that *LS* is designed to teach, ranked in order of their *emphasis* (importance).
- A set of m scenes $\{S_1, S_2 ..., S_m\}$ define prerequisite scenes of *LS*, which the student is required to complete before *LS* is made available.
- A set of k pairings $\{\{T_1, O_1\}\{T_2, O_2\}, ..., \{T_k, O_k\}\}$ describe a collection of test criteria and required outcomes.
- A boolean flag s indicates whether or not learning performance should be assessed using code similarity analysis based on a threshold score z.
- A set of r fragments $\{F_1, F_2 ..., F_r\}$ describe code fragments which are required to be present in a *valid* solution of *LS*.
- A set of x model solutions $\{A_1, A_2 ..., A_x\}$ represent valid (code) solutions to *LS*.

To assess the validity of a student's code as a possible solution to *LS*, the code is analysed over a number of stages (Fig. 1). In the first two stages of the *Interpreter*, the code is analysed for syntax and runtime errors by passing it directly to the javac compiler. If errors are detected at either of these stages, then the code is passed to the *Corrector* module where the corrective feedback functionalities are invoked and tailored advice is returned to the student (either through game character or console).

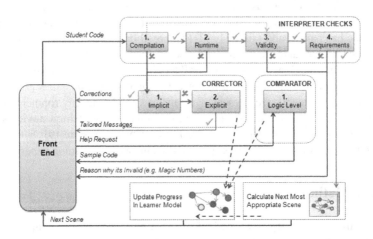

Fig. 1. Overview of Corrective Feedback and Code Assessment Features

The third stage verifies the validity of the students solution against $LS\{k\}$ (and $LS\{x\}$ if $LS\{s=1\}$) to ensure that it functions correctly. The final (optional) stage is a requirement check where the presence of the set of required fragments is verified (e.g., $LS\{r:\{$"while", "if(x<10)"$\}\}$). If the student's code passes all the test stages but is not an exact match of any $A_i \in LS\{x\}$ then it is stored pending further analysis by an expert instructor. If it is a valid solution, then it can be added to $LS\{x\}$. This reduces the instructor's workload considerably, as they are not required to identify and manually author all possible solutions to a given programming problem.

3.2   Explicit Corrective Feedback

Debugging is a key programming skill. However, many novices can struggle with 'ambiguous' and unspecific compiler messages [21], i.e., the feedback returned does not always accurately describe the fault in the code (Table 1). Considering that novices are heavily reliant upon compiler feedback and guidance to compensate for their lack of programming experience, unspecific compiler messages pose a serious issue. Simply acting upon the feedback provided could result in the introduction of further errors, which confuse the student. Also, lab time is lost on syntax correction instead of problem solving (for students) and teaching (for instructors). To address these issues, we extend the *rewriting* technique of traditional tutoring systems further to provide explicit corrective feedback. By using source code analysis techniques to tailor compiler messages to a student's code, we can explain the problem more clearly to students, allowing them to develop a deeper understanding of the cause of errors.

From an implementation perspective, our system includes a database of common errors (Table 1) grouped by error class. If the interpreter reports an error from the javac compiler, then the error class is identified and a set of possible causes are retrieved from the database. We currently only consider the first error thrown. Using the line and column information provided, the corresponding fragment at fault is extracted and compared to the fragments in the database. If a match is found, tailored advice is supplied to the student along with the standard compiler error class. This ensures that any experts assisting the student can perform diagnosis. If there is no match, a generalised layman's terms message is returned and the fragment is added to the database pending an expert instructor to specify advice. As with the reuse of student solutions to programming tasks, this allows our system to become semi self-populating rather than requiring an instructor to manually author examples and feedback of all possible causes of error. This allows the system to continually expand to cover a greater range of errors.

Table 1. Common Java Errors from a Programming Course [15] and possible causes

Error Class	Code Fragment	Actual Error
cannot find symbol	`String = new String();`	No variable name.
	`return s.Length();`	Misspelt method name.
; expected	`x = x + 3:`	Used colon not semi colon.
	`String y = "is" x;`	Missing concatenation '+'.
class or interface expected	`For(int i=0; i<5; i++) {}`	Case on keyword 'for'.
	`{ calc(int x, int y); }`	Adding parameter types in call.
<identifier> expected	`public void int getX()`	Extra keyword in signature.
not a statement	`String x = "a" + "b" ; "c";`	Extra semi-colon.
{ expected	`public class My Class`	Space in the class name.

3.3   Implicit Corrective Feedback

As with [25], we attempt to provide automatic error correction of some of the syntax errors, in particular automatically correcting spelling and case mistakes involving

Java keywords (e.g., int) and common Java classes (e.g., String). This implicit correc-tive feedback instructs the students how to correct problems on the syntax level. Cur-rently, this functionality is only invoked if the compiler produces a 'cannot find symbol' error. When an error of this type is detected, the system first extracts the token at fault using line and column information provided by javac. The Levenshtein distance of the token and each of possible replacements is computed to produce a ranked list of substitutions ordered by least distance (run time of $O(\ln//m/)$). The token at fault is replaced with the highest ranked substitution and the code is recompiled. If the 'cannot find symbol' error has been removed, then the system asks the student if they think the correction is valid. This ensures that the student is actively made aware of the error in their code and is guided to correct it. If the error is still present, then the next ranked substitution is applied until the list is exhausted. If the system is unable to correct the student's error through substitutions, then the code is passed to the compiler message customiser for further analysis.

3.4   Program Logic Level Corrective Feedback

Our final form of corrective feedback supports the student in correcting problems at the program logic level. As novices may encounter difficulties in completing coding tasks, our system is capable of suggesting possible solutions based on their similarity to the student's code. Defining similarity of two code fragments that perform the same under all possible conditions is unfeasible. So, we consider a simpler definition. To compare the *structure* of the student's code to the set of possible solutions $LS\{x\}$, we have chosen to use a tree-based approach [22]. This allows us to perform code comparison through precise node-by-node analysis to identify the most appropriate code resembling what the student has already created, rather than supplying a single generic model answer. Specifically, we use a *tree edit distance* algorithm [26], which performs well in a similar project to determine the similarity between classes [23].

Let V be a set of vertices, and E a set of edges. For two ordered trees $Z_1 = (V_1, E_1)$ and $Z_2 = (V_2, E_2)$, we define three valid elementary operations on Z_1 and Z_2: the *dele-tion* of a leaf vertex $v \in V_1$, the *substitution* of a vertex $w \in V_2$ for a vertex $v \in V_1$ and the *insertion* into Z_2 of a new vertex $w \notin V_2$ as a new leaf. A cost function is applied to each operation. The edit distance is the lowest cost sequence of operations needed to transform Z_1 into Z_2. By constructing an *edit graph* of Z_1 and Z_2, the problem of find-ing a *valid* transformation from Z_1 to Z_2 can be reduced to finding the shortest path through the graph. This has a run time of $O(|V_1||V_2|)$ requiring $O(|V_1||V_2|)$ additional space [26]. From an implementation perspective, a set of reduced Abstract Syntax Trees (AST's) of $LS\{x\}$ and the AST of the student's code (P) are first generated by using Eclipse JDT. These trees are then passed to a reducer class, which prunes the search space based on the average number of vertices in each $A_i \in \{A_1, ..., A_x\}$. For example, let $Z_1 = A_i$ and $Z_2 = P$. If on average $|V_1| = 50$ and $|V_2| = 30$, then all A_i with $|V| >$ a pre-defined threshold could be removed, as an excessive amount of edit opera-tions would be required to transform Z_1 to Z_2. Following reductions, the edit distance is calculated on the reduced set of model AST's to determine the closest match to the student's code, which is then provided.

3.5   Concept Visualization

To convey programming concepts and constraints to novice students in a more visual and interactive manner than a conventional e-learning system [1, 7-8, 13-14, 25, 28] we intend to use a game content construction learning interface as a support. We currently use this interface for concept visualisation. Future work will be to extend the interface to include game-based tasks. However, unlike standard applications of computer games within programming courses, our approach is not to simply include games as a method of rewarding learning progress. Nor do we simply sugar-coat the learning process by combining them with traditional programming tasks. Instead, the uniqueness of our approach is to transform well designed game content construction tasks into programming tasks such that the student can learn programming through task completion. Through observing the game state, novices can obtain a greater understanding of concepts and the execution state [9] than through the use of traditional static course materials alone. Furthermore, the use of games for concept visualisation provides a strong motivational tool, where novices can see immediate results of code execution without first having to master a large amount of syntax [2].

The game scenario can also be customised, thus allowing for a greater variety of different examples and increasing the motivational capability further. For instance, to teach object creation one of our implemented learning scenes is set in a garage near a racing track (Fig. 2). When the scene commences, the mechanic explains how his car (object) was created from a specific blueprint (class). To demonstrate object creation the student is required to create new wheel objects and add them to the car.

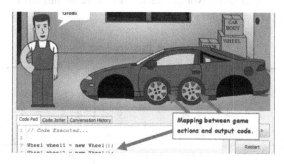

Fig. 2. Sample Learning Scene Demonstrating Object Creation

This is performed by right clicking on a box of 'Wheel' in the corner of the room and selecting 'new Wheel()' from the popup menu. As these actions are performed, the corresponding fragments of course code are generated and displayed in the box below the game interface, providing the student with an implicit example of the concept and demonstrating the corresponding syntax required.

4   Evaluation

Preliminary Findings. To determine whether students would be interested in using a game-based approach to learn programming, we have conducted a preliminary survey of recent students who completed the *Introduction to Programming* (IP) course at our university. A total of 54 students completed the online survey, 29 completed the course in 2011 and 25 in 2010. Findings indicated a high level of student interest in using a game-based approach, with only 11% of students indicating no interest or felt the approach would have been unsuitable for IP. 82% felt that a game-based approach would have been more interesting than current laboratory tasks, with 63% indicating they would have practiced programming more in their own time if a game-based approach was used. Additionally, 74% reported that unspecific error messages had been a hindrance at some point in the course.

User Experience. To assess the suitability of our system, we have conducted a user study on a prototype. The main research questions we asked included: Would the techniques presented provide better support to students in understanding programming concepts than traditional tools such as BlueJ or Eclipse? Does the approach convey concepts such as method calling in a clear manner? Would the system be more appropriate for a novice programmer than IDE's? The participants included six members of the universities Learning Technologies Team (LTT) and six demonstrators. The LTT regularly provides training and advice to staff on aspects of e-learning and is involved in developing tools to support education, such as Blackboard extensions. Participants were invited to either a group or individual session which lasted for about 30 minutes. Each session included discussion and two demonstrations of each support method and concept visualisation. Participants were asked to provide an overall grade out of five indicating whether or not a feature would aid the students understanding of coding concepts and syntax (Table 2).

Table 2. Results from the User Study

	Implicit Feedback	Explicit Feedback	Logic Level Feedback	Concept Visualisation	Actions to Source	Game-Based Tasks
LTT (n=6)	4.17	4.50	4.00	4.50	4.50	4.33
Demonstrator (n=6)	4.00	4.17	3.33	4.33	4.67	4.17
Overall Average (/5)	**4.09**	**4.34**	**3.67**	**4.42**	**4.59**	**4.25**

Qualitative feedbacks collected were mainly positive. Most participants believed that the auto-correction of errors would be a useful support to novices. Several suggested that the functionality should be invoked after a student has attempted to correct the mistake instead of immediately. Error message customisation was deemed to be the most useful corrective feedback technique as it could provide students more practical advice than what they currently receive through javac. The game-like concept visualisation of coding concepts such as method calling proved to be a popular idea to support novices (10/12 positive) and the mapping between game actions to output source code was viewed as an effective method of demonstrating the effect of code execution to novices (9/12 positive). Overall, participants indicated that they saw value in the techniques for teaching novice programmers with 8/12 indicating the system would be more appropriate for novices than BlueJ and 10/12 more appropriate than a conventional IDE.

User Criticism. The main criticisms of our approach were related to the scaling up issue, as when a student migrates to a regular IDE, the additional supports would be lost. A suggested solution to this issue was to integrate the functionality directly into an IDE or to always provide the generic error message along with customised support.

5   Conclusion

In this paper, we have presented our work on a method and prototype system designed to teach programming concepts through combining several forms of corrective feedback with motivational game-like concept visualisation. Unlike traditional programming tasks, our approach goes beyond simple 'fill in the gap' exercises and can provide real-time context specific feedback to students through source code analysis - providing greater support to novices than standard compiler messages. Unlike static course materials, the use of concept visualisation allows novices to rapidly develop an understanding of coding concepts and program dynamics through a set of clear, visual examples. This also provides a strong source of motivation by allowing novices to obtain 'instant results' despite only applying little syntax. We have evaluated and confirmed the feasibility of the approach from both instructor (educational potential) and student perspectives (interest). Future work will include extending concept visualisation further to support game-based challenges specifically designed to teach algorithms through problem-based learning, along with the development of a corresponding pedagogical interface [29]. Additionally, the potential benefits of using a token-based approach to evaluate coding similarity will be investigated in terms of runtime and accuracy. Finally, the educational effectiveness of the approach will be evaluated from an end-user perspective.

References

1. Abu Naser, S.: JEE-Tutor: An Intelligent Tutoring System for Java Expression Evaluation. Information Technology 7(3), 528–532 (2008)
2. Anderson, E., McLoughlin, L.: Critters in the Classroom: A 3D Computer-Game-Like Tool for Teaching Programming to Computer Animation Students. In: Proc. ACM SIGGRAPH Educators Program, Article 7 (2007)
3. Bayliss, J., Strout, S.: Games as a Flavour of CS1. ACM SIGCSE Bulletin 38(1), 500–504 (2006)
4. Bennedsen, J., Caspersen, M.: Failure Rates in Introductory Programming. ACM SIGCSE Bulletin 39(2), 32–36 (2007)
5. Bierre, K., Ventura, P., Phelps, A., Egert, C.: Motivating OOP by Blowing Things Up: An Exercise in Cooperation and Competition in an Introductory Java Programming Course. ACM SIGCSE Bulletin 38(1), 354–358 (2006)
6. Bloom, B.: The 2-Sigma Problem: The Search for Methods of Group Instruction as Effective as One-To-One Tutoring. Educational Researcher 13(6), 4–16 (1984)

7. Butz, C., Hua, S., Maguire, R.: A Web-Based Bayesian Intelligent Tutoring System for Computer Programming. Web Intelligence and Agent Systems 4(1), 77–97 (2006)
8. Daly, C., Horgan, J.: An Automated Learning System for Java Programming. IEEE Trans. Education 47(1), 10–17 (2004)
9. Dann, W., Cooper, S., Pausch, R.: Making the Connection: Programming with Animated Small World. ACM SIGCSE Bulletin 32(1), 41–44 (2000)
10. Gee, J.: Learning by Design: Games as Learning Machines. Interactive Educational Multimedia 8(1), 15–23 (2004)
11. Gomes, A., Mendes, A.: Learning to Program – Difficulties and Solutions. In: Proc. Engineering Education (2007)
12. Hattie, J., Timperley, H.: The Power of Feedback. Review of Educational Research 77(1), 81–112 (2007)
13. Hsiao, I., Sosnovsky, S., Brusilovsky, P.: Guiding Students to the Right Questions: Adaptive Navigation Support in an e-Learning system for Java Programming. Comp. Assisted Learning 26(1), 270–283 (2010)
14. Holland, J., Mitrovic, A., Martin., B.: J-LATTE: A Constraint-Based Tutor for Java. In: Proc. Computers in Education, pp. 142–146 (2009)
15. Jackson, J., Cobb, M., Carver, C.: Identifying Top Java Errors for Novice Programmers. In: Proc. Frontiers in Education, pp. T4C-24-27 (2005)
16. Jenkins, T.: On the Difficulty of Learning to Program. In: Proc. the LTSN Centre for Information and Computer Sciences, pp. 53–58 (2002)
17. Kelleher, C., Pausch, R.: Taxonomy of Programming Environments and Languages for Novice Programmers. ACM Computing Surveys 37(2), 83–137 (2005)
18. Leutenegger, S., Edgington, J.: A Games First Approach to Teaching Introductory Programming. ACM SIGCSE Bulletin 39(1), 115–118 (2007)
19. Li, F., Lau, R., Dharmendran, P.: An Adaptive Course Generation Framework. International Journal of Distance Education Technologies 8(3), 47–64 (2010)
20. Narciss, S., Huth, K.: Fostering Achievement and Motivation with Bug-Related Tutoring Feedback in a Computer-Based Training for Written Subtraction. Learning and Instruction 16(4), 310–322 (2006)
21. Nienaltowski, M., Pedroni, M., Meyer, B.: Compiler Error Messages: What Can Help Novices? ACM SIGCSE Bulletin 40(1), 168–172 (2008)
22. Roy, C., Cordy, J., Koschke, R.: Comparison and Evaluation of Code Clone Detection Techniques and Tools: A Qualitative Approach. Science of Computer Programming 74(7), 470–495 (2009)
23. Sager, T., et al.: Detecting Similar Java classes using Tree Algorithms. In: Proc. Workshop on Mining Software Repositories, pp. 65–71 (2006)
24. Schooler, L., Anderson, J.: The Disruptive Potential of Immediate Feedback. In: Proc. Conference of the Cognitive Science Society, pp. 702–708 (1990)
25. Sykes, E.: Development Process Model for the Java Intelligent Tutoring System. Interactive Learning Research 18(3), 399–410 (2007)
26. Valiente, G.: Algorithms on Trees and Graphs. Springer, Heidelberg (2002)
27. Virvou, M., Katsionis, G., Manos, K.: Combining Software Games with Education: Evaluation of its Educational Effectiveness. Educational Tech. & Soc. 8(2), 54–65 (2005)
28. Wang, F.L., Wong, T.-L.: Designing Programming Exercises with Computer Assisted Instruction. In: Fong, J., Kwan, R., Wang, F.L. (eds.) ICHL 2008. LNCS, vol. 5169, pp. 283–293. Springer, Heidelberg (2008)
29. Watson, C., Li, F., Lau, R.: A Pedagogical Interface for Authoring Adaptive e-Learning Courses. In: Proc. MTDL, pp. 13–18 (2010)

Extensible Multi-platform Educational Game Framework

Eugenio J. Marchiori[1], Ángel Serrano[1], Javier Torrente[1],
Iván Martínez-Ortiz[1], and Baltasar Fernández-Manjón[1,2]

[1] Facultad de Informática, Universidad Complutense de Madrid,
28040 Madrid, Spain
[2] Laboratory of Computer Science, Massachusetts General Hospital,
Harvard University, Boston, USA
aserrano@e-ucm.es,
{jtorrente,imartinez,balta,emarchiori}@fdi.ucm.es

Abstract. This paper presents an extensible multi-platform educational game framework. This new framework enhances the *point-and-click* adventure game model used in a preexisting educational game framework (eAdventure) by extending it with new game metaphors and interactions. These include mini-games (e.g. puzzles, stories, word-games) suited for a greater variety of subjects (e.g. math, history, science) that are configured through a plug-in architecture. Targeting multiple platforms allows for the transparent deployment and use of the developed games in new mobile devices (e.g. tablets) and other systems of growing interest in the educational community. Unifying these aspects into one platform is a challenging task because it must implement the appropriate balance between expressivity, game production costs and possibilities to re-use successful educational game models. The basic adventure metaphor is used as a backbone to provide a strong narrative to drive games and engage the students.

Keywords: Educational game framework, plug-in architecture, adventure games, multi-platform, serious games.

1 Introduction

Educational video games are available in very different flavours, going from simple (and inexpensive) puzzle games to complex (but costly) 3D immersive environments. Different genres are also available, but authors like Amory *et al.* [1] or Dickey [2] point out that the adventure game genre is especially well suited for educational use, because these games promote reflection and improve intrinsic motivation, and thus facilitate the acquisition of knowledge.

Several advantages can be achieved by narrowing the gaming field to specific formulas of proven educational value. First, successful gaming models such as *point-and-click* adventures can be reused, helping to reduce the risk that the lack of rigorous research proving games' educational gain imposes [3]. Second, specific and easy-to-use authoring tools and frameworks can be created and used, which reduces development costs and complexity [4]. These advantages can be of particular

H. Leung et al. (Eds.): ICWL 2011, LNCS 7048, pp. 21–30, 2011.

importance in settings where the high development cost is used as an argument against the use of educational games [5].

However, constraining the game genre too much creates its own set of problems. Technical solutions applied in education must be flexible and adaptable in order to fit local needs, teachers' pedagogical approaches, and particularities of each subject or domain (e.g. [6]). Extending the gaming model with new functionality is usually required to meet the requirements of each use case (e.g. puzzles, word games or math challenges). These specific extensions can increase the perceived complexity the tools, increasing the difficulty of creating and maintaining the games, so it should be done only as needed and not for the general case.

We are applying these ideas in the development of the next generation of the eAdventure educational gaming platform[1] (i.e. eAdventure 2.0, formerly <e-Adventure>). eAdventure is a research project that started in 2005 with the aim of providing educators with a game authoring tool specially devised for education. Since its origins, eAdventure has been focused in the *point-and-click* adventure game genre (games like *Monkey Island*^{TM} or *Myst*^{TM} are classic examples of adventure games). Now the platform is an established product and we are using the input gathered from educators, users and our experience developing and deploying games to improve it.

In this paper we present the approach behind eAdventure 2.0, which allows for the inclusion of other successful game approaches while keeping the focus on adventure and story driven games. eAdventure 2.0 is still a single unified (though hybrid) platform that allows for simple reuse of existing games, and promotes new game development in a cost effective way. A plug-in architecture allows for the incorporation of the new features, allowing not only the customization of the games, but also the customization of the platform for specific use cases, while avoiding the platform overload for general use. These extra features can be new game genres or metaphors, such as puzzles, *fill-in-the-blanks* exercises, simple simulations or other interactive mini-games. More approaches and metaphors can be developed through the use of an API (Application Programming Interface) provided by the eAdventure 2.0 platform. To prepare for changing behaviors in today students and gamers, this platform allows for the automatic deployment of games in different target platforms, ranging from traditional PCs, to web browsers and new mobile devices (i.e. Android *smartphones* and tablets).

This paper is structured as follows: section 2 presents the motivation behind the extensible hybrid platform. Section 3 shows the basic architecture to support this platform. Later, section 4 presents the implementation of the new architecture using available technologies. Finally, section 5 presents some use cases for the new platform advantages and section 6 presents the final remarks.

2   Motivation: Hybrid Educational Game Model

During the last 5 years the eAdventure platform (formerly <e-Adventure>) has been under intense development and use. Currently in its 1.3 version, the platform has

---

[1] http://e-adventure.e-ucm.es

grown to meet the demands and requests of users. This platform was designed for the development of "adventure games" [7] and was used in several experiments with teachers and students [8], as well as in other academic settings.

Experience using the platform has shown that there are many limiting factors that cannot be addressed within the current eAdventure architecture, stimulating a new approach. We propose a new model (Fig. 1) where plug-ins were introduced in the game editor to add flexibility in the creation or modification of adventure games complemented by mini-games. The new model also extends the system to easily export these games into different platforms, including new mobile devices (e.g. Android tablets)

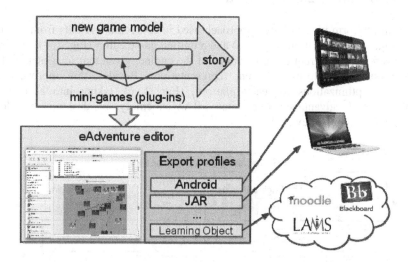

Fig. 1. Abstract model of the eAdventure 2.0 platform for the creation of story-driven adventure games complemented with mini-games

Teachers who wish to replicate simple games to test specific skills or increase the expressiveness of the platform in other ways usually expect and demand mini-games, plug-ins and pre-made components. The use of mini-games complements the current "adventure" gaming model, by allowing the story (the core of adventure games) to become the driving force that takes the player through the different puzzles and challenges. This changes the game model, from a purely adventure game metaphor, to a hybrid game genre. Several plug-ins are included with the eAdventure 2.0 platform. These range from simple puzzle games to more complex plug-ins to support accessibility aspects within the games. Besides, expert users or those with programming knowledge can create new plug-ins targeting the platform by the use of the API.

Moreover, the e-learning community shows a growing interest in mobile devices (e.g. tablets), as well as emerging web technologies. Targeting these platforms within the old approach required the creation of specific versions of eAdventure that increase the cost, create compatibility problems and are hard to maintain by the eAdventure development team. A new platform-agnostic engine core helps to deal with all these problems.

Other platforms are taking similar approaches, like the *Adventure Maker*[2] and *Raptivity*[3] systems. The *Adventure Maker* platform allows for the creation of 2D adventure games and provides a plug-in architecture. However, it does not provide educational tools (e.g. in-game evaluation features), not all games are cross-platform (just the simplest of them being playable on *iPhone* devices), and only provides a single game metaphor. The *Raptivity* system is more focused on educational content, it is very easy to use and provides many different puzzles or game metaphors. However, the creation of rich adventure games is not currently possible.

3   eAdventure 2.0 Architecture

The multi-platform plug-in based approach used in eAdventure results from a single core engine implementation (Fig. 2, a) and a unified game editor (Fig. 2, d). Different platforms require different customizations of the engine, given that images and other assets must use platform-dependent representations. Besides, this approach also allows for optimizations for each platform (Fig. 2, c), taking into account its constraints and advantages (e.g. more RAM memory in desktops vs. local installations in mobile devices).

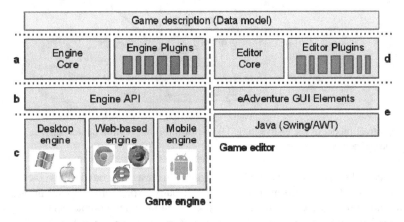

Fig. 2. Overview of the basic eAdventure engine and editor architectures. This includes: (a), engine core and plug-ins: (b), engine API; (c), specific platform implementations; (d), editor core and plug-ins; and (e), editor GUI (Graphic User Interface).

The engine exposes an API to the plug-ins (Fig. 2, b) that allows each particular plug-in implementation to target multiple platforms simultaneously, ensuring that the plug-in, in most cases, will not affect the multi-platform compatibility. At the same time, this API allows for new elements to be registered for the specific platform in which they are needed, in case of specific asset representations (e.g. specific video codec support).

---

[2] http://www.adventuremaker.com/
[3] http://www.raptivity.com/

This way, the game description (an instance of the abstract game data model) is represented by elements in the eAdventure engine core (e.g. frame animations) or those available through engine plug-ins (e.g. video player). In the engine, these elements use a common API, some parts of which are implemented for the specific underlying platform. The editor uses a set of core components, that allows for the direct use of the basic game elements (e.g. game character) and editor plug-ins that allow for the edition of complex elements (e.g. conversations). To provide a common *look&feel* to all editor plug-ins, a set of GUI elements is provided which includes the common elements required in game edition (i.e. graphic asset management, image and animation preview, etc).

Plug-ins can be added at both the engine and editor levels, adding flexibility to the development process and opening new opportunities to include new value-added features. From the end-user perspective, engine plug-ins introduce elements that need specific representations during the game (e.g. support for specific accessibility features), while editor plug-ins aim to improve usability, reduce the time needed to create a game, or facilitate the reuse and adaptation of complex gaming structures (e.g. conversations are made up of several independent lines, questions, etc.). From the technical perspective, engine plug-ins can help to extend the functionality of the system in different ways, such as adding new accessibility mechanisms or helping to increase compatibility (e.g. a plug-in can allow specific assets to be used in all platforms). Editor plug-ins are mostly used to represent the same information with different degrees of flexibility/complexity in the editor.

4   eAdventure 2.0 Implementation

This section presents the technical solutions used in the implementation of the eAdventure architecture. The most relevant of these include the definition of the API, how dependency injection has been used to achieve modular code, the definition and implementation of an extensible data model and the representation of such a data model at run-time through the use of a dynamic model based on game objects.

4.1   API Definition

To ease the platform extensibility and the support for plug-in development, a high-level API was defined including all the general interfaces describing eAdventure games and game elements. Every part of an eAdventure project is defined using elements available in the API, thus exposing the full functionality of the system for plug-in development. It must be noted that the use of the API in itself is limited to expert users (i.e. programmers) who may want to increase the functionality of the platform, while regular users of the platform (i.e. game creators) need not be aware of its complexity.

For example, the API includes a platform agnostic definition of colours, positions and other parameters within games. At the same time different assets such as images or animations have specific interfaces defined in the API that allow for different implementations of these elements. In addition, the basic game scene model, which includes different elements, is also accessible through the API, allowing for specific extensions (i.e. the implementation of plug-ins).

4.2   Dependency Injection

To deal with the complexity of platforms and devices in eAdventure, links between interfaces from the API and concrete implementations are established through dependency injection. This creates highly decupled code that allows for better testing, simple configuration of different platform-specific code (though configuration files) and favours code modularity. In our approach, Google Guice[4] is used, which works through configuration modules. Dependency injection is transparent for the user.

One configuration module is used for each of the platforms where eAdventure is supported. For example, the system provides a *RuntimeImageAssetRenderer* interface, which provides methods to render image assets in the games. Rendering is not accomplished in the same way in a Desktop platform as in a mobile platform like *Android*. However, we can use *RuntimeImageAssetRenderer* interface and its methods without caring about the concrete implementation, which is injected at run-time.

4.3   Data Model

The data model is represented by a tree structure that is stored using a serialized xml representation. This xml, although complex, is human-readable which can assist expert users during the creation of games.

Every data element extends the *EAdElement* basic unit (Fig. 3, a). There is no computation logic within these units as we apply the MVC (Model-View-Controller) pattern. Besides, to perform the serialization in an automatic way, Java *annotations* are used to mark the persistent parameters that are to be stored in the XML.

4.4   Dynamic Game Model: Game Objects

The data model is interpreted within the engine core to create the game. Every EAdElement is translated into a dynamic game object (GameObject, Fig. 3, c) that can be drawn and manipulated by the game engine. The specific GameObject for each EAdElement is obtained though a Game Object Factory (Fig. 3, b). Implementing the Factory pattern, combined with the dependency injection technique, allows for the easy addition of new EAdElement types with specific GameObject representations.

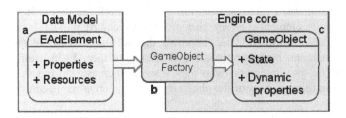

Fig. 3. EAdElements (a), which define the game model, are used to create *GameObjects* (c), through a *Game Object Factory* (b). These new elements hold the dynamic state, which changes during the game. The data contained by the *EAdElement* will not change during the game.

---

[4] http://code.google.com/p/google-guice/

As *EAdElement* is the minimal unit in the data model, the game object is the basic unit at the engine core. It has a graphical representation, and holds all the game logic, including user interaction. But still it is an abstract element, because rendering mechanisms need to be defined in every supported platform.

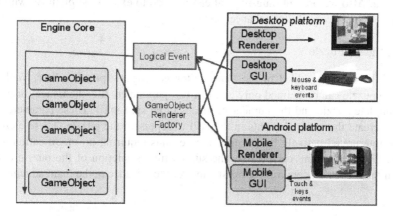

Fig. 4. GameObject is an abstract element in the engine core. Must be interpreted for the different platforms to make it available to the user, through rendering, for GUI interactions.

Each platform manages the rendering for every individual game object (Fig. 4). The GUI events sent from the different devices are translated into platform-independent logical event that can be directly interpreted by the *GameObject*.

4.5   Adding Plug-ins

The eAdventure core platform can be extended through plug-ins. An eAdventure plug-in is a set of classes and interfaces extending and using the API. Plug-ins are programmed as independent units that are loaded at start-up in both the editor and the engine (dynamic plug-in installation is not supported). Each plug-in must have a descriptor file that identifies the initialization class that must be called either in the editor or engine.

Two distinct types of plug-ins are considered: editor plug-ins and engine plug-ins. Editor plug-ins are used to manipulate and edit structures already defined by the API or even other plug-ins. These plug-ins increase the usability of the editor (e.g. by providing ready made components) and increase the productivity of the user (e.g. by simplifying the creation of some repeated elements). As an example, the eAdventure platform includes several editor plug-ins to allow the creation of in-game basic types of puzzles. Each of these puzzles are made of basic game objects, but the plug-in editor deals with the composition of these elements in more complex structures. Engine plug-ins can add new functions to the game engine (e.g. different styles of rendering for some game object) or new data elements with their corresponding interpretation during run-time.

5   Case Studies

eAdventure 2.0 allows for the creation of complex and varied educational games that can run in multiple platforms. An example of how to include jigsaw puzzles is presented. Also we present plug-ins that can be used to extend the platform with new features such as accessibility enhancements.

5.1   Jigsaw Puzzle

One of the plug-ins added to the main editor is a jigsaw puzzle editor. With this editor, a puzzle can be defined only giving a few parameters (i.e. the image formed by the complete puzzle and the number of pieces to be split into). These parameters are used to create the basic elements in the API to represent the puzzle. These elements can be interpreted natively by the engine core, thus requiring no modification to the engine. From the game perspective, the successful completion of the puzzle can be used in the game as a condition to be met in order to advance in the main adventure.

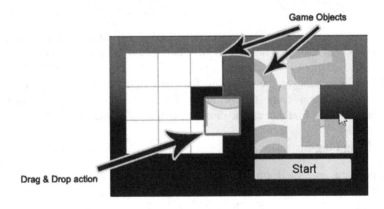

Fig. 5. Jigsaw *Puzzle* is interpreted as a group of standard *Game Objects*. Each of these elements has associated a series of actions (e.g. drag & drop), all defined by the API.

5.2   Adding Accessibility Features

Engine plug-ins were used to enhanced the accessibility of the platform. One of the stereotypes considered was people with low vision. One of the typical problems that people with low vision have is that they perceive an altered brightness of the colors. To deal with that it is necessary to render the game using a high contrast combination profile that allows them to distinguish game elements (objects and characters) from the background. While this problem is relatively simple to solve in text-based applications (e.g. the Web) it is much harder in highly interactive visual applications like games where images with heterogeneous distributions of colors are the most frequent type of content. In these applications how each element is rendered cannot be decided in isolation, but the whole context of the application must be considered (i.e. the interrelation between elements is important).

Other considerations must also be taken into account. For example, some elements of the game interface (e.g. buttons) need to be larger, along with the font size, which is especially challenging to deal with if the text is embedded directly in one of the game images.

To deal with these needs we added new accessibility features to the eAdventure platform using the plug-in model. When the system identifies that the user needs a low-vision configuration, scene backgrounds are rendered using a low-brightness filter and game elements are rendered using a high-brightness filter. Game elements that are not relevant in that moment are also rendered using the background filter (see Fig. 6).

Fig. 6. From left to right, first image shows a scene rendered in normal mode. Second image shows the same scene with low-vision rendering activated. The last image shows the scene when an object is selected (all others are rendered as part of the background to improve usability).

6   Final Remarks

The new eAdventure model allows for a hybrid game model creation that combines new game genres with the adventure game metaphor as a backbone. This increases the game expressivity but at the same time maintains the simplicity of game creation and maintenance, achieved though the use of plug-ins.

The plug-in architecture facilitates the development of the whole platform and allows the evaluation of new features in educational games from both technical and pedagogical perspectives.

Next steps in the project are to increase the number of plug-ins available to simplify the development of more complete educational games. For example, we are considering the development of new plug-ins to introduce social features to the platform such as game leader-boards, achievement badges and others to ease the inclusion of new sorts of media into educational video games.

Acknowledgements. The Ministry of Education (grants Movilidad I-D+i PR2010-0070 and TIN2010-21735-C02-02) and the Ministry of Industry (grants TSI-020110-2009-170, TSI-020312-2009-27) have partially supported this work, as well as the Complutense University of Madrid and the Regional Government of Madrid (research group GR35/10-A and project e-Madrid S2009/TIC-1650), and the PROACTIVE EU project (505469-2009-LLP-ES-KA3-KA3MP) and the GALA EU Network of Excellence in serious games (FP7-ICT-2009-5-258169).

References

1. Amory, A., Naicker, K., Vincent, J., Adams, C.: The Use of Computer Games as an Educational Tool: Identification of Appropriate Game Types and Game Elements. British Journal of Educational Technology 30(4), 311–321 (1999)
2. Dickey, M.D.: Engaging by design: How engagement strategies in popular computer and video games can inform instructional design. Educational Technology Research and Development 53(2), 67–83 (2005)
3. Hays, R.T.: The effectiveness of instructional games: a literature review and discussion. Technical Report 2005–2004 for the Naval Air Center Training Systems Division: Orlando, FL (2005)
4. Torrente, J., Moreno-Ger, P., Fernández-Manjón, B., Sierra, J.L.: Instructor-oriented Authoring Tools for Educational Videogames. In: 8th International Conference on Advanced Learning Technologies (ICALT 2008), Santander, Spain. IEEE Computer Society Press (2008)
5. Federation of American Scientists. Summit on Educational Games: Harnessing the power of video games for learning (2006),
   http://www.fas.org/gamesummit/Resources/
   Summit%20on%20Educational%20Games.pdf
6. Baltra, A.: Language Learning through Computer Adventure Games. Simulation Gaming 21(4), 445–452 (1990)
7. Moreno-Ger, P., Martinez-Ortiz, I., Fernández-Manjón, B.: The <e-Game> project: Facilitating the Development of Educational Adventure Games. Cognition and Exploratory Learning in the Digital age (CELDA 2005), Porto, Portugal, IADIS (2005)
8. Moreno-Ger, P., Torrente, J., Bustamante, J., Fernández-Galaz, C., Fernández-Manjón, B., Comas-Rengifo, M.D.: Application of a low-cost web-based simulation to improve students' practical skills in medical education. Int. J. Med. Inform. 79, 459–467 (2010)

A Study of Peer Discourse in Computer-Supported Collaborative Learning Environment

Ken W. Li

Department of Information and Communications Technology
Hong Kong Institute of Vocational Education (Tsing Yi)
20 Tsing Yi Road, Tsing Island, Hong Kong, China
kenli@vtc.edu.hk

Abstract. Working with peers at computers may cultivate social interaction but what patterns of student-student talk are associated with statistical thinking in an IT environment are not well studied. An observation study focusing on social interaction was therefore conducted in the context of statistics classroom teaching. The observation study drew on Mercer's work [9] to categorise student-student talk as exploratory, cumulative, or disputational. Most talk was of the exploratory type, characterised by reasoning and statistical thinking, and only a few instances were classified as cumulative when students were attempting straightforward learning tasks or maintaining harmonious social relations. No instances of disputational talk were observed. A finer grained analysis of students' talk, using an adaptation of Kumpulainens's framework [1], identified some forms of talk that were used for maintaining social interaction, while other forms were associated with making reasoning explicit and activating higher order thinking for a variety of sophisticated tasks, for instance, deducing practical implications for regression parameters.

Keywords: social interaction, statistical thinking, exploratory talk, cumulative talk, disputational talk.

1 Introduction

The attention of most teachers and students has been drawn to eye-appealing and dynamic features offered by IT as well as its powerful and interactive computational capabilities. They perceive educational software embellished with animation, narration, structured hints, instantaneous feedback and the provision of information and factual knowledge as a vehicle for transmitting knowledge to students and/or individualising learning to suit each student's learning needs or pace. However, these are only of partial relevance to the role of IT in reordering the context of education [5]. Also, individualisation of learning is not consistent with Vygotsky's sociocultural theory [11] in which learning is conceived as a social process leading to an exchange of personal views, sharing of information, insights and ideas and offers of mutual assistance. For this reason, Jones and Mercer [5] and Mercer [9] believed that IT has much to do with re-organising an environment in which students and teachers or students among themselves develop learning partnerships to socially construct

H. Leung et al. (Eds.): ICWL 2011, LNCS 7048, pp. 31–40, 2011.

knowledge through peer collaboration, classroom talk and social interaction. Many researchers (e.g., [4]-[9], and so forth) interested in how IT supports social processes in learning have made of use of concepts from Vygotsky's sociocultural theory [11].

Although there is no definite answer to what is the best way to teach students using IT in a classroom, sociocultural perspectives offer certain guidelines for developing a model of teaching and learning in an IT environment in the way that should allow students to take more control over their learning by working collaboratively with peers and thus constructing knowledge through sharing ideas and resolving conflicting views (see [8]). In this paper, an empirical study was conducted to address the research question of how IT supports student-student talk and assists in developing understanding in a statistics classroom.

2   Research Design

Since the empirical study was set within a classroom, the research design and associated methods of collection and analysis of data were selected for their relevance to teachers and students as research participants. The participants included a teacher and 58 students enrolling in Year 2 of the Higher Diploma in Applied Statistics and Computing course in the Hong Kong Institute of Vocational Education. All the students had attained the elementary level of probabilistic and statistical concepts in their Year 1 study. Among the students, 31 were females and 27 were males, ranging in age from 19 to 22.

This cohort of students was selected because Regression Modelling is a module taught in their Year 2 study in which the teacher planned for improving classroom teaching practice by means of developing and adopting a model of statistical thinking and a cognitive model of correlation comprehension within an IT environment in which web resources and Excel were utilised with an emphasis on social processes of learning (refer to [2] and [12]). The delivery of the module follows a pattern of 2-hour lectures supported by 1-hour computing laboratory sessions in each of fifteen weeks. The lectures were delivered to the whole class in a lecture theatre equipped with IT equipment, software and audio-video aids.

The students had been divided into three tutorial groups for course administration and management since their Year 1 study. To increase students' opportunities for peer learning and collaboration, the students within each tutorial group were subdivided into collaborating groups: 2-person groups and a 3-person group when necessary (i.e., where group size is an odd number). Students were assigned laboratory exercises demanding the analysis, design or implementation of the solutions in a computing laboratory.

Data were gathered through an observation study aiming at examining what typical form of social interaction was beneficial to teaching and learning and how such social interaction might be useful according to sociocultural perspectives on learning. In an observation study, verbal speech and peer interaction were audiotaped.

3   Methodology of Data Analysis

The students' conversations were transcribed in full, with relevant excerpts being selected for analysis within a Vygotskian framework [10]. Peer talk was initially analysed with the aid of the framework of Fisher [3] and Mercer [9], who studied how each of the categories of exploratory, cumulative and disputational talk was developed; and how different talk categories were associated with different outcomes in collaborative learning.

Furthermore, the nature of peer talk and the contents of their dialogue were analysed qualitatively based on Kumpulainen's classifications of collaborative talk [1]: informative, compositional, interrogative, judgmental, organizational, responsive, reproductional, affectional, argumentational, expositional, heuristic, experiential, hypothetical, imaginative and intentional. Only those categories of talk that were relevant to the context of a statistics classroom were used. Table 1 shows how these categories of talk are expressed during regression modelling work.

Table 1. Classifications of talk during statistical work (modified from [1])

Classifications	Description
Informative	Seeking factual information or knowledge previously learnt.
Compositional	Deducing practical implications for regression parameters involving discussion of data context, scatterplots graphing and hypothesis testing.
Interrogative	Seeking learning partners' feedback or approval when puzzling about their own work.
Judgmental	Conveying one's agreement or disagreement.
Organisational	Orgainising ideas and wording when presenting statistical work or constructing persuasive lines of statistical reasoning.
External thinking	Articulating one's thought when presenting statistical output aloud.
Responsive	Showing one's participation in learning activities or expressing one's agreement to a less extent.
Reproductional	Repeating learning partners' response and one's own response without any elaboration or critical evaluation.
Affectional	Expressing one's personal feelings, for example, task accomplishment.
Argumentational	Challenging someone's proposal or defending one's argument with concrete evidence.
Expositional	Discovering things unfamiliar or unanticipated without detailed planning, such as interacting with data, studying problem context, looking for alternative approaches, etc.
Hypothetical	Proposing statistical ideas without providing any evidence or explanation.
Heuristic	Formulating or regulating strategies for appraising correlation and model fitting, refining a regression model, etc.

4   Research Findings

The analysis that follows uses excerpts from the conversations of one pair of female students, identified by their initials, P.L. and K.W. who worked together to accomplish two major tasks in a computer laboratory. These tasks were chosen because some students were not fully aware that correlation analysis was an effective statistical method for studying a linear relationship between two variables, thus potentially laying foundations for fitting data to a regression model. They experimented with given regression data so as to discuss its strength and direction of linear relationship.

4.1   Conceptual Understanding of the Strength of Data Relationship

K.W. and P.L. discussed how the correlation coefficient changed when manipulating scatters of data and how this reflected changes in the strength of the data relationship.

Excerpt

1.	P.L.:	What does the strength (of data relationship) mean? (**Interrogative**)
2.	K.W.:	Wait! Let me go to the page (Section 12.2.1) first. (**Responsive**)
3.	P.L.:	OK! Should we just discuss the strength? (**Interrogative**)
4.	K.W.:	Study the strength of linear relationship between two variables. (**Responsive**)
5.	P.L.:	Study the strength of linear relationship between two variables. (**Reproductional**)

After P.L. had read the task inaudibly, *"Go to Section 12.2.1, study the strength of linear relationship between two variables"*, she realised she did not understand the meaning of strength of data relationship. She consciously initiated a search for the meaning so she asked, *"What does the strength (of data relationship) mean?"* to get the meaning clear prior to attempting subsequent tasks.

Excerpt

6.	K.W.:	We did that in the lecture yesterday. I remember if it (the button of a visualisation tool) goes left hand side, it will be (data have) a negative relation(ship). (**Informative**)
7.	P.L.:	Yes, when it (data trend) goes to ... (**Responsive**)
8.	K.W.:	It is a negative relationship, correlation and the slope will become negative. (**Expositional**)
9.	P.L.:	Yes. (**Responsive**)

K.W. next recalled correlation concepts discussed in the last lecture. P.L. and K.W. then used the interactive tool offered by the website, http://www.seeingstatistics.com as a means of exploring the strength as well as the direction of the data relationship.

The tool enabled students to see vividly how their correlation changed as they manipulated the scattering of data. The function of K.W.'s dialogue here was *informative* when she recalled how to quantify correlation associated with data patterns in a scatterplot. P.L. attempted to illustrate a negative correlation but was interrupted by K.W. And K.W. pointed out that the correlation and the slope of the line fitting the data in their scatterplot were both negative, a proposal with which P.L. agreed.

Using the interactive tool, K.W. further explored the *"strength of linear relationship of data"* concept. They extended their vision to reading the value of r from a scatterplot. Apparently, the tool enriched their understanding of correlation as mapping a graphical representation of correlation into a numerical representation. K.W. asked P.L. what r was. P.L. answered and sought K.W.'s social approval because she was unsure of her answer. The high amount of the use of the *interrogative* function in their conversation showed they checked their understanding with one another to make sure they grasped the concept correctly. The *judgmental* function was also displayed in P.L.'s talk, as she was vocal in expressing her agreement. She also supplemented K.W.'s partial answer as a social mode of thinking. Her agreement was significant in getting herself and her learning partner more involved in thinking about the *data strength*.

Excerpt

10.	K.W.:	It is more and more negatively correlated when the … (**Expositional**)
11.	P.L.:	When the correlation coefficient … (**Expositional**)
12.	K.W.:	When the button (of the visualisation tool) moves to the right (left). (**Expositional**)
13.	P.L.:	When the correlation coefficient, r becomes −1 and the slope becomes negative. (**Expositional**)
14.	K.W.:	What is the switched sign? (**Interrogative**)
15.	P.L.:	The changes of r … (**Expositional**)
16.	K.W.:	r is what? (**Interrogative**)
17.	P.L.:	r is a correlation coefficient, isn't it? (**Interrogative**)
18.	K.W.:	Oh! I see. So when the correlation coefficient … (**Interrogative**)
19.	P.L.:	Yes, (the correlation) increases. (**Responsive**)
20.	K.W.:	The correlation increases and tends to 1, the slope gets … (**Interrogative**)
21.	P.L.:	Positive (**External thinking**)
22.	K.W.:	Yes, becomes positive (**Responsive**)
23.	P.L.:	Yes. (**Judgmental**)
24.	K.W.:	… more and more positively correlated. (**Responsive**)
25.	P.L.:	Yes. (**Judgmental**)

P.L. had her own interpretation of *"strength of linear relationship of data"* but this was found to be wrong. In the next segment, K.W. clarified P.L.'s misunderstanding when she mixed up two concepts that quantify a data relationship, "strength" and "direction".

Excerpt

26.	P.L.:	Is this the strength? (**Interrogative**)
27.	K.W.:	The strength means (irrespective of) whether it's negatively scattered or is positively correlated. The strength refers to data dispersion (scattering). (**Informative**)
28.	P.L.:	Oh! That's the data dispersion. (**Expositional**)
29.	K.W.:	I'm not talking upward or downward (slope). Does it mean the negative (value of r) more dispersed (scattered)? (**Interrogative**)
30.	P.L.:	Not upward or downward, right? Not the direction, right? (Interrogative)
31.	K.W.:	You can still mention the direction of data relationship. (**Informative**)
32.	P.L.:	Does it mean when the more negative correlation, the more dispersion (scattering) is in the data? (**Interrogative**)
33.	K.W.:	No, the r-value is from -1 to 1. When it tends to (and is) very close to -1, the correlation (points) is very close together. The points are very close together which means the strength is strong. (**External thinking**)
34.	P.L.:	Yes, I know. That is to check whether or not the data are dispersed (scattered). (**Responsive**)
35.	K.W.:	No, not dispersed (scattered), they are close together. Also, when it (the correlation) is very close to 1, the points are also very close together. (**Argumentional**)
36.	P.L.:	Oh, I see! (**Responsive**)
37.	K.W.:	When the number (correlation) is around 0, ... (**Expositional**)
38.	P.L.:	Very dispersion (dispersed) (**Responsive**)
39.	K.W.:	Yes, very dispersion. The value's (correlation coefficient) in the middle ... (**Expositional**)
40.	P.L.:	I understand what you mean. (**Affectional**) OK! We can do (Section) 12.2.2.

In fact, the major difficulty P.L. encountered is related to her unidirectional representation of a numerical value as illustrated in her two questions, *"Does it mean the negative (value of r) more dispersed (scattered)?"* and *"Does it mean when the more negative correlation, the more dispersion is in the data?"* Obviously, these two questions were related to a simple quantifying concept, a negative value was construed as being less than a positive value, and hence her inference was that a negative *r* has more dispersion. P.L.'s misconception was dispelled by K.W. who assertively re-iterated how data scattering was related to and illuminated the strength of data relationship (Excerpts 33 and 35).

Based on Mercer's categories [9], the talk between K.W. and P.L. changed from *cumulative* to *exploratory* and displayed a lot of explicit reasoning when the learning task moved on to studying the strength of data relationship. When interacting with the data patterns, P.L. aimed at understanding the meaning of the "strength" of data relationship, whereas K.W. succeeded in her attempt to review the concept of data strength. Excerpts 6-25 illustrated that K.W. used expressive language to develop conceptual understanding and K.W.'s improved understanding resulted from a joint communicative accomplishment in which P.L. supplemented K.W.'s answers from time to time. K.W. expressed lucid knowledge of data strength (see Excerpt 27) but P.L. confused "strength" with "direction" of data relationship (see Excerpts 32 and 34). K.W. offered greater assistance to P.L. in developing her knowledge and understanding by adopting an interpretive strategy rather than repeating her explanations. The strategy K.W. employed primarily involved the first cycle of the pattern recognition-interpretive process in the Cognitive Model of Correlation Comprehension [2] in which she initially contrasted the spatial association between pairs of data and subsequently inspected whether the data cloud (the scatter of data) condensed and exhibited a straight line that was neither vertical nor horizontal, that is, an interpretive-integrative process. Based on this strategy, she manipulated different scatterings of data to illustrate the concept of "strength". Nevertheless, P.L. did not accept K.W.'s elaborations without justification. Instead, P.L. critically evaluated what was being explained by K.W. by interrogation and in doing so became more involved with knowledge construction in order to consolidate her own understanding. They built up shared understanding as their talk moved to higher level functions. K.W. gained a more refined level of understanding as she got the opportunity to check and elaborate what she already knew, while P.L. strived for a clear understanding.

As before, K.W.'s talk exhibited a variety of functions to clarify P.L.'s misconceptions about the strength of the data relationship. P.L.'s utterances were relatively more *interrogative* and *responsive* in nature because she was in pursuit of the meaning of correlation and used *questioning* to help herself get the concept clear and also showed she was listening to K.W. *Expositional* talk was also important as the students used expressive language to interact with and manipulate the data and comment on the value of r. Overall, in this segment of dialogue, there was increased use of *expositional* talk consistent with its *exploratory* tone (as in [9]). Interrogation and response were still present, but no longer accompanied by the social reinforcement of *reproductional* and *affectional* talk.

4.2   Conceptual Understanding of the Direction of Data Relationship

After K.W. and P.L. found they had a firm grasp of the *"strength of linear relationship of data"* concept, they further discussed how the correlation coefficient changed with respect to the direction of the data relationship when manipulating scatters of data. P.L. and K.W. moved on to the next task in Laboratory Exercise 1, "Go to Section 12.2.2, study the direction of linear relationship between two variables". Getting to know whether or not data form pattern(s) is a prerequisite for justifying the direction of the data relationship. K.W. and P.L. took turns to illustrate the *"direction of data relationship"* concept.

Excerpt

41.	P.L. & K.W.:	Study the direction of linear relationship between two variables. (**Unclassified**)
42.	K.W.:	Direction? Direction? Now we should tell whether it's (the data patterns) going upward or downward. (**Interrogative**)
43.	P.L.:	Yes. (**Responsive**)
44.	K.W.:	We can see that when the r is .... (**External thinking**)

45.	P.L.:	very close to –1 (**Expositional**)
46.	K.W.:	… very close to –1, it is a downward slope. (**Responsive**)
47.	P.L.:	Yes. (**Responsive**)
48.	K.W.:	And this is its direction. The correlation increases … (**Expositional**)
49.	P.L.:	to +1 (**Expositional**)
50.	K.W.:	… very close to +1, the slope is … (**External thinking**)
51.	P.L.:	positive (**Expositional**)
52.	K.W.:	… going upward (**Expositional**)
53.	P.L.:	going upward (**Reproductional**)
54.	K.W.:	Yes, it is a positive slope. (**Expositional**)
55.	P.L.:	Yes. (**Responsive**)
56.	K.W.:	OK? (**Interrogative**)
57.	P.L.:	OK! (**Responsive**)
58.	K.W.:	We've done that. (**Affectional**)
59.	P.L.:	Yes. (**Responsive**)

K.W. questioned herself to articulate her thoughts for how they should check the direction of the data relationship, *"Now we should tell whether it's (the data patterns) going upward or downward"* (Excerpt 42). P.L. responded to confirm the way of checking the direction K.W. proposed, *"Yes"* (Excerpt 43). The students appeared to be interacting closely with each other's thinking to reckon on the data patterns by finishing each other's sentences (Excerpts 44-52), thereby predominantly using *expositional* talk, together with a few *responsive* utterances for expressing their agreement and their participation. P.L.'s response (Excerpt 53) was *reproductional* in nature as repeating K.W.'s response but without any elaboration. K.W. wanted to conclude the direction of the data relationship using *expositional* talk (Excerpt 54). The remaining Excerpts 55-59 were mainly *responsive* and only K.W. expressed task accomplishment using *affectional* talk (Excerpt 58). K.W. also wanted to confirm P.L.'s understanding, *"OK?"* (Excerpt 56), as P.L. had previously displayed confusion between "strength" and "direction" concepts. They were involved in making personal judgments of the data trend (direction) with the aid of an interactive tool and related discussions. They were able to map the sign of the numerical representation of r onto the slope of a line fitting the data. There was a high degree of mutuality in this learning process as the two students came to a clear understanding of conceptual meaning of the "direction" of data relationship.

Using Mercer's framework [9], their dialogue was categorised as *exploratory* talk in which P.L. and K.W. both engaged critically but constructively with each other's ideas. This is evident in the pattern of predominantly *expositional, interrogative – responsive* and *external thinking* functions. P.L. was more confident and proactive at deriving her answers successfully. It was observed that she substantiated her answers by using a mouse to trace the path of neighbouring data points that is, (x_1 , y_1) and (x_2 , y_2), (x_2 , y_2) and (x_3 , y_3), … , (x_{n-1} , y_{n-1}) and (x_n , y_n) where

(x_{n-1}, y_{n-1}) and (x_n, y_n) are the co-ordinates of the second last and the last points of the data set respectively. This was consistent with the second cycle of the pattern recognition-integrative process in the Cognitive Model of Correlation Comprehension ([2]). However she skipped the second cycle of interpretive-integrative process to check data linearity because the laboratory exercise was confined to studying linear relationship between two variables. She checked each slope associated with each pair of neighbouring data points, that is, the third cycle of the pattern recognition-integrative process ([2]). She then summarised slopes associated with pair of neighbouring data points to determine whether the linear relationship was positive (upward slope) or negative (downward slope).

To sum up, their *exploratory* talk was typically talk which requested clarification with responses which provided elaborations and justifications as the learning task moved on to studying the direction of the data relationship. K.W.'s talk displayed various functions but was mainly *expositional, external thinking* and *interrogative* in nature when taking the proactive role of appraising the direction of data relationship. *Expositional* talk was used when she proposed partial answers. *External thinking* was used for articulating her thoughts, and *interrogative* talk was used for asking P.L. to propose ways to tackle the problem and confirm P.L.'s own understanding. P.L. seldom asked questions but actively participated in the appraisal task. She followed K.W.'s proposal and suggested some answers resulting from her own insight. That was why her talk was mostly *responsive* and *expositional*.

5   Conclusion

With regard to student-student talk, the evidence presented here suggests that students were active participants and held a common conception of what could be achieved cooperatively. Almost all of the talk analysed in this paper was relevant to the tasks at hand, and there was no evidence of Mercer's disputational pattern of talk, where opinions are presented and disagreements emerge without attempt at justification. Most of the students' talk was exploratory and focused on a particular theme related to the task, or segment of a task, that students were tackling. Exploratory talk was observed when it was necessary for students to use higher order thinking to accomplish more sophisticated learning tasks. In the context of regression modelling, students talked about what to do and how to do it, what worked (and what did not) and why, in order to make joint decisions that led to progress. A few instances of cumulative talk were observed, when straightforward tasks such as scatterplot comprehension were attempted. In these circumstances, students proposed ideas or accepted the ideas of their learning partners without finding it necessary to give or seek justification. So both exploratory and cumulative talk proved to be valuable for knowledge construction. Moreover, group interaction was associated with positive affective responses so that these tasks and the talk that they promoted may have been beneficial in building social relationships and fostering rapport between students.

Analysis of talk in the statistics classroom aimed to portray the nature and role of classroom talk in the teaching and learning process, but the analysis may be over-interpreted or under-interpreted. This is possibly because a few collaborating groups of students rather than all were selected for audiotaping their talk at the time they collaboratively worked at computers. One reason for not audiotaping all groups of students was related to the limited resources available. Another reason concerned the anxiety of that may have been felt by some collaborating groups of students at having their peer talk audiotaped. Some students were reluctant to talk or spoke softly so that their voices could hardly be heard. Each of these reasons reduced the coverage in the observation study and may have resulted in some distortion of the findings.

Acknowledgments. The author would like to thank Prof. Gary McClelland at Colorado University for his permission to use the webbook, Seeing Statistics at http://www.seeingstatistics.com.

References

1. Kumpulainen, K.: Children's Talk during Collaborative Writing at the Computer. Reading 28(2), 6–9 (1994)
2. Li, K., Goos, M.: Reinforcing Students' Correlation Comprehension. International Journal of Learning 17(11), 261–274 (2011)
3. Fisher, E.: Educationally Important Types of Children's Talk. In: Corson, D.J (series ed.), Wegerif, R., Scrimshaw, P (vol. eds.) Language and Education Library: Computers and Talk in the Primary Classroom, vol. 12, pp. 22–37. Multilingual Matters Ltd., Clevedon (1997)
4. Goos, M.: Technology as a Tool for Transforming Mathematical Tasks. In: Galbraith, P., Blum, W., Booker, G., Huntley, I.D. (eds.) Mathematical Modelling: Teaching and Assessment in a Technology-Rich World, pp. 103–113. Horwood Publishing, Chichester (1998)
5. Jones, A., Mercer, N.: Theories of Learning and Information Technology. In: Scrimshaw, P. (ed.) Language, Classrooms and Computers, pp. 11–26. Routledge, London (1993)
6. Light, P.: Collaborative Learning with Computers. In: Scrimshaw, P. (ed.) Language, Classrooms and Computers, pp. 40–54. Routledge, London (1993)
7. Scrimshaw, P.: Teachers, Learners and Computers. In: Scrimshaw, P. (ed.) Language, Classrooms and Computers, pp. 3–10. Routledge, London (1993)
8. Wegerif, R., Scrimshaw, P.: Introduction: Computers in the Classroom Context. In: Corson, D.J (series ed.), Wegerif, R., Scrimshaw, P (vol. eds.) Language and Education Library: Computers and Talk in the Primary Classroom, vol. 12, pp. 1–9. Multilingual Matters Ltd., Clevedon (1997)
9. Mercer, N.: The Guided Construction of Knowledge. Multilingual Matters Ltd., Clevedon (1995)
10. Vygotsky, L.S.: Thought and Language. MIT Press, Massachusetts (1962)
11. Vygotsky, L.S.: Mind in Society. Harvard University Press, Massachusetts (1978)
12. Li, K.: A Pedagogy Model for an IT Environment. In: Kong, S.C., Ogata, H. (eds.) The 17th International Conference of on Computers in Education. The Asia-Pacific Society for Computers in Education, Hong Kong (2009)

eMUSE - Integrating Web 2.0 Tools in a Social Learning Environment

Elvira Popescu and Dan Cioiu

University of Craiova, Software Engineering Department
A.I. Cuza 13, 200585 Craiova, Romania
popescu_elvira@software.ucv.ro

Abstract. Traditional teaching methods should be adapted to accommodate the learning needs of the new generation of digital native students. One approach is to provide support for social learning by integrating Web 2.0 tools in educational settings. This paper focuses on a platform specifically built to this end: eMUSE (empowering **M**ash**U**ps for **S**ocial **E**-learning), which aggregates several social media components by means of mashups. In addition, the platform provides learner tracking functionality, by retrieving students' actions with each tool and storing them in a local database for further processing. Thus eMUSE offers value-added services for both students and teachers: common access point to facilitate tools' management; help students keep track of their contributions as well as their peers'; a simple way for instructors to monitor the class activity as well as quickly check, visualize and grade each student's contributions. The paper includes a comprehensive rationale underlying eMUSE, a description of the platform architecture and functionalities, as well as an initial experimental validation.

Keywords: social learning, Web 2.0, mashups, learner tracking.

1 Introduction

The generation of students we are teaching today was raised in the context of digital technologies, in a world of communication and wide availability of information. According to [15], these so called "digital natives" have different patterns of work, attention and learning preferences. Therefore, the traditional teaching methods should be adapted to the needs of this new "Internet generation", offering support for social learning.

A simple way to achieve this is the integration of Web 2.0 tools (also known as social software tools, e.g., blogs, wikis, social bookmarking systems, media sharing tools) in the learning process. Up to the present, there are many papers which report on the successful use of these Web 2.0 tools in educational settings [3], [7], [10], [12], [13]. While not all studies are positive, many researchers obtained encouraging results with respect to student satisfaction, knowledge gain and/or learning efficiency. This can be explained by the fact that the principles Web 2.0 is based on (user-centered, participative architecture, openness, interaction, social networks, collaboration) are in line with modern educational theories such

H. Leung et al. (Eds.): ICWL 2011, LNCS 7048, pp. 41–50, 2011.

as socio-constructivism [16]. According to it, knowledge cannot be transmitted but has to be constructed by the individual, by means of collaborative efforts of groups of learners. Furthermore, with Web 2.0, the user is not just content consumer but also content generator (often in a collaborative manner). This is in line with contribution-based pedagogies which state that collaboratively creating learning resources and sharing them with others are promising practices through which students can learn efficiently [7].

The majority of the experiments reported so far involve a single Web 2.0 tool and were realized in an ad-hoc manner [10]. However, using a combination of these tools could be more adequate for some learning scenarios, e.g.: i) a social bookmarking application for finding, storing, tagging and sharing links to resources of interest for a project; and ii) a wiki for collaboratively writing the project documentation; and iii) a blog for posting about the project progress, experience exchange, help requests, critical and constructive feedback to peers. Obviously, this places a lot of burden on the teacher, who needs to set up the learning space from scratch and then continuously monitor students' activity on several scattered tools. Hence the need for a platform that would integrate a wide range of social media components, providing also more support to the students and teachers: common access point to facilitate tool management; help students keep track of their contributions as well as their peers'; a simple way for instructors to keep track of the class activity as well as quickly monitor, visualize and grade each student's contributions. This led us to conceive, design and build such a social learning environment, which we called eMUSE (empowering MashUps for Social E-learning). The name comes from the underlying technology: the Web 2.0 tools were integrated into the platform by means of mashups.

A more detailed rationale underlying eMUSE is presented in the following section. Subsequently, an overview of the platform architecture, functionalities and implementation is included in section 3. Section 4 covers the positioning of eMUSE with respect to other Web 2.0-enhanced learning spaces, as well as an initial experimental evaluation of the platform. Finally, the paper ends with some conclusions and future research directions.

2   eMUSE Rationale

The eMUSE platform that we envisaged had to offer the following functionalities:

1. provide integrated access to all the Web 2.0 tools selected by the instructor for the course at hand: common access point, detailed usage instructions, summary of the latest activity
2. retrieve students' actions with each tool and store them in a local database
3. offer a summary of each student's activity, including graphical visualization, evolution over time, comparisons with peers, as well as aggregated data
4. compute a score based on the recorded student activity (following instructor-defined criteria)
5. provide basic administrative services (authentication service, enroll students to the course, edit profile etc.).

The main rationale for introducing eMUSE was to cater for the learning needs of digital native students. However, when designing the platform, we also had in mind the needs of the instructor, as well as the researcher, as detailed in the following subsections.

2.1   eMUSE for the Learner

The fact that students have a place where they can access their own accounts to all Web 2.0 tools required for the course, as well as the accounts of their peers, provides an **ease of access** as well as a reduction in the time and effort needed for the tool management task.

Furthermore, having all the tools integrated in one platform creates a **sense of community** between learners, which is deemed paramount in academic settings, increasing both student success and student retention rates [6]. Relying on eMUSE as a course support tool provides the necessary social interaction.

Another advantage of eMUSE is that it integrates Web 2.0 tools that learners are already **familiar** with from out-of-school activities [12], like Blogger, MediaWiki, Twitter, Delicious, YouTube etc. Thus, students have the opportunity to use the pedagogically valuable tools in a semi-formal framework, in collaboration with their peers, inside the eMUSE platform. In this sense, eMUSE is somewhat similar to **Personal Learning Environments**, like MUPPLE [17]. Unlike these systems, however, the control over the selection of tools that will be used for a course belongs to the instructor, not to the learner. This can be seen as a positive aspect, relieving the burden on the student, since "too much freedom and lack of structure can create chaos, which hinders the learning process" [9]. Furthermore, even when learners do not encounter problems in choosing the right tools for collaborative work, synchronization of work is difficult and time-consuming [9]. Therefore, having a common access point and a continuously updated overview of the most recent peer activity is beneficial for the students.

One of the meta-skills that students need to learn is to take initiative and responsibility for their own learning [9]. This could be boosted by the opportunity to visualize their own progress, as well as to position themselves with respect to the other peers. eMUSE is thus offering an important support for **self-monitoring and self-evaluation**, which in turn may spur learning.

The scores which can be computed by the system based on students' actions with the Web 2.0 tools provide the necessary incentive for the more result-oriented and exam-oriented students. Since these scores also include some explanations, the students are provided with the necessary **feedback** as well, which is extremely important in informal learning [9].

By providing scores, as well as instant comparative evaluation of learners' work (in quantitative terms), the platform responds to the digital native students' need for **"quick gratification"** [15]. eMUSE is thus in line with Vassileva's recommendations that learning environments should try to "tie learning more explicitly to social rewards in terms of marks and credentials" [15].

Due to the provision of comparative evaluations and continuously updated overviews of latest activity, **competitiveness** is also enhanced; as reported in

[7], students are "pushed" by finding out that a peer has published a blog post and they no longer wait until the deadline to make their contribution.

Furthermore, the platform takes advantage of the fact that many of today's students have a **social motivation for learning** (e.g., finding a piece of information to impress one's peers, offering help in a group task) [15], by encouraging participation and contributions.

2.2 eMUSE for the Instructor

First of all, instructors may choose from a **variety of tools** that they can integrate in their course (currently seven Web 2.0 tools are included - Blogger, MediaWiki, Twitter, Delicious, YouTube, Picasa, SlideShare - but more can be envisaged). Thus, a **wide range of pedagogical scenarios** can be designed, corresponding to the particularities of the course as well as teacher's preferences. Clear instructional guidelines can be provided to the students by means of the usage help files associated to each tool.

The platform offers instructors the degree of control needed, providing continuous **monitoring of students' activity**. This is one of the main advantages of our platform versus similar systems, which do not collect and store students' actions with the Web 2.0 tools.

This tracking and monitoring functionality of eMUSE can prove valuable also from an institutional point of view. As Sclater pointed out, "Institutions need to be careful that they do not lose the opportunity to track what students are doing. If they fail to record valuable data on how students are using learning tools and content, it will be far more difficult to enhance the courses and provide remedial assistance to learners with difficulties" [14].

The **suggestive graphical visualization** functionality of the students' actions with the Web 2.0 tools proves very helpful for the teacher. By simply looking at the students' contributions over time, the instructor can get the big picture, spot the problems and follow the class progress. Moreover, since all the data are stored in a local database, they are readily available for **further processing and analysis**; based on the results, teachers may choose to improve the next edition of the course.

Instructors may use the scores automatically computed by the platform as a component in their grading scheme or at least as an orientation. Since these scores are based on quantitative aspects only, they should definitely be doubled by manual analysis of the quality of students' contributions; however, the scores could be a valuable indicator in themselves and a **support for teachers in the evaluation/grading process**.

2.3 eMUSE for the Researcher

Despite the growing number of papers on the subject, the full potential of Web 2.0 for education is yet to be established and many questions still lie ahead, as summarized in [8]. The majority of the experiments reported so far involve a single Web 2.0 tool and were realized in an ad-hoc manner [10]. Hence, the need for a platform which can provide the required **support for systematic research**: i) various Web 2.0 tools which can be integrated in different combinations and pedagogical scenarios; ii) graphical visualizations of the students' activity; iii) collecting and storing students' actions, making them readily available for further analysis and processing (e.g., statistical analysis, data mining). eMUSE meets all these conditions and we believe it will prove very helpful in our systematic research endeavors.

3   Implementation Overview

The first step towards the creation of eMUSE was to select the most suitable Web 2.0 tools to be integrated into the system, which meet two requirements: i) have a demonstrated pedagogical value (according to case studies reported in the literature); ii) offer technical support for mashup integration (well documented and maintained APIs, RSS feeds etc.). We therefore decided to add the following tools in the first version of eMUSE: blog (Blogger), wiki (MediaWiki), social bookmarking tool (Delicious), microblogging tool (Twitter), media sharing tools (YouTube, Picasa, SlideShare). Naturally, the range of social media components could be subsequently extended.

The integration of the Web 2.0 tools into the platform was done by means of **mashups**, ensuring a lightweight architecture, with loosely-coupled components. A mashup represents a combination of data and/or functionalities from two or more external sources to create a new Web application. Paper [1] presents a review of mashup applications in various domains; examples of e-learning applications include: [2], [4], [17]. Generally, accessing data and functionalities can be done by several methods: i) APIs (Application Programming Interface) based on REST (Representational State Transfer); ii) RSS (Really Simple Syndication) or Atom feed integration; iii) Screen scraping [11]. In our case, the access to the tools was mostly made by means of open APIs (in case of YouTube, SlideShare, Picasa and Twitter), but also directly through feeds when this was more convenient (in case of Blogger and Delicious) or even by direct access to the database (in case of the locally installed MediaWiki).

According to [11], mashups do more than simply integrate services and content, typically adding value to the user, producing enriched results; it is also the case of our eMUSE system, as reflected in its name (empowering MashUps for Social E-learning). More specifically, the platform integrates a learner tracking functionality, i.e., all student actions performed within the Web 2.0 tools are retrieved and recorded in the platform's database (together with a description and an associated timestamp). The list of actions includes: *post_blog_entry, post_blog_comment, upload_youtube_video, post_delicious_bookmark, add_delicious_friend_to_network, add_slideshare_document, create_picasa_album, post_tweet, revise_wiki_page, upload_wiki_file* etc. These are further processed and offered to the learner and/or instructor in aggregated forms, in a graphical representation. Figure 1 presents a schematic architecture of the integration of tools in the eMUSE platform, together with the additional learner tracking and visualization functionalities. As far as the implementation is concerned, Java-based and XML technologies were employed, with MySQL used as DBMS and Apache Tomcat as servlet container.

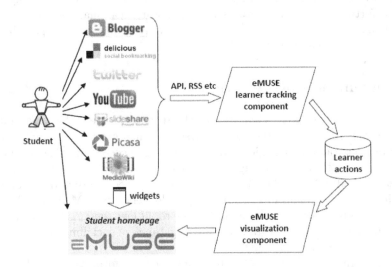

Fig. 1. eMUSE schematic architecture - learner tracking module

From the students' point of view, eMUSE offers the following main functionalities:

- an integrated learning space, with a common access point to all the Web 2.0 tools selected by the instructor, including updates of the latest peer activity
- a summary of each student's involvement, including pie/bar/line charts, evolution over time, comparisons with peers, as well as aggregated data
- a preliminary score computed based on the recorded student activity, following instructor-defined criteria.

A screenshot of the platform (representing the student home page) can be seen in Figure 2.

As far as the instructor is concerned, eMUSE acts as a control panel, with the following main functionalities:

- student management (course enrolment, centralized access to students' accounts on each Web 2.0 tool, grading information)
- collect data on students' activity, search and browse students' actions, visualize course statistics, detailed charts of student involvement and comparative evaluation
- configure grading scheme: define grading categories (i.e., individual contributions, peer feedback, communication skills etc.) and assign different weights to each action type inside each category, based on the particularities of the course; the overall score will be a weighted sum of all defined categories.

A screenshot of the platform illustrating a part of these functionalities (i.e., the graphical visualizations of the students' activity) can be seen in Figure 3.

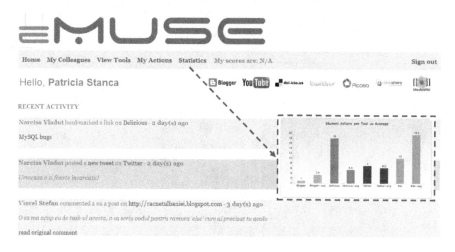

Fig. 2. eMUSE student home page, including an overview of latest peer activity. From the top menu, the student may choose to see: i) the list of peers and their corresponding tool accounts; ii) the list of available tools, including detailed usage instructions; iii) the list of her actions, filtered by several criteria; iv) graphical visualizations of her activity (as previewed in the dotted box on the right side).

4   eMUSE Validation

4.1   Comparison with Similar Platforms

In the introduction section we reported on several experimental studies involving the use of Web 2.0 tools in education; however, most of them included only one social media tool, which was integrated ad-hoc into the course (no dedicated platform was used) [10]. There are nevertheless other initiatives, designed at aggregating several social media tools:

- Some of them are general purpose platforms, such as: Netvibes or iGoogle (personalized dashboards including user-defined social media modules), Elgg [5] (a social engine which delivers building blocks that can be used to create social networks and applications). The main advantage of eMUSE compared to these platforms is that it was specifically designed for e-learning, therefore providing dedicated functionalities (learner tracking, evaluation and grading, etc.).
- Some learning management systems (LMS) nowadays integrate social media tools (e.g., blog and wiki in Moodle or Sakai). However, the range of available components is limited and they are built-in tools, often providing less functionalities than a fully-fledged external Web 2.0 application (which students are already familiar with). Moreover, eMUSE is not aimed at replacing an LMS; it is designed as a dedicated support tool for social interaction and collaborative learning, which could be integrated with any course / project and could be run in parallel with an LMS.

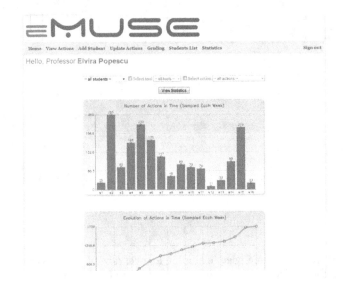

Fig. 3. eMUSE screenshot - instructor perspective of course statistics

– Recently, there have appeared the so-called "mash-up personal learning environments", platforms that support learners in building their own PLE; MUPPLE [17] and PLEF [2] are two such examples. These platforms mainly support learners in assembling various feeds and widgets in a single interface (either manually or by means of learner interaction scripts). By contrast, in eMUSE the components are chosen by the teacher in the context of a course. In addition, the platform offers value-added services, by collecting and analyzing students' activity with these tools and providing support to the instructor in the monitoring and evaluation process.

Hence eMUSE occupies a well defined niche in the landscape of Web 2.0-enhanced learning spaces, answering the specific needs outlined in section 2.

4.2   Experimental Validation

In order to experimentally validate the platform, we used it as support tool for collaborative learning in the context of an undergraduate course on "Web Applications' Design". 45 students were enrolled in the course, unfolding in the first semester of the 2010-2011 academic year at the University of Craiova, Romania. The project assignment was team-based, performed in a blended mode, with weekly face-to-face meetings and with the requirement to use eMUSE (and the integrated Web 2.0 tools) for the project tasks. At the end of the semester the platform recorded over 1800 student actions. A detailed statistical analysis of the recorded data is currently underway; in what follows, we will report on the subjective data collected by means of the satisfaction questionnaires applied to the students at the end of the study.

The results revealed that 75.55% of the students found the platform "useful" or "very useful"; 88.88% of the students found the platform motivating at least to a moderate extent and 68.88% were enthusiastic about using the platform for other courses. Detailed results are illustrated in Figure 4.

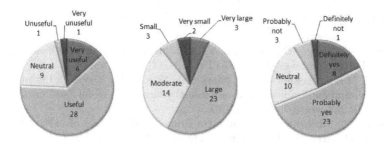

Fig. 4. Distribution of students' answers to the following questions: i) *Do you consider the platform useful?* (left chart); ii) *To which extent was eMUSE motivating for you?* (middle chart); iii) *Would you like to use eMUSE for future courses?* (right chart)

When asked to comment on the advantages of the platform, most students mentioned: i) the increased motivation (e.g., "can help motivate one if he sees he's behind peers"); ii) the opportunity to monitor own progress and compare it to the others (e.g., "I get a big picture of all my contributions", "I can see my contribution relative to the others"); iii) better management of the social media tools (e.g., "easier access to accounts", "easier to keep track of all the tools"). The biggest disadvantage spotted by the students was the fact that all the summaries and statistics are quantitative only and this could lead to an inflation of low-quality contributions ("post hunting" as one student put it). However, this actually happened only in a limited number of cases, since students were clearly informed that in the end it will be the quality of their contributions that will matter most towards their final grade.

5   Conclusion

The paper described our endeavor to build a social learning environment prototype (eMUSE), starting with a comprehensive rationale, followed by a detailed description of the platforms' architecture and functionalities. A theoretical comparison with other Web 2.0-enhanced learning spaces, as well as an initial experimental study involving 45 students, were performed in order to evaluate the platform.

A more in-depth analysis of the experimental results obtained is our next research direction; we want to investigate the effects of eMUSE on students' activity, on the usage patterns of the Web 2.0 tools, as well as on the learning gain. We also plan to perform more extensive studies, with a larger number of students from different backgrounds, with various settings and instructional scenarios.

Acknowledgments. This work was supported by the strategic grant POSDRU/ 89/1.5/S/61968, Project ID 61968 (2009), co-financed by the European Social Fund within the Sectorial Operational Program Human Resources Development 2007 - 2013.

References

1. Beemer, B., Gregg, D.: Mashups: A Literature Review and Classification Framework. Future Internet 1(1), 59–87 (2009)
2. Chatti, M.A., Agustiawan, M.R., Jarke, M., Specht, M.: Toward a Personal Learning Environment Framework. International Journal of Virtual and Personal Learning Environments 1(4), 66–85 (2010)
3. Conole, G., Alevizou, P.: A Literature Review of the Use of Web 2.0 Tools in Higher Education. Technical report, The Open University, UK (2010), http://www.heacademy.ac.uk/assets/EvidenceNet/Conole_Alevizou_2010.pdf
4. Drachsler, H., Pecceu, D., Arts, T., Hutten, E., Rutledge, L., van Rosmalen, P., Hummel, H., Koper, R.: ReMashed – Recommendations for Mash-Up Personal Learning Environments. In: Cress, U., Dimitrova, V., Specht, M. (eds.) EC-TEL 2009. LNCS, vol. 5794, pp. 788–793. Springer, Heidelberg (2009)
5. Elgg - Open source network engine, http://www.elgg.org/
6. Finkelstein, S.L., Powell, E., Hicks, A., Doran, K., Charugulla, S.R., Barnes, T.: SNAG: Using Social Networking Games to Increase Student Retention in Computer Science. In: Proc. ITiCSE 2010, pp. 142–146. ACM, New York (2010)
7. Hain, S., Back, A.: Personal Learning Journal - Course Design for Using Weblogs in Higher Education. The Electronic Journal of e-Learning 6(3), 189–196 (2008)
8. Hemmi, A., Bayne, S., Land, R.: The Appropriation and Repurposing of Social Technologies in Higher Education. J. Comput. Assist. Learning 25(1), 19–30 (2009)
9. Herder, E., Marenzi, I.: Trends in Connecting Learners. First Research & Technology Scouting Report. STELLAR project deliverable (2010), http://hdl.handle.net/1820/2824
10. Homola, M., Kubincova, Z.: Taking Advantage of Web 2.0 in Organized Education (A Survey). In: Proc. ICL 2009, pp. 741–752 (2009)
11. Ort, E., Brydon, S., Basler, M.: Mashup Styles (2007), http://java.sun.com/developer/technicalArticles/J2EE/mashup_1
12. Popescu, E.: Students' Acceptance of Web 2.0 Technologies in Higher Education: Findings from a Survey in a Romanian University. In: Proc. DEXA 2010 Workshops, pp. 92–96 (2010)
13. Popescu, E., Manafu, L.: Repurposing a Wiki for Collaborative Learning - Pedagogical and Technical View. In: Proc. ICSTCC 2011 (in press, 2011)
14. Sclater, N.: Web 2.0, Personal Learning Environments, and the Future of Learning Management Systems. Educause Research Bulletin 13 (2008)
15. Vassileva, J.: Toward Social Learning Environments. IEEE Trans. Learning Technologies 1(4), 199–214 (2008)
16. Vygotsky, L.S.: Mind in Society. Harvard University Press, Cambridge (1978)
17. Wild, F.: Mash-Up Personal Learning Environments. iCamp project deliverable (2009), http://www.icamp.eu/wp-content/uploads/2009/01/d34_icamp_final.pdf

Learn-as-you-go: New Ways of Cloud-Based Micro-learning for the Mobile Web

Dejan Kovachev, Yiwei Cao, Ralf Klamma, and Matthias Jarke

Information Systems and Databases, RWTH Aachen University,
Ahornstr. 55, 52056 Aachen, Germany
{cao,kovachev,klamma,jarke}@dbis.rwth-aachen.de

Abstract. *Micro-learning* refers to short-term learning activities on small learning units. In our contemporary mobile/web society, micro-learning pertains to small pieces of knowledge based on web resources. Micro-learning falls into the group of informal learning processes. The existing web and mobile services have great potential to support informal learning processes, especially micro-learning. However, several specific aspects need to be considered. In this paper, we propose a micro-learning model based on three technical aspects: (i) ubiquitous learning resource acquisition; (ii) cloud-based data management; and (iii) tag-based regulation of learning processes and content. A micro-learning prototype consisting of an Android application and a web browser add-on is evaluated in the use case of bilingual vocabulary learning. The initial prototype evaluation study shows promising results in enhanced flexibility in personal learning content creation and increased efficiency in filling knowledge gaps.

Keywords: micro-learning, Web 2.0, tagging, OCR, cloud computing, data synchronization, self-regulated learning, web scraping.

1 Introduction

People gain their main knowledge from high-quality, specially designed, learning materials like books or in courses at schools. However, gaps in personal knowledge always exist, which can only be identified through a real-life practice, when we feel difference of what we know and what we want to know. That knowledge is not indispensable, but it feels like a mental itch. We try to fill the knowledge gaps because that is how we scratch the itch [17]. We call these pieces of personal knowledge *micro-knowledge*.

Nowadays, mobile and web technologies are developing new ways for learning and knowledge attaining. People use Web 2.0 platforms such as Wikipedia and (micro-)blogs additionally to augment the existing course materials for formal learning and education. Furthermore, smartphone applications and mobile Web make learning content be well accessible anywhere at any time. The convergence of the Web and mobile platforms currently is an enabling factor for novel informal learning methods such as micro-learning. *Micro-learning* refers originally to taking short-term-focused learning activities on small learning content units

H. Leung et al. (Eds.): ICWL 2011, LNCS 7048, pp. 51–61, 2011.

[9]. We refine micro-learning as a learning activity on small pieces of knowledge based on web resources. Micro-learning differs from micro-blogging (e.g. Twitter) in way that the later is more about disseminating information (a single resource) to other people, and the former is about collecting personally relevant information (several resources) from many sources and using that collection to cover personal knowledge gaps. Micro-learning consists of a fast, convenient and instant capture of the self-identified knowledge gaps, understanding them with the help of online resources, creation of a learning object out of these online resources and integration of that learning object into small learning activities interwoven into our daily life.

Our research on micro-learning is motivated by the following considerations. First, exploiting the ever growing web content as a primary source for personal knowledge enrichment requires usage of many independent online services to acquire the relevant information. A combination of heterogeneous digital resources or fragments is required. Second, personal learning content is a subject to a "evolution". Many of the learning systems consider relatively static learning content with less adaptiveness. But in case of micro-learning, learning content changes constantly. Users enrich learning content with new web resources. Third, the learning phases (plan, learn and reflect) in micro-learning span over different spatio-temporal settings. There is a disparity of the periods (and available devices) when people encounter the knowledge gaps and when they have time to learn and reflect. Therefore, different devices should be supported. Fourth, switching context from the primary activity to a learning process causes distraction from the main activities. People should be able to acquire the information artifacts quickly and learn them at suitable time, without much interruption. Fifth, since micro-learning involves heterogeneous content, pre-defined data models and learning processes would not fit. Tagging offers a simple but yet powerful mechanism to organize, save and distribute learning content and to regulate personal learning processes [8].

In order to support learners' micro-learning activities, we conceptualize a micro-learning model with three technical foci. We have developed tools for ubiquitous acquisition of digital learning resources both on a desktop web browser and a smartphone. Furthermore, we apply cloud-based approaches to micro-learning synchronized between Web and mobile learning environments. Cloud technologies are applied to augment and synchronize data processing capacities on smartphones [12]. Finally, we use tags for micro-learning in different learning phases based on the tagging model in our previous research [2]. This tagging concept is proposed to meet challenges in learning resource management and learning process support. As a proof of concept we have applied the implemented tools in the use case of vocabulary learning.

2   Description of the Use Case

We have chosen language learning because it is a subtle process which takes long time and constant effort. The mastery of a language involves series of micro-learning such as vocabulary, idioms, phrases, etc. We illustrate the bilingual learning scenario for micro-learning requirements analysis. The targeted user group is non-native speakers of two languages which are being learned in parallel. The bilingual vocabulary learning depicts the increased usage of online services' usage, and thereupon the increased complexity of system requirements.

Language learning is not a standalone process and needs assistant means. We aim to enable users to capture the language knowledge gaps and to practice/learn on their mobile devices. Learners often encounter unknown words which are translated in that moment but are often forgotten afterwards. Learners should establish a meaning-form link between the unknown word and native language quickly, and then use multiple learning strategies and deep elaboration to make the retention become a long-term memory [18,7]. Additionally, the bilingual explanation has a relatively greater effectiveness than the monolingual through a verified experiment of using computerized bilingual dictionaries. However, it requires links of all three languages, i.e. the native and the two other non-native.

The scenario "a German in China": *Sophie is a native German speaker who lives and works for an international company in Shanghai, China. She needs to master English for career and to improve Chinese for everyday life. Therefore, she uses any chance to capture and learn unknown vocabulary and phrases. She uses her smartphone to capture new words at any encounter. She makes notes of new words at surfing the Web. Often she doesn't have time to learn new words comprehensively at work, but while commuting in the metropolis she has much time, so she can learn and practice using her smartphone. The smartphone screen size limits the creation of learning objects, but desktop or laptop web browser offers Sophie more user-friendly possibilities to manage her learning resources with contextualized vocabulary examples and explanatory multimedia. The boundary between web and mobile still exists for her to access vocabulary on various platforms. She wishes a seamless mobile and web learning environment.*

3   Related Work

Gathering and saving web content is important in Web 2.0. Popular tools like Delicious provide a convenient means to organize web links of our interest by bookmarking whole pages which are usually overfilled with unnecessary content like advertisements or decorations. However, in learning cases, there is a clear need to scrap only the most important information and persist it into the personal learning objects. The idea to collect online resources from different web sites is not brand new. Web scrapers have been invented to extract fragments within web pages (e.g., weather forecasts, stock quotes, and news article summaries) and to re-purpose them in personalized ways [10]. The existing (semi-)automatized tools [16] for grabbing data from web sites are focused more on extracting structured data from e-commerce sites, therefore, their usability for learning purposes is limited. Our tools allow users to grab any fragments from web pages that are best contribute to his/her understanding.

Additionally, tags have been employed widely for learning resource management in learning environments [20]. Use of tags offers learners complete flexibility to describe and organize their learning resources. Research shows that learners use tags to describe resource provenance [20,22], learning content [5], and learning goals [14]. Vuorikari et al. [21] stress the crucial roles of tags for web-based educational resources. Tags used for learning content depend highly on learning content domains. A tag analysis on learning goals conducted in [14] presents a list of goal-related tags. Experiments show that some verbs e.g. want, need, plan, like, take, solve have a higher occurrence frequency than tags like question and exam etc. We base our approach on the state of the art of tagging models and apply it to micro-learning, which is explained in details in Sec. 4.3.

Some tools for second language learning such as ROLE Project Language Learning Widget [23] are good, however, mostly web based. Mobile-only solutions of synchronization technologies are often too generic and don't support the learning processes. Mobile second language learning tools like CAMCLL [1] have drawn much attention. MicroMandarin [4] has applied micro-learning concept for language learning on mobile phones as well. Both CAMCLL and MicroMandarin focus well on enhanced context-awareness of language learning by using, while other learning resources are not considered. However, they are limited by the services they include. Our tools allow the user to use any web resource or service and to grab the relevant information.

In short, our approach is able to help learners micro-learn through cloud storage, automatic learning resource synchronization, and flexible tagging models for self-regulated learning processes. Cross-platform learning on the mobile and Web 2.0 is supported.

4   System Overview

Based on the scenario and the surveyed issues, the main components of our system are discussed in this section.

4.1   Ubiquitous Learning Content Creation and Enhancement

Ubiquitous communication and computing technologies enable smartphones to be widely used to acquire instant knowledge anywhere anytime. They are good for instant learning content acquisition (images, videos, sound, location), but devices with bigger displays (laptops, desktops) are more convenient for enhancement and completion of the learning objects from a learners' perspective. Therefore, we exploit smartphones for instant context-enriched content acquisition and as tools for informal learning, and desktop web browsers with extensions to manage and enrich personal learning content.

Mobile OCR Input. Novel methods like Optical Character Recognition (OCR) help alleviate some of the inherited issues of their small computing devices. OCR refers to the process for acquisition of text and layout information, through analyzing and processing of image files. Compared to the traditional input way of typing, OCR technique has many advantages such as speed and high efficiency for large texts. Furthermore, in the case of Asian or Arabic alphabets OCR eases the input of characters and words. Several mobile products are trying to commercialize this convenient approach[1].

In our system the OCR technique is used as a tool to catch the source words from document and we implement this component based on the open-source project "Wordsnap"[2]. This input method allows users to input the words they want to query or learn in a more convenient way when they read printed documents.

Web Scrapping. Our web browser add-on uses client side DOM-parsing web scraper to ease the selection of content fragments from multiple web pages. The tool highlights the information chunks on the web page and lets the user select only relevant parts (text, paragraphs, divs, images, videos, etc.) out of it. Fig. 1 shows how parts of different web pages were selected by the user that he/she thinks they are most relevant in the current context, and are added to the learning object. The user can then use other web pages to enrich the learning object, e.g. images from Flickr or videos from YouTube, in order to make it more understandable and explanatory.

4.2   Cloud-Based Data Synchronization

One of the biggest challenges in multimedia application development is device heterogeneity. Users are likely to own many types of devices. Switching from one device to another, users would expect to have ubiquitous access to their multimedia content. Cloud computing is a promising solution to managing heterogeneous learning content, i.e. images, text, web pages excerpts, links, videos, etc. and delivery of computing and storage services as utility.

In our case, the cloud features a personal learning content vault for each user. It handles data storage, data processing, and adaptive content delivery to different devices. These cloud learning services run on top of the scalable multimedia cloud infrastructure, which is more described in our previous research work [13].

In general, in informal learning the acquisition and learning phases happen on different devices. For example, unknown phrases are heard during conversation and recorded on the smartphone, and further understanding is carried on a desktop or laptop computer. Therefore, a seamless integration of web-based tools with mobile applications is required for the purpose of enabling learning anywhere at any time [15]. The content and metadata both should be up-to-date using data synchronization technologies.

In the whole system design smartphones are not the only way to add data to the personal learning vault, i.e. it is exposed through a REST API for other clients to access and change the data. However, providing such access requires methods for synchronization of the data between all clients. For better network

---

[1] http://www.pleco.com/

[2] http://www.bitquill.net/trac/wiki/Android/OCR

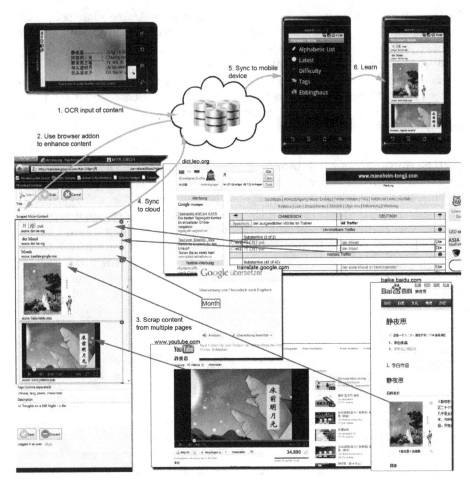

Fig. 1. Microlearn workflow. The user inputs difficult-to-type Chinese characters via OCR, thus initializing a learning object which is synchronized to the cloud (top left). The browser add-on (down left) helps getting relevant content from several web sites (down right). The augmented object is synced back to the cloud. The user can learn using rich-content learning objects on the mobile device (top right).

traffic efficiency, an incremental synchronization technique is implemented. The small mobile devices have a local partial replica of the user's learning content synchronized with the cloud personal learning content vault which is also accessible from the Web.

4.3   Tagging for Micro-learning

Since the created content has arbitrary structures and is heterogeneous, tagging is a powerful and flexible approach to organizing the content and the learning processes in a personalized manner. We propose a micro-learning model based on the three core learning processes: plan, learn, and reflect (see Figure 2). They are controlled by tags falling in six groups. Context, frequency, recentness, and preference are identified as important mind set by Gillbert [6]. We extend them with semantics and feedback to support the whole learning process spanning from planning, and learning, to reflecting processes. Each core process is supported by three categories of tags directly, which is depicted in dark dash lines. The light dash lines show the indirect connections between the tag categories and learning processes, which is not specific for learning and will be explained later. A set of Web 2.0 operations are listed beside each tag categories. We argue these Web 2.0 operations give learning resources a special type of tag as well. We have grouped the tag survey results from [11,19] and list the potential tags as an example in the rectangles.

(i) **Context:** "environmental" issues related to whole learning processes including spatial, temporal, device-related, as well as social or community context (including languages). Temporal information such as "to learn this week" and community recommendation are directly used for the planning and reflecting phase. Though learning context is often mentioned in literature, context tags are not directly applied at the learning phase.

(ii) **Frequency:** specially related to time plan ("when I have time") and users' learning wishes/activities to indicate the frequency for repeatedness and priority categories. Tags such as "to read" or "to learn" show the necessity of repeatedness for learning content at the beginning phase. Other tags like "monthly" and "weekly" can be used after learners get feedback and experience about the learning content.

(iii) **Recentness:** related to the latest status of learning content and learning activities. The recentness of learning categories can be extracted automatically. This tag category can be used at the planning and learning phases. In addition, the more recently the knowledge is learned, the better it is held in learners' memory. It is connected to the learning performance indirectly.

(iv) **Semantics:** domain specific tags and for knowledge description. Learners can set categories of knowledge through tags. However, semantics intertwines with context so tightly that it is difficult to differentiate sometimes.

(v) **Preference:** learners' subjective/affective opinion about learning content. This information can be well tagged at the learning and reflecting phases. It is unable to be grasped well at the planning phase, thus they are indirectly connected.

(vi) **Feedback:** the status of achievement, including feedback from learners themselves and others. Learners can set notification or get notification by others.

4.4   Using the Tools for Learning

We explain how these tools can be used in the aforementioned scenario.

Sophie reads some stories from a paper book. Some words are not clear to her. She inputs the Chinese characters, which are difficult for her to enter them using keyboard but easier with the OCR module. It recognizes the characters

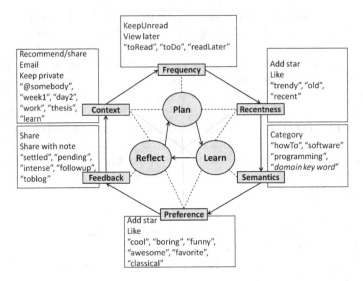

Fig. 2. Tagging based micro-learning model

and uses Google translation to display initial translation and Sophie gets some initial understanding, which are error-prone. Then she tags it with 'check-later' among other tags. When she has more time at home in front of her desktop computer she opens the learning objects containing 'check-later' tag and she gets the freshly initialized learning object from her smartphone. She uses different web pages and services to fully understand the meaning in English and German at the same time. Using the browser add-on she attaches different explanatory multimedia fragments from the Web to the learning object. She tags the object tags about the content and with 'learn-as-you-go', 'repeat-weekly' in order to steer the reflection process. After saved this learning object synchronizes with the cloud and thereupon to all her devices. Next day, when she commutes she can reflect upon the personally-created understandable learning content. She gets notifications after one week to repeat the same content again.

Although the tagging model for micro-learning still has ambiguity and drawbacks, it serves as a first guideline for tag-regulated micro-learning system development. With regard to our bilingual learning scenario, we illustrate the application of this model in vocabulary and knowledge learning process with flashcards. The well-known flashcards as a component of Leitner Systems are applied mainly at reflecting phase of micro knowledge. *Feedback* tags such as "settled" or "pending" etc. are applied to show the learning progress. *Context* tags can be used to identify the learning context ranging from mobile to static, e.g. vocabulary for "learn-as-you-go" or in which language for bilingual learning. *Frequency* tags are used next. *Recentness* according to the time when learning activities take place is important for repeating of micro-knowledge on flashcard. Content of micro knowledge itself can be tagged with *semantics* tags. Additional *preference* tags can be applied to categorize learning content.

5   Evaluation

We developed an Android application that features translation, OCR input of text, tagging of learning content, reinforcement learning model and synchronization with the cloud. Furthermore, we developed a browser add-on that enables users to enhance the learning objects with rich multimedia content and to further refine the learning content management.

In order to obtain a comprehensive evaluation of the prototype and get the result of the users' feedback to summarize advantages and disadvantages, referring to Chen et al. [3], we have adopted a series of simplified questions of system operations to measure if these tools is able to satisfy the needs of users. Ten students who studied more than one foreign language were asked to use the tool for a period of time and to use it for bilingual vocabulary learning. Only 2 out of the 10 students had used a smartphone for learning purposes before. The students then answered a questionnaire.

The evaluation of the current version revealed positive feedback for supporting bilingual vocabulary learning, synchronization of learning content, usage of online resources for learning content creation and enhancement, and usage of multiple strategies for vocabulary learning (time, tags, language, difficulty, Ebbinghaus). The drawbacks of the system are slower OCR recognition than typing for Latin script languages, issues with color printouts (but for Asian scripts the value of using OCR input is huge). With the development of the OCR technology we could improve the function of OCR to get a more powerful learning tool. Currently, some applications depended on object recognition from images have already emerged such as Google Goggles.

6   Conclusions and Future Work

We envision the micro-learning concept based on mobile web learning as a new trend for future learning. New user experience for micro-learning content capture with novel input methods e.g. OCR help learners capture micro knowledge conveniently and easily. The cloud approach with advanced data synchronization technologies lowers the barriers in cross-platform learning processes and knowledge management. The tagging model for micro-learning supports various learning phases: plan, learn, and reflect.

The micro-learn model is implemented for a proof of concept and can be extended to each learning phase. At planning, knowledge capture should become more intelligent information scrapping on the Web, and enhanced context and activity capturing with OCR improvements on the mobile. At learning, XMPP-based technologies could be employed to enhance collaborative learning in the cloud among learner communities. At reflecting, context-aware learning content organization and reuse can be developed on learners' reflection.

Acknowledgments. This work is supported by the German excellence research cluster UMIC, EU FP7 IP ROLE project and B-IT Research School.

References

1. Al-Mekhlafi, K., Hu, X., Zheng, Z.: An Approach to Context-Aware Mobile Chinese Language Learning for Foreign Students. In: Eighth International Conference on Mobile Business (ICMB 2009), pp. 340–346. IEEE (June 2009)
2. Cao, Y., Kovachev, D., Klamma, R., Lau, R.W.H.: Enhancing Personal Learning Environments by Context-Aware Tagging. In: Luo, X., Spaniol, M., Wang, L., Li, Q., Nejdl, W., Zhang, W. (eds.) ICWL 2010. LNCS, vol. 6483, pp. 11–20. Springer, Heidelberg (2010)
3. Chen, C.-M., Li, Y.-L., Chen, M.-C.: Personalized Context-Aware Ubiquitous Learning System for Supporting Effectively English Vocabulary Learning. In: Proceedings of the 7th IEEE International Conference on Advanced Learning Technologies (ICALT 2007), pp. 628–630. IEEE (July 2007)
4. Edge, D., Searle, E., Chiu, K., Zhao, J., Landay, J.A.: MicroMandarin: Mobile Language Learning in Context. In: Proc. of CHI 2011, pp. 3169–3178. ACM (2011)
5. Gasevic, D., Zouaq, A., Torniai, C., Jovanovic, J., Hatala, M.: An Approach to Folksonomy-based Ontology Maintenance for Learning Environments. IEEE Transactions on Learning Technologies (99), 1–14 (2011)
6. Gilbert, D.: Stumbling on Happiness. Vintage (2007)
7. Gu, Y., Johnson, R.K.: Vocabulary Learning Strategies and Language Learning Outcomes. Language Learning 46(4), 643–679 (1996)
8. Heckner, M., Neubauer, T., Wolff, C.: Tree, funny, to_read, google: What are tags supposed to achieve? a comparative analysis of user keywords for different digital resource types. In: Proceeding of the 2008 ACM Workshop on Search in Social Media, pp. 3–10. ACM (2008)
9. Hug, T.: Micro Learning and Narration - Exploring Possibilities of Utilization of Narrations and Storytelling for the Designing of "micro units" and Didactical Micro-learning Arrangements. In: The Fourth Media in Transition Conference (MiT4), Cambridge, MA, USA (May 2005)
10. Huynh, D.F., Mazzocchi, S., Karger, D.R.: Piggy Bank: Experience the Semantic Web Inside Your Web Browser. In: Gil, Y., Motta, E., Benjamins, V.R., Musen, M.A. (eds.) ISWC 2005. LNCS, vol. 3729, pp. 413–430. Springer, Heidelberg (2005)
11. Kipp, M.E.: @toread and cool: Subjective, affective and associative factors in tagging. In: Canadian Association for Information Science/L'Association canadienne des sciences de l'information (CAIS/ACSI), June 5-8 (2008)
12. Kovachev, D., Cao, Y., Klamma, R.: Augmenting Pervasive Environments with an XMPP-based Mobile Cloud Middleware. In: Proceedings of the International Workshop on Mobile Computing and Clouds (MobiCloud 2010) in Conjunction with MobiCASE 2010, Santa Clara, CA, USA. Springer, Heidelberg (2010)
13. Kovachev, D., Klamma, R.: A Cloud Multimedia Platform. In: Proceedings of the 11th Int'l Workshop of the Multimedia Metadata Community (WISMA 2010), Barcelona, Spain, pp. 61–64. CEUR (2010)
14. Krenge, J., Petrushyna, Z., Kravcik, M., Klamma, R.: Identification of learning goals in forum-based communities. In: Proceedings of the 11th International Conference on Advanced Learning Technologies (ICALT 2011), Athens, Georgia, USA, July 6-8. IEEE Computer Society, Los Alamitos (2011) (page to appear)
15. Lagerspetz, E., Tarkoma, S., Lindholm, T.: Dessy: Search and Synchronization on the Move. In: Proceedings of the 11th International Conference on Mobile Data Management (MDM 2010), pp. 215–217 (May 2010)

16. Liu, B., Grossman, R., Zhai, Y.: Mining Data Records in Web Pages. In: Proceedings of the 9th ACM SIGKDD, pp. 601–606. ACM (2003)

17. Loewenstein, G.: The Psychology of Curiosity: A Review and Reinterpretation. Psychological Bulletin 116(1), 75–98 (1994)

18. Schmitt, N.: Review Article: Instructed Second Language Vocabulary Learning. Language Teaching Research 12(3), 329–363 (2008)

19. Sen, S., Lam, S.K., Rashid, A.M., Cosley, D., Frankowski, D., Osterhouse, J., Harper, F.M., Riedl, J.: Tagging, Communities, Vocabulary, Evolution. In: Proceedings of the 2006 20th Anniversary Conference on Computer Supported Cooperative Work, pp. 181–190. ACM (2006)

20. Tiropanis, T., Davis, H., Millard, D., Weal, M.: Semantic Technologies for Learning and Teaching in the Web 2.0 Era. IEEE Intelligent Systems 24(6), 49–53 (2009)

21. Vuorikari, R., Poldoja, H., Koper, R.: Comparison of Tagging in an Educational Context - Any Chances of Interplay? Int'l J. Technology Enhanced Learning 2(1/2), 111–131 (2010)

22. Wang, P., Gao, H.: Exploring Social Annotations for E-learning. In: Int'l Conf. on Comp. Sci. and Soft. Eng., vol. 5, pp. 222–225. IEEE (2008)

23. Wolpers, M., Friedrich, M., Shen, R., Ullrich, C., Klamma, R., Renzel, D.: Early Experiences with Responsive Open Learning Environments. Journal of Universal Computer Science (J.UCS), Proc. of I-KNOW 2010, Graz, Austria, 391–402 (September 2010)

Web 2.0 with Alert Support for Busy Parents in Suzuki Method of Children Music Teaching

Cheuk-Ting Chan[1] and Dickson K.W. Chiu[2]

[1] Department of Music, Hong Kong Baptist University
[2] Dickson Computer Systems, 7 Victory Avenue, Homantin, Hong Kong
chancheukting2002@yahoo.com.hk, dicksonchiu@ieee.org

Abstract. Suzuki believed that learning environment would determine the success and failure of students in music. Therefore, he not only provided teachers with useful and logical teaching skills, but also stressed on the importance of parents' participation as a "home teacher". In this paper, we propose a Web 2.0 learning platform (WASSAP) to support Suzuki method of music education, especially aiming at supporting busy parents who do not have adequate time to accompany their child in person to learn. Alerts are used as a mechanism to facilitate communications among parents, teachers, and peers.

Keywords: Web 2.0, alert management, children learning, parent support.

1 Introduction

Shinichi Suzuki [15] was a renowned Japanese music educator who had a profound influence on music education in his own country and throughout the world. Suzuki advocates a logical and developmentally sound approach to instrumental learning. Thousand of parents and teachers in more than 40 countries, had been inspired by Suzuki method in helping their children in learning musical instruments. His methodology has been developed and expanded for various kinds of instruments such as violin, cello, flute, oboe, guitar, and harp [8].

As music teachers and instrumental tutors, the authors always try to adopt various teaching method in their daily teaching, aiming at enhancing students' learning effectiveness on grasping the instrumental skills and their motivation in learning music. However, the mere effort of the music instructor is inadequate. Parental support and participation have significant influence in facilitating children's motivation and interest in learning music.

Suzuki believed that learning environment will determine the success and failure of the students. Therefore, he not only provided teachers with useful and logical teaching skills, but also stressed on the importance of the parents as a "home teacher", who can always participate in children's learning process and build up a supportive learning environment to their children. Although, the idea of parental involvement suggested by Suzuki is inspiring, its implementation often faces various difficulties in metropolises like Hong Kong. This is because many parents are too busy working with non-fixed hours and frequent need to travel [10], resulting in inadequate involvement with their children's learning.

H. Leung et al. (Eds.): ICWL 2011, LNCS 7048, pp. 62–71, 2011.
© Springer-Verlag Berlin Heidelberg 2011

To overcome these limitations, we propose some remedies for overcoming these limitations through information and communications technology (ICT) assistance provided via our "Web 2.0 with Alert Support for Suzuki Approach Platform" (WASSAP), which provides a virtual musical environment for teachers, students, and parents. Remarkably, we employ an Alert Management System (AMS) to facilitate their communications.

The rest of paper is organized as follows. Section 2 introduces background and related work, while Section 3 reviews Suzuki method of music education. Section 4 points out some limitations in implementing Suzuki method with busy parents. Section 5 outlines our WASSAP system architecture. Section 6 discusses how our WASSAP facilities the education process according to Suzuki method before we conclude with our future work directions.

2   Background and Related Work

Hidi and Harakiewicz [9] emphasized that learning environment affects students' interest in learning music. Marjoribanks and Mboya [13] suggested that teachers need to understand the relationship between family background and students' interest in order to motivate students in learning music. Likewise, Ceci et al. [3] emphasized that family background is the key factor in influencing children's music learning outcomes, which is also dependent on how well an understanding of family background is incorporated into children's learning experiences.

Coleman [4] refined the definition of family background generally as parents' opportunity of creating supportive learning environments and the relationships between adults and children. In Suzuki method, he put much emphasis on building a strong partnership of parent, teacher and child, which is known as "Suzuki triangle", in which he enlisted the aid of parents as home teachers and emphasized the strong influence of parents in motivating and helping children's learning in music.

For Web 2.0, McLean et al. [14] pointed out that the term Web 2.0 does not refer to new technical standards, but to new ways of using the Internet as a platform for interactive applications. A distinguishing characteristic of Web 2.0 is the use of online social networking technologies to create value through mass user participation, such as Really Simple Syndication (RSS) to rapidly disseminate awareness of new information, Blogs to describe new trends, Wikis to share knowledge and podcasts to make information available "on the move". However, as far as we know to date, there are no other comprehensive websites that explore Web 2.0 functionalities to support teachers, students, and parents.

Further, we advocate the use of an Alert Management System (AMS) component for the management of notifications and associated communications in information systems [2], which originates from a medical application. We also apply it for a distance education application for the case of Open University of Hong Kong [1], as well as many other commercial applications. Therefore, we include an AMS for our Web 2.0 music learning application for mobile busy working parents.

3   Requirements Overview of Suzuki Method

There are three main areas in Suzuki method, namely, philosophy, curriculum, and technical concepts. Each area will be discussed in more details in following subsections to illustrate our system requirements.

3.1   Philosophy of Suzuki Method

A "Mother tongue" approach to Children's Music Learning: As observed by Suzuki, children usually learn their native tongues without much difficulty in their first few years of life by listening and imitating their mothers' voices, despite the great complexity of language [6]. Therefore, Suzuki thought that the process of language learning should be universal and could be applied in music education.

All Children have Talent: Suzuki [15] believed that every child has a potential to become musical and their potential is often unlimited: musical ability is not an inborn talent but a common ability that can be developed. Therefore, any child who is properly trained can develop musical ability, just as all children develop the ability to speak their mother tongue.

Environment Rather than Genetics Determine Students' Success and Failure: A good learning environment is the most important determinant of a student's achievement in music learning. Children with a warm and supportive learning environment tend to be more successful. Therefore, building such a musical environment by parents is the key to the students' success.

3.2   Curriculum of Suzuki Method

Careful and Sequential Planning of Curriculum: Teachers are suggested to design a series of musical pieces to introduce and review musical techniques in a progressive way. Musical techniques should be disguised in musical selections that are interesting and attractive to the children and their families. Much of the motivation for learning comes from the desire to learn new pieces in the repertoire.

Avoiding Dry Technical Exercises: Teachers should avoid teaching dry technical exercises. New technical skills and musical concepts should be introduced and disguised in the context of familiar musical pieces because this makes the students' acquisition much easier. In addition, teachers should make sure each student is capable of handling old techniques before introducing a new one. On the other hand, breaking each new skill into the smallest possible steps can help the students manage them easily.

3.3   Technical Concepts of Suzuki Method

Begin Lessons Early: Suzuki noted how young children can easily master the complicated behaviors as the intricacies of speech or using chopsticks at their early ages. Children can in fact learn these behaviors much more easily than adults. Suzuki concluded that children should receive formal musical training at an age of three or four, and probably begin to learn musical instruments by four years old or even earlier.

Positive Reinforcement by Parents: When a child learns to talk, they learn it by listening to their parents' voice and imitating their speech. Parents often function very effectively as teachers. Therefore, Suzuki strongly invited the aid of a parent as an assistant teacher to help guide the child's practice at home.

Daily Listening to Recordings: Daily listening to recordings of relevant pieces helps children learn the melodies and appreciate good sound of the instruments. Listening also aids in developing skills on grasping an accurate pitch and rhythmic pulse.

Learning by Ear before Reading Music Notations: Suzuki was inspired by his observation that children learn to speak their native language with great proficiency long before they learn to read. Similarly, he emphasized the development of children listening skills at a very young age and teaching them to play entire works by ear before they learn to read music. Children are taught to read only after their ability to speak has been well established. In the same way, students should develop basic competence on their instruments before being taught to read music. This sequence of instruction enables both the teacher and student to focus on the development of good posture, beautiful tone, accurate intonation, and musical phrasing.

One-point Learning: Teachers should focus on only one technique at a time, temporarily overlooking others so that teachers do not overwhelm a child with instructions about several different things at once. In addition, technical skills are broken down into the smallest possible steps so that information is introduced in a way that is understood by both the parent and child.

Individual Lessons vs. Group Classes: Children should attend individual lessons, so that students can learn at their own paces. Teachers should reinforce important skills introduced at private lessons. On the other hand, Suzuki pointed out the social benefits of group classes. Peer learning promotes social interaction and enhance motivation among the children, sharing challenges with peers. This also creates a system of peer-support, in which children can learn from the more experienced. Peer learning also provides students with opportunities to experience how to play together as well as a tremendous aid in motivating students to practice at home.

4   Participation Problems of Busy Parents

Based on the mother-tongue approach, Suzuki believed that parents have a huge amount of influence on facilitating children's music learning. Suzuki emphasized the important role of parents acting as "home teachers", who guide and assist their children to practice at home. Parents should act as home teachers by taking part in the following activities in order to understand what the child is expected to do and fostering the musical environment by attending concerts and playing recordings at home. These include co-operating with the music instructors, giving positive encouragement to their children, attending child's lesson, and learning to play the instrument before the child.

Because of the crucial role of parent support, we review some of the typical problem that we observed in Hong Kong. Most parents are always busy and exhausted with their daily jobs; most of them have little involvement in their children's learning. In addition, we point out some problems of such parents usually encountered when they are getting involvement in their children's music education process. The observation is mainly based on our experience in teaching music in a school and as private instrumental tutors, as well as discussions with parents.

Over Relying on Household Helpers: Parents with different educational level may have different impacts on their children's music learning. Parents who have higher educational level are more motivated in taking part in their children's daily activities. Due to their heavy workload, many busy parents hire foreign household helpers to look after their children. Such helpers merely play a role of "accompanying", i.e., bringing the children to music center, waiting for them, and bringing them back home. Usually, they do not understand what the children did in the music course, and neither do the parents. As busy parents often rely too much on these helpers, they seldom communicate with the music instructors, not fully understanding what the children are expected to learn.

Parents are Short-Sighted towards the Values of Music Learning: The attitude of parents may influence the children's achievement in music learning. Many parents share one common purpose for encouraging their children in learning musical instrument: to pave the way for seeking a greater opportunity to be admitted to a better school. Their vision towards the children's music learning is short-sighted and their expectation to their children's achievement is "materialistic" as well. Children from such family background usually become less motivated to achieve long-term goals in music education.

Lack of Adequate Knowledge in Acting as a Home Teacher: Marjoribanks [12] indicated that parents in lower social-status groups often have particularly high aspirations for their children, but they may be unable to put into practice those processes that realize their aspirations. Many busy parents with lower educational level are lacking adequate knowledge in monitoring and supervising their children's learning at home. Neither can they know how to act as a home teacher, nor get familiar with the instruments and the music. They hesitate to express their personal affection, seldom give positive encouragement, and do not know how to appraise their children's performance.

Too Much Other Entertainment: In metropolis like Hong Kong, there are too much entertainment such as going to cinema, singing Karaoke, playing TV games, Web browsing, and so on. Many people's leisure time is mostly occupied with such entertainments and it is difficult for a child and even an adult to concentrate in learning music, which is often not regarded as entertainment. Therefore, it is difficult to persuade parents to attend concerts or play recordings at home frequently.

5   System Architecture

Fig. 5 shows the system architecture of our WASSAP design, based on our AMS core [1]. As the AMS manages only the alert, domain-specific application logic is required for a complete system. Upon data or process service requests, the application logic generates alerts with the necessary specifications to the AMS such as requesting a teacher's assistant, parent event notification, etc. These alerts are channeled through the user prescribed channels (such as SMS, email, instant messaging, etc.) according to their preferences and schedules [2]. Any subsequent processing that depends on the result of an external or human service (e.g., a teacher or preprocessing some video clips) may have to wait till it finishes (as signaled by the AMS); otherwise the workflow can continue. Users can respond to alerts or use our WASSAP through different devices such as desktop computers, laptops, mobile phone, and so on. On the other hand, the application logic is triggered by the Process Execution Module of the AMS to carry out timely appropriate actions in response to incoming alerts. The following introduces the modules inside the application logic to realize various required assistance for Suzuki method.

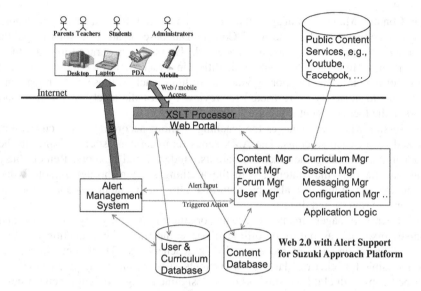

Fig. 1. WASSAP Architecture

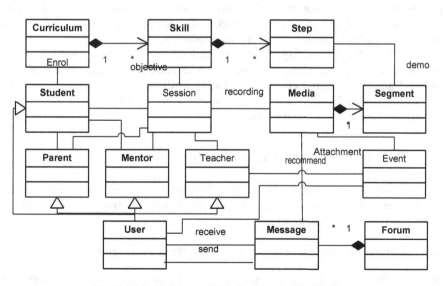

Fig. 2. Main Entities and Relationships in WASSAP

The Curriculum Manager is the key application logic of our platform. According to Suzuki method, teachers should create a curriculum (such as at a certain level for a certain instrument), targeting a series of progressive skills. Each new skill is broken down into the smallest possible steps. All the skills and steps should be linked to interesting contents that are managed the Content Manager, which could be scores, video, audio clips, etc. Fig. 2 illustrates the main entities and relationships of our WASSAP

The Content Manager manages the contents required for our platform. Those contents are either stored in the local Content Database or are just links to public content sources such as YouTube and Facebook. Users are encouraged to share their clips that they think good in public facilities in order to attract more volunteer mentors for the children. Temporary video recordings, such as those of each teaching session, should normally be restricted for review by just the teachers, students, and mentors in the local Content Database.

The Session Manager manages the teaching sessions according to the curriculum and schedules of each students. The AMS sends reminders and start messages to the relevant users, including the teachers, parents, students, and mentors. Remote busy parents and mentors may interact with the teaching session through remote video conferencing. Sessions can also be recorded into the Content Database for the participants to review and discuss.

The Event Manager manages events organized typically by teachers and administrators, such as online or offline music competitions, introduction of other content appreciation sessions recommended by teachers, etc. The Event Manager is also responsible for other regular education events, such as reminding parents to listen prescribed clips with children, submission of assignment (e.g., student practice clips), and so on. Such reminders will be routed through the AMS.

The Forum Manager manages all user discussions in our platform, including private group discussions and comments as well as public and general topical discussion divided into areas of specification. The Messaging Manager managers all user to user on-line chats as well as off-line messages.

The User Manager manages all user accounts, such as their profile, security information, and preferences. This include their preferences of the types of alerts received and their desired channels, including SMS, instant messaging, email, etc. The Configuration Manager allows the administrators to set up system-wide defaults and system configuration parameters.

6   Parent Assistance Offered by Our Platform

In this section, we discuss how our platform creates an interactive musical environment that overcomes time and space limitations of busy parents to facilitate Suzuki method to music education.

6.1   Communicating and Cooperating with Music Instructors

Music teachers are taking an important role of educators. They should attempt more chances to communicate with the parents and explain more to them about parents' powerful influence on children's success, arousing their awareness of long-term benefit of music learning to the personal growth. Music teachers should always encourage parents to communicate with them too, so that parents can adequately understand their children's progress and performance in the lessons. Our platform provides forums for event announcement and personal messaging for achieving such purposes.

Music teachers are encouraged to give comments about the child's performance after each lesson. This also aims in creating a care and opening an communication channel between parents and teachers. Instead of relying on the helper, direct electronic communications provide much better interactions, and they are also recorded in our system for easy progress monitoring. This encourages both parents and children to be involved and enhance their motivation in seeking for improvement in the learning process. For example, teachers and parents can discuss whether the children have enjoyed a particular piece and found a scale or exercise challenging. Children in higher kindergarten and primary schools can even participate directly to share their own experience.

6.2   Increase Parental Involvement in Their Children's Learning Progress

Even though parents may have inadequate time to attend child's lesson during weekdays, they should always show their interests and care about their children's learning progress, maintaining an open, warm and supportive home atmosphere, seeking chances for informal conversations with the children about everyday events, learning interests, difficulties they encountered in the lesson and setting their common goals in the achievement in music learning. The AMS of our platform can alert the parents of the start of lessons and events, as well as provide video conferencing to support interactions of remote parents with teaching sessions and the recording of the sessions for parents' review.

As discussed, Suzuki method emphasis much on listening. Therefore, parents should spend more time in sharing music media with their children. As performances of the children's teacher will create a deeper impression to the children, we suggest teachers to share their own recording clips via our platform, so that parents can view these clips will their children. Some of these clips can also be used to facilitate their parents to practice music with their children at home. Teachers may prescribe media for their daily listening and practice via our platform together with the appropriate reminder alerts. Such clips aim to help children learn the melodies, appreciate good sounds and phrasing, develop correct posture, and grasp accurate pitch and rhythm.

6.3   Fostering a Virtual Musical Environment

Music teachers are encouraged to foster a musical environment by organizing various kinds of events and activities, such as bringing students and parents to public concerts, taking part in performances and competitions, etc. As busy parents and students may not have such time, teachers may select appropriate concert video clips from YouTube and other public video sharing sources and share such links via our platform.

Virtual music competition can be arranged simply by uploading students' recorded performances to our platform. Discussions among teachers, parents, and even older students can be also encouraged through our platform. All the notification of the above-mentioned events and important messages can be adequately supported by our AMS.

Music teachers can also assign capable senior students as mentors to assist the younger children. The attendance of advanced students at sessions (either physical or electronic) on beginners' pieces not only creates atmosphere of generosity and cooperation, but also enhances the motivation among the children, sharing challenges with peers.

As currently many parents and older children often consider Web browsing and interacting on Internet platforms entertainment, the overall image of our platform is expected to reduce much of the resistance and possibly to arouse more interest instead.

7   Conclusion

It is important for both parents and teachers to have more contributions to the musical environment of children, because their musical development may depend on the emphasis given to musical activity and on the opportunities in exposing to music. Despite of the busy city environment such as in Hong Kong, we have presented our "Web 2.0 with Alert Support for Suzuki Approach Platform" (WASSAP) to help teachers, students, and parents to streamline music learning processes according to the Suzuki approach. We have also introduced our system design and discussed how this could be realized. We advocate the use of contemporary Web 2.0 and ICT, which could typically help busy mobile people in learning participation, overcoming much restrictions of time and space. This is particularly applicable in metropolises with higher computing penetration as well as high-bandwidth broadband and wireless infrastructure.

As for further work, we plan to carry out these remedies in our professional practices and would like to evaluate the effectiveness with a comparative field study. For technical advancement, we are exploring the application of ontology and other social networking technologies for this purpose.

References

1. Chiu, D.K.W., Choi, S.P.M., Wang, M., Kafeza, E.: Towards Ubiquitous Communication Support for Distance Education with Alert Management. Educational Technology & Society 11(2), 92–106 (2008)
2. Chiu, D.K.W., Kafeza, M., Cheung, S.C., Kafeza, E., Hung, P.C.K.: Alerts in Healthcare Applications: Process and Data Integration. International Journal of Healthcare Information Systems and Informatics 4(2), 36–56 (2009)
3. Ceci, S.J., Rosenblum, T., de Bruyn, E., Lee, D.Y.: A bioecological model of human development. In: Sternberg, R.J., Grigorenko, E.I. (eds.) Intelligence, Heredity, and Environment, pp. 303–322. Cambridge University Press, Cambridge (1997)
4. Coleman, J.S.: Family, school, and social capital. In: Saha, L.J. (ed.) International Encyclopedia of the Sociology of Education, pp. 623–625. Pergamon, Oxford (1997)

5. Cook, C.A.: Suzuki Education In Action: A story of Talent Training From Japan. Exposition Press, New York (1970)
6. Derling, N., Steinberg, L.: Parenting styles as context: An integrative model. Psychological Bulletin 113, 487–496 (1993)
7. Griffin, R.: The Suzuki approach applied to guitar pedagogy. Thesis (D.M.A.), University of Miami (1989)
8. Hackett, P., Lindeman, C.: The musical classroom: backgrounds, models, and skills for elementary teaching. Person Education, London (2004)
9. Hidi, S., Harackiewicz, J.M.: Motivating the academically unmotivated: A critical issue for the 21st century. Review of Educational Research 70, 151–179 (2002)
10. Ho, W.C.: Musical behaviour of young Hong Kong students. Educational Research Journal 17(2), 197–217 (2002)
11. Lee, S.L.: The Suzuki beginner: a teacher's guide to the Suzuki principles of violin. Thesis (Ph.D.), University of Washington (1992)
12. Marjoribanks, K.: Family and school capital: Towards a context theory of students' school outcomes. Kluwer Academic, Dordrecht (2002)
13. Marjoribanks, K., Mboya, M.: Learning Environments, goal orientations, and interest in Music. Journal of Research in Music Education 52(2), 155–166 (2004)
14. McLean, R., Richards, B.H., Wardman, J.I.: The effect of Web 2.0 on the future of medical practice and education: Darwikinian evolution or folksonomic revolution? Med. J. Aust. 187, 174–177 (2007)
15. Suzuki, S.: The Suzuki Concept: An introduction to a successful method for early music education. Diablo Press, Berkeley (1973)

Interrelation between Trust and Sharing Attitudes in Distributed Personal Learning Environments: The Case Study of LePress PLE

Sónia C. Sousa, Vladimir Tomberg, David R. Lamas, and Mart Laanpere

Tallinn University, Institute of Informatics, Narva Road 25,
Tallinn 10120, Estonia
{scs,vtomberg,drl,martl}@tlu.ee

Abstract. This paper focuses on relations between learners' generic level of trust in online environments and their attitudes towards openness and sharing in a blog-based personal learning environment LePress. The main rationale of this study was inspired by the changes present in today's education, where the use of blogs as Personal Learning Environments is becoming an emerging trend in higher education. We claim that by understanding interrelation of trust and attitudes towards sharing within this open and flexible environments, we will be able to contribute to the design decisions regarding the LePress, which lead to increasing the participation of individuals and communities in inherent formal and informal learning processes in a number of contexts. Major contributions of this paper are towards understanding (1) the relationship between trust and teacher/learners attitudes towards sharing in a blog-based personal learning environment and (2) the correlation between users trust level and expectations towards affordances of online learning tools.

Keywords: trust, blogs, learning flow, Wordpress, LePress, Personal Learning Environments.

1   Introduction

This study explores the influence of generic level of trust to attitudes of learners towards openness and sharing in distributed Personal Learning Environments (PLE). Our aim is to provide a broader understanding of the nature of the relationship between learners' attitudes and expectations towards sharing and trust when in open learning context. This is due to the belief that the trust elements within distributed PLEs can somehow beneficiate each individual, a structured group or a community' sharing attitudes and behaviors.

This paper starts by providing a brief literature review on recent changes in online learning environments and trust-related issues in online communities. Our focus is narrowed down to the use of blogs as PLEs in formal higher education context. The next part of the paper introduces a blog-based PLE called LePress, which is an enhancement of the most popular blog engine WordPress. The final part of the paper summarizes the results from survey, which was carried out among 32 LePress users in two different higher education institutions.

H. Leung et al. (Eds.): ICWL 2011, LNCS 7048, pp. 72–81, 2011.

2   Online Learning Environments and Trust Issues

Learning, nowadays, can no longer be seen as a passive activity, it becomes an autonomous activity, where learners are openly responsible for the learning processes as well as for actively participating towards it.

A tendency towards a more individual-centered approaches whereas group-centered activities, creates context and where each individual contributes to the intellectual climate and the technological infrastructure of society, rather than the effects of media itself [5].

The view of the Internet as we seen a decade ago, as a mere repository of information and data has no longer exists. Especially, within this increasingly availability of user-generated content mechanisms in the World Wide Web and the increasing growth of social networking services, like the Web 2.0, or read-write Web.

The tools had transformed the Internet into a hub of socialization and are more then ever before representing the logical extension of our human tendencies toward togetherness. These tools are somehow tailoring our society and culture in general. These technologically enhanced social contexts represent new identities that are being formed and evolving individually or collectively and each one is tailored by each individual's diversity [6].

One consequence of that is that nowadays we can find very difficult to solely rely on face-to-face communications. And as the penetration of these social computing tools (like blogs, wikis, social bookmarking, virtual worlds, podcasts, RSS feeds, media sharing, and social networking sites) are becoming increasingly high we find new opportunities for individuals or groups to launch new collaborative approaches and form new social engagement contexts through the World Wide Web [4].

The change communication tools in has been shaping our society and changing the way we relate, organize our work and learn in general. In sum, this new social media approaches have been enabling the creation of a new social and cultural diversity, in other words have been shaping a new social and cultural space where is possible to communicate, work, interact or form new relationships without physical or temporal frontiers [12].

These emerging, increasingly digitalized lifestyles are suitable for individuals who are competent users of technology and capable of self-actualization. This kind of individuals need to feel safe and accepted in their relationship space in order for them to be willing to participate and engage in a mutual dialogue [14,11].

As any relationship (formed virtually or in face to face contexts) needs for environments with a particular history of trust, varied motives, mistakes and forgiveness that need to be created and maintained. In those contexts a careless communication potentially leads to lack of character, personality, familiarity which curbs the sharing values, gender, age, people's roles, social status – dimensions which are normally relied upon to determine people's trust based attitudes or decisions [7].

Another raising trend in today's higher education is the tendency to use Personal Learning Environments instead of, or in parrallel with traditional Learning Management Systems. In spite of we still see a tendency for universities to use different types of Learning Management Systems (LMS), mostly due to the already existing maturity of the inherent concepts. As well as because of the fact that LMS are now stable environments featuring high availability, scalability, usability, interoperability, stability, security performance [8].

There is an increasing tendency to agree that the adoption of Personal Learning Environments might result in a quantum leap over LMS based approaches, especially within the technology enhanced learning community of researchers. As envisioned, PLE facilitate learner-based constructivist learning processes and promote the usage of open resources, and Web 2.0 tools by opposition to the teacher-centric tactics enabled by typical, Web 1.0 associated LMS [9].

We argue that trust can represent an important key role in facilitating or hindering the adoption of blog-based Personal Learning Environments and open educational resources. We beilieve that trust affects individuals' predisposition to interact, by shaping their willingness to rely on others, or by influencing their ability to believe that other's actions will eventually lead to expected results [10]. As well trust can influence individuals' beliefs, attitudes and behaviors towards learning and sharing process, as it is a key element for provide cooperation and collaboration practices [14, 13, 11] Therefore, we propose that developers of blog-based learning environments should take into account the potential impact of trust-related factors to the attitudes and expectations of users.

3   LePress

Blogs are considered as a popular platform for using as PLE; they allow learners to build their learning portfolios by sharing, reading and reflecting on the learning experiences. Modern blogging platforms allow mixing multimedia information from different sources directly in blog posts.

LePress is an open-source software plug-in for popular WordPress blogging platform, it was developed in the Institute of Informatics, Tallinn University. As its name implies (LePress is a short version of Learning WordPress), LePress is intended for adding specific learning-related functionalities into WordPress. There exist a plenty of different Wordpress plug-ins which support different aspects of online learning. A specific feature of LePress is built-in support for managing learning related workflows (or learning flows) for course enrollment and assessment of learning outcomes.

Wilson [1] sees personal blogs as the key component of PLE that can be connected with institutions through using specially designed 'Course Coordination Space'. There is no strict definition of such space, it can be implemented in many forms, but this should be a lightweight software solution capable for providing courses' provisioning, scheduling, and monitoring. The possibility to ensure user support is another critical functionality of course coordination space. Following this design we developed LePress for providing a connection between the formal universities' learning courses and informal PLEs distributed among blogs of teachers and students. The native functionalities of LePress cover almost all tasks intended for Course coordination space.

LePress allows teachers to create courses on the base of their WordPress blogs and register students in them. In addition to various ways of using blogs in course works [2, 3] in LePress teacher can also produce special posts that are considered by the system as assignments or learning tasks. Being automatically notified about new assignments and deadlines the students can publish their homeworks in their own blogs. These posts automatically gathered by LePress and delivered to dedicated gradebook, accessbile only by the teacher. Teacher in turn can assess these submissions, grade them and send personal feedback.

LePress uses non-destructive approach to existing workflows in WordPress. Actually the users continue to work with their blogs in usual way by posting the own and commenting other's posts. The only additional task is to use dedicated categories for course-related posts and selected posts in teacher's blog as assignments [15].

LePress is not a unique WordPress plug-in for organizing courses, but it is very different in its design. Currently there are two other popular plug-ins that declare the functionality of course management on the base of WordPress, namely BuddyPress Courseware and Learninglog.

BuddyPress Courseware proposes a big scale approach. It offers for teachers a lot of versatile functionalities trying to find a possible substitution almost for any functionality of traditional LMS. Filling of variety different types of formal documentations like a course description, books register, or course bibliography is typically a strong requirement for the university course preparation process. However these and many other formal activities hardly can be considered as mandatory part of teaching process in PLE. Such kind of information is more expected to be presented at the institutional side, for example university can publish the course related data using XCRI (eXchanging Course-Related Information) standard syntax.

Attractiveness of blogs for end-users (in our case for teachers and students) often originates from simplicity and usability of blogs, therefore constructing complex data structures with large amount of functionalities on the top of the personal blog seems as disputable approach. The first question is why we need to build the fully functional traditional LMS on the top of the blogs, while many excellent 'pure' LMS are already produced and used in universities? What are advantages of such approach in terms of pedagogy and implementation of course workflow?

BuddyPress Courseware and Learninglog plug-ins have a mandatory requirement of prerequisite installation of additional BuddyPress plug-in which can be considered as another limitation. The popular plug-in BuddyPress provides for WordPress several features of social network. Use of BuddyPress is a pointless activity in single-user WordPress blog; it is designed to be installed on the top of special multiuser WordPress (WPMU) or WordPress version 3 with networking activated. After installation of BuddyPress local users can be organized into groups, add each other to friends, send messages and use forums for intercommunications. The mentioned above plug-ins for coursework implementation must be installed on the top of BuddyPress to use its group-management functionality. However this solution has some disadvantages. The main problem is an impossibility to add into the course any students from the blogs that belong outside of WPMU or WordPress network; only registered in specific WPMU or in the WordPress network local users can be added into groups. Currently there is only one possibility to link external blog into BuddyPress group, it is subscribing to RSS feed by installing a special additional plug-in. Though this runaround do not allows an external user to be a true group participant.

This limitation makes it difficult to organize courses with participants who use personal blogs dispersed on different hosting servers. As there is no way to add participants from outside of specific software instance, it transforms an open blog-based PLE into a traditional closed learning management system.

The need for using an additional software instance (BuddyPress) is the second shortcoming of mentioned above solutions, because installation and managing of current version of BuddyPress is not an easy task. Also this software has several known compatibility issues. A necessary of administration of additional software requires from teachers extra workload and technical skills.

In contrast to the other existing educational extensions for Wordpress for, LePress is designed as a Course Coordination Space and thereby it provides a connection between formal university courses and PLE. Students can run their own LePress-enhanced blog on a separate server or choose a central WPMU server hosted by the university. This allows an owner of external WordPress blog who already uses it as e-Portfolio to instantly join into the courses announced in another blog.

4   Research Approach

The aim of this study was to identify interrelation between general trust level and attitudes towards sharing within open, blog-based learning environments. To achieve this aim, two research questions were formulated:

1. What are the student's attitudes and expectations towards (a) sharing learning resources via the public Web, (b) sharing the assignment submissions and teacher's feedback with fellow students; and (c) participating in the negotiation of shared meaning?
2. How is the generic trust level of LePress users related with their attitudes towards affordances they expect from an online learning environment?

The questionnaire contained 18 questions and was divided in four parts: demographic and background information questions; attitudes towards sharing; trust related issues online; the affordances of online learning environments. The survey was written in English, Russian and Estonian. Responses from thirty-two students (from two higher education institutions) were collected from which we used twenty-nine completed ones for data analysis purpose, eleven in Russian, eighteen in Estonian. Thirteen respondents were female and sixteen male, age range varied between 18 and 52 years. All students have been taking at least one course, which was taught in blended mode using a blog-based Personal Learning Environment LePress.

5   Results

The following paragraphs summarizes the survey results in relation to: general learners Internet activity patterns; their sharing patterns; predisposition to relate or interact online; the learning environment; the feedback given; and learning activities.

General Internet Activity Patterns – results analysis shows that most uses the Internet to interact with others online in a daily base (82.76%). Also, reveled that people find activities like "reading and sending e-mail" (65.52%) as the most useful activity in the Internet, see f. This activity is followed by "Search for information [search engines, etc] " (31.03%), "Learning, sharing ideas in formal education contexts [school, institutions, etc]" (24.14%) and "Organizing or initiate activities, meetings, events". Finally comes "Sharing documents [doc, pictures, videos, music] " and "Chatting and Socializing".

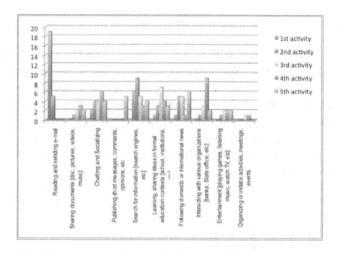

Fig. 1. Rank of activities consider more useful in online contexts

Students' Attitudes towards Sharing Learning Resources and Information – in here we observe people's predisposition to share in distinct online relationships contexts. More specifically, observe people's predisposition to share within a more close relationship context (e.g. friends, family and co-workers) and when in a more open one (e.g. acquaintances, student/teacher and strangers). Those sharing context where raised on issues like (1) sharing learning resources; (2) sharing personal information; (3) exchange comments and messages; and (4) on sharing Facebook status message. Results indicate a clear preference towards participating and sharing in groups with more close relationship than those with loose and open relationship.

Students' Attitudes towards Trusting in a Specific Online Person – when asked student's the question "what make you trust in a particular person online" the answers showed a tendency to consider vey important issues like: if the person is honorable (34,48%) and capable to respect them (31,03%). Where also consider important to know that person with whom they are going to communicate with (37.93%) and to share similar interest and preferences (34.48%).

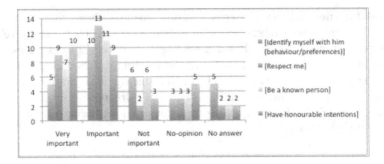

Fig. 2. What make you trust in a particular online person?

Students' Attitudes towards Willingness to Engage in a Give and Take Action – the most considered features that make them be willing engage in a more give and take action are the sense of honesty in the people with whom they will share (48,28%) and receive the information (37,93%). In other words believing that he or she will be a reliable source of information. Also, a sense of mutual respect and affinity is considered a very important feature (31,03%). Willingness to share (85,52%) and feeling of empathy and sympathy (41,38%) are considering important features as well, see figure below.

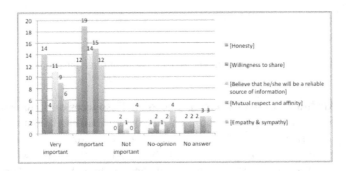

Fig. 3. What is the most important feature that makes you willing to engage in a give and take action online?

Most Important Condition to Be Willing to Interact with Another Person Online – is to know how they behave, especially if they behave in a friendly and transparent manner (44,83%) and again honest (44,83%) is also an important factor. Another important issue to make them willing to interact online with someone else is the feeling of relative security in the relation (34,48%) but in the other hand they did not consider predictability and important factor (51,72%). Important features also consider here are the sense of belonging (27,59%) and mutual respect (37,93%). See figure below.

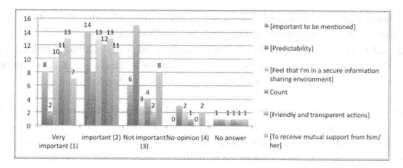

Fig. 4. What is the most important feature that makes you willing to engage in a give and take action online?

The finally and fourth part of the survey, addresses questions regarding the learning environment and raised issues that in general are related with: students' sharing beliefs when in open learning contexts and the level of control and availability of the course resources. Also addresses students' beliefs towards open communication and open learning processes reliability and credibility.

Students' Attitudes Towards the Open Learning Environment – students' seem to agree that a blog-based learning environment is a good learning tool and don't mind that other's can read their coursework materials (44,83%). Also the majority agrees that a blog-based learning environment makes the learning process transparent and shareable (37,93%).

Students' Sharing Beliefs towards the Open Learning Environment – student's don't mind sharing the resources (files, references, my personal notes) collected and created in the process of study on the public Web (31.03%). Not even mind if someone (e.g. her boss, 10 years from now) will find his or her old homework submissions on the public web (44.83%).

Students' Beliefs towards the Level of Control and Availability of the Course Resources – most students strongly agree that prefer to have their learning resources available on the public Web (31.03%) and not locked into an online learning environment (20.69%). Some though, seams undecided about keeping or not teacher's homework comments private by default or not. But, agreed that a student should be able to define access restrictions to his/her resources (41.38%) although seam neither agree or disagree if learners should have control over some learning main components like defining learning goals, selecting learning strategies, finding learning resources, choosing evaluation methods and indicators, choosing topics (44.83%).

Students' Beliefs towards the Learning Processes Reliability and Credibility – majority believes that by keeping all learning activities open attracts other Web users (especially external experts and practitioners) to participate in the course and share their knowledge (37.93%). But, somehow they seam undecided if by keeping their homework submissions public, others students can then make their valuable comments. Next and final group of questions aims to understand users' attitudes towards online learning environment affordances, specifically towards the learning cooperation and collaboration related practices; and of the technologies features.

Students' Attitudes towards Technological Related Features – from the technological point of view 37,93% of students consider very important for an online learning environment to include possibilities like: searching and annotating artefacts (e.g. tagging). Also is very important to include tools that allow creation and editing features (34.48%) or allow uploading and managing files (44.83%). Asynchronous text-based communications (e.g. forum), Self-tests (no record, no grading); Multiple-choice tests and content package and concept mapping tools are also considered as important features for online learning environment affordances.

Students' Attitudes towards the Learning Cooperation and Collaboration Related Practices – from a more cooperative and collaborative perspective students' consider important to provide Collaborative writing and drawing (e.g. online shared whiteboard) tools, built-in workflows (e.g. reviewing and publishing), self-reflection are referred as important features of an online learning environment. Providing tools for versioning of documents, or possibilities to practice in virtual labs; or to simulate experiences; or practicing with interactive models should also be included. As well as the possibility for forming sub-groups, group assignments and for Project/time management.

6   Conclusions

The main contribution of this study is exploration of intersection of areas such as trust, personal learning environments and learners' attitudes towards open learning environments.

For designing LePress course environment, the most important and promising results of survey is preference of the students to use learning resources available on the public Web and readiness of students to use for distributed PLE tools like LePress. On the other hand results point out that trust is an important factor in the learning process. An online learning environment should facilitate the learner in determining the quality of the relationship, i.e. if the other person acts in an honorable way and respect the relation, if they share similar interest are important issues to trust someone online. Trust affects also the learner's perceiving if other person behavior, especially if they are friendly, transparent and honest will help them to be more willing to share. And finally, the learners with higher levels of trust seem to be more willing to engage themselves in sharing activities online.

Acknowledgments. This research was funded by targeted research grant No. 0130159s08 from the Estonian Ministry of Education and Research.

References

1. Wilson, S.: PLEs and the institution, Scott's Workblog (2007),
   `http://zope.cetis.ac.uk/members/scott/`
   `blogview?entry=20071113120959`
2. March, T.: Revisiting WebQuests in a Web 2 World. How developments in technology and pedagogy combine to scaffold personal learning. Interactive Educational Multimedia (Band 15) (2007)
3. Attwell, G.: Personal Learning Environments – the future of elearning? eLearning Papers 2(1) (January 2007)
4. Nielsen Online: Global Faces and Networked Places. A Nielsen report on Social Networking's New Global Footprint (2009),
   `http://blog.nielsen.com/nielsenwire/`
   `wp-content/uploads/2009/03/nielsen_globalfaces_mar09.pdf`
5. McLuhan, M.: Understanding Media: The extensions of Man. Routledge, London (1994)
6. Putnam, E.: Diversity and community in the twenty-first century. The 2006 Johan Skytte prize lecture. Scandinavian Political Studies (2007),
   `http://www.utoronto.ca/ethnicstudies/Putnam.pdf`
7. Preece, J.: Etiquette, empathy and trust in communities of practice: Stepping-stones to social capital. Journal of Universal Computer Science 10(3), 194–202 (2001)
8. Hall, J.L.: Assessing Learning Management Systems. In: Chief Learning Officer,
   `http://pttmedia.com/newmedia_knowhow/KnowHow_Deploy/LMS/`
   `Docs/Assessing_LMS.doc` (accessed January 2010)
9. Dron, J., Anderson, T.: Lost in social space: Information retrieval issues in Web 1.5. Journal of Digital Information 10 (2009)
10. Mishra, A.K.: Organizational responses to crisis: The centrality of trust. In: Kramer, R., Tyler, T. (eds.) Trust in Organizations: Frontiers of Theory and Research, pp. 261–287. SAGE publications Inc., California (1996)
11. Gambetta, D.: Trust making and breaking co-operative relations. In: Gambetta, D. (ed.) Can We Trust Trust?, pp. 213–237. Basil Blackwell (1998)
12. Weaver, A., Morrison, B.: Social networking. Computer 41(2), 97–100 (2008)
13. Tschannen-Moran, M.: Collaboration and the need for trust. Journal of Educational Administration 39(4), 308–331 (2001)
14. Bachrach, M., Gambetta, D.: Trust as Type Detection. In: Castelfranchi, C. (ed.) Trust and Deception in Virtual Societies, pp. 1–22. Kluwer Academic Publishers (2001)
15. Tomberg, V., Laanpere, M., Lamas, D.: Learning Flow Management and Semantic Data Exchange between Blog-Based Personal Learning Environments. In: Leitner, G., Hitz, M., Holzinger, A. (eds.) USAB 2010. LNCS, vol. 6389, pp. 340–352. Springer, Heidelberg (2010)

Positive Influence Dominating Set
in E-Learning Social Networks

Guangyuan Wang, Hua Wang, Xiaohui Tao, and Ji Zhang

Department of Maths and Computing of USQ
Toowoomba. Queensland, Australia
{guangyuan.wang,hua.wang,xiaohui.tao,ji.zhang}@usq.edu.au

Abstract. In recent years, the development of E-learning is rapid. Learning efficiency can be greatly improved if E-learning users' social networks properties can be effectively utilized. However, the nodes in most research models are the same type. The focus of our study is on E-learners' positive influence between their relationship. In this paper, we proposed a new model and selection algorithm named Weight Positive Influence Dominating Set (WPIDS) and analyzed its efficiency through a case study. By comparing the differences between WPIDS and that of Positive Influence Dominating Set (PIDS), we found that our model and algorithm are more effective than those of PIDS.

Keywords: E-learning, Weight Positive Dominating Set, Algorithm.

1 Introduction

As the internet becomes widespread, E-learning communities become more and more popular [1]. E-learning is an attractive and efficient way for modern education. In such learning environments, almost all the resources are provided through the computers and networks and students can learn anytime and anywhere. Tutors and students interaction and collaboration also plays an important role in E-learning procedure. These online users share the same interest and purpose which provides a powerful medium of communicating, sharing and disseminating information and spreading influence beyond the traditional social interactions within a traditional social network setting.

Some research has been done to understand the properties of E-learning. Many educators and researchers have proposed their designs, described their implementation and shared their experiences from different points of view on E-learning environments [2, 3, 4, 29]. In fact, the relationship between the E-learning users composes an online social network. In this paper, we explore the E-learning system social networks structure to help E-learning users to improve their achievements during the E-learning process. In E-learning programs the tutors and students compose the set of users. There are some different studying groups according to their interest and purpose. The fact is that each user has different learning ability and it is very important to divide groups such that there are plenty of tutors or excellent students in each group to have positive influence

H. Leung et al. (Eds.): ICWL 2011, LNCS 7048, pp. 82–91, 2011.
© Springer-Verlag Berlin Heidelberg 2011

to help others. For example, a user can be an authority such as a tutor who has heavy positive influence on others, an excellent student, an average student, or a poor student according to their academic records. An excellent student has positive influence on his direct friends (called outgoing neighbors), but he might turn into a poor student and has negative influence on his outgoing neighbors if many of his friends are poor students, and vice versa.

On the other hand, due to the financial limitations in budget, it is impossible to set lots of tutors in the study program. These issues are very intricate and complex problems that require a system-level approach where the dynamics of positive and negative influence resulting from individual-to-individual and from individual-to-group interactions as well as the evolving status of individuals can be fully captured. Therefore, how to choose a subset of users to be part of the positive set so that the effect of the positive users can positively affect other users through the whole group under consideration during learning programs becomes the key item of inquiry. In an effort to address this issue, the specific problem we study in this paper is the following: given an online E-learning system and the set of users. We identify a subset of the individuals within the E-learning online social network to participate in an education/intervention program such that the education/intervention can result in a globally positive impact on the entire users.

We assume that 1) if the total arc weights of an individual's incoming neighbors have positive impact on him, then the probability that this individual positively impact others in the social network is high. 2) education/intervention program can convert a negative influential individual to a positive influential person. 3) there are some authority users (tutors) with no incoming arcs which means that they are positive users without others' influence. Our first assumption comes from an extensive body of evidence suggesting that one of the most powerful predictors of negative/habitual behavior in individuals is whether an individual has friends who also engage in that behavior[5, 33]. Due to outside competition in terms of personality traits attained from peer influence, the more neighbors/ friends exerting positive influence, an individual has, the more likely he is to impact others in a positive way. Our second assumption comes from the work in [6, 7, 33], where nearly every individual in the feedback intervention program showed an improving grades in studying. The third assumption comes from the fact that the tutors is authorities in the study program who can not be affected by other students' negative influence. With the above three assumptions, the problem is equivalent to selecting a subset of the individuals to participate in the E-learning program such that each individual in the social network has more positive influence than negative influence.

The main idea is how to effectively utilize positive users to affect the whole users. The contribution of this paper is as follows:

- We propose a new Weight Positive Influence Dominating Set (WPIDS) model in an E-learning community which reasonably utilizes its online social network structure to help E-learning users to improve their achievements.

- We propose and evaluate the WPIDS selection algorithm with a real-world case study and compare the differences between WPIDS and PIDS.
- We analyze the causes why our WPIDS model is better than PIDS model.

The rest of this paper is organized as follows. In Section 2, we define the WPIDS problem. Section 3 describes some related work. In section 4, we present the WPIDS selection algorithm. Section 5 shows a case study. Section 6 concludes this paper and discusses our future work.

2 Problem Definitions

In this section, we formulate the WPIDS problem in the E-learning online social networks. As an intuitive scenario, we consider a small learning group composed of Bob, Chris, Don and Tom. Bob is a tutor and others are negative students and Chris who has the biggest influence among these three students. The problem is how to choose the smallest number of students to have positive impact on others to improve their achievements. In the above example, we can choose both Bob and Chris as the WPIDS and Bob should strengthen influence on Chris. If Chris can become an excellent student she can positively influence other students. We will use the following network model to illustrate the E-learning online social network in context of the improving achievement issue: A digraph $G = (V; A; C; W)$ is used to represent the E-learning online social network. V is the set of nodes in which each node is a user in the E-learning systems. A is the set of arcs in which each direct arc represents the existence of a social connection/influence between the two endpoints. C is the compartment vector that saves the compartment of each node. The compartment of a node decides whether it has positive or negative influence on its outgoing neighbors. For example, for the improving E-learning users' achievements problem, the compartment of each node is one of the followings: authority (tutor), excellent student, average student, or poor student. A node in the authority or excellent student compartment has positive influence and all nodes in any of the other two compartments have negative influence. W is a set of weight values corresponding to arcs belong to A. Each arc's value is decided by the frequency of the two persons' interactions.

Definition 1 *(E-learner Social Network). An E-learner Social Network is a weighted digraph $G = (V; A; C; W)$. V is the set of nodes in which each node is a user in the system. A is the set of arcs between the vertices: $A = \{(u, v)|u, v \in V$ and the user u influences the user $v\}$. C is the compartment vector that saves the compartment of each node. The compartment of a node decides whether it has positive or negative influence on its outgoing neighbors. W is a set of weight values corresponding to arcs belong to A. The weight value W of an arc (u, v) is defined as:*

- *$w(u, v) \in [-1, 0)$, if the user u is a negative user;*
- *$w(u, v) \in [0, 1]$, if the user u is a positive user.* ☐

Definition 2 *(WPIDS). With the above E-learner social network model, the Weight Positive Influence Dominating Set (WPIDS) of an E-learner online social network G is defined as finding a subset P of V such that any node u in V is dominated by its total incoming neighbors' arcs weight not less than zero. That is,*

$$\forall u \in G, \sum_{v \in N^-(u)} w(u,v) \geq 0,$$

where $N^-(u) = \{v | (v,u) \in A\}$ is the incoming neighbor nodes of node u. □

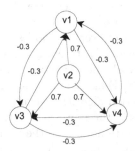

Fig. 1. An Example of WPIDS Graph Model with an Authority

Example 2.1. *An example of WPIDS is shown in Fig. 1. Let node v_2 represents an authority (tutor) and nodes v_1, v_3, v_4 represent non-positive students, and let $w(v_2, v_1) = w(v_2, v_3) = w(v_2, v_4) = 0.7$, other arcs weight values are -0.3. According to the definition of WPIDS, the total incoming arcs weight values of nodes v_1, v_3, v_4 are 0.1. So node v_2 is a WPIDS which shows the key person's influence.*

3   Related Work

Most of the current research in E-learning system fall in several categories: one is to explore on how to construct the E-learning environments, such as the work in [8]. G.K. Tegos et al presented a general of the E-learning system and proposed a component-based web-environment [8]. S. Garruzzo [9, 10] described their multi-agent E-learning platform. The agents in tutor system can provide adaptive service by exploiting the device agents associated with the E-learning web site and the teacher agents. As information security is becoming more and more important, there are also many E-learning systems developed for information security curricula [11, 27, 28, 30, 31]. These paper presented different designs concept from E-learning modules to information security curricula to construct an E-learning system.

On the other hand, it will greatly improve learning efficiency if credible study materials can be accurately identified in the E-learning community, so citation analysis has been widely used for bibliometrics ranking (e.g. [12], [13], [14], [15], [25]). They can be separated into two classes depending on what type of the nodes represent in the graph model. The nodes in the citation graph represent publications [12, 13] or journals and authors [14, 15, 25].

Some research has been done to understand the E-learning online social network properties [16, 17, 18] and how to effectively utilize social networks to spread ideas and information within a group [19]. Among these issues, dominating problems in a network have gained popularity since its wide application background. Whilst domination in undirected graphs have been studied extensively [21, 26], domination in directed graphs (digraphs) have not yet gained the same amount of attention from researchers. For domination in digraph, the research of [22, 23, 24] study the properties of the minimum dominating sets upon some characterized digraphs. However, the nodes and links in their models are mostly equal status, which are mostly studying location problems. Jon. Kleinberg et al study online social networks in which relationships can be either positive or negative [32]. In paper [26] Feng. Wang et al explored a Positive Influence Dominating Set (PIDS) selection algorithm to utilize online social networks to help alleviate social problems in the physical world. They proposed dominating set problems in different property nodes and they utilized online social networks to help alleviate social problems such as drinking, smoking or drug. However, they don't consider the influence of direction and degree factors between their relationship. Another drawback in paper [26] is they overlook the key persons' heavy influence during the procedure. Our work focuses on these reasonable factors between their relationship. We study a typical real-world E-learning social network and explores how to utilize E-learning networks topology properties to help E-learners to improve their achievements.

4   WPIDS Selection Algorithm

In this section, we present a WPIDS selection algorithm for the based arc Weight Positive Dominating Set problem formalized in the earlier section. First we define and explain a few terms and definitions used in the description of our algorithm. Each node can have either positive or negative impact on its outgoing neighbor nodes. We call a positive node with positive impact on his outgoing neighbors and a negative node with negative impact on his outgoing neighbors. The level of a node's positive effect is its positive outgoing arc weight value. The same holds for the level of a node's negative effect. The compartment of a node decides whether a node is a positive or a negative node. For example, in the context of E-learning, a node in the authority or excellent user compartment is a positive node and a node in any other compartment is a negative node. Nodes that are chosen into the WPIDS are marked as positive nodes. Thus a node u of a node $v's$ incoming neighbor is a positive neighbor if u is initially a positive node or u is selected into the WPIDS. The effect value of a positive user $u's$ outgoing arc weight $w(u, v)$ has become $|w(u, v)|$. A PIDS P of a graph G is a subset of nodes in G such that any node u in G is dominated by at least $\lceil \frac{d(u)}{2} \rceil$ nodes in P where

$d(u)$ is the degree of node u. A WPIDS P of a graph G is a subset of nodes in G such that any node u in G is positively dominated by its incoming neighbors. That is, any node u in V is dominated by its total incoming neighbors' arcs weight not less than zero.

The main idea of WPIDS algorithm is as follows: first prune the original graph by removing the initial positive nodes and choose the nodes into positive set if they are such that the definition of WPIDS, then update the positive set and their outgoing arc weights, give a ascending order of the remainder nodes according to their total outgoing arcs weight. We use a greedy algorithm to select the node with the smallest total outgoing arcs weight values into the dominating set, repeat the above procedures until all nodes in the original graph are positively dominated by their incoming neighbors. The computing complexity of our approximation algorithm is $O(n^2)$. Algorithm 1 gives the details of the WPIDS algorithm. Compartment vector C contains the nodes that are initially in positive compartment.

Algorithm 1. Arc Weight Positive Influence Dominating Set Selection Algorithm

---

Input: A digraph $G = (V, A, C, W)$ where V is the set of nodes, A is the set of arcs that capture the social interaction of the nodes, C is the set of nodes that are initially in positive compartment.

Output: A subset $P \cup C$ of V such that any node u in V has been positively dominated. i.e. each node's sum of incoming arc weights is non-negative.

1 Initialize the status of all nodes in V to NEGATIVE and P to empty;
2 Let $V' = V - C$ and set the status of nodes in C to POSITIVE;
3 Calculate the sum of total incoming arcs weight of each node in V;
4 T is the set of nodes in V' that have been positively dominated;
5 Let $V' = V' - T$;
6 While not every node in V' has been positively dominated;
7 Choose the node with the smallest weight value in V' into the P set, set the status of nodes in P to positive which have absolute values of outgoing arc weights;
8 Repeat step 3-7;
9 End of while;
10 The nodes in set $P \cup C$ are positive influence dominating set of G, and the positive influence value of each node is also calculated.

Example 4.1. *Fig. 2 shows how to operate our WPIDS algorithm 1, which is almost the same as Fig. 1 except one more negative node v_5 and let $w(v_4, v_5) = w(v_5, v_4) = -0.2$. According to our Algorithm 1, node v_4 has the smallest total outgoing arcs weight value (-0.8) and other nodes' total outgoing arcs weight values is -0.6, so node v_4 is selected as a positive node. The arc weight $w(v_4, v_5)$ becomes 0.2 which can positively dominate node v_5. The set $\{v_2, v_4\}$ is the WPIDS which can positively dominate the whole nodes.*

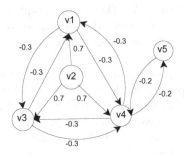

Fig. 2. An Example of WPIDS Selection Algorithm Graph Model

5 Case Study

5.1 A Real-world Case

In this section we use a real-world studying group (Fig. 3) to discuss the differences between WPIDS and PIDS selection algorithms. The studied case is depicted in Fig. 3. The scenario undergraduates are picked up from an computer science class[1], where Bob is a tutor and other person are non-positive students in an small E-learning group. Ann is a quiet and introverted girl who has limited influence to others. In Fig. 3, the arcs weight values are the same as in Fig. 2 and Ann has -0.1 influence value to Don. According to our WPIDS definition, Bob and Kris are the WPIDS. If we get rid of the arc's weights and direction Don and Kris are the PIDS according to its definition [26].

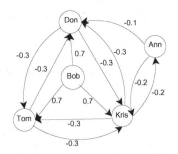

Fig. 3. A Case Study of WPIDS Selection Algorithm Group Model

5.2 Discussions

So from the case study of Fig. 3, we can see that the WPIDS in our model has some different real meanings from the PIDS in paper [26]. One of our improvements is that we consider the reasonable partition of persons who attended the

---

[1] From the authors' university. For privacy reasons, the students have been renamed.

program. Either in E-learning program or social influence in online communities we should consider the authorities' effect such as tutors or correctional officers who have heavy positive influence on other persons and they should be without interference from others. In other words, they are the key persons who play important roles during the program. Due to Ann's special situation, Kris should be selected into WPIDS to positively influence Ann instead of other persons. This solution shows the importance of directions. That is, the relationships between users are not equal. For example, the influence of relationship between tutors and students can be considered one-way. The fact is that the degree of influence between two persons is different and should be considered. Besides, our definition of the dominating problem is more reasonable than that of PIDS since one person's neighbors' level of influence is the decisive factor instead of the number of one's neighbors. So in order to positively dominate the whole group we can strengthen influence on the key persons instead of increasing the number of positive persons. So through these discussion we can draw a conclusion our WPIDS model is more reasonable and effective than PIDS model in paper [26].

6   Conclusions and Future Work

In this paper, we introduced and studied the problem of how to utilize online social network as a medium to improve users' achievements in E-learning system. We proposed the WPIDS selection algorithm to evaluate the effect of educating a subset of the entire target group susceptible to a social problem. The case study has revealed that the WPIDS model and algorithm are more effective than those of PIDS [26]. Since the tutors play important roles in the E-learning community the size of WPIDS is smaller than that of PIDS in a large online social networks.

To deeply understand the effect of WPIDS, we will compare our WPIDS algorithm with the PIDS algorithm in empirical experiments in future work. Since it is very important to specify the reasonable arc weight values of the E-learning users' influence and the cost of each tutor, we will also study the models under these factors to consider the positive influence dominating set problem.

References

1. Giannoukos, I., Lykourentzou, I., Mpardis, G., et al.: Collaborative e-learning environments enhanced by wiki technologies. In: Proceedings of the 1st International Conference on Pervasive Technologies Related to Assistive Environments, Article No 59. ACM, Athens (2008)
2. Shi, H.C., Revithis, S., Chen, S.S.: An agent enabling personalized learning in e-learning environments. In: Proceedings of the First International Joint Conference on Autonomous Agents and Multiagent Systems: Part 2, pp. 847–848. ACM, Bologna (2002)
3. Aghaee, N.G., Fatahi, S., Ören, T.I.: Agents with personality and emotional filters for an e-learning environment. In: Proceedings of the 2008 Spring Simulation Multiconference, Article No. 5. ACM, Ottawa (2008)

4. Lee, H.M., Park, D., Hong, M.: An instant messenger system for learner analysis in e-learning environment. In: Proceedings of the 9th ACM SIGITE Conference on Information Technology Education, pp. 51–52. ACM, Cincinnati (2008)
5. Jaccard, J., Blanton, H., Dodge, T.: Peer influences on risk behavior: Analysis of the effects of a close friend. J. Developmental Psychology 41(1), 135–147 (2005)
6. Larimer, M.E., Cronce, J.M.: Identification, prevention and treatment: A review of individual-focused strategies to reduce problematic alcohol consumption by college students. J. Stud Alcohol Suppl. 14, 148–163 (2002)
7. Walters, S.T., Bennett, M.E.: Addressing drinking among college students: A review of the empirical literature. J. Alcoholism Treatment Quarterly 18(1), 61–71 (2000)
8. Tegos, G.K., Stoyanova, D.V., Onkov, K.Z.: E-learning of trend modeling in a web-environment. J. ACM SIGCSE Bulletin 37(2), 70–74 (2005)
9. Garruzzo, S., Rosaci, D., Same, G.M.L.: MASHA-EL: A Multi-Agent System for Supporting Adaptive E-Learning. In: Proceedings of 19th IEEE International Conference on Tools with Artificial Intelligence (ICTAI), pp. 103–110 (2007)
10. Garruzzo, S., Rosaci, D., Same, G.M.L.: ISABEL: A Multi Agent e-Learning System That Supports Multiple Devices. In: Proceedings of IEEE/WIC/ACM International Conference on Intelligent Agent Technology (IAT), pp. 485–488 (2007)
11. Yuand, D.Q., Zhong, J.L.: Designing a comprehensive open network laboratory courseware. Journal of Computing Sciences in Colleges 24(1), 174–181 (2008)
12. Fu, L.D., Aliferis, C.: Models for predicting and explaining citation count of biomedical articles. In: AMIA Annual Symposium Proceedings, pp. 222–226 (2008)
13. He, Q., Pei, J., Kifer, D.: Context-aware Citation Recommendation. In: WWW 2010: Proceedings of the 19th International Conference on World Wide Web, pp. 421–430 (2010)
14. Nicolaisen, J.: Bibliometrics and citation analysis: From the science citation index to cybermetrics. JASIST 61(1), 205–207 (2010)
15. Robinson, M.D.: Applied bibliometrics: Using citation analysis in the journal submission process. JASIS 42(4), 308–310 (1991)
16. Mislove, A., Marcon, G.K.P., Druschel, P., Bhattacharjee, B.: Measurement and analysis of online social networks. In: Proceedings of the 7th ACM SIGCOMM Conference on Internet Measurement Conference (IMC), pp. 29–42 (2007)
17. Nazir, A., Raza, S., Chuah, C.N.: Unveiling facebook: A measurement study of social network based applications. In: Proceedings of ACM SIGCOMM Internet Measurement Conference (IMC). ACM, Vouliagmeni (2008)
18. Anagnostopoulos, A., Kumar, R., Mahdian, M.: Influence and correlation in social networks. In: Proceedings of the 14th ACM SIGKDD International Conference on Knowledge Discovery and Data Mining (KDD), pp. 7–15 (2008)
19. Kempe, D., Kleinberg, J., Tardos, E.: Maximizing the spread of influence through a social network. In: Proceedings of the ninth ACM SIGKDD International Conference on Knowledge Discovery and Data Mining (KDD), pp. 137–146 (2003)
20. Haynes, T.W., Hedetniemi, S.T., Slater, P.J.: Fundamentals of Domination in Graphs. Marcel Dekker, New York (1998)
21. Velzen, B.V.: Dominating set game. CentER Discussion Paper No. 2003-39, Tilbarg University, Center of Economic Research (2003)
22. Chartrand, G., Dankelmann, P., Schultz, M., Swart, H.C.: Twin domination in digraphs. J. Ars Comb. 67 (2003)
23. Chartrand, G., Harary, F., Yue, B.Q.: On the out-domination and in- domination numbers of a digraph. J. Discrete Mathematics 197, 179–183 (1999)

24. Ghosal, J., Laskar, R., Pillone, D.: Topics on domination in directed graphs. In: Haynes, T.W., Hedetniemi, S.T., Slater, P.J. (eds.) Domination in Graphs: Advanced Topics. Marcel Dekker, New York (1998)

25. Wei, W., Lee, J., King, I.: Measuring credibility of users in an e-learning environment. In: WWW 2007: Proceedings of the 16th International Conference on World Wide Web, pp. 1279–1280 (2007)

26. Wang, F., Camacho, E., Xu, K.: Positive influence dominating set in online social networks. In: COCOA, pp. 313–321 (2009)

27. Li, C.C., Pickard, J., et al.: A practical study on networking equipment emulation. Journal of Computing Sciences in Colleges 24(2), 137–143 (2008)

28. Lahoud, H.A., Tang, X.: Information security labs in IDS/IPS for distance education. In: Proceedings of the 7th Conference on Information Technology Education, Minneapolis, Minnesota, USA, pp. 47–52 (2006)

29. Wang, H., Zhang, Y., Cao, J.: Effective collaboration with information sharing in virtual universities. J. IEEE Transactions on Knowledge and Data Engineering 21(6), 840–853 (2009)

30. Wang, H., Sun, L.: Trust-involved access control in collaborative open social networks. In: Proceedings of 4th International Conference on Network and System Security (NSS), pp. 239–246 (2010)

31. Sun, L., Wang, H.: Towards Identify Anonymization in Large Survey Rating Data. In: Proceedings of the 4th International Conference on Network and System Security (NSS), pp. 99–104 (2010)

32. Leskovec, J., Huttenlocher, D., Kleinberg, J.: Predicting Positive and Negative Links in Online Social Networks. In: Proceedings of the 19th International Conference on World Wide Web (WWW), Raleigh, North Carolina, USA (2010)

33. Crandall, D., Cosley, D., Huttenlocher, D., Kleinberg, J., Suri, S.: Feedback Effects between Similarity and Social Influence in Online Communities. In: Proceeding of the 14th ACM SIGKDD International Conference on Knowledge Discovery and Data Mining, Las Vegas, Nevada, USA (2008)

Social Tagging to Enhance Collaborative Learning

Élise Lavoué

Université de Lyon, CNRS
Université Jean Moulin Lyon 3, MAGELLAN, LIRIS, UMR5205
Elise.Lavoue@univ-lyon3.fr

Abstract. In this paper, we investigate how social tagging could be used in Education as a support for learning processes. We first summarize the results of recent works on the effect of the use of social tagging for knowledge building and learning. We show that few educational tag-based systems intentionally use tagging to enhance learning. We then describe a Tag-based Collaborative System (TaCS), meant for supporting social and collaborative learning thanks to tagging, and detail the learning processes expected by the use of the system. We conducted an exploratory study to observe (1) the evolution of the students' tags as an indicator of the learning of new concepts and (2) the evolution of the tags assigned to documents as an indicator of the learning of new conceptual relations. The results show that the students make their tags and their relations to documents evolve, mainly due to two activities: the comparison of individual and collective tag clouds and the negotiation for an agreement on a common tag cloud in the groups.

Keywords: Tagging systems, educational systems, collaborative learning.

1   Introduction

Social tagging is the activity of annotating and classifying digital resources with keywords (tags as metadata). It is used by most of web-based information systems for the collaborative indexing of massive amount of information [1]. However little is known about how Web 2.0 technologies, particularly social tagging, may directly interact with individuals at the knowledge and cognitive level [2]. In this paper, we are interested in the use of tagging in Education as a support for learning processes. Our research are based on some recent works [3, 4] described in section 2, which tend to explain how social tagging supports cognitive and social learning processes. We show that tag-based systems are mainly used in Education as a means of indexing and searching for information but that they are rarely used intentionally as a means of supporting collaborative learning processes. Section 3 is dedicated to the description of a Tag-based Collaborative System (TaCS) we have developed. This system is meant for supporting learning processes thanks to tagging. It helps learners to understand and be familiar with a domain of interest thanks to the tags they assign to their documents. We finally detail in section 4 the results of a pilot study conducted in real conditions during five weeks.

H. Leung et al. (Eds.): ICWL 2011, LNCS 7048, pp. 92–101, 2011.

2   Learning Processes and Tag-Based Educational Systems

2.1   Social Tagging and Cognitive Processes

Glahn, Specht and Koper suggest using tagging for educational issues, mainly for reflection activities [5]. Within the distributed cognition framework, Fu studies the interactions between the internal and external representations of concepts, tags and documents when a user is engaged in iterative explore-and-comprehend cycles [3]. The results suggest (1) that the interactions between internal concepts and external tags gradually lead to the sharing and assimilation of conceptual structures and (2) that social tagging systems are then a means for social exchange of knowledge structures. Based on these works, Kimmerle, Cress and Held [4] presents a model that defines learning and knowledge building as a co-evolution of cognitive and social systems while users tag. Their theoretical framework distinguishes four processes:

- *Externalization*: learners externalize their knowledge on a resource by assigning tags to it. To create tags, users have to articulate their own cognitive concepts and to translate them into keywords. This cognitive effort can arouse an individual learning.
- *Internalization*: by navigating in the information space using the tag clouds, users collect information relating to a tag. On the one hand, they learn tags used by the others and as a consequence how the others classify their resources. On the other hand, tags show new interconnections between concepts for users. It can lead to the incorporation of the concepts of the community and to the modification of the individual cognitive structures of users.
- *Assimilation*: by discovering and using new tags (and the associated concepts) that are in agreement with their knowledge, users can widen their knowledge but do not develop new different concepts.
- *Accommodation*: users can question and modify their cognitive concepts by learning that their associations on a specific domain are rather different, inadequate, or even false. It can occur when users realize that the other users use tags that are very different from theirs, what implies that specific resources or tags are bound to very different concepts.

2.2   Tag-Based Educational Systems

Social tagging systems are usually used to facilitate the collaborative indexation of massive quantity of information and to improve their access [6]. Connotea and CiteULike are examples of online reference management and social bookmarking services for assisting scientists, researchers and academics in storing, organizing, sharing and discovering links to academic scientific and research papers. Tag clouds are also used as an indexation and search tool by communities of teachers, as in the Cloudworks Web site [7], created for teachers to discuss their practices and ideas of educational design. The ASK - LOST 2.0 system [8] uses tags to index all types of digital educational resources (images, videos, texts, URL). Dahl & Vossen [9] apply social tagging to the context of e-learning repositories: the metadata repository share.loc and the content repository Learnr.

Some works are interested in tags for other educational applications. The social annotation and tagging systems OATS [10] and SparTag.us [11] allow highlighting a part of a text and tagging this content. For every annotated text, users can see their assigned tags as well as the most assigned tags by other users. It is also possible to see the cloud of the most used tags. However, these tools do not allow a collaborative work, since every student annotates and tags individually the text. The online collaborative system TACO [12], based on tags, has been developed to support language learning. This system is designed to improve the understanding of written English and more exactly to develop capacities of critical thinking. A forum is linked to each tag to allow learners to criticize them and to exchange ideas. This system is especially meant for helping teachers to assess precisely their students thanks to an automatic score mechanism applied on their tags.

In conclusion, usually only the community effect of tags (the use by a large number of users) is used for the indexation and the search for information. Only the TACO environment was really meant for collaborative learning, with negotiation and criticism of tags, but it is very specific to language learning. Our approach is not specific to a discipline and suggests using tags and tag clouds as negotiation and comparison objects within learning groups. We based on this approach to develop the TaCS platform described in the following section.

3   TaCS: A Tag-Based Collaborative System for Learning

In this part, we describe the Tag-based Collaborative System (TaCS) and the learning processes expected with its use. It is based on the content management system Joomla!. We have integrated existing components that we have modified and we have also developed a specific component to offer the functionalities described below.

3.1   Documents and Tags Management

Learners have a personal space in which they can create and manage documents and tags (see Fig. 1). A document is a text with its reference (the file or the link of the Web page where the text was extracted). Learners have to assign at least one tag that identifies the main concept or idea of their document. Tags are displayed under the shape of clouds. For each tag is indicated the number of times it has been used (the more the tags are used, the more the size and the font weight are big in the tag cloud). On the same interface, learners can see the tags currently used to describe documents (explicit information), the deleted tags (among those used to describe documents) and the tags used to navigate on the platform (implicit information).

TaCS is meant for collaborative activities, usually carried out by groups of four or five students. That explains why we distinguish three types of actors: the learner, the group and the class. Learners have access to their own documents and tag clouds from their space; to the documents and the tag clouds of their group from the group space; to the tag clouds of the class from the class space.

User menu   Navigation menu: individual space, group space and class space

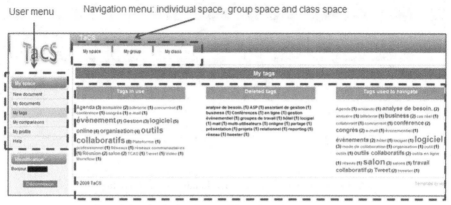

A user's tag clouds: tags in use, deleted tags, tags used to navigate

Fig. 1. Tag clouds of a student on TaCS (implicit and explicit information)

By asking learners to assign tags to documents, we expect them to think about the documents they create, to understand their content and to apply their ability to synthesize by identifying the keywords (tags) summarizing the main ideas and concepts. The difficulty of assigning tags to documents could bring learners to question the relevance of the document with regard to the domain studied. Furthermore, by giving learners the possibility to visualize their own tag clouds, we aim at bringing them to have a reflexive approach and to question their appreciation of the subject concerned. They can for example detect a gap between the approach they think to have and the image reflected by the tag cloud. The implicit information (deleted tags and tags used to navigate) also reflect for learners an image of their actions: they can realize for example that they often use a tag to navigate while they have never used it to describe a document.

3.2   Comparison of Tag Clouds and Statistics

The TaCS platform offers several functionalities to compare tags. From their own space, learners can compare their tag cloud with the tag cloud of their group (see Fig. 2). From the group space, learners can compare the tag cloud of their group with the tag cloud of the class (including the tags of all the groups). These comparisons concern the name and the degree of use of the tags. As explained in [3], a tag cloud can be considered as a simplified external representation of the internal concepts of learners or as a shared external knowledge structure of the group and the class. We think that the comparison of their own tags with those of their group or those of their group with those of the class could bring learners to assimilate new concepts and to question their own concepts. That could bring learners to create and/or delete documents and/or tags.

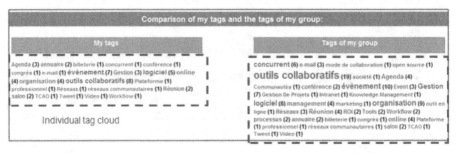

Fig. 2. Comparison of learners' individual and collective tag clouds

The system also displays some statistics:

- On the activity of the group: tags to define, number of used and deleted tags, number of created and deleted documents (for the group and for each member). These statistics give learners a means of situating themselves within their group.
- On the activity of the class: number of used and deleted tags, number of created and deleted documents by the class and by the group. These statistics give groups a means of situating themselves within the class.

3.3   Details on Documents and Tags

The distinction between documents and tags aims at bringing learners to realize that tags have as much importance as documents. Learners have access to the details of tags as well as the details of documents. The details are:

- For a tag: the learners that have used it, the associated documents and its definition. This definition can be created collaboratively by all the members of a group, thanks to the comment tool described in section 3.4.
- For a document: its editor, its title, its date of creation, its text, its references and the assigned tags.

We think that the visualization of explicit tag-document relations (tags assigned to document, documents associated with a tag by learners in a same group) could bring learners to discover and assimilate new conceptual relations and possibly to question and to modify their existing conceptual relations. That could lead to the creation of documents bound to a tag and/or to the association of new tags to a document.

3.4   A Community Space

TaCS offers community functionalities to bring conviviality and to favor the exchanges, the mutual aid and the negotiation between learners: a comment tool linked to each document and to each tag ; a voting system on documents and on comments ; a learner's profile ; a forum for each group (not accessible to the others), as well as for the class.

As explained in section 4.1, members of a same group are asked to build a set of documents and a model of indexation of the group (tag cloud). Learners of a group have to negotiate to reach agreement, especially to define a common definition of every tag. They also need to share their expertise on the domain, for example by means of forum, and to criticize and to evaluate the submissions of the other learners through comments and votes. By doing these activities, we would like learners to acquire and develop collaborative skills, such as to negotiate, to share and to criticize.

4   A Pilot Study of TaCS

We carried out an exploratory study, which attempted to gather evidence to support the usability and the utility of the TaCS platform as a support for the learning processes detailed in section 2.1. We also wanted to identify potential uses of the platform, maybe not previously meant. More precisely, we studied the effects of comparing tag clouds on students' activities and the effects of social tagging on the group dynamics.

4.1   Method - Experimental Data

This exploratory study was a part of a course about "Collaborative Information Systems" of a 5th year in University, from 11 November 2010 to 16 December 2010. The students had to study the case of a company, which organizes events abroad. They had to design a collaborative information system to facilitate the work of the employees of this company. The students were asked to search for documents on which they base their study, to tag them and to reach a common definition of every tag. They had access to the TaCS functionalities according to five phases so as to be able to observe the effect of the different functionality on the students' activities and to make hypothesis on the learning processes that occurred. We make it clearer that the expected learning processes were not exposed to the students, which means that they had access to the functionalities according to these phases but we did not ask them to use the functionalities with a specific intention. Each phase described below lasted a week:

- *Phase 1: Individual search for documents.* The students searched individually for interesting documents related to the case study and tagged them. Learners had access to their own space to create documents and to visualize their tag clouds.
- *Phase 2: Visualization of the tag cloud of the group.* The learners could compare their tag cloud with the tag cloud of their group. The aim was to bring students to modify their own tags or to create new documents.
- *Phase 3: Access to all the documents of the group.* The students had access to all the documents of their group, to the forum and to the list of the members of their group with their profile. They were able to discuss the documents and to vote for them thanks to the comment and vote functionalities. The aim was to bring learners to share all the documents within their group and to keep only those they estimated relevant to the case study.

- *Phase 4: Access to the statistics and the details of the tags of the group.* The statistics of the group were made accessible on its space (see section 3.3). Learners could also see for each tag the learners that had used it, the associated documents and its definition. This information aimed at giving learners a means of situating themselves within their group.
- *Phase 5: Visualization of the tag cloud and the statistics of the class.* The students had access to the tag cloud of the class to compare it with the one of their group and to the statistics of the class (see section 3.3). Each group could modify its documents and assigned tags.

This study was conducted with 17 students and the groups of learners were composed of 4 or 5 students. The results detailed come from two types of data:

- Use tracks: a specific tool was used to collect the use tracks according to the evaluation criteria (e.g. submitted and deleted documents; used and deleted tags at each phase).
- Questionnaire: this was filled anonymously to collect the learners' opinions and explanations regarding the used or unused functionalities and the learning processes they think they have applied. Among the 17 students, 13 filled in the questionnaire (47 questions).

4.2 Results and Interpretation

We observed a rather high level of participation on TaCS. 201 documents, 354 distinct tags and 969 tag-document relations (association of a tag with a document) were created. This participation can be explained in particular by the fact that the learners were globally satisfied by the ease of use (considered very good or good by 8 respondents and bad by 1) and the general quality of the interface (considered very good or good by 10 respondents, against 3 rather good).

Concerning the utility of documents, a considerable part of the created documents had been deleted at the end of the study (61 documents). We notice that almost all of the documents did not evolve after the first phase (by deletion or addition). At the first phase of individual work, the students created 180 documents among the 201 final documents. Furthermore, they deleted 57 documents during the first phase (among the 61 deleted documents during the study). So we can suppose that the fact of assigning tags to documents (aim of the first phase) brought the students to understand the proposed documents, to question them and to delete those they considered less relevant. We can also conclude that the collective activities and the comparison with the documents and tags of the other groups had no influence on the evolution of the documents.

We observe that the students revised their tags since 251 tags among the 354 distinct submitted tags were deleted at the end of the course. They also questioned the relations because at the end of the scenario 407 relations were deleted. According to the answers to the questionnaire, the learners made their tags evolve mainly for two reasons: after comparison with the tags of the members of their group and by a collective decision of the group. The answers to the questionnaire show that the comparison of the learners' tags with those of their group mainly (1) allowed the students to have a view of the others' work, (2) led them to question themselves and (3) led them to make their tags evolve.

We studied the evolution of the distinct tags proposed by each group at each phase of the study, as an indicator of the evolution of the concepts identified by the learners as being relevant to the case study (see Fig. 3). We were also interested in the evolution of the tag-document relations, what can help us to determine if students questioned their conceptual relations:

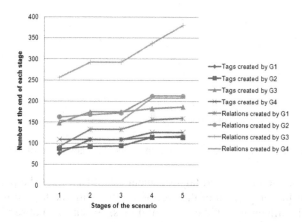

Fig. 3. Tags and tag-document relations created at each phase of the study

- The majority of the tags and relations were created during the first phase, what seems normal because it is the phase where the students created the documents and assigned their tags. This result confirms that the students tried to summarize their documents by tags from the first phase of individual work.
- A significant part of the tags and tag-document relations was created during the phase 2. It explains by the fact that the learners had access to the tags of the others, what confirms that the comparison had an influence on the creation of tags.
- The phase 3 had only a very low influence on the creation and the deletion of tags and their relations to documents. It leads us to conclude that the sharing of documents between students of a same group has an influence neither on the evolution of documents nor on those of their tags and relations to documents.
- Another significant part of the tags and their relations to documents were created during the phase 4. We also observe that most of the tags and tag-document relations have been deleted during the phase 4 (see Fig. 4). So during this phase the students not only deleted the tags and relations that they did not consider being relevant to the case study, they also created new tags and relations. We deduce that the negotiation within the group led students to question their tags and tag-document relations. These results also highlight the fact that most of the learners' motivation come from the dynamics inside the group. It is confirmed by the respondents who think that they have applied the expected collaborative skills: criti-

cism of the other members' submissions (documents and tags) (11 yes, 1 no and 1 NR); negotiation of tags (10 yes, 1 no and 2 NR), negotiation of the definition of tags (10 yes and 3 no) and documents (11 yes, 1 no and 1 NR).

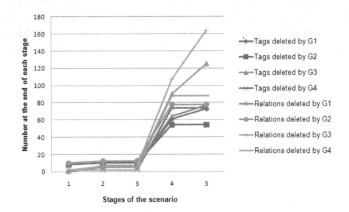

Fig. 4. Tags and tag-document relations deleted at each phase of the study

- The low evolution of tags and tag-document relations during the phase 5 leads us to think that the comparison of the tags of a group with the tags of the whole class has only little influence on the evolution of tags. We can also observe that students are especially interested in the work within their group and that they do not compare much themselves with the other groups. This is an interesting result that can question the need of a space for the class.

5   Conclusion and Future Work

With this study, we observed that the sharing of documents between the students of a same group has an influence neither on the evolution of documents nor on those of their tags and relations to documents. Regarding the expected learning processes, we notice that the students effectively questioned their tags (more than documents), mainly due to a comparison with those of the other members of their group. The criticism and the negotiation within the groups also seem to provoke a questioning and a modification of tags and documents. We thus suggest that tags could be more used on educational web-based systems, so as to support learning processes such as synthesis of the main ideas and concepts of a text; students' reflection on their own internal concepts; assimilation of new concepts; and creation of new conceptual relations. We advance that tags and tag clouds can be used within groups of students as negotiation and comparison objects to enhance the learning of new concepts and conceptual relations within collaborative activities.

This work opens up several possibilities. The first one is to analyze in detail the relevance of the tags assigned to documents and their evolution at each phase of the scenario, according to the offered functionalities. We are comparing the tags created by students with keywords extracted automatically from the text of documents (with text-mining tools). This analysis will allow us to finely study the utility of the functionalities of the TaCS platform. From a long-term perspective, we think that tags could also be used to help teachers to monitor learning activities and to evaluate students (individually and collectively). Tag clouds are indicators which could reflect the learners' acquisition of the concepts of a domain and the learning processes they applied. Tags could also be used to collect metadata on learners to be able to personalize their learning activities.

References

1. Yeung, C.-M.A., Gibbins, N., Shadbolt, N.: Contextualising tags in collaborative tagging systems. In: Proceedings of the 20th ACM Conference on Hypertext and Hypermedia, pp. 251–260. ACM, Torino (2009)
2. Held, C., Cress, U.: Learning by Foraging: The Impact of Social Tags on Knowledge Acquisition. In: Cress, U., Dimitrova, V., Specht, M. (eds.) EC-TEL 2009. LNCS, vol. 5794, pp. 254–266. Springer, Heidelberg (2009)
3. Fu, W.-T.: The microstructures of social tagging: a rational model. In: Proceedings of the ACM Conference on Computer Supported Cooperative Work (CSCW 2008), pp. 229–238. ACM, San Diego (2008)
4. Kimmerle, J., Cress, U., Held, C.: The interplay between individual and collective knowledge: technologies for organisational learning and knowledge building. Knowl. Manage. Res. Pract. 8, 33–44 (2010)
5. Glahn, C., Specht, M., Koper, R.: Implications of Writing, Reading, and Tagging on the Web for Reflection Support in Informal Learning. In: Dillenbourg, P., Specht, M. (eds.) EC-TEL 2008. LNCS, vol. 5192, pp. 110–121. Springer, Heidelberg (2008)
6. Millen, D., Feinberg, J., Kerr, B.: Dogear: Social bookmarking in the enterprise. In: Proceedings of the 24th International Conference on Human Factors in Computing Systems (CHI 2006), pp. 111–120. ACM, Montreal (2006)
7. Conole, G., Culver, J.: The design of Cloudworks: Applying social networking practice to foster the exchange of learning and teaching ideas and designs. Computers & Education 54, 679–692 (2010)
8. Kalamatianos, A., Zervas, P., Sampson, D.G.: ASK-LOST 2.0: A Web-Based Tool for Social Tagging of Digital Educational Resources. In: Proceedings of the Ninth IEEE International Conference on Advanced Learning Technologies (ICALT 2009), pp. 157–159. IEEE Computer Society, Riga (2009)
9. Dahl, D., Vossen, G.: Evolution of learning folksonomies: social tagging in e-learning repositories. International Journal of Technology Enhanced Learning 1, 35–46 (2008)
10. Bateman, S., Brooks, C., Mccalla, G., Brusilovsky, P.: Applying Collaborative Tagging to E-Learning. In: Proceedings of the 16th International World Wide Web Conference (WWW2007), Banff, Alberta, Canada (2007)
11. Nelson, L., Held, C., Pirolli, P., Hong, L., Schiano, D., Chi, E.H.: With a little help from my friends: examining the impact of social annotations in sensemaking tasks. In: Proceedings of the 27th International Conference on Human Factors in Computing Systems (CHI 2009), pp. 1795–1798. ACM, Boston (2009)
12. Chen, J.-M., Chen, M.-C., Sun, Y.S.: A novel approach for enhancing student reading comprehension and assisting teacher assessment of literacy. Computers & Education 55, 1367–1382 (2010)

A Framework to Enrich Student Interaction via Cross-Institutional Microblogging

Suku Sinnappan and Samar Zutshi

Faculty of Higher Education Lilydale, Melbourne 3140, Victoria, Australia
{ssinnappan,szutshi}@swinburne.edu.au

Abstract. This paper introduces a framework for collaborative microblogging that we believe is useful in enriching student interaction, both in-class and outside of contact hours. The framework is called Microblogging for Community of Inquiry (MiCoI). MiCoI is based on our experience using microblogging in an undergraduate Information Systems unit to facilitate a Community of Inquiry (CoI). In our experiment we demonstrated the existence of CoI with collaboration between an Australian and American tertiary institution using Twitter as the microblogging platform. The results were encouraging and were highlighted by the opportunity of cross-institutional interaction, reduced barrier to student engagement driven by social elements and additional channels to facilitate CoI. MiCoI is extended from this experiment and is designed to be applicable to any microblogging platform.

Keywords: Microblogging, Community of Inquiry, Twitter, Tertiary institution.

1   Introduction

The use of microblogging has become very popular. However, until recently, its usage in higher education has been largely limited to informal, social interaction. This paper presents findings from an initial study that suggests that microblogging can facilitate all aspects of a Community of Inquiry (CoI). Encouraged by the findings, and based on our reflection, we propose a framework (MiCoI) to facilitate CoI in higher education by facilitating learning activities that require students to interact with their peers as well as other student cohorts. This paper presents some key findings from our trial use of microblogging to facilitate a CoI and also presents our initial framework for further usage of microblogging in higher education.

2   Microblogging and Community of Inquiry

In this section, we provide a brief background regarding the use of microblogging for education. We also introduce the CoI framework and discuss our rationale for adopting microblogging as a tool to facilitate CoI.

H. Leung et al. (Eds.): ICWL 2011, LNCS 7048, pp. 102–111, 2011.

2.1   Microblogging and Twitter

A microblogging platform allows users to post brief messages for public view, which appear in reverse chronological order. Microblogging combines aspects of blogging and social networking and as such is considered one of the "social media". Microblogging has become very popular since the inception of Twitter in 2007. Despite several other microblogging platforms having become available, Twitter remains the most popular and in the literature reference is often made directly to the use of Twitter for education rather than to the use of microblogging e.g. [1, 2, 3].

The key features of microblogging are the ability to publish posts that are very brief (up to 140 characters in the case of Twitter), the ability to include abbreviated hypertext links and the ease and mobility with which such posts can be made.

The preliminary studies in the education literature on the use of microblogging in education suggest that it has significant potential. For example, a report describing the use of Twitter to complement a traditional LMS found that it encouraged free-flowing, just-in-time social interactions between students and staff [1]. [4] concluded that there was great potential for microblogging as a tool to support informal learning and it also allowed for the staff to provide feedback and get a feel for the overall "learning climate." [5] found that there were a number of potential applications such as for peer-to-peer support and administration.

However educators have recognised some drawbacks in Twitter usage, such as the possibility of it being distracting and addictive [6], cited by [1]. This may be related to findings around Twitter usage more broadly, e.g. [7] and [8] which emphasised the social aspects of Twitter usage. [9] analysed a random sample of 3379 tweets and produced nine message categories by extending work done by [7] to evaluate message content. The study found that there were two types of users. The first (80% of the users) largely disseminates messages about themselves. The second (20%) are more informative and involved with their followers. Educators acknowledge the possibility that Twitter usage could potentially suffer from various drawbacks, however in general their findings suggest that the potential benefits outweigh the drawbacks [7,10].

An interesting aspect of using microblogging to complement a traditional LMS is the fact that students can take the discussion beyond the barriers of the traditional classroom. Most LMSs allow access to the discussion only to fellow students in the Topical discussions and debates can benefit from more open discussion, e.g. with students from other courses and institutions or by tapping into discussions and debates in the wider society.

2.2   The Community of Inquiry Model

The Community of Inquiry (CoI) model proposed by [11] provides a conceptual framework for characterising the higher education experience. The CoI model proposes that learning occurs through the interaction of three elements, viz. cognitive presence, social presence and teaching presence. Cognitive presence refers to the extent to which the participants in the community are able to construct meaning through their communication. Social presence is the extent to which participants in the CoI project their personal characteristics to the community, beyond a simple notion of a sense of belonging [12]. The teaching presence refers to the dual functions of educational experience design and facilitation. While the educational experience design is largely within the purview of the staff, the facilitation function can be shared by the staff and students.

In principle, social media applications, such as microblogging, could be leveraged to enhance all three types of presence in an educational setting. Cognitive presence can be enhanced through social media based on students' ability to build meaning through ongoing communication involving individual and social exploration of ideas to develop understanding of a particular issue. Social presence is significantly enriched based on students' capability to present their ideas and identity while developing valuable links with the community. Finally, teaching presence can be enhanced by allowing informal and personal facilitation by staff and students.

2.3   CoI and Microblogging

[11] originally proposed the CoI framework in the context of ensuring that the critical components of higher education identified were in fact carried over to distance and online courses using computer-mediated communication (CMC), i.e. asynchronous discussion boards. However, subsequent work has adapted the framework for use in "blended learning" i.e. courses where a significant degree of CMC complements face-to-face communication [13] A report describing the use of Twitter to complement a traditional LMS found that it encouraged free-flowing, just-in-time social interactions between students and staff, thus enhancing the social presence aspect of the CoI [1]. Microblogging, while having what is sometimes referred to as a "real-time" characteristic, still remains asynchronous and thus is compatible with the original CoI principles. The fundamental differences from "classical" asynchronous interaction include much briefer messages and less explicit "thread" structures in most user interfaces used. Next section presents the case study which is central to MiCoI presented in Section 4. The lessons learned from the case study are critical in adjudicating as to how MiCoI should be implemented.

3   Case Study

3.1   Background, Methodology and Results

The usage of Twitter as part of tertiary learning is growing and is increasingly a common scene. However, most institutions use Twitter for social information exchange rather than deep pedagogical use. To explore this further we experimented the usage of Twitter based on the Community of Inquiry (CoI) approach. The experiment used a second-year undergraduate unit on eBusiness delivered primarily in a face-to-face mode with a LMS for online support. Twitter was used as the microblogging platform due to its popularity and the instructors' familiarity with the platform. The basic experiment involved setting up in-class tutorial activities that were suitable as the basis of students posting their thoughts and questions as tweets. The purpose of doing so was to encourage student interaction across the traditional tutorial-based boundaries. In-class activities included scaffolding in the use of twitter and appropriately tagging tweets using "hashtags." Also, collaboration was undertaken with an American instructor running a similar unit to ensure that there were periods of overlap where both the Australian and the American cohorts were covering similar topics in the curriculum. They were therefore able to interact with each other using microblogging in an ad-hoc, real-time manner on the topics of privacy, ethics and censorship (topics common to both curricula) over a four-week period.

The data set analysed for this study is the list of tweets tagged as being relevant to the curriculum-related discussions that met at least one of two criteria. The first criterion is that the tweet was annotated with at least one of the hashtags "#leb215" and "#cse2642" (corresponding to the two unit codes). The dataset includes tweets by both the American students and staff (referred to hereafter as Cohort 1) and the Australian students and staff (Cohort 2).

A content-analysis approach using a coding scheme adopted from [14] was used to analyse the tweets. The coding scheme used is summarised in Tables 1-3, which use the elements and indicators from [14]. Our adaptation of the coding scheme for the microblogging environment is illustrated via the examples and coding guidelines in the same tables. Up to two categories were assigned to each tweet; a "primary" category which seemed most applicable and, where necessary, a "secondary" category. This form of categorization is comparable to research such as [9] and [15] Given that this experiment was a non-assessable component, the response was considered encouraging from both cohorts as approximately 57% from Cohort 1 and 60% from Cohort 2 participated. In total there were 324 tweets.

Table 1. Coding Scheme for Cognitive presence, adapted from [14]

Category (Code)	Indicator	Brief coding guidelines	Example Tweet
Triggering event (CTP)	New topic introduced, Sense of puzzlement	Includes new resource and opinion or ask for comment	I found an article about WikiLeaks http://yhoo.it/hrJ6dN #cse2642
Exploration (CEX)	Information exchange	Comments on previously raised resource, expresses an opinion on a previous tweet, expression of opinion with no linked resource	Some peoples in the government want to get WikiLeaks branded as a terrorist organization #cse2642
Integration (CIN)	Connecting ideas	Draws connections from multiple tweets, multiple @s AND multiple URLs, multiple hashtags and multiple URLS	@Iserguy @VickyBlueWoody Do AUS parents need edu on how2censor??? http://tinyurl.com/25dd66w http://tinyurl.com/2g529bx #cse2642 #leb215
Resolution (CRE)	Apply new ideas	Resolves an issue, brings a discussion to a close, uses ideas from learning material to settle an argument.	N/A

Table 2. Coding Scheme for Social presence, adapted from [14]

Category (Code)	Indicator	Brief coding guidelines	Example Tweet
Affective (SAF)	Expressing emotions	Emoticons, text-based expressions of humour eg LOL, LMAO, emotionally loaded words like ridiculous, includes emotionally laden value judgements e.g fantastic, brilliant	http://bit.ly/99BFZo This my not be ethical but I still LOL'ed so hard over the ignorance contained in this article #cse2642
Open communication (SOC)	Risk-free expression	Bold statements, controversial statements (indicates a level of comfort making them), personal confessions	@dr_at_work the theory "never against a government" seems perfect in China. lol
Group cohesion (SGC)	Encouraging collaboration	Replies with an opinion, or asks for clarification, e.g. RT with agreement, RT with disagreement, @mention, multiple @mentions, reply with URL	@Iserguy I think it does, it doesn't allow for every side to freely express themselves #cse2642 #leb215

Table 3. Coding Scheme for Teaching presence, adapted from [14]

Category (Code)	Indicator	Brief coding guidelines	Example Tweet
Design and organization (TDO)	Setting curriculum and methods	Communication on the units, methods, etc Typically staff-staff communication.	@stefaniemarkham saying hi from down under. looks like #cse2642 is going well. we #LEB215 will soon participate in your discussions.
Facilitating discourse (TFD)	Sharing personal meaning	typically retweet or reply with extra/counter resources, soliciting clatrification, asking for explanation	RT @Reeseandchips: @Armein78 violent video gmes make children mre aggrssive #leb215 #cse2642 - what does this say..http://bit.ly/9IFcgW
Direct instruction (TDI)	Focusing discussion	Provides guidelines on topic and/or format of discussion	@waacyweng can you retweet and add #leb215 in all ur tweets with #cse2642 students

3.2   Analysis and Discussion

Beyond Social Presence

The first finding from the data is that the Twitter usage considered through the CoI lens strongly indicated a cognitive presence, over and above the social presence. This can be seen in the aggregates shown in Table 4, where cognitive components (67%) outweighed the social components (25%). This may seem to contradict the descriptive statistics from previous studies on Twitter messages, such as [7, 8, 9] which claims that Twitter is used for none other than social purposes. Our findings support [1] where an improved student engagement can be seen.

Encouraging Levels of Participation

On average this experiment had almost 60% participation from both cohorts (47 out of 80 students) and the findings demonstrate a healthy composition of CoI components across both cohorts. Though this was not an assessable component, the number of tweets and the richness of each tweet suggest that students were keen to participate and contribute. Another factor supporting this is the fact that the discussion continued for a longer period than the duration of the assigned learning activities.

Limited Teaching Presence Exhibited by Students

Although there was 7.6% teaching presence as shown in Table 4, most of the tweets corresponding to teaching instructions were made by the instructors. This suggests that a low teaching presence from students was exhibited in the tweets. Students could exhibit teaching presence by leading discussions and supporting peers with learning activities. In a more mature CoI, we would expect that a larger number of participants could potentially contribute to the discussion in a manner that would indicate teaching presence. This could be facilitated in the future by designing learning activities that would encourage students to take lead roles for a stipulated time.

Limitations

There were several limitations to this experiment. First, we had a small sample size of 47 participants across both cohorts. This could have introduced some bias to the study, as more students would have resorted to more 'noise' and non-class discussion eventuating in a different composition of CoI components. Second, though both cohorts were using Twitter independently throughout the semester this experiment only ran for 4 weeks where they were asked to collaborate and exchange messages. A longer experiment would have yielded more representative data on both the cohorts and their progress throughout the semester.

Table 4. Percentage of tweets for each CoI element

CoI Element	Cohort 1 (%)	Cohort 2 (%)	Both cohorts (%)
Cognitive Presence	37.05	30.46	67.51
Social Presence	11.39	13.43	24.82
Teaching Presence	0.00	6.95	7.67
Total	48.44	50.84	100

4   The MiCoI Framework

The case study in Section 3 provided a good benchmark on how to extend the usage of Twitter for pedagogical usage and despite the uptake of Twitter as noted in [16] there have been few reported examples of microblogging usage in a CoI context in tertiary education. Therefore, based on our experience and findings from the case study, we propose a framework (MiCoI) which offers guidelines for educators intending to broaden their students' horizons. This is achieved by having them interact with other students and possibly external experts and the wider online community in real time, thus enriching the student experience. Research has linked the importance of social presence to a range of critical factors such as student satisfaction and development of a community of peers [2].

The MiCoI framework is designed with the intention to suit any microblogging platform. The design is based upon the common features seen in microblogging platforms such as usage of limited characters (such as 140), the ability to follow and un-follow any users within the platform, ability to involve one or many users within a message, direct messaging and forming groups. The framework proceeds through three phases, a Planning phase (educator-educator interaction prior to teaching and learning activities), an Implementation phase (student-student and student-staff interaction, actual learning and teaching activities, and Monitoring phase (educators monitor exchange of information and encourage discussion among student). These two phases are discussed below.

4.1   Planning Phase

Topics, Duration and Collaboration

The planning phase requires an educator intending to use microblogging to identify possible topics that lend themselves particularly well to debate and discussion and in which students would benefit from exposure to a wide variety of opinions and in near-real time interaction. This is important to set the criteria for cognitive presence. Having identified a number of such topics, the next step is to find one or more educators (intra-institution or inter-institution) who would find such topics to be of interest to their students. The group of similar discipline educators would then identify possible overlaps in their semester times such that their respective students are able to engage in cross-cohort discussions. The educators would then collaboratively synchronise the key topics, and select appropriate in-class activities. There activities then are shared among the educators. It would also be possible for different educators to take lead at different times as the group collaborates. This will ensure that the discussion load is distributed and facilitated well. Further during this phase as well educators need to collaboratively agree on procedures and protocols for microblogging usage.

Platform and Tools

First is in the selection of the microblogging platform. There are several platforms such as Twitter, Jaiku, Pownce, Plurk,Tumblr, Laconica etc. This is important as different applications have different features and which would need to suit the educator's requirements and familiarity to guide students through the collaboration. Further, accessing microblogging application within class would be free but this would not be the same of students decide to access via their mobiles as they will have to pay for the message sent.

Choosing the right platform would also help managing the microblog communication and information flow as the platform in itself has limited features. For example, the Twitter platform can be used via the default web interface. However, a custom tool like TweetDeck provides more options to manage communication via Twitter. It allows longer messages with feature called long update. Tweetdeck also allows users to track messages based on certain keywords and hashtags which is useful for engaging in concurrent discussions with many students at the same time. The custom tool itself may require other supporting software (e.g. Tweetdeck requires Adobe AIR which allows web applications to operate as standalone client applications without the constraints of a browser). The educator is required to ensure that lab computers have the appropriate software, as student accounts typically have limited installation privileges. This might pose an obstacle to the introduction of a new technology in class.

Learning Activity Design
To encourage usage and help familiarize the educator needs to plan simple, in-class learning activities allowing students to explore the software environment. For example as part of the learning activity students could be asked to research about the latest trends of green technology within Australia. Upon obtaining the information they will be required to post their findings to be shared with others using pre-specified hashtags for example #greenIT and #unitcode. Students will be allowed to post as many messages as they want but are required to meet a minimum requirement. Educators can further probe and extend their findings to meet the objective of the learning activity.

4.2   Implementation Phase

In the implementation phase, the students and educators engage in the planned in-class activities and post microblogs accordingly. The implementation phase runs for the period planned for in the previous phase. If inter-cohort collaboration around common topics of interest is planned for, this interval could be for several weeks.

A key aspect of the implementation phase is familiarisation with the microblogging platform preliminary socialisation with each other. Introduction in class supported by appropriate learning activities are crucial to build understanding and the know-how approaching how to use microblogging for academic discussion.

Initially, students are instructed on how to create an account with the platform chosen. This allows students with no pre-existing account to get started. It also allows students with pre-existing accounts to create a new one for educational use alone, if they so wish. The students then notify the cohort of their user name. This will allow others in the class to follow them, including the educators. Students are then encouraged to communicate freely and use the features of the microblogging platform. This is an important stage especially for students who have never microblogged before.

Prior to commencing the collaboration between various cohorts under MiCoI, students need to be able to organise messages meaningfully, sent and receive direct messages, and to follow dialogues. They should also be conversant to include peers in a dialogue (e.g. using the @mention in Twitter), and create a group (e.g. using the list in Twitter). This will allow students to discuss relevant topics, share messages, share resources through links and form groups.

We think that within the implementation phase the educators should also set up an information repository using LMS. The information repository acts as a back-up to all discussions transpired with the microblogging platform in case of an emergency where student cannot access the internet. To do this, educators need to have a requirement whereby students log all their messages on microblog into the LMS every week. Weekly record is envisaged to help continue the thought process and disruption to internet connection will not hamper the ongoing discussions.

4.3   Monitoring and Evaluation

The third and final phase is called the Monitoring phase and is critical to ensure that the intention of the collaboration is achieved. Monitoring is actually concurrent with the implementation phase, while evaluation can occur at the end of an implementation phase. Here, educators need to be aware of what is being discussed and clarify student messages to align them as closely as possible to the objectives of the unit. Given the open nature of the internet and microblogging platform it is common for students to go astray to discuss irrelevant topics as mentioned in [6]. Here educators need to ensure that a healthy balance of CoI elements is present in their weekly discussion. This would mean that there are all three elements of CoI with a reasonable emphasis on the Cognitive elements (CRE, CTP, CIX and CEX).

To ensure this balance the messages needs to be weekly informally analysed. Educators also stand to benefit from this weekly exercise as they get to know how the class has progressed to meet the unit's requirement.

5   Conclusion and Future Work

This work supports and extends research done by [10,4,1,2,] showing that mircoblogging has potential for pedagogical use to enhance and complement all "presences" in CoI. Based on our previous work we propose microblogging framework that can be used to create a CoI. Though the case study only included two institutions the findings are significant towards extending the research done on microblogging within the tertiary education space. This especially, when many tertiary institutions currently use microblogging limited to only social activities [16]. Further, this also encourages other educators who are intending to adopt microblogging to facilitate their teaching and learning activities as it was reported that many educators shy away from microblogging when it comes to classroom activities [16]. We are the first known study to have used microblogging to form CoI between an Australian and American tertiary institution. In future, authors might extend the idea of MiCoI to include other higher education institutions over a longer period of time to validate the framework and demonstrate outside class learning in asynchronous and real time.

References

1. Dunlap, J.C., Lowenthal, P.R.: Tweeting the Night Away: Using Twitter to Enhance Social Presence. J. Info. Sys. Ed. 20 (2009a)
2. Dunlap, J.C., Lowenthal, P.R.: Horton Hears a Tweet. Educause Qtly. 32 (2009b), http://www.educause.edu/EDUCAUSE+Quarterly/EDUCAUSEQuarterly MagazineVolum/HortonHearsaTweet/192955
3. Rodens, M.: What the tweet? Twitter as a Useful Educational and Professional Development Tool. Communicating For Learners, Spring #2 (2011)
4. Ebner, M., Lienhardt, C., Rohs, M., Meyer, I.: Microblogs in Higher Education – A chance to facilitate informal and process-oriented learning? Comp. & Ed. 55, 92–100 (2010)
5. Badge, J., Johnson, S., Moseley, A., Cann, A.: Observing Emerging Student Networks on a Microblogging Service. JOLT 7(1) (March 2011), http://jolt.merlot.org/vol7no1/cann_0311.htm
6. Grosseck, G., Holotescu, C.: Can we use Twitter for Educational Activities? In: 4th International Scientific Conference, eLearning and Software for Education, Bucharest, Romania (2008)
7. Java, A., Song, X., Finin, T., Tseng, B.: Why we twitter: understanding microblogging usage and communities. In: 9th WebKDD and 1st SNA-KDD 2007 Workshop on Web Mining and Social Network Analysis. ACMPress (2007)
8. Krishnamurthy, B., Gill, P., Arlitt, M.: A few chirps about twitter. In: First Workshop on Online Social Networks WOSP 2008. ACM Press (2008)
9. Naaman, M., Boase, J., Lai, C.: Is it really about me?: message content in social awareness streams. In: 2010 ACM Conference on Computer Supported Cooperative Work, CSCW 2010. ACM Press (2010)
10. Junco, R., Heiberger, G., Loken, E.: The effect of Twitter on college student engagement and grades. Journal of Computer Assisted Learning (2010), doi:10.1111/j.1365-2729.2010.00387.x
11. Garrison, D.R., Anderson, T., Archer, W.: Critical Inquiry in a Text-based Environment: Computer Conferencing in Higher Education. Internet and Higher Ed. 2, 87–105 (2000)
12. Garrison, D.R., Anderson, T., Archer, W.: The first decade of the community of inquiry framework: A retrospective. Internet and Higher Ed. 13, 5–9 (2009)
13. Garrison, D.R., Vaughan, N.: Blended Learning in Higher Education: Framework, Principles, and Guidelines. Jossey-Bass, San Francisco (2007)
14. Garrison, D.R., Cleveland-Innes, M., Koole, M., Kappelman, J.: Revisiting methodological issues in transcript analysis: Negotiating coding and reliability. Internet and Higher Ed. 9, 1–8 (2006)
15. Sinnappan, S., Farrell, C., Stewart, E.: Priceless Tweets! A Study on Twitter Messages Posted During Crisis: Black Saturday. In: 21st Australasian Conference on Information Systems (2010), http://aisel.aisnet.org/acis2010/39
16. Faculty-Focus. Twitter in higher education 2010: Usage habits and trends of today's college faculty. Annual Survey on the Popular Microblogging Technology (2010), http://www.facultyfocus.com/free-reports/ twitter-in-higher-education-2010-usage-habits- and-trends-of-todays-college-faculty/ (retrieved June 24, 2011)

ICT-Based School Collaboration, Teachers' Networks and their Opportunities for Teachers' Professional Development - A Case Study on eTwinning

Riina Vuorikari[1], Adriana Berlanga[4], Romina Cachia[2], Yiwei Cao[3], Sibren Fetter[4], Anne Gilleran[1], Ralf Klamma[3], Yves Punie[2], Santi Scimeca[1], Peter Sloep[4], and Zinayida Petrushyna

[1] European Schoolnet,
Rue de Treves, 61
1040 Brussels, Belgium
{Riina.Vuorikari,Anne.Gilleran,Santi.Scimeca}@eun.org
[2] Information Society Unit, Institute of Prospective Technological Studies,
Edificio Expo - c/ Inca Garcilaso 3
Sevilla - 41092
{Romina.Cachia,Yves.Punie}@ec.europa.eu
[3] RWTH Aachen University
Ahornstr. 55
52056 Aachen Germany
{cao,klamma}@dbis.rwth-aachen.de
[4] The Open University of the Netherlands
Valkenburgerweg 177
6419 AT Heerlen, Netherlands
{Adriana.Berlanga,Sibren.Fetter,Peter.Sleop}@ou.nl

Abstract. In this paper we first investigate how eTwinning and national and local teachers' professional development schemes interact. eTwinning is the community for schools in Europe that promotes teacher and school collaboration through the use of Information and Communication Technologies (ICT) under the European Union's Lifelong Learning Programme. The eTwinning Portal hosts more than 137,000 teachers who interact with each other on the European-scale. Second, using this authentic data, we discuss how novel research methods such as Social Network Analysis, information visualisation techniques and future scenario forecasting are used to study eTwinning in the Tellnet-project aiming to sustain and support dynamic teacher networks as a platform for formal and informal teachers' professional development in the future.

Keywords: school collaboration, information and communication technologies, teachers, professional development, social network analysis, information visualisation.

1 Introduction

In many ways, nowadays' teachers in schools can be considered caught with one foot in the future and another one in past [1]. On the one hand, developments of

H. Leung et al. (Eds.): ICWL 2011, LNCS 7048, pp. 112–121, 2011.

technologies, tools and the vast take-up of such applications imply that teachers need to keep abreast of technology developments in order to keep up with their students' knowledge of new technologies. On the other hand, most teachers still have to work in school environments where policies are outdated and curricula no longer cover the skills required for today's societies.

New opportunities brought about by networking tools are enabling teachers to network and collaborate with other teachers from anywhere, at any time. For example, [2] focuses on addressing professional development through the study of teachers' professional networks. Similarly, a survey conducted in the US found that teachers believe that collaborative professional development activities, such as networking with other teachers outside school, is more effective and helpful as professional development than traditional forms of training [3]. Recent studies have focused on eTwinning [4] as a possible professional development network for teachers [5, 6]. The eTwinning action is defined as the community for schools in Europe. It promotes teacher and school collaboration through the use of Information and Communication Technologies (ICT) allowing both formal and informal opportunities for professional development. For teachers who participate in the eTwinning action, it offers a high potential for up-skilling in areas of European key competences [7], e.g., communication in foreign languages, digital competence, and interpersonal, intercultural and social competences.

Therefore, it becomes interesting and important to gain deeper understanding on how such teachers' social networks actually support and foster teachers' professional development. Moreover, understanding how the dynamic and multidirectional flow of social influence within such networks could better be harnessed to engage a wider scale of practitioners. This would guarantee that new pedagogical practices and opportunities for professional development would not remain as isolated "islands of innovation" [8].

The main questions examined in this paper are two-fold. First, we focus on eTwinning and ask: What can eTwinning contribute to professional development, and what type of relationships can be found between eTwinning and teachers' professional development schemes at the local and national level? Second, we look into the social network aspect of eTwinning and explain how through Social Network Analysis (SNA), visualisation techniques and a number of other complimentary methods, it can be studied to better understand how to support in-service teachers in their changing role in teaching and learning, and how to encourage new forms of professional development.

For this paper, we adopt the following definition of teachers' professional development: "Professional development is defined as activities that develop an individual's skills, knowledge, expertise and other characteristics as a teacher. This definition recognises that development can be provided in many ways, ranging from the formal to the informal. It can be made available through external expertise in the form of courses, workshops or formal qualification programmes, through collaboration between schools or teachers across schools or within the schools in which teachers work" [9, p.49]. Section 2 looks into eTwinning professional development opportunities, whereas Section 3 focuses on eTwinning as a social network giving some examples of the new study [10].

2   Multimodality of eTwinning Professional Development Opportunities

Since 2005, eTwinning has been one of the most successful actions of the school education programme (Comenius) under the European Union's Lifelong Learning Programme. In autumn 2011, thirty-two countries in Europe participate in eTwinning and the eTwinning platform hosts more than 137,000 registered members.

As stated earlier, eTwinning is regarded as the community for schools in Europe. Teachers from all participating countries can register on the Portal and use the eTwinning online tools to find each other, meet virtually, exchange ideas and practice examples, team up in eTwinning Groups, learn together in Learning Events and engage in online-based projects. The eTwinning online tools are provided by the Central Support Service (CSS), the coordinating body of eTwinning run by European Schoolnet. Additionally, each country involved has a National Support Service (NSS) that represents and promotes the eTwinning action by providing training and support (face-to-face, by phone and online), organising meetings and national competitions, and running media and public relations campaigns.

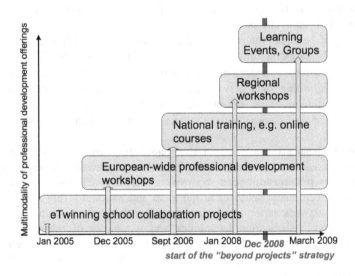

Fig. 1. The development of eTwinning Professional Development offerings

Since the beginning of eTwinning in 2005, creating an eTwinning project has been the main focus of the action. A minimum of two schools from at least two European countries create a project and use ICT to carry out their work. As teachers and schools communicate and collaborate via the Internet, there are no grants or administrative conditions connected to the scheme and face-to-face meetings are not required. Such school collaboration is already a well-known concept and much practiced in many schools around the world. The novelty of eTwinning, however, is to offer an umbrella under which these widely scattered isolated practices are gathered under a solid framework, and thus allowing better opportunities for sharing practices and further networking.

Figure 1 depicts the evolution and multimodality of eTwinning professional training activities summarising the evolution of eTwinning and its opportunities for professional development. Since December 2005, European-wide Professional Development Workshops (PDW) have been offered to eTwinning teachers. They are aimed at individuals who want to learn more about eTwinning and develop their skills in European collaboration using ICT. Aims of these workshops also include tackling some of the key competences at the European level, e.g., communication in foreign languages, digital competence, and interpersonal, intercultural and social competences. The introduction of the eTwinning Groups on a pilot basis in late 2008 and online Learning Events in 2009 offered new opportunities in the area of professional development and brought together specific interest groups for networking and sharing purposes. This was part of a *beyond school projects* strategy with the aim of transforming eTwinning from a partnership tool to a virtual community for teachers in Europe [11].

Lastly, in 2006, some of the first national training session began taking place, mixing face-to-face with online methods. During the school year 2008-2009, all NSS were asked to report on their eTwinning professional training events and activities. It was estimated that more than 28,000 European teachers participated in these events in one way or another. They include all types of events, mostly face-to-face, ranging from half a day to three-day events such as PDWs, annual and national eTwinning conferences, eTwinning prize ceremonies, training workshops, lectures and presentations. This reflects that eTwinning is a blended network, a network which combines face-to-face interactions with online interactions taking place on the eTwinning platform and using ICT for communication and collaboration.

To study the relationship between eTwinning and professional development, the National Support Services were surveyed on synergies between the two schemes. Out of twenty-eight countries for which we were able to gather the information, in seven (7) countries eTwinning activities can be fully taken into account for formal professional development and in nine (9) countries, the situation was the opposite: there was no link between eTwinning and formal professional development. In eleven (11) countries, some synergies were found [6]. To summarise, we can conclude that in 58% of the twenty-eight eTwinning countries, eTwinning can be used at least to some extent to support the goals of professional development programmes.

A clearer picture can also be drawn of how eTwinning interacts with both *formal* and *informal* professional development opportunities. In this case, by *formal* professional development we mean that the needs and goals of a national and/or local professional development programme strongly interact with eTwinning. This results, for example, in an eTwinning online course that is offered to teachers as part of the other general professional development offerings. By *informal* professional development we mean that teacher's involvement in an eTwinning project, for example, is recognised to support the goals of a national and/or local professional development programme, and therefore teacher's participation in such a project can count, in a way or another, towards *formal* recognition, e.g., career credits or advancement in the teacher's career. These synergies are summarised in Table 1.

Table 1. Formal and informal recognition in eTwinning in synergies with formal and informal professional development in all participating countries

	Formal professional development	Informal professional development
Formal recognition, e.g., career credits, fulfilment of professional duty	e.g., teachers who participate in an eTwinning online course provided by NSS get accredited career points.	e.g., teachers who participate in an eTwinning project get accredited career points.
Informal recognition e.g., peer recognition, intrinsic motivation	e.g., teachers' participating in formal professional development programmes become voluntary eTwinning "mentors".	e.g., peer recognition among colleagues resulting from a successful eTwinning project.

Apart from *formal* recognition, the value of *informal* recognition that teachers get from being part of eTwinning is also notable. This *informal* recognition manifests itself in different ways and is hard to measure. Most importantly, it seems that teachers participating in eTwinning activities can gain positive status within their own work environment (e.g., school), and also outside (e.g., parents' interest in their project). *Informal* recognition can be personal self-fulfilment, for example, the satisfaction of learning new skills and perspectives through eTwinning. Moreover, it can be translated into behaviour in the work environment, e.g. a well developed and active professional development culture in the school makes it easy for a teacher to participate in eTwinning activities outside of the school. Lastly, intrinsic motivational factors such as "fun" to participate in eTwinning are notable, and interplay with other issues such as recognition by colleagues and absence of bureaucracy, in the process of participating.

Using the OECD definition of professional development as presented in the beginning, we can summarise that eTwinning can develop "individual's skills, knowledge, expertise and other characteristics as a teacher". Often teachers start an eTwinning project without thinking of it as a professional development activity, but in the course of the project they realise that they are gaining new skills and competences. Even if eTwinning is not a trigger for professional development, it is an added value. The challenge for the future is to find the means for eTwinning to become that trigger.

3   Getting to Scale - Growing beyond Innovators

Since its inception, eTwinning statistics have been gathered on the eTwinning Portal using different methods such as user registration; the interaction of users with the different tools and website analytics to monitor visitors on the site [5]. The number of registered teachers, registered schools and participation in eTwinning projects has constituted the core statistics. Using such absolute figures it is easy to monitor how teachers engage in eTwinning projects; however, these figures give only a limited understanding of eTwinning's success and uptake within the entire teacher population of a given country.

Table 2. eTwinning reach = the registered users of a country / teacher population within this country

Country	Teachers (OECD 2007)	Registered users on eTwinning in May 2010	eTwinning Reach	
			May 2010	May 2011
Austria	100,984	914	0.90%	1.06%
Belgium	189,930	1,382	0.70%	0.90%
Czech Republic	105,818	2,935	2.80%	3.73%
Estonia	17,423	1,320	7.60%	9.74%
Finland	68,442	1,472	2.20%	2.83%
France	707,609	9,298	1.30%	1.86%
Germany	835,980	4,606	0.60%	0.75%
Greece	148,627	3,225	2.20%	2.65%
Hungary	135,030	1,003	0.70%	1.01%
Iceland	6,218	274	4.40%	7.16%
Ireland	60,718	671	1.10%	1.43%
Italy	723,870	7,365	1.00%	1.36%
Luxembourg	6,973	103	1.50%	1.74%
Netherlands	245,876	1,684	0.70%	0.93%
Norway	89,480	1,042	1.20%	1.52%
Poland	521,037	9,895	1.90%	2.57%
Portugal	157,239	2,239	1.40%	1.90%
Slovakia	63,184	2,111	3.30%	4.46%
Slovenia	22,290	564	2.50%	3.70%
Spain	484,289	7,966	1.60%	2.23%
Sweden	140,326	1,992	1.40%	1.98%
Turkey	590,494	5,941	1.00%	3.62%
United Kingdom	788,575	8,549	1.10%	1.52%
Average:	-	-	*1.90%*	*2.64%*

As opposed to using the number of teachers who signed up on the eTwinning Portal as a point of reference, new perspectives can be gained by using the entire teacher population in a given country for this purpose (Table 2). This makes it possible to see how eTwinning has been taken up in relation to the entire teacher population, giving more indication about the spread and success of the eTwinning action within the country. Therefore, we use *eTwinning reach* as a relative indicator of teachers who are knowledgeable about eTwinning in a given country, a manifestation of which is that they have signed up on the Portal.

The following method is used: *eTwinning reach* = the registered users of a country / teacher population within this country. eTwinning reach is rooted in the popular idea of Diffusion of Innovations [12], "a theory of how, why, and at what rate new ideas and technology spread through cultures." To calculate eTwinning reach, the OECD data[1] from 2007 (OECD statistics of educational personnel) and the eTwinning data from May 2010 and May 2011 are used. Out of thirty-two eTwinning countries, OECD statistics can be found for twenty-three of them, which represent 86% of the entire eTwinning population, and covers the countries that have been part of eTwinning for about the same duration (i.e., not all participating countries joined eTwinning at the same moment). It should be noted that this leaves discrepancy in the accuracy of data; however, it serves as a good proxy for our purpose.

On the two right-hand columns of Table 2, the data for eTwinning reach are presented. On average, in May 2010, 1.9% of the teacher population in countries indicated in Table 2 had registered on the eTwinning Portal. In May 2011, the average had increased to 2,64% of the teachers' population in Europe. In general, rather small countries show higher percentages: Estonia, Iceland, Slovakia, Slovenia and Finland, but also the Czech Republic have reached beyond 2.5% of their teacher population. Similar indicators can be calculated not only for teachers, but also for schools.

We can observe that on average, in May 2010, the eTwinning action concerns 2,64% of the potential teaching population within the participating countries. According to Rogers' model of diffusion of innovation (1962), eTwinning in most countries still remains limited to teachers who are "innovators" in using ICT for cross-country school collaboration. Some countries have passed the 2.5% milestone of "innovators" (e.g., Estonia, Iceland, Slovakia, the Czech Republic, Greece, Slovakia, Slovenia, Finland and Turkey) and are currently targeting the segment of "early adopters" within their teacher population. Several of these countries have a relatively small population, although the Czech Republic has over 10 million and Turkey over 70 million inhabitants. If the premise is that teachers' collaboration network such as eTwinning provide a suitable support for competence development [13], therefore, it is important to understand the dynamic and multidirectional flow of social influence within such networks.

3.1 Creating Connections Which Did Not Exist before – between Teachers in Europe

eTwinning is nowadays in a transitional phase, since 2008, its aim has broadened more towards the delivery and maintenance of a social network for teachers [4]. The eTwinning platform has also gone through major changes over the period and new social networking features have been added to the platform to allow new ways of interaction.

---

[1] http://stats.oecd.org/

The Lifelong Learning Project Tellnet [10] aims at exploring and supporting eTwinning as a lifelong learning system and studying it using novel tools such as network theory, Social Network Analysis (SNA) and scenario building to forecast alternative future visions. According to network theories, any social relationships can be seen consisting of nodes and connections [14]. In eTwinning, for example, an individual teacher or a school can be considered as a node and the various activities between them as connections. Information visualisation techniques, on the other hand, can be used to visually represent these connections. First studies using SNA and network visualisation of eTwinning were reported in [15] when the network consisted of 45,000 schools.

Table 3. eTwinning network clusters

Cluster size (N eTwinners)	N times identified
8807	1
3669	1
3175	1
1172	1
100-1000	9
10-100	136
2-9	2627
Total:	**2776**

Through these novel methods, the Tellnet project identifies the main networks, hubs and communities of practices that are effective in sharing practices, encouraging innovation and creativity at schools, and engaging new members. The eTwinning platform is used to extract data based on interactions between the participating teachers, currently more than 137,000 teachers in Europe, and various networks are detected where teachers are the nodes and the interaction among them create the ties: (1) Project Collaboration Network where the ties between nodes are eTwinning projects that eTwinners have collaborated on; (2) Contact-list Network where the ties between nodes are contacts that eTwinners have added to their contact-list for potential project partnerships; (3) Messaging Network where the ties between nodes are the wall messages that eTwinners have written to each other's wall using the internal messaging system on the platform. Moreover, different levels of intensity can be assigned to these relationships between participants.

First studies conducted on the eTwinning network aim at detecting and understanding its structure. In [16], the Project Collaboration Network was identified to consist of 2776 separate clusters (Table 3) that are formed through eTwinners' project collaboration. Four (4) gigantic clusters create the main core of the eTwinning Project Collaboration Network, the biggest cluster contains 8807 eTwinners, and there are a number of smaller clusters. The clustering formation shows that the biggest component is created by eTwinners who have collaborated with each other in a high number of projects over a long period of time. These partnerships create complex ties between participants. The modularity of the clustering was calculated based on density-based clustering algorithm by Newman [17], indicating the quality of the cluster; a fraction of any node's connections within its cluster (internal edges) and its connections to other clusters [18]. Empirical observations indicate that a modularity greater than 0.3 corresponds to significant community structures. In our analysis, modularity of 0.4 was observed, corresponding to significant community structures.

Therefore, the first Tellnet studies show that whereas the eTwinning Project Collaboration Network is strongly dependent on a core group, it is nevertheless a large and well-interconnected group indicating some possibility of strong community of practitioners.

4   Conclusions and Future Work

In this paper we have focused on the potential of teachers' social network to support and sustain teachers' professional development using a case study of the eTwinning action. We discussed some novel research methods used to study eTwinning in the Tellnet-project such as SNA, information visualisation and future scenario forecasting, giving some first samples of that research.

The future research should focus on how such novel research could support both practitioners (e.g. teachers) and policy-makes to sustain and support dynamic collaboration networks as a platform for formal and informal teachers' professional development in the future.

Acknowledgements. The research for this paper has been partly funded with the support from the European Commission by the Lifelong Learning Project Tellnet, Teachers' Lifelong Learning Network. The views reflect the views only of the authors, and the Commission cannot be held responsible for any use which may be made of the information contained therein.

References

1. Caroll, T., Resta, P.: Redefining teacher education for digital-age learners. In: Summit report from the Invitational Summit on Redefining Teacher Education for Digital-Age Learners (2010),
   http://redefineteachered.org/sites/default/files/
   SummitReport.pdf?q=summitreport
2. Hofman, R.H., Dijkstra, B.J.: Effective teacher professionalization in networks? Teaching and Teacher Education 26(4), 1031–1040 (2010)
3. US Department of Education. Teacher quality. A report on the preparation and qualifications of public school teachers Washington DC. National Center for Education Statistics (1999)
4. eTwinning. The eTwinning action, http://www.eTwinning.net; statistics
   http://www.etwinning.net/en/pub/news/press_corner/
   statistics.cfm

5. Crawley, C., Gilleran, A., Scimeca, S., Vuorikari, R., Wastiau, P.: Beyond School Projects, A report on eTwinning 2008-2009. Central Support Service for eTwinning (CSS), European Schoolnet (2009),
http://resources.eun.org/etwinning/25/
EN_eTwinning_165x230_Report.pdf

6. Vuorikari, R.: eTwinning Report 2010: Teachers professional development: an overview of current practice. Central Support Service for eTwinning (CSS), European Schoolnet (2010),
http://desktop.etwinning.net/library/desktop/resources/
5/55/955/43955/etwinning_report_teachers_professional
_development_en.pdf

7. Official Journal. Recommendation of the European Parliament and of the Council, of 18 December 2006, on key competences for lifelong learning. L 394 of 30.12.2006 (2006)

8. Forkosh-Baruch, A., Nachmias, R., Mioduser, D., Tubin, D.: Islands of Innovation and School-Wide Implementations. Two Patterns of ICT-based Pedagogical Innovations in Schools. An Interdisciplinary Journal on Humans in ICT Environments 1(2), 202–215 (2005)

9. OECD. Creating Effective Teaching and Learning Environments: First results from TALIS (2009)

10. Tellnet. Teachers Lifelong Learning Network, http://www.tellnet.eun.org

11. Crawley, C., Gerhard, P., Gilleran, A., Joyce, A. (eds.): eTwinning 2.0 Building the community for schools in Europe. European Schoolnet (2010)

12. Rogers, E.M.: Diffusion of innovations. Simon and Schuster (1962)

13. Koper, R., Rusman, E., Sloep, P.: Effective Learning Networks. Lifelong learning in Europe 1, 18–27 (2005)

14. Wasserman, S., Faust, K.: Social Network Analysis: Methods and Applications. Cambridge University Press, New York (1994)

15. Breuer, R., Klamma, R., Cao, Y., Vuorikari, R.: Social Network Analysis of 45,000 Schools: A Case Study of Technology Enhanced Learning in Europe. In: Learning in the Synergy of Multiple Disciplines, pp. 166–180 (2009),
http://dx.doi.org/10.1007/978-3-642-04636-0_18

16. Fetter, S., Berlanga, A.J., Sloep, P., Vuorikari, R.: Major trends arising from the network (Project deliverable D 3.1). Teachers Lifelong Learning Network. Brussels, Belgium, European Schoolnet (2011),
http://tellnet.eun.org/web/tellnet/project-document

17. Newman, M.E.J.: Fast algorithm for detecting community structure in networks. Phys. Rev. E 69(6), 66133 (2004)

18. Pham, M., Cao, Y., Klamma, R., Jarke, M.: A Clustering Approach for Collaborative Filtering Recommendation Using Social Network Analysis. Journal of Universal Computer Science 17(4) (2011),
http://www.jucs.org/jucs_17_4/a_clustering_approach_for

Web-Based Self- and Peer-Assessment
of Teachers' Educational Technology Competencies

Hans Põldoja, Terje Väljataga, Kairit Tammets, and Mart Laanpere

Tallinn University, Institute of Informatics, Narva mnt 25,
10120 Tallinn, Estonia
{Hans.Poldoja,Terje.Valjataga,Kairit.Tammets,
Mart.Laanpere}@tlu.ee

Abstract. Although there are several competency frameworks for measuring teachers' educational technology competencies, there is a lack of Web-based assessment tools that allow authentic assessment. This paper addresses the design challenges for assessing teacher's educational technology competencies. The empirical part describes the participatory design process for developing a Web-based self- and peer-assessment tool. The presented conceptual design describes a system where teachers can solve competency tests that contain various self-test, peer-assessment and self-reflection tasks. The tasks are assessed using the performance indicators and assessment rubric that are based on the ISTE NETS for Teachers competency model.

Keywords: educational technology competencies, self-assessment, peer-assessment, conceptual design.

1   Introduction

In last decades many countries have invested considerable sums to information and communication technology (ICT) in schools. However, successful use of ICT in schools requires not only investments in infrastructure but also advancements in teachers' skills to integrate these new tools into learning and teaching. In order to establish systematic support mechanisms for teachers' professional development it is necessary to indicate the competencies that are needed for using ICT in schools.

Generic ICT competency frameworks such as International Computer Driving Licence (ICDL) [1] do not cover all the competencies that are needed for educational use of ICT. Therefore several international initiatives are aiming at developing educational technology competency frameworks for teachers. These competency frameworks are outlined in section 2. They often serve as a basis for developing national educational technology competency models. In the this study we understand competency as "a set of personal characteristics (e.g. skills, knowledge, attitudes) that an individual possesses or needs to develop in order to perform an activity within a specific context. Performance may range from the basic level of proficiency to the highest levels of excellence." [2].

H. Leung et al. (Eds.): ICWL 2011, LNCS 7048, pp. 122–131, 2011.

Our research is carried out in the context of teacher education in Estonia. The national Educational Technology Competency Model (ETCM) [3] for teachers is presented in section 3.1. While many teachers have participated the professional development courses on using educational technology, there is a low awareness of educational technology competencies. In order to plan teachers' professional development and training needs it is necessary to measure their level of educational technology competencies. One option to assess the educational technology competencies is to use a Web-based assessment tool. However, ETCM contains also complex performance indicators that cannot be assessed using simple automated tests. Other assessment methods such as self- or peer assessment are needed to assess these competencies. This paper addresses the following research problem: to what extent and how could be teachers' educational technology competencies assessed using a Web-based tool?

Together with the assessment methodology we are designing and developing a web-based assessment tool named DigiMina (*DigitalMe* in Estonian). In section 3 we discuss the main design challenges for assessing teachers' educational technology competencies. Section 4 describes the participatory design research methodology that is used in this study. In section 5 we present the first empirical results in a form of conceptual design.

2   Teachers' Educational Technology Competencies

There are several initiatives and approaches aiming at developing standards, which can be a basis for measuring teachers' educational technology competencies. In this section we will shortly discuss three of them.

The International Computer Driving License (ICDL) started as a European initiative but has currently expanded to 148 countries. ICDL certifies that the holder has knowledge of basic concepts of Information Technology (IT). Modules like concept of ICT, using personal computer and managing files, word processing, spreadsheets, databases, presentations and communication have to be completed in order to achieve the basic level of digital literacy [1]. Testing takes place in testing centers and is organized as performing the required tasks from each module.

European Schoolnet [4] conducted the survey by analyzing the polices of European Teachers' ICT competencies and points out that although ICDL is commonly agreed certification, it is too much focused on generic ICT skills. Because of this, ICDL framework is neglecting dimensions, which are pedagogically significant [5] and is leaving out important contextual information. In addition, ICDL was criticized for poor support for tracking of informal learning that happens outside the school environment.

UNESCO ICT Competency Framework for Teachers (ICT-CFT) aims at improving teachers' practice using ICT in professional activities by providing a set of guidelines for creating national-level competency models. The framework addresses six sub-domains of the teachers' work: policy and vision, curriculum and assessment, pedagogy, ICT, organization and administration, and teacher professional development [6].

National Educational Technology Standards for Teachers (NETS-T) is a competency model developed in 2008 by the International Society for Technology in Education (ISTE) [7]. ISTE NETS-T aims to make teachers as role models for students with regard to digital-age knowledge work skills. The main advantage of ISTE NETS-T is support for standard-based performance assessment in the similar way for teachers, school administrators and students. ISTE NETS-T acknowledges the importance of developing and assessing competencies in the authentic context of teachers' work.

Each of the discussed competency frameworks has its benefits in specific context. ICDL provides globally acknowledged and easy-to-implement generic ICT skill tests for teachers, whereas UNESCO and ISTE have more contextualized, competency- and performance-based approach. Many countries have implemented the competency-based approach while evaluating teachers' ICT competencies. For example, in Netherlands the ICT competencies for teachers have taken ISTE NETS-T as a baseline. Their competency model is structured in a matrix format, each cell representing a teacher's interaction with pupils, colleagues and environment. The competencies are clustered into several sub-domains: pedagogy, curriculum, professional development, organization, policies, ethics, innovation and technical aspects [8]. In United Kingdom, evaluation of the teachers ICT competencies is more focused on generic ICT skills. Online simulator-based ICT tests have been developed as a part of Qualified Teacher Status (QTS) exam. The ICT test for QTS is designed to assess skills relevant to all teachers, teaching various subjects in primary and secondary schools [9].

Estonian policy-makers have chosen ISTE NETS-T as the most suitable framework for developing the national educational technology competency model for teachers (ETCM). This recently finalized competency model serves as the basis for developing competency tests also for DigiMina project.

3   Design Challenges for Assessing Teachers' Educational Technology Competencies

In the following section we will analyze the main design challenges for Web-based assessment of teachers' educational technology competencies. The analysis is addressing these challenges in relation of three different sub-domains: (1) how to define performance indicators of all competencies in ETCM, (2) how to select appropriate methods and instruments for assessing competencies, and (3) how to implement selected assessment methods in a Web-based tool.

3.1   Educational Technology Competency Model for Estonian Teachers

Teachers' Educational Technology Competency Model (ETCM) is based on ISTE NETS-T 2008, it was adapted for the Estonian context by a group of experts in 2011. The model aims at in-service teachers' competency development in primary, secondary, vocational and higher education level. The model consists of five core areas of educational technology competencies in the digital age:

1. Facilitating and inspiring learners in a digital environment
2. Designing and developing learning experiences and learning environments
3. Modeling and designing work environments
4. Promoting and modeling digital citizenship and responsibility
5. Engaging in professional growth

Each of these competencies includes 3-4 sub-competencies, which define the particular area of competency more precisely. Competencies need to be recognized in practice through the fulfillment of clearly established performance criteria [10], which allows to judge whether or not mastery of a competency has been attained. For assessment purposes this model has been extended into an assessment matrix. We have identified 5 levels of competencies appropriate for different stages of professional development in teacher education. The assessment matrix consists of competency benchmarks across 5 levels of teachers' professional development emphasizing competency benchmarks from the beginner to the expert level.

The main difference in comparison to the previous competency models is its emphasis on facilitating and supporting learners to use technology for developing their creativity, personal learning environment, learning habits and skills, but also highlighting ethical issues and changing social structures and behaviors in digital era.

The first design challenge for DigiMina is to define performance indicators for each competency in ETCM, especially the ones related with facilitating and inspiring the students and promoting digital citizenship.

3.2   Measuring Educational Technology Competencies

Measuring educational technology competencies is a challenging task, which is seen in several attempts to develop frameworks and models. According to Calvani et al. [5] there are no adequate instruments to assess and promote educational technology competencies. Cumming and Maxwell [11] put emphasis on two major theoretical considerations. The first relates to conceptions of validity, with emphasis on the appropriateness of assessment tasks as indicators of standards, and on the appropriateness of interpretation of assessment outcomes as indicators of learning [11]. Assessment methodology and instruments must be reliable, valid, flexible, but also affordable with respect to time and costs. Methodology together with assessment instrument must ensure that assessment decisions involve the evaluation of sufficient evidence to judge the level of competency of the teacher.

Reliability in our context is understood as a measure of the reproducibility, consistency and accuracy of an assessing methodology [12]. The methodology must demonstrate similar outcomes for teachers with equal competency at different times or places, regardless of the assessor conducting the assessment.

Validity, on the other hand, focuses on whether an assessment methodology and its instrument actually succeeds in evaluating the competencies that it is designed to evaluate [12]. Validity refers to the extent to which the interpretation and use of an assessment outcome can be supported by evidence. In order to assess whether a teacher is competent, they are judged against competency standards (assessment matrix) or competency benchmarks developed by a group of experts. A competency standard is comprised of individual units of competency that include the essential information needed to assess a teacher. However, there is a question what sort of evidence needs to be collected in order to assess and make judgments on which benchmark a teacher meets.

For instance, for measuring clinical competencies, Miller [13] has developed a pyramid of competencies, which is a simple conceptual model outlining the issues involved when analyzing validity. The pyramid consists of four levels:

1. knows – basic facts
2. knows how – applied knowledge
3. shows how – performance assessment in vitro
4. does – performance assessment in vivo

Such a conceptual model has also a potential in the context of teacher education and their educational technology competencies. Taking the model as a basis and looking at the ways of how educational technology competencies have been assessed, the literature overview shows that the majority of assessment models and tests focus on the first basic level – assessing a pure technological knowledge and skills with basic computer-based multiple choice tests. Developing such tests is rather time consuming, but they guarantee high reliability because of the large number of items that can be easily tested and marked [12]. The main drawback of these tests is seen in their decontextualization, lack of authenticity in tasks and assessment of the most trivial parts of knowledge.

For assessing educational technology competency advancement such an approach has some limitations and has led to an increasing focus on more sophisticated assessment methods such as testing "knows how" — i.e., the assessment of knowledge as applied to problem solving or educational technology reasoning and decision-making in specific contexts. Thus, the test items must be problem-based and situated in authentic context.

Level 3, 'shows how' in Miller's pyramid, can be assessed by practical examinations, observed long or short cases. The only way to assess level 4, "does", is to observe the person at work in the real world. Our focus is on level 2 'knows how'.

Difficulties in setting up "knows how" tests involve combining the application of knowledge with the large range of problems [12]. "Equally, reference to the context in which competencies are acquired is important, as is reference to the context in which they will subsequently be applied" (p.9) [10]. Educational technology competencies cannot be separated from the practical contexts in which they are acquired and applied.

DigiMina project has taken a focus on developing a methodology and an assessment instrument, which emphasize contextualized problem-based cases anchored in authentic settings of teachers' work, but at the same time allow automatic feedback from the instrument as much as possible based on multiple choice formats such as single best answer, extended matching, etc.

The second design challenge for DigiMina project is to define methodologically sound self- and peer assessment test items for each performance indicator, allowing to measure each competency in valid and reliable manner.

3.3   Web-Based Assessment of Competencies

As authentic context for performance is one of main defining aspects of competency [2], authentic assessment methods seem to be the most suitable for measuring the level of competency. Quite often, authentic assessment methods are contrasted with standardized testing and other forms of computer-assisted assessment [14]. Yet, the authenticity of the assessment could be implemented in various ways, without a need to avoid computer-assisted assessment tools. Gulikers et al [15] have suggested a five-dimensional framework for authentic assessment, defining five different aspects of enhancing the authenticity of assessment:

- tasks: meaningful, relevant, typical, complex, ownership of problem and solution space;
- physical context: similar to professional work space and time frame, professional tools;
- social context: similar to social context of professional practice (incl. decision making);
- form: demonstration and presentation of professionally relevant results, multiple indicators;
- criteria: used in professional practice, related to realistic process/product, explicit.

Using the DigiMina software as hypothesis, we claim that authenticity could be built in the Web-based assessment tool by addressing all five dimensions of Guliker's framework.

The third challenge of DigiMina project is to combine the requirements for authentic assessment of competencies with the limited possibilities of online testing tools.

4   Methodology

The design process follows the research-based design methodology [16]. In this methodology the design process is divided into four iterative stages which may take place partly in parallel: (1) contextual inquiry, (2) participatory design, (3) product design, and (4) production of software as hypothesis.

The main aim of contextual inquiry phase is to define the context and the design challenges. In case of DigiMina the main context is teacher education with special focus on novice teachers who are doing their induction year in schools. The design challenge is to enable teachers to evaluate their educational technology competencies. In this phase we used personas [17] as a method to describe the goals and motivations of archetypal users. We developed five personas that cover our expected user groups: (1) teacher training master student, (2) novice teacher, (3) experienced teacher, (4) educational technologist of a school and (5) trainings manager. These personas served as a basis for writing the scenarios.

The second phase of research-based design process is participatory design, involving potential users of the system in design sessions. In order to communicate the design ideas with our stakeholders we need simple and non-technical communication tools. One such communication method is scenario-based design [18] where typical use cases are described as simple stories of people and their activities. These stories can be used in a participatory design session to evoke ideas and discussion. We prepared four main scenarios that addressed directly the above mentioned design challenges: (1) master student is evaluating her educational technology competencies, (2) peer assessment of problem solving tasks, (3) educational technologist of a school is getting an overview of teachers' educational technology competencies and (4) training manager is compiling a training group with sufficient level of competencies.

The scenarios were evaluated in two participatory design sessions. The first session included 3 novice teachers. The second session included an expert teacher and a teacher trainer. The first design session focused on the first two scenarios, the second design session included all four scenarios. While the participants found the scenarios realistic they pointed out several details that could be changed in the scenarios. The design sessions indicated need for two additional personas: facilitator of master students and novice teachers, and a teacher trainer. As an outcome of the participatory design phase we have defined the main concepts of DigiMina. These are discussed in the next section.

Currently we are in the third phase of research-based design process. The aim of product design phase is to define the use cases and basic interaction. This is done through agile user stories [19] and prototyping. User stories have been mapped to the information architecture diagram. We have developed a set of paper prototypes and high-fidelity prototypes about main pages of the system. These prototypes will be evaluated with the users before moving to the production phase.

5   Conceptual Design of DigiMina

The conceptual design of DigiMina is presented as a concept map (see Fig. 1). Key concepts are emphasized in bold and explained in details in the following section. This conceptual map covers both the user interface vocabulary and concepts related to educational technology competencies.

Competency Test. The central feature of the system is a competency test that is taken by the users. One of the usability issues with competency test is a large number of tasks. There are 19 competencies in 5 groups. Each competency is assessed in 5 level scale. We have taken several steps to solve this issue. Before starting the competency test users can pre-evaluate their competency level in 5 competency groups. When taking the test they will receive tasks at the specified competency level. Also it is possible to save the test and continue answering later.

Competency test can be taken several times to measure the advancement in educational technology competencies. In a typical scenario the first competency test is taken during educational technology course in the university, second test in the induction year in a school and additional tests when working as a teacher. All the results can be compared with the earlier results.

Tasks. Competency test contains tasks that are mapped to performance indicators. These performance indicators are specified with the assessment rubric. The tasks are divided into three types according to the assessment method: (1) automatically assessed self-test items, (2) peer-assessment tasks and (3) self-reflection tasks. Whenever possible, we tried to compose a self-test item for each competency (succeeded in 29 cases), but often it would have compromised the authenticity of the tasks, so we had to create either peer-assessment (23 cases) or self-reflection task (41 cases) instead. An example of a self-test task could be a multiple-response item based on a screencast that shows how a teacher is publishing a learning object into a repository, while making several small mistakes in the process. An example of a peer-assessment task expects the teacher to adapt a given study guide to her own working context (age range, subject area, software). Adapted study guide will be submitted to qualitative peer-assessment procedure by another teacher. An example of a self-reflection task expects the teacher to reflect on the process and results of her experience of creating digital learning resources based on one real-life example.

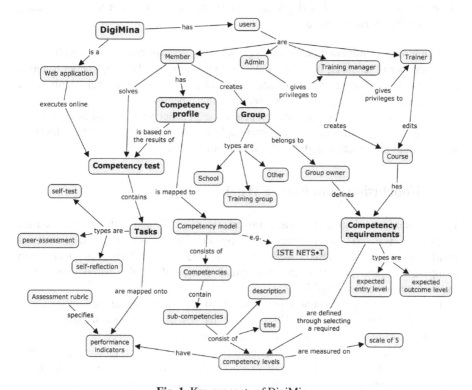

Fig. 1. Key concepts of DigiMina

Peer-assessed tasks are typically used in higher competency levels where the user has to write a solution to authentic problem. In that case the answer has to be evaluated by another DigiMina user with the same or higher competency level. In case if teacher students and novice teachers this can be one of their group members.

The scope of DigiMina is limited to delivery of competency tests and tasks. Tasks are created in a specialized question and test authoring tool TATS and stored in a format compatible with IMS Question & Test Interoperability Specification [20].

Competency Profile. When the user has completed all the tasks the system will display her competency profile. This includes a diagram that displays her competency level in all 19 competencies. In the competency profile it is possible to compare your competency levels with the average competency level of various groups (other novice teachers, other teachers in your school, other teachers in your subject, all DigiMina users, etc). It is possible to make the competency profile public or share it with selected people.

Group. In order to connect teacher students from the same course or teachers from the same school it is possible to create groups. The creator of the group (typically facilitator of the course or educational technologist of the school) is able to see the competency profiles of other group members and various statistics about the competencies. In a school setting DigiMina can be used to find out teachers' training needs in educational technology.

Competency Requirements. When DigiMina will contain competency profiles of a large number of teachers, it will become a valuable tool for planning teacher trainings and organizing training groups. Educational technology related teacher trainings can be described with competency requirements that specify expected entry level and expected outcome level in certain competencies. Teacher trainers will be able to see the competency profiles of teachers who apply for the trainings. In a school level the group owner can create specific competency requirements.

6   Conclusions and Future Work

Educational technology competency frameworks play an important role in systematic support of teachers' professional development. This paper analyzed the design challenges for Web-based assessment of teachers' educational technology competencies and presented the conceptual design of a Web-based competency assessment tool called DigiMina.

DigiMina is designed not as a monolithic Web application, but as one component in a larger digital ecosystem of distributed tools that teachers are using in their everyday work in the digital age. For instance, the test items are not developed inside DigiMina, but are imported from test item authoring tool TATS or Learning Object Repositories. Teachers' competency profiles created with DigiMina can be linked and embedded to other social media systems and integrated into national teachers' portal (e.g. for providing more relevant recommendations on professional development courses).

The next iteration of our research-based design focuses on evaluating the set of assessment tasks and developing the Web-based competency assessment tool. In addition to supporting teachers' professional development DigiMina assessment tool will provide a valuable data set for further research on teachers' educational technology competencies.

Acknowledgments. This research was funded by Estonian Ministry of Education and Research targeted research grant No. 0130159s08.

References

1. ECDL Foundation (2011), `http://www.ecdl.org/`
2. Sampson, D., Fytros, D.: Competence Models in Technology-enhanced Competence-based Learning. In: Adelsberger, H.H., Kinshuk, P.J.M., Sampson, D. (eds.) International Handbook on Information Technologies for Education and Training. Springer, Heidelberg (2008)
3. Educational Technology Competency Model (2011), `http://www.tiigrihype.ee/?dl=53`
4. European Schoolnet: Assessment Schemes for Teachers ICT competence (2005), `http://www-old.eun.org/insight-pdf/special_reports/PIC_Report_Assessment %20schemes_insightn.pdf`
5. Calvani, A., Cartelli, A., Fini, A., Ranieri, M.: Models and Instruments for Assessing Digital Competence at School. Journal of e-Learning and Knowledge Society 4, 183–193 (2008)
6. UNESCO: ICT Competency Standards for Teachers: Implementation Guidelines (2008), `http://unesdoc.unesco.org/images/0015/001562/156209e.pdf`
7. ISTE: NETS for Teachers (2008), `http://www.iste.org/standards/nets-for-teachers/nets-for-teachers-2008.aspx`
8. Hogenbirk, P., de Rijcke, F. (eds.): Teachers: It clicks Professional development for good ICT practice. The Inspectorate of Education, Utrecht (2006)
9. McDougall, A.: Models and Practices in Teacher Education Programs for Teaching with and about IT. In: Voogt, J., Knezek, G. (eds.) International Handbook of Information Technology in Primary and Secondary Education, pp. 461–474. Springer US, Boston (2008)
10. de Pablos Pons, J.: Repositori institucional: Higher Education and the Knowledge Society. Information and Digital Competencies. RUSC. Revista de Universidad y Sociedad del Conocimiento. 7, 6–15 (2010)
11. Cumming, J.J., Maxwell, G.: Contextualising Authentic Assessment. Assessment in Education: Principles, Policy & Practice 6, 177–194 (1999)
12. Wass, V., Van der Vleuten, C., Shatzer, J., Jones, R.: Assessment of clinical competence. The Lancet 357, 945–949 (2001)
13. Miller, G.E.: The assessment of clinical skills/competence/performance. Academic Medicine 67, S63–S67 (1990)
14. Lombardi, M.M.: Making the Grade: The Role of Assessment in Authentic Learning. EDUCAUSE Learning Initiative (2008)
15. Gulikers, J.T.M., Bastiaens, T.J., Kirschner, P.A.: A Five-Dimensional Framework for Authentic Assessment. Educational Technology Research & Development 52, 67–86 (2004)
16. Leinonen, T., Toikkanen, T., Silvfast, K.: Software as hypothesis: research-based design methodology. In: Proceedings of the Tenth Anniversary Conference on Participatory Design 2008, pp. 61–70. Indiana University, Indianapolis (2008)
17. Cooper, A., Reimann, R., Cronin, D.: About Face 3: The Essentials of Interaction Design. Wiley Publishing, Inc., Indianapolis (2007)
18. Carroll, J.M.: Making Use: Scenario-Based Design of Human-Computer Interactions. The MIT Press, Cambridge (2000)
19. Cohn, M.: User Stories Applied: For Agile Software Development. Addison-Wesley, Boston (2004)
20. Tomberg, V., Laanpere, M.: Implementing Distributed Architecture of Online Assessment Tools Based on IMS QTI ver.2. In: Lazarinis, F., Green, S., Pearson, E. (eds.) Handbook of Research on E-Learning Standards and Interoperability: Frameworks and Issues, pp. 41–58. IGI Global (2011)

Designing the Competence-Driven Teacher Accreditation

Kairit Tammets[1], Kai Pata[1], Mart Laanpere[1], Vladimir Tomberg[1],
Dragan Gašević[2], and Melody Siadaty[2]

[1] Centre for Educational Technology, Institute of Informatics, Tallinn University
Narva road 25, 10120, Tallinn, Estonia
{kairit,kpata,martl,vtomberg}@tlu.ee
[2] Athabasca University & Simon Fraser University, Canada
dgasevic@acm.org, melody siadaty@sfu.ca

Abstract. For supporting technology-enhanced in-service teacher accreditation for professional competences, this case study in Estonian context investigates the applicability of an organizational knowledge-management (KM) model extended by the principles of self-regulated learning. The survey findings revealed the existing state, open challenges, and potential barriers of supporting teachers' lifelong learning activities with the new model. An activity scenario and a set of software services supporting the harmonization of teachers' accreditation with the model were developed via a participatory design process with the teachers. The evaluation indicated that organizational, intra- and inter-personal scaffolds embedded in services were used concurrently in each accreditation activity.

Keywords: accreditation, e-portfolio, competence development, learning path.

1   Introduction

In this paper, we focus on designing a technology-enhanced accreditation process of teachers' professional competences. The general vision of the European teaching profession outlines that teachers should be lifelong learners who continue their professional development throughout their careers [1]. However, teachers' professionalism is at crossroad - one possible future scenario leads to constrained professionalism of teachers, due to the rigid and formal accreditation standards; another scenario calls for maintaining and pursuing professionalism through teachers' participation in their community of practice [2]. According to the first scenario, formal accreditation standards would enable periodic evaluation of a set of measurable indicators concerning teachers' work and their conformity to the requirements of their rank on the basis of self- and external assessment. According to the second scenario, teachers' professional growth could also be promoted by reorganizing the teacher accreditation processes in such a way that the process would integrate learning and knowledge-building (LKB) activities of teachers in their day-to-day practice. This second scenario is in line with the assumption that learning in the professional context may be conceptualized as an internal and practically unobservable process that results in changes of teachers' beliefs, attitudes, or competences [3]. In this paper, we investigate technological support for the second approach to the accreditation process. We investigate

H. Leung et al. (Eds.): ICWL 2011, LNCS 7048, pp. 132–141, 2011.

how an organizational knowledge management model [4] could be extended to organizational learning and knowledge building (LKB) for supporting the accreditation process for Estonian teachers. Taking into consideration the national practices of teachers' accreditation process and Estonian practice, we propose that the procedure would be more efficient, if it would promote life-long learning, be more performance-based, and technologically supported.

2   Technology-Enhanced Accreditation of Teachers' Competences

2.1   Accreditation of Teachers' Competences in Estonia

In the literature, there is no consensus on the process of teacher evaluation and several different terms are used such as teacher certification, accreditation, and attestation. Teacher certification usually refers to an initial evaluation of a teacher's professional competences in the beginning of their professional career [5]. Teacher accreditation is a procedure for regulating career advancement within profession and/or for justifying the decision for experienced teachers' salary increase [6]. In the context of our study, we define accreditation as the procedure for regulating career advancement within profession [7]. The aim of the teacher accreditation is to support teachers' professional development and career possibilities by periodical self-evaluation and external-evaluation exercises. So, teachers' self-directed reflective practices should be part of accreditation process in addition to the competence standard-based procedures. In this paper, we show that the current accreditation process does not encourage teachers to integrate their everyday LKB activities as part of the accreditation.

2.2   Learning and Knowledge Building (LKB) Model for Accreditation

Teachers, teacher trainers, and the organizations responsible for teacher accreditation and standards form an extended professional learning community. A Learning and Knowledge Building (LKB) model developed by the IntelLEO project (http://www.intelleo.eu) for supporting temporal LKB in extended organizations [8, 9] could be used for supporting teachers' accreditation. This model is based on the systemic knowledge management model in organizations [4], and contains four phases of knowledge conversion: socialization, externalization, combination and internalization (SECI phases). Naeve, et al. [10] have used SECI phases for describing learning process at workplace, focusing on reflective practices in networking and collaboration. The LKB model adds the focus on self-directed planning and reflection for competence development in the professional community to the SECI activities. Teachers' professional development activities in a professional learning community have been formerly mapped onto the SECI phases [11]. In the accreditation context, the following aspects must be highlighted:

In this model, a competence-oriented approach is pursued so that the accreditation procedure starts from the planning of the competence development. For this reason, we start describing the SECI phases from the internalization (I) phase. The *internalization* phase involves mainly individual planning and learning activities like planning and reflecting on what competences and goals teachers have previously achieved and what they would like to achieve. Secondly, it is important to notice that learning new competences happens in a social context; therefore the *socialization (S)* phase of accreditation aims to support teachers to participate in social networks across boundaries, talking about, sharing, and taking ownership of norms and visions of the teachers' professional community. In the *externalization (E)* phase of the accreditation, teachers should also reflect about the activities that were significant for their learning, and document the learning paths that enabled them to arrive to certain competences.

Currently, while developing the teachers' competence standards and accreditation norms, it is not considered that the professional community of teachers would constantly evolve the competences. Integrating the *combination* (C) phase into the accreditation process would allow for considering the community's contributions in the standard development.

2.3 Technological Support for Teacher Accreditation

Modern society presumes more or less that a teacher uses some technology for professional development and life-long learning [12]. Many studies have demonstrated advantages of the use of e-portfolios in supporting teachers' professional development in that e-portfolio is an electronic collection of evidence that shows a person's learning journey over time [13]. In Estonia, the Elgg[1]-based e-portfolio-community portal Koolielu[2] has recently been developed for teachers. Koolielu provides individual e-portfolios, as well as, LKB opportunities in communities. In the competence-based teacher assessment, it is common to use e-portfolios with selected evidence of performances and products in various contexts, accompanied by teachers' comments and reflections [14]. Based on the LKB model (Sec. 2.2), three types of scaffolds are needed to support LKB in SECI phases during the teacher accreditation:

- *Intra-personal scaffolds* – while using e-portfolios, individuals should have a possibility to plan their learning goals and reflect on their learning paths based on professional teacher competences;

- *Inter-personal scaffolds* – individuals should be able to learn competences from other individuals' learning paths in the professional community and discuss with other individuals about their competence development;

- *Organizational-scaffolds* – individuals should align their personal learning goals with the required competence standards in the community and contribute to the development of competence standards and normative learning paths.

However, e-portfolio services currently available in professional communities still lack functionalities that would support self-directed competence development in the extended organizational context. For filling this technological gap, the IntelLEO project, among other services, developed the Learning Planner (LP) and the Organizational Policy (OPT) services. These services, if integrated with the e-portfolio functionalities, would enable teachers to be better embedded into the context of the professional community while performing LKB in the accreditation process. The description of the services in accreditation process context is provided in Sec. 4.2.

---

[1] http://www.elgg.org/
[2] http://www.koolielu.ee

3   Methodology

3.1   Research Design

We used a participatory design approach [9] for developing the technology-enhanced support of the teacher accreditation process. The aim of implementing the participatory design elements in the process of developing the technological solution was to bring the teachers closer to the development process, and to stress the importance of collaboration between teachers and developers [15]. Hence, the approach enabled us to turn the traditional designer-user relationship upside down, viewing the teachers as experts and the designers as technical consultants [16].

The study for designing the accreditation process according to the SECI phases of the LKB model contained the following steps:

a) Identifying the needs for changes in the accreditation process. A web-based survey and interviews were conducted among Estonian teachers.

b) Designing the accreditation scenario and scaffolding services. Based on the LKB model, the usage scenario for accreditation was created with the stakeholders. The needs-analysis results and the scenario were used for guiding the development of the LP and OPT services.

c) Evaluating the accreditation scenario and prototypes. LP and OPT services were evaluated in the context of the accreditation scenario.

3.2   Data Collection and Analysis

A web-based Likert-scale survey was developed that contained twelve statements, based on the knowledge conversion SECI phases of our LKB model. The survey sample consisted of 53 teachers from Estonian schools all over the country. Five respondents were men and 48 female. The questionnaire was conducted in April 2010 and the participation was voluntary. The respondents were asked to select their response to each statement in terms of their activities in the accreditation context using a five-point scale ranging from 'strongly disagree' (1) to 'strongly agree' (5). The means (M) and standard deviations (SD) were calculated for each question.

We developed an unstructured design interview that was conducted using the LKB model schema in the discussions with the teachers. The questions were focusing on the: a) artifacts and documents to be presented to the accreditation committee; b) processes related to preparing and presenting the accreditation e-portfolio; c) role of technology; and d) barriers related to the accreditation process. The design interviews were held with three in-service teachers from Estonian Teachers' Association who were experts in the accreditation field. These teachers were also involved in the development of the accreditation scenario.

The evaluation of the LP service was conducted with nine teachers from Estonian schools who were familiar with the accreditation activities. The LP functionalities were grouped according to the intra-personal, organizational and inter-personal scaffolding elements. The evaluation questions tested the teachers' perceived value of the functionalities with respect to the LKB activities from the SECI phases. After using the LP service, the respondents were asked to connect the LKB activities with the service's functionalities using the numbered screenshots of the service. For each LKB activity, the percentage indicating the perceived usefulness of the functionalities of each tool by the respondent group was calculated. The OPT service works in harmony with the LP but is not directly accessed by teachers, and was therefore not evaluated in this study.

4   Results

First, we discuss the current LKB activities in the accreditation context along with the respective limitations and barriers. Then, we describe the designed web-based services developed in terms of accreditation scenarios (Section 4.2.2). Finally, we present results of the evaluation of prototypes of the services in the accreditation context.

4.1   Critical Gaps and Controversies in the Current Accreditation Policy

We have combined the results of the survey with the results from the interview to provide the description of the limitations of the accreditation process.

4.1.1   Internalization: Planning Personal Competence Development and Learning from Others

Generally, it was found from the survey that learning from colleagues' e-portfolios was considered a useful aspect for the respondents, as it would enable them to see how their colleagues have composed their accreditation e-portfolios (M=3.46; SD=1.67). The teachers admitted that their colleagues' feedback to the e-portfolio reflections could support their development (M=3.31; SD=1.73), but they would rather not take the feedback into consideration when planning their professional development (M=2.94; SD=1.61).

The interviews also revealed an important limitation of the current accreditation process in terms of supporting the professional development of teachers. First, it does not support life-long learning. The accreditation portfolio is presented to the commission either as paper-based or just sent as text-documents. The portfolio does not include reflections or web-based learning materials as evidences of teacher's professional performance. Neither does it include plans for the next working period. In the future, when a teacher would like to apply for the next rank, she/he has no systematic recordings reflecting what was presented to the commission during the last time of accreditation, or the new plans, which were made for the upcoming period.

4.1.2   Socialization: Networking and Feedback from Colleagues

Teachers considered socialization an important aspect in their accreditation context – they can receive feedback on their performance, and it would support their professional development (M=3.31; SD=1.73). What makes the feedback aspect interesting is that although teachers admitted that getting feedback on their performance is supportive for their professional development, they were not very interested in giving feedback on their colleagues' reflections (M=2.5; SD=1.36). The interviews also pointed out that missing feedback is one of the important limitations of the current accreditation process. The accreditation commission members let the teacher know if the next rank has been nominated, but no feedback is given if any of the aspects were performed especially well, and what should be improved in the future.

4.1.3 Externalization: Documentation of Knowledge and Competences

The teachers had quite a high opinion (M=4.08; SD=1.37) that reflections about professional activities would support their development. On the other hand, interest in documenting the moments of the professional competence development as reflections was low (M=2.31; SD=1.43). It means that teachers can theoretically see what is useful for them, but they do not have a habit of documenting their knowledge and competences. This might be the most critical barrier in reorganizing the accreditation process. The need for reflections as part of the accreditation requirements was also discussed in the interviews with the stakeholders from Estonian Teachers' Association. They stated that teachers, who pass the accreditation process, currently just have to list all the evidences of passing the training courses or about guiding the youth organizations, but they are not expected to reflect about their teaching activities.

4.1.4 Combination: Share Documents with Colleagues

Results from the study revealed that sharing the learning resources, lesson plans and tasks with colleagues is not a habit among the teachers (M=2.12; SD=1.58). In general, the teachers were not very interested in their e-portfolios being published and used by other teachers for learning purposes (M=2.75; SD=1.84). The missing sharing and reusing culture among teachers might be another barrier for reorganizing the accreditation process according to the LKB model.

The teachers, who answered the questionnaire, know well what kind of LKB activities could support their professional development, but currently they do not do these activities. One of the reasons might be that current accreditation process is too formal, bureaucratic and does not support teachers' intrinsically motivated LKB, and therefore, there is a lack of collaboration, providing feedback, and sharing the knowledge about competences among teachers.

4.2 Technology Needs to Enhance Teachers' Accreditation Process

The IntelLEO project has provided a set of new Web services that are based on the SECI model. Below, we describe two of the IntelLEO core services, which are the most relevant for teachers in the context of accreditation.

The LP service is a personal tool for planning and documenting personal learning paths toward achieving certain competences, defined as sets of envisaged or completed learning activities together with related knowledge assets, events and resources. LP provides users with technical support for the three main types of scaffolds as introduced in Sec. 2.3. Here, we briefly overview some of LP functionalities for: i) Intra-personal scaffolds (in PS in Fig. 1A) - Users can manage and plan their learning goals; document their learning experiences including new competences (e.g., "Describing learning mesh-ups" in Fig. 1A), learning paths, learning activities or knowledge assets; ii) Inter-personal scaffolds – Documented experiences can be shared with other users (e.g., "Describing learning mash-ups" becomes a user-created competences in OS of Fig. 1B); personal learning goals from PS can be shared with colleagues, so that they can collaboratively edit learning experiences; or relevant colleagues can be discovered and followed (Fig. 1C), similar to Twitter, where the colleagues activities are shown in Social Wave (Fig 1D); and iii) organizational-scaffolds – users can align personal goals with organizational objectives (e.g., by selecting competences from OS such as "Composing learning resources in Fig. 1E and placing them into PS as shown in Fig. 1); or receiving recommendations for the most suitable competences and learning paths, ranked based on users' user model and current learning context (OS in Fig. 1).

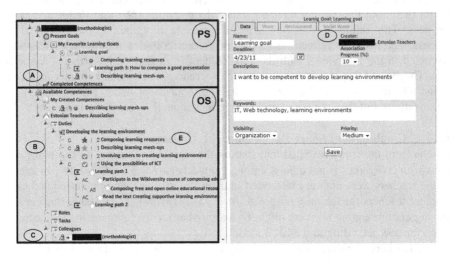

Fig. 1. Learning Planner: PS – Personal Space; OS – Organizational Space

The OPT services are used to define needs and requirements at the organizational and administrative levels such as specifying the organizational structure and job positions, binding job positions to a set of competence definitions, harmonizing the set of internal competences with the ones of other organizations (e.g., university), or setting incentives for competence management. Functionalities of these services are grouped into four different modules: i) *Competence Management Module* where the competences, related to the organization can be defined and modified; ii) *Organizational Management Module* where the roles within the organization can be defined; iii) *Learning Management Module (LMM)* where the Learning path templates can be prepared, taking into consideration the roles and competences used in the organization. Such templates designed in LMM propose initial recommendations for users in the LP service; iv) *Inter-organizational Management Module* where the competences between organizations can be mapped and harmonized; and v) *Motivation Management Module* which defines the motivation policies at the organizational level.

The LP supports competence development process of individuals and the OPT assures that individuals' knowledge sharing process is compliant with the organization's culture, rules and norms. Combining LP and OPT with the e-portfolio functionality might support the professional development and accreditation process, efficiently.

4.2.1.   Accreditation Scenarios

A scenario illustrating how to use the developed LKB model in the accreditation process in teacher development context was developed in the participatory design sessions together with teachers.

An accreditation specialist at the National Examinations and Qualifications Centre develops the formative evaluation learning path template by using the OPT. Additionally, the learning path activities will be associated with appropriate competences described in the Standard of Teacher's Professional Competence, with the same tool.

Teacher Jane has decided to pass the accreditation process in order to get the next rank in her teacher career. Jane uses e-portfolio for the accreditation process. She finds from her LP a recommended accreditation-oriented learning path template that has been prepared by an accreditation specialist using the OPT. First, she defines her learning goals. Then, she explores her colleagues' existing accreditation learning paths in order to learn from them. Jane also decides to create a group with LP, where other teachers, who are preparing themselves to pass the accreditation process, could share their experiences and support each other. To provide evidence for each competence, Jane describes her learning activities and uploads files or adds Web links as evidences of her competences. All activities should be explained with reflections. In LP, all the activities in the accreditation template have to be connected to one or many competences from the competence standard accessed via the OPT. Finally, Jane should plan her professional development for the next professional period. The created content (reflections, evidences, certifications) may be visible only for the owner (teacher), only for selected users or groups (e.g. the commission). After Jane has shared the access to the commission, the commission is expected to give feedback on each of the competence-based activities in Jane's e-portfolio by writing a reflective evaluation and suggestions for the future.

4.3   Evaluation Results of Software Prototypes in the Accreditation Context

Evaluating the prototypes of the IntelLEO services with nine Estonian teachers, revealed how different functionalities might co-support the LKB activities related with the accreditation process in each SECI phase (see Fig.2). To simplify the overview, in the figure, we coloured the functionalities according to organizational scaffolds (black), intra-personal scaffolds (white), and inter-personal scaffolds (grey).

In **the Internalization phase**, the most useful functionalities for *planning their personal learning goals* were intra-personal scaffolds such as "My favourite learning goals", "Personal learning paths", and "Adding new assets to personal learning paths" (50%). The activity of *harmonizing personal learning goals with those of their organization* was mainly (56%) influenced by three organizational scaffolding functions, and intra-personal scaffolding functions (32%) indicating that self-directed planning for accreditation should be embedded into the context of the requirements from the professional community. The inter-personal scaffolds (48%) appeared to be very important in the internalization phase for *learning from colleagues*. It seems that the learning paths and assets from the colleagues should be harmonized with the organizational competences before they are accepted as personal goals. However, this finding needs to be clarified via interviews.

The Socialization phase was represented with the activity *socializing and networking with colleagues*. It was found that this activity was mostly (67%) supported by the inter-personal scaffolding functionalities such as "rating and commenting assets and learning paths", "visibility and authorship of the assets/learning paths" and by "the social analytics". Yet, even in the socialization phase, the organizational and intra-personal scaffolds were of some importance to the teachers (25%).

In **the Externalization phase**, teachers used the three types of scaffolds equally (67%) while *documenting their knowledge and competences*. The most important functionalities in the externalization phase seemed to be "competence description", and possibility of adding and editing "personal learning paths" and "new assets". In **the Combination phase**, the activity *sharing documents with colleagues* was firstly supported by the inter-personal (48%) and by intra-personal scaffolds (35%).

It appeared that teachers combined organizational, inter- and intra-personal scaffolding functionalities of the LP for different LKB activities in the accreditation process. These types of scaffolds are simultaneously needed and should be used concurrently in every LKB activity in an accreditation process.

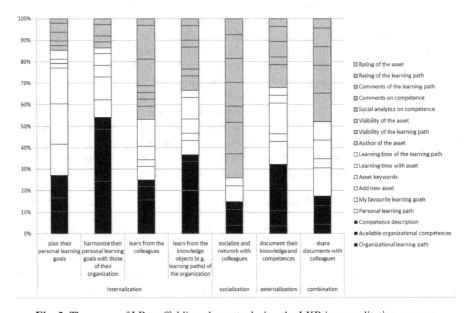

Fig. 2. The usage of LP scaffolding elements during the LKB in accreditation process

5   Conclusion

While one possible future scenario of teacher professionalism to the managerial notion of evidence-based accreditation is based rigid and formal standards, an alternative scenario calls for maintaining and pursuing professionalism through teachers' participation in the community of practice, through collaborative learning and knowledge building activities. According to the latter approach, teachers' professional growth could also be promoted by reorganizing the teacher accreditation processes in such a way that on-the-job LKB activities of teachers is also taken into account. In this paper, we showed how to technologically support the second approach for accreditation. We propose to integrate the LKB model derived from Nonaka and Takeuchi [4] as part of the accreditation process for Estonian teachers. Taking into consideration the national practices of teachers' accreditation process and Estonian practice, we propose that the procedure would be more efficient, if it would follow life-long learning aspects, be more performance-based, and technologically supported.

Acknowledgements. MER targeted research 0130159s08 and IntelLEO project (no. 231590) funded the study. This document does not represent the opinion of the EC, and the EC is not responsible for any use that might be made of its content.

References

1. Common European Principles for Teacher Competences and Qualifications. European Commission (2005)
2. Hargreaves, A.: Four Ages of Professionalism and Professional Learning. Teachers and Teaching: History and Practice 6(2), 151–182 (2000)
3. Bereiter, C., Scardmalia, M.: Learning to Work Creatively with Knowledge. In: De Corte, E., Verschaffel, L., Entwistle, N., van Merrienboer, J. (eds.) Unravelling Basic Components and Dimensions of Powerful Learning Environments. EARLI Advances in Learning and Instruction Series (2003)
4. Nonaka, I., Takeuchi, H.: The knowledge-creating company: How Japanese companies create the dynamics of innovation. Oxford University Press, Oxford (1995)
5. Heine, H.: Teacher Certification Systems. Research into practice 2006, pp. 7–30. Pacific Resources for Education and Learning, Honolulu (2006)
6. Männamaa, I.: Assessing Teachers' Performance in Pre- and Primary Schools in Estonia. In: Schonfeld, H., O'Brien, S., Walsh, T. (eds.) Questions of Quality, pp. 225–230. Centre for Early Childhood Development & Education, Dublin (2005)
7. Helleve, I.: Theoretical Foundations of Teachers' Professional Development. In: Lindberg, Olofson (eds.) Online Learning Communities and Teacher Professional Development: Methods for Improved Education Delivery (1- 19). IGI-Global, US (2009)
8. Stokic, D., Pata., K., Devedžic, V., et al.: Intelligent Learning Extended Organizations. In: Proceedings of 8 9 TELearn 2008, Hanoi, Vietnam. CD Edition (2008)
9. Kieslinger, B., Pata, K., Fabian, C.M.: Participatory Design Approach for the Support of Collaborative Learning and Knowledge Building in Networked Organizations. International Journal of Advanced Corporate Learning 2(3) (2009)
10. Naeve, A., Yli-Luoma, P., Kravcik, M., Lytras, M.D.: A modelling approach to study learning processes with a focus on knowledge creation. International Journal Technology Enhanced Learning 1(1/2), 1–34 (2008)
11. Pata, K., Laanpere, M.: Supporting cross-institutional knowledge-building with Web 2.0 enhanced digital portfolios. In: Proc. 8th IEEE International Conference on Advanced Learning Technologies, Santander, Cantabria, Spain, pp. 798–800 (2008)
12. European Commission, Improving the Quality of Teacher Education - Conclusions of the Council and of the Representatives of the Governments of the Member States, meeting within the Council (2007)
13. Barrett, H.: Balancing the Two Faces of ePortfolios. Educação, Formação & Tecnologias 3(1), 6–14 (2010)
14. Wolf, K., Dietz, M.: Teaching portfolios: purposes and possibilities. Teacher Education Quarterly 25, 9–22 (1998)
15. Muller, M.J.: Participatory Design: The Third Space in HCI. In: The Human-Computer Interaction Handbook: Fundamentals, Evolving Technologies and Emerging Applications. L, Erlbaum Associates Inc., New York (2002)
16. Schuler, D., Namioka, A.: Participatory Design: Principles and the Practices. Lawrence Erlabum Associates, Inc. (1993)

Occupational Guidance through ELECTRE Method

Stefanos Ougiaroglou and Ioannis Kazanidis

[1] Dept. of Applied Informatics, University of Macedonia, 54006 Thessaloniki, Greece
stoug@uom.gr
[2] Dept. of Accountancy, Kavala Institute of Technology, 65404 Kavala, Greece
kazanidis@teikav.edu.gr

Abstract. Many students do not manage to complete their higher education studies because they chose an university department whose curriculum consists of courses that are out of their interest. If the selection of their studies is done with more caution and knowledge might lead to better decision making. This paper presents a web-based decision support system which allows the student to indicate the degree of interest for courses in secondary education that they has been taught. The system, using the multicreteria analysis method ELECTRE, presents a possible, ranked based on student's interests, university departments list.

Keywords: ELECTRE, occupational guidance, decision support system, higher education.

1   Introduction

Secondary education graduates are invited to choose the university department where they are going to continue their studies. In Greece, they have to complete a form stating their preferences in higher education departments. However, often the process of completing the department list is based on some specific factors that lead students to a higher education department, the knowledge domain of which, in fact is out of their interest. Examples of such factors are: (i) Lack of accurate information and proper guidance, (ii). Influence from relatives (eg parents' professional and expectations), (iii) selecting courses based on placement rather than actual intellectual interests and skills.

As a consequence many students are often asked to complete a curriculum of a university department which consists of courses that do not interest them. This leads many of them to abandon their studies or to continue by facing various learning difficulties and finally obtain their diploma expecting just a job. It is very likely, these students had another, successful evolution in another science, if they were led to complete their statement with more caution and knowledge.

One way that might help students take a right decision for their studies, is to carefully study the curricula of universities and their departments on the basis of having attended courses in secondary education, and choose the courses that really interest them. However, such a procedure is difficult and time consuming.

This paper proposes the use of an intelligent decision support system which allows the students to indicate their degree of interest for courses in secondary education that

H. Leung et al. (Eds.): ICWL 2011, LNCS 7048, pp. 142–147, 2011.

they has been taught. Afterwards based on multiciteria analysis method ELECTRE I [1], it presents a possible, ranked based on special interests, Higher Education departments categories list. The need for such an application arose after the completing a relevant questionnaire [2] by students. The proposed system helps the students, based on the degree of preference shown for courses of their secondary education studies or possibly even on subjects outside the official curriculum, identifies the higher education departments of which will be required to carry out a curriculum consisted of courses that are related to their interests. This decision support system is a web-based interactive application, which was given the name ELECTRE in School Occupational Guidance (ESOG).

2   Multicreteria Analysis Methods

An important part of decision support systems are those which based on multicriteria analysis methods. These methods based in the principle that complicated problems of decision-making, are not possible to be solved monodimensionally. On the other hand, all the criteria that influence the process of decision-making, is necessary to be taken into account, and to be combined for the solution of each problem.

Multicriteria analysis methods are used for various assessments and evaluations. Their use is necessary if we should take into account various parameters of a problem, none of which is more important than the other, to make a decision. A multicriteria analysis method usually incorporates the charachteristics: (i) it is necessary to define criteria that characterized problems in an integrated manner, (ii) alternative solutions, so-called actions have to be developed, representing alternatives, projects, plan variants or any other entities that have to be compared or ranked, (iii) afterwards decision makers define each criterion weight, (iv) each criterion has a preference type, representing "formalization of decision makers behavior" and (v) according to the defined criteria, input data for each action is defined as an absolute value represented in incomparable units.

An important multi-criteria method is ELECTRE. The acronym ELECTRE stands for: ELimination Et Choix Traduisant la REalité (ELimination and Choice Expressing REality). ELECTRE is a family of multi-criteria decision analysis methods that include ELECTRE I [1], ELECTRE II [3,4], ELECTRE III [5], ELECTRE IV [6], ELECTRE IS [7] and ELECTRE TRI [8]. All the above ELECTRE methods act in two stages. Initially, one or several outranking relations are developed, which aims at comparing in a comprehensive way each pair of actions while on the second stage, an exploitation procedure elaborates the recommendations obtained in the first stage making consistent exploration and analysis in support of decision makers. In this study, ELECTRE I is adopted in order to guide the students to indicate the appropriate university department. For this reason it is presented in Section 3.

3   ESOG System

In this paper, multicreteria analysis was applied in order to aid students to decide which Higher Education (HE) department is better to choose for their higher education studies. According to the adopted framework initially students state their liking degree in Secondary Education Courses (SE) through an appropriate questionnaire (a form with questions such as "How interesting is the course"), and afterwards the ELECTRE in School Occupational Guidance (ESOG) system utilizes the ELECTRE I method and produces a ranked list of the best possible decisions for each student.

Initially the Secondary Education courses are considered as the criteria of the ELECTRE I method, while the possible solutions of the problem (decisions) were assigned to categories of Higher Education departments. In order ELECTRE I method be able to produce a ranked list based on student interests, a value that indicates how important is each criterion (SE course) for any of the alternative decisions (HE departments' categories) shall be assigned (values 1-5). These values are called weights. In ESOG, the appropriate weights and the grouping of HE departments into categories have been determined by occupational guidance experts taking into account the curriculums of Greek university departments.

ELECTRE I method, for each course that is rated by the student, creates a two-dimensional NxN array, where N is the number of possible decisions (12 HE departments categories). Any decision i is compared to the weighting of the remaining N-1 j decisions. If the coefficient of decision i is greater than the coefficient of j decision (i ≠ j), then the degree of students choice for this course is entered in the corresponding cell of the array, otherwise the value zero is assigned. In this way they are created as many arrays as the number of student answers to the questionnaire. It is easily conceivable that no values entered in the cells of the main diagonal of these tables. We can imagine these arrays as a three-dimensional array (*CompArray [][][]*) NxNxM where M the number of courses.

The next step is to find the summary of students liking degree which is represented in values from 1 to 5, which 1 corresponds to lowest interest from the student and 5 to highest. These values are assigned into a new variable *SumGrades*. In addition the summary of the corresponding cells of all levels of the three-dimensional table (*SumArray [][]*) is calculated and if the quotient of division of particular sum with variable SumGrades is bigger than a predetermined threshold T (we defined T=0.6), then this value is assigned into a corresponding cell of a new two-dimensional table (*BoolArray [][]*), otherwise the zero value is assigned into the same cell. T ∈ [0.5,1] represents the strictness of the evaluation. Values close to 1 mean that in order to confirm the claim of a criterion set there should be almost an agreement in all of them. On the other hand small threshold values let method confirm criteria claims with less strictness.

Finally, the sum of lines and columns of table BoolArray [] [] is calculated and is stored in two monodimensional tables (*RowSum []* and *ColSum []* respectively). The final list of HE departments categories, results on removing the values of *ColSum []* table cells from the corresponding values of *RowSum []* table. The produced table includes the values that show how match the corresponding category of HE departments suit to student interests. Finally the algorithm sorts the table values in ascending order while at the same time keeps the match with the equivalences departments' categories, and produces a final ranking interests list of HE departments' categories. The steps of the ELECTRE I algorithm as it was adapted by ESOG system are briefly presented in Figure 1.

ESOG_ELECTRE_Algorithm (*Weight*[][], *Degree*[], *N*, *M*)

!*M*: courses number, *N*: HE Department Categories,

!*Weight*: per course and per departments category (Values 1-5)

!*Degree*: Liking student degrees (Values 1-5)

for $i = 1$ **to** M

    for $j = 1$ **to** N

        for $k = 1$ **to** N

            if $i \neq j$ **then**

                if $Weight[i][j] \geq Weight[i][k]$ **then**

                    $CompArray[j][k][i] \leftarrow Degree[i]$

                else

                    $CompArray[j][k][i] \leftarrow 0$

Set to 0 the Table *RowSum*[] and *ColSum*[] values

for $j = 1$ **to** N

    for $k = 1$ **to** N

$$SumArray[j][k] \leftarrow \frac{\sum_{i=1}^{M} CompArray[j][k][i]}{\sum_{i=1}^{M} Degree[i]}$$

    if $SumArray[j][k] \geq 0{,}6$ **then**

      $BoolArray[j][k] \leftarrow 1$

    Else

      $BoolArray[j][k] \leftarrow 0$

    $RowSum[j] \leftarrow RowSum[j] + BoolArray[j][k]$

    $ColSum[k] \leftarrow ColSum[k] + BoolArray[j][k]$

for $i = 1$ **to** N

    $ELECTRERank[i] \leftarrow RowSum[i] - ColSum[i]$

Sort (*ELECTRERank*[])

Print: *ELECTRE*Rank[]

Fig. 1. Steps of ELECTRE I algorithm in ESOG system

The process outlined in Figure 1, becomes more easily comprehensible studying Figure 2, which shows an application example of the ELECTRE I. In this particular example there are two sets: SE Courses = {X, Y, Z} and categories of HE departments = {A, B, C}. Observing the output list it is obvious that the student, in accordance with his/her interests, suits more (positive relation) with category A, does not suit by no means (negative relation) with category C, while in the middle (neutral relation) is category B.

ESOG web application is available at http://users.sch.gr/stoug/esog/studentform.php. In brief ESOG system initially prompts students to state their school, class and gender and through an HTML form. Then, it prints a questionnaire of 24 SE courses where student can define the interest in each one of them through a five grade likert scale (1: No Interest–5: High Interest). When the student completes the questionnaire form, ELECTRE I is executed and the system produces the ranked list of 12 HE departments' categories in accordance to student interests. This list includes in the following order the ranking position of department category, the title of department category and the total value of degrees corresponds to each one of them. These values show how much the student suits with the corresponding category of HE departments. Hence, student should not take into consideration only the ranking but also the degrees that assembles each category (e.g. the first category can have a very big difference in degrees from the second). The HE departments' categories are also possible to have been marked with negative values, fact that shows that the student does not suit by no means with the corresponding category of HE departments.

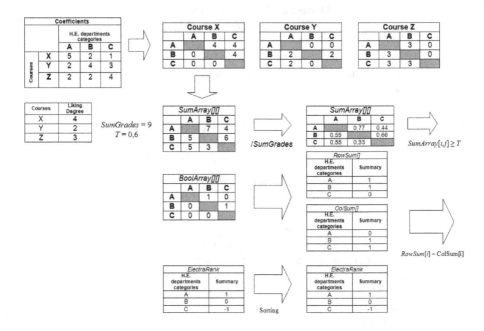

Fig. 2. Example of ELECTRE I application

ESOG system is implemented using a three tier architecture. PHP is used for system intelligence while the MySQL server is used for system database. The ESOG system is hosted in the Greek Panhellenic Network. Finally it is worth mentioning that ESOG is an adaptive system since it provides an administrator interface that allows the system administrators (they can be school managers, teachers, occupational guidance experts etc.) to dynamically determine the SE courses that will be included in the questionnaire, the HE departments categories and the corresponding ELECTRE weighs. Moreover, the administrator web interface provides various statistics about the ESOG questionnaire and its results.

4   Conclusion and Future Work

This work attempted to introduce the multicriteria analysis methods in school occupational guidance. In particular it introduced the ESOG web based system which adopt the ELECTRE method in order to produce a list of the most suited HE departments for each SE student according to his interests in SE courses. In addition, it underlines that the science of information technology and concretely the stream that deals with the decisions support systems, can help the occupational orientation of students. A right decision of higher education department will help student succeed more on his studies since the curriculum courses will be on their interest. This will increase their motivation on the courses and as a consequence the learning performance.

Although that the literature confirms that ELECTRE method is widely considered as an effective and efficient decision aid with a broad range of applications, student that uses an application of software such as ESOG so that it get help in their decisions in critical transient stages of their life, should not rely their decision only in the system's proposed suggestions. It should be helped by occupational adviser, trying to discover how their interests were created, which factors are influenced them and also not to consider that these factors may change in other stages of their life. These facts should be mentioned to the students prior the use of ESOG system, so that the latter be able to exploit the system with the best possible way.

Since ESOG is an adaptive web-based application it can be used to guide the students even in other similar decisions as for example to choose a direction during their secondary education studies (Positive, Theoretical, Technological) or choose mandatory courses. In the future we are planning to operate ESOG application in a large scale and record students' choices as well as the proposed decisions. This data will help further evaluate the system and its efficiency and will also let school teachers and occupational guidance experts guide students on their occupation selection.

References

1. Roy, B.: Classement at Choix en Presence de Points de Vue Multiples (la Methode ELECTRE). Rev. Franc. Inform, et Rech. Oper. 2(8), 57–75 (1968)
2. Mastrogiannis, N.: Methodological framework of knowledge mining support from data with the use of principles of multicreriria decisions analysis (in Greek). PhD Dissertation, University of Patras, Greece (2009)
3. Roy, B., Bertier, P.: La méthode ELECTRE II. Note de travail 142, SEMAMETRA Metra International (1971)
4. Roy, B., Bertier, P.: La méthode ELECTRE II – Une application au médiaplanning. In: Ross, M. (ed.) OR 1972, pp. 291–302. North-Holland Publishing Company, Amsterdam (1973)
5. Roy, B.: ELECTRE III: Un algorithme de classements fondé sur une représentation floue des préférences en présence de critéres multiples. Cahiers du CERO 20(1), 3–24 (1978)
6. Hugonnard, J., Roy, B.: Le plan déxtension du métro en banlieue parisienne, un cas type dápplication de lánalyse multicritére. Les Cahiers Scientifiques de la Revue Transports 6, 77–108 (1982)
7. Roy, B., Skalka, J.: ELECTRE IS: Aspects méthodologiques et guide dútilisation. Document du LAMSADE 30, Université Paris Dauphine (1984)
8. Roy, B., Bouyssou, D.: Comparison of two decision-aid models applied to a nuclear plant siting example. European Journal of Operational Research 25, 200–215 (1986)

A Competence Bartering Platform for Learners

Freddy Limpens and Denis Gillet

EPFL, REACT Group
http://react.epfl.ch/
{Freddy.Limpens,Denis.Gillet}@epfl.ch

Abstract. This paper introduces the concept of a currency-free competence exchange platform in the context of communities of self-regulated learners exploiting personal learning environments. In a life-long perspective, learners can be seen as potential teachers of the skills they collect and develop all along their experience. Currently, spontaneous assistance is a common practice but remains limited to acquaintance groups. Our goal is to foster the emergence of self-driven communities by enabling learners to make available or find competences, to arrange coaching sessions, and to get reusable credits in return. This paper details our investigations on competence models and decentralized credit systems on which the design of our Competence Bartering Platform is grounded.

1 Introduction

This work is part of the ROLE european project[1], which provides a theoretical model and technological framework for building learning environments that are user-centered, context sensitive, and shareable. In this vision, self-directed learners are able to compose autonomously bundles of lightweight tools (widgets) and use them in collaborative web spaces. The aim of this paper is to describe an extension of this already existing framework for helping learners to develop their competences by taking part in a currency-free bartering scheme of coaching services. In this setting, learners turn into providers of their competences and give *coaching* sessions to their peers in exchange of reusable credit units (hence the term *currency free*).

We position our approach as a compromise between formal and informal competence development. A formal approach to competence development can be found for instance in [4] who provide a conceptual framework to formalize learning path and help learners in defining and assessing their proficiency in the competences they acquire. Informal competence exchange can be observed among students when they support each other, but these exchanges are neither recorded nor formally encouraged and remain within the limits of small acquaintance groups. Outside of the academic realm, some skills exchange networks appeared in the 70's and 80's. In 1971, Héber-Suffrin founded the first RERS (French for Reciprocal Skills Exchange Network[2]) where primary school

---

[1] http://www.role-project.eu/
[2] http://www.rers-asso.org/

H. Leung et al. (Eds.): ICWL 2011, LNCS 7048, pp. 148–153, 2011.

pupils could have the chance to teach their peer one skill they had. These informal exchanges were seen as a basis for a community of skills and knowledge sharing. Later were created LETS (Local Exchange and Trading Systems [5]) where members could trade skills, in the form of services, in a multilateral way and in exchange of credit units. More recent but similar Web-based community sites allow their members to exchange skills in the form of jobs or services (*skillsbox.com, swapaskill.com*) or in the form of teaching sessions (*formarezo.com*). In all these online platforms members advertise on the skills they have to offer or are looking for. In swapaskill.*com*, people with matching *wants* and *haves* swap one service for another, wheras *skillsbox.com* and *formarezo.com* use multilateral trade where members exchange skills or teaching sessions for credits. In a similar fashion, *p2pu.org* is an online university run by its students, who can occasionaly lead study groups organized in faculties and followed remotely from anywhere in the world. As a result, *p2pu.org,* which meets a growing success, delivers official competence records that are gaining more and more recogniton[3].

With the Competence Bartering Platform, learners who turn into teacher to coach their fellows would then get official recognition of their skills that they can easily value in their CV. In addition, they'll get credits they could invest to get new competences from their peers. The multilateral exchange principle allowed by the use of community currencies would enable to overcome the implicit bilateral exchange scheme whereby A helps B who helps A in return. This type of currency-free scheme also tackle the shortage of cash and enable students to take valuable coaching sessions that go beyond informal tips given by their fellows. And as a result of its greater flexibility in comparison with academic teaching, this platform makes available Just In Time - Just On Topic learning [1].

In this paper we will first detail a typical scenario of usage of our Competence Bartering Platform. Following a brief overview of the platform, we will detail our investigation on competence and decentralized credit model that ground our approach before concluding.

2   Scenario of Usage

Tom has just entered Cambridge University and started a Master degree in Advanced Web Development. In his first project, he is supposed to know Ruby programming language[4]. Unfortunately, among his acquaintances, none are proficient in Ruby, but one suggests he should have a look at the Competence Bartering Platform.

He first checks what is available among the registered users with the Search Competence Widget and finds Sandra, who indicated Ruby as one of her competences. To start using the system, he has to 1) fill in at least one competence he owns and make it publicly available. For this he uses the CV Editor widget that, in addition, allows him to export this data in the form of a nicely typed CV. 2)

---

[3] Provinding certifications backed by Mozilla fund.
   http://p2pu.org/en/schools/school-of-webcraft/
[4] http://www.ruby-lang.org

He opens an Educational Credit Unit (ECU) account where, as a newcomer, he is offered 10 credits.

Tom is now able to contact, with the chat widget, Sandra, and they agree on a meeting date for an introductory session on Ruby. After this session, Sandra sends a "billing" order to Tom through the ECU management widget and then Tom proceeds to the "payment" through the same widget. Tom is now able to assess the support he got from Sandra on Ruby. This assessment will then come as a complement to the records Sandra shows to support her competence as a "Ruby coach".

As Tom has extended his competence profile, he is quickly contacted by other peers to give coaching sessions. After the completion of his master degree, Tom has a positive balance on his ECU account. He found a position in a London area company where he will be able to use his ECUs by "purchasing" coaching sessions to his co-workers.

3   Overview of the Competence Bartering Platform

The Competence Bartering Platform (CBP) we envision will be made of a set of widgets, based on OpenSocial gadget specifications[5], and dedicated services, which will be implemented as extensions to the container Apache Shindig[6]. These components will extend the ROLE SDK[7], which bundles a set of ROLE services and libraries and is meant to be plug-able to existing collaborative or learning environment such as EPFL's Graaasp[8] or moodle.org.

3.1   Collecting Competences

To non intrusively collect competence data, we will provide our users a *CV Editor* widget where users can edit and update their personal information with the possibility to export a CV. The information provided is then sent to the Shindig user service extended to support competence data. In our model, a person owns a competence when s/he is able to combine his/her knowledge and skills autonomously in a given context. A competence is captured by the combination of URI of a DBPedia[9] concept denoting the scope or topic, and an indication of the level taken from the EQF reference scale[10]. Using DBPedia knowledge base allows in turn to provide extra search and retrieval features thanks to its built-in semantic relations. Optionally, more detailed information can be added, such as evidence records, official references, etc. To encode this data, we proposed an extension for both OpenSocial standards (with an extension to the OpenSocial Social Data Specification[11]) and RDF (with an extension of the Cognitive

---

[5] http://opensocial-resources.googlecode.com/svn/spec/1.0/Core-Gadget.xml

[6] http://shindig.apache.org

[7] A first version is already available at http://sourceforge.net/projects/role-project/

[8] http://graaasp.epfl.ch/

[9] RDF port of WikiPedia, http://dbpedia.org/

[10] http://www.emcq.eu/index.php?page=the-eqf-reference-levels

[11] http://opensocial-resources.googlecode.com/svn/spec/1.1/Social-Data.xml

Characteristics Ontology[12])[13]. Regarding the privacy of the competence data, we adopt the strategy featured in the Graaasp platform where access rights are divided into three categories: 1) public: everyone can access; 2) close: only established contact of the owner can access, but data remain searchable. E.g. if someone, who is not a contact of the owner, searches for a competence, the system will indicate that someone possesses this searched-for competence and will request the owner approval before disclosing his/her contact information; 3) hidden: only the owner can access and search this data.

3.2   Search Competences and Start Trading

Since competence data will be included in the personal profile of users with adequate privacy control, the CBP will be able to use directly the search and recommendation services of the ROLE SDK. A dedicated widget will also be proposed and will outputs a list of relevant persons for a given competence. Once the relevant person has been found, users can pick up from the ROLE Widget Store a set of communication and collaboration tools that can be used to arrange a meeting or work remotely[14]. In order to avoid over estimation of the claimed competences, users will be able to provide an assessment of the competence of their coach. These peer-based assessments will then come as a complement to the self-provided proofs of competence. In this way, mutual ratings would not work as a global rating mechanism that can influence user's reputation. Indeed, shy users protective of their reputation might then refrain on providing competences that they truly own, thus lowering the amount of offers, a crucial criteria of success.

3.3   Decentralized Credit System

Providers of coaching sessions can ask in return reusable "Educational Credit Units" (ECU) using the *Credit and trades management* widget. This tool rely on the *Credit Management* service that secure transactions and safe-keep user's credits. This service will be based on the Ripple[15] decentralized credit system, which consists in a network where transactions are transmitted as IOUs[16] between trusted members, following the model of [3]. Such a decentralized credit system is more robust than a centralized system and also allows cross-communities transactions and transfers of credit. Ripple system has been initially designed by Fugger[17] to overcome the devaluation of community currencies, used in LETS

---

[12] http://smiy.sourceforge.net/cco/spec/cognitivecharacteristics.html

[13] These extensions are documented in the ROLE deliverable D4.4, see
http://www.role-project.eu/Deliverables

[14] http://www.role-widgetstore.eu/widgets/Collaborate%20%2526%20Communicate

[15] http://ripple-project.org

[16] Short for "I Owe You", informal acknowledgment of debts. See
http://en.wikipedia.org/wiki/IOU

[17] http://ripple-project.org/decentralizedcurrency.pdf

systems e.g., when some members take more than they give to the community. Moreover, [2] showed that such credit networks can bring as much credit liquidity as centralized currency systems.

This type of decentralized system however assumes the existence of a trust network, which is problematic for a cold start. A possible workaround consists in providing a temporary trusted authority to serve as intermediary for the first transactions. These authorities could be managed by the organizations hosting the CBP and would simply have to maintain a node in a credit network system and have each of their members to trust this central authority node. With trust links appearing along the process, these intermediary nodes would become unnecessary for future transactions and would not harm the ecosystem when shutting down.

4   Conclusion

From universities to professional organizations and institutions, students and corporate partners can be seen as both learners (consumers) and teachers (provider) of the competence they collect during their career. This paper introduces the ROLE Competence Bartering Platform (CBP) that offers learners to gain new competences by trading their own competences with their fellows in exchange of credit units. Technically, this platform comes as an extension of the ROLE framework that already provides the technology aimed at upgrading existing collaborative platforms towards responsive and open learning environments. To achieve a greater level of interoperability, we comply to OpenSocial and RDF standards and propose to extend them to support competence description and cross-platform exchange. To ensure that the credit units exchanged between competence providers and competence consumers are reusable across communities and along the career of learners, we propose to use a decentralized system based on credit networks. To overcome the requirement of trust links for such a system to work efficiently, local authorities can maintain a node that can serve as a temporary intermediary between peers that do not yet trust each other. Then, as trust evolves with successful transactions, the intermediary peers are no longer required for most of the exchanges. The ROLE CBP thus ties together a competence management system plugged to collaborative platforms and a decentralized credit system in order to foster the effective development of competence of the learners in a new framework we can call cloud coaching.

References

1. Boyd, G.: Editorial: Quatts, virtual currency for gaming and bartering education on the web. British Journal of Educational Technology 33, 361–363 (2002)
2. Dandekar, P., Ashish Goel, R.G., Post, I.: Liquidity in credit networks: A little trust goes a long way. In: Workshop on the Economics of Networks, Systems, and Computation (2010)

3. Ghosh, A., Mahdian, M., Reeves, D.M., Pennock, D.M., Fugger, R.: Mechanism Design on Trust Networks. In: Deng, X., Graham, F.C. (eds.) WINE 2007. LNCS, vol. 4858, pp. 257–268. Springer, Heidelberg (2007)
4. Janssen, J., Berlanga, A., Vogten, H., Koper, R.: Towards a learning path specification. International Journal of Continuing Engineering Education and Lifelong Learning 18(1), 77–97 (2008)
5. Linton, M.: The letsystem design manual (1994),
   http://www.gmlets.u-net.com/design/

Rule-Based Reasoning for Building Learner Model in Programming Tutoring System

Boban Vesin[1], Mirjana Ivanović[2],
Aleksandra Klašnja-Milićević[1], and Zoran Budimac[2]

[1] Higher School of Professional Business Studies, Novi Sad, Serbia
{vesinboban,aklasnja}@yahoo.com
[2] Faculty of Science, Department of Mathematics and Informatics, Novi Sad, Serbia
{mira,zjb}@dmi.uns.ac.rs

Abstract. Semantic Web provides huge potential and opportunities for developing the next generation of e-learning systems. Although ontologies have a set of basic implicit reasoning mechanisms derived from the description logic, they need rules to make further inferences and to express relations that cannot be represented by ontological reasoning. We implemented an adaptive and intelligent web-based PRogramming TUtoring System – Protus. One of the most important features of Protus is the adaptation of the presentation and navigation of a course material based on particular learner knowledge. This system aims at automatically guiding the learner's activities and recommend relevant actions during the learning process. This paper describes the functionality, structure and implementation of a learner model used in Protus as well as syntax of SWRL rules implemented for on-the-fly update of learner model ontology.

Keywords: Semantic Web, rules, SWRL, tutoring system.

1   Introduction

Semantic Web seems to be a promising technological foundation for the next generation of e-learning systems [1]. The main objective of the Semantic Web [2] is to describe Web resources in a way that allows machines to understand and process them. Ontology, generally defined as a representation of a shared conceptualization of a particular domain, is a major component of the Semantic Web. The initial work on implementing ontologies as the backbone of e-learning systems is presented in [3]. Since that time, many authors have proposed the usage of ontologies in different aspects of e-learning [4]. Ontologies allow specifying formally and explicitly the concepts that appear in a concrete domain, their properties and relationships [5]. Furthermore, they are especially useful in educational environments, as they enable people and/or software agents to share a common understanding of the knowledge structure.

Although ontologies have a set of basic implicit reasoning mechanisms derived from the description logic which they are typically based on, they need rules to make further inferences and to express relations that cannot be represented by ontological

H. Leung et al. (Eds.): ICWL 2011, LNCS 7048, pp. 154–163, 2011.

reasoning [6]. Thus, ontologies require a rule system to derive/use further information that cannot be captured by them, and rule systems require ontologies in order to have a shared definition of the concepts and relations mentioned in the rules. Rules also add expressiveness to the representation formalism, reasoning on the instances, and they can be orthogonal to the description logic [7]. Moreover, rules can be defined to complement and extend ontologies, in the form of expressing constraints, reacting to events/changes, discovering new knowledge, transforming data, etc.

In order to provide individual adaptation in the tutoring systems it is necessary to store the information about the learners (goals, preferences, knowledge, etc.) to be used for adaptation purposes. This information constitutes the learner model [8]. To achieve the goal of personalized adaptive learning, prior knowledge helps to distinguish what learners already know and what they do not know [9]. The learner model represents the state of knowledge of the learner in the concerned subject and helps in deciding the correct teaching strategy to be used for the learner.

In the previous works realized an adaptive and intelligent web-based PRogramming TUtoring System – Protus that applies recommendation and adaptive hypermedia [10]. This system is realized as a general tutoring system for different programming languages, but it completely tested for an introductory Java programming course. The implemented system aims at automatically guiding the learner's activities and recommend relevant links and actions to him/her during the learning process.

The learner knowledge base in Protus is represented by an overlay model in which the current state of a learner's knowledge level is described as a subset of the overall architecture. The learner model includes learner's personal information, background, goals, and learning style as well as his/her competence levels for each concept node and each unit in the content tree, and an overall subject competence level.

The main objective of the paper is to propose a new features of Protus that will allow rule-based reasoning. The learner modeling is derived from the knowledge contained in the ontology. Various conditions are captured in the body of SWRL rules. As a result of the firing of rules, updates to learner model are generated and data about learner's navigation and progress through course is collected. This data can be further used to implement the concept of adapted content and adapted navigation.

In this work we will present the Protus learner model, its architecture, ontology and SWRL (Semantic Web Rule Language) [11] rules for updating the learner model.

The rest of the paper is organized as follows. In the second section appropriate related work is discussed. Section 3 describes the used technologies. Details about learner modeling in Protus are presented in Section 4. Section 5 presents implemented SWRL rules. Section 6 brings conclusions and indicates directions of further research.

2   Related Work

Recently, a lot of research efforts have been focused on applying Semantic Web technologies to different aspects of e-learning [4]. A wide range of educational software that implements ontology-based components has been developed, but the most of these systems use ontologies only for representation of concepts, knowledge or learners data

[5, 12] while details about rule-based reasoning are omitted. A model of a web-based personalized intelligent tutoring system with a learner model is presented in [13]. That model makes use of learners' knowledge levels, psychological characteristics and learning styles in order to construct and update learner details [14].

Main attention, in agent-based approach [15], is paid to the usage of ontologies for agent communication and formal description of learning components and processing strategies. Several aspects of usage of ontologies for selecting and utilization of instructional strategies can enhance power of thinking and problem solving.

Authors in [16] described an iterative methodology in order to develop and carry out the maintenance of web-based courses. They apply association rule mining technique (*if-then* recommendation rules) in order to discover interesting information through learners' activities.

The learner model of adaptive learning system based on Semantic Web has been presented in [17]. This model mainly considers three factors including learner study style, cognition level, interest and hobby and so on. The authors used Protégé to set up learner model ontology and used data mining technology to update learner model.

Other examples of an ontology-based learner models and description of the adaptation mechanisms are presented in [18-21]. These works show that the most relevant difficulty in the knowledge modeling in e-learning systems is related to the Semantic Web structures (such as ontologies). These ontologies can be exploited not only to organize learning objects and to state their inter-relationship but also to build personalized learning paths and to maintain up to date learner cognitive states.

The most of the systems concentrate more on advancing a learner's state of knowledge than on analyzing and improving the learner's cognitive state. Besides, that does not facilitate the definition and execution of rules that provide constant updating of learner model. Architecture for learner model ontology supported by several SWRL rules is described in this paper. Such approach brings acceptable solution for the personalization process. Further we present a way of linking semantics and content, and implementation of rule-based reasoning, within learner modeling in Protus. Appropriate SWRL rules are defined and executed in order to accomplish effective and scalable learner modeling in Protus.

3   Used Semantic Web Technology

With the rapid development of the semantic web the usage of ontologies is becoming common [22]. The Ontology Web Language (OWL) [23] standard is propelling this trend toward large scale application in different domains. However, the utility of the ontologies is limited by the processing mechanisms that are smoothly integrated with this form of representation. The SWRL is proposed as an important step in this direction, building on the experience of the previous work on Rule Markup Language - RuleML [11]. Eventually the availability of standardized rule language for the semantic web will make it possible to use both ontologies and rules as a basis for innovative applications that are connected to the semantic web.

SWRL is a language targeted to introduce inference rules in knowledge models represented in OWL [24]. SWRL [11] is probably the most popular formalism in Web community. The main advantage of SWRL is the simplicity, while extending the expressiveness of OWL. Its syntax and semantics is compatible with OWL, since they are both combined in the same logical language. Most of the existing rule-based applications for the Web have adopted SWRL approach in order to express rules [25].

Protégé is ontology editor and knowledge-base framework [26]. It provides graphical user interface for easy management of ontology. The Protégé OWL Plug-in provides a SWRL editor, which enables the formalization of SWRL rules in conjunction with OWL ontologies. Other ontology can be imported to achieve knowledge reuse.

Jess is a Java framework for editing and applying rules and it contains a scripting environment and a rule engine [27]. Recently, the evolution of rule technologies on the Web has led Jess to rebound its practical value in the community of Web developers (obtains integration with paradigms like Java servlets or applets).

4   Learner Modeling

Building of the learner model and tracking related cognitive processes are important aspects in providing personalization. The learner model is a representation of data about an individual learner that is essential for an adaptive system. The system uses that data from learner model in order to predict the learner's behavior, and thereby adapt to his/her individual needs. Learner model is a collection of static and dynamic data about the learner [28]. Static data include personal data, specific course objectives, etc. Dynamic data include scores, time spent on specific lesson, marks, etc. Also, learner model contains a data about this/her performance and learning history.

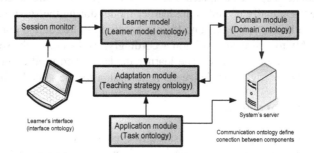

Fig. 1. Global architecture of Protus

Learner model in Protus presents crucial element of global Semantic Web infrastructure (figure 1). Educational ontologies for different purposes was included in the system, such as for presenting a domain (*domain ontology*), building learner model (*learner model ontology*), presenting of activities in the system (*task ontology*), specifying pedagogical actions and behaviors (*teaching strategy ontology*), defining the semantics of message content languages (*communication ontology*) and specifying behaviors and techniques at the learner interface level (*interface ontology*).

Data from learner model in Protus is classified along three layers [29]:

- *Objective information*: personal data, previous knowledge, preferences, etc. The learner edits this data during his/her registration on the system.
- *Learner's performance:* data about level of knowledge of the subject domain, his/her misconceptions, progress and the overall performance for particular learner.
- *Learning history*: information about lessons and tests learner has already studied, his/her interaction with system, the assessments he/she underwent, etc.

In order to accomplish successful categorization of learners we tracked characteristics of the learner and collected a variety of useful information:

- about the learner, including cognitive, affective and social characteristics,
- about the learner's perspectives on the content itself: feedback on the content, knowledge of the content (as determined, for example, by a test administered during the learner's interactions with the system),
- about the technical context of use: characteristics of the learner's environment,
- about learner's interaction with content: observed metrics such as dwell time, number of keystrokes, patterns of access, etc.

The learner model is initialized by a simple but carefully designed questionnaire which is presented to the learner in first session [10]. The initial overall competence level is decided by checking the learner grades of prerequisite courses and previous experience data, if available. The learning styles are assessed by tracking learning behavior. The learners are allowed to set and modify their learning preferences and goals [29]. The competence level of each concept is dynamically updated at each interaction, which is then used to update the competence levels of the related leaf units in the content tree. The competence levels of non-leaf units are determined.

Protus system gradually re-builds the learner model during the session, in order to keep track of the learner's actions and his/her progress, to detect and correct his/ her errors and possibly to redirect the session accordingly. At the end of the session, all of learners' preferences are recorded. The learner model is then used along with other information and knowledge to initialize the next session for the same learner [29].

4.1   Learner Model Ontology

The learner model ontology was built using Protégé and presents a means for storing personal preferences and data about the learner's mastery of domain concepts [29]. The information is regularly updated according to the learner's interactions with the content and is used by the adaptation module of Protus to draw conclusions and decisions. Figure 2. illustrates this ontology. This ontology offers the opportunity to map all information about the learner, from confidential data (password), to a knowledge evolution history. The top class of learner model ontology is *User* class, which has metadata such as Identifier, Name, Last name, Gender, Address, etc. Subclasses of the *User* class are *Teacher* and *Learner* (represent details about teacher and learner). The class *Learner* consists of: *Performance*, *PersonalInfo*, and *LearningStyle* components. These three classes are related to association through *hasPerformance*, *hasInfo*, and *hasLearningStyle* properties. Class *LearningStyle* represents the preferred learning style for particular learner, according to Felder-Silverman Learning Style Model (sequential/global, active/reflective, visual/verbal and sensing/intuitive) [30].

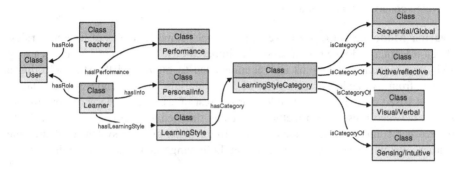

Fig. 2. Learner model ontology of Protus

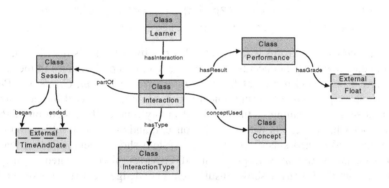

Fig. 3. Ontology for learner observation and modeling

At run time, learner interactions can be used to draw conclusions about his/her possible interests, goals, tasks and knowledge, in order to provide personalization. Ontology for learner observations should therefore provide a structure of information about possible learner interaction. Figure 3. depicts such ontology as a part of *Learner model ontology*. Learner performance is maintained according to a class *Interaction*. *Interaction* is based on actions taken by specific learner, during specific *Session*. *Interaction* implies a *Concept* learned from the experience, which is represented by *conceptUsed* property. Interaction has a certain value for *Performance*, which is in this context defined as a floating point number and restricted to the interval from 1 to 5. This ontology is responsible for updating the *Learner model ontology*.

5   Rule-Based Reasoning

Implemented ontologies have a set of basic implicit reasoning mechanisms derived from the description logic but they need rules to make further inferences and to create useful relations [31]. Thus, rule systems require taxonomies in order to have a shared definition of the concepts and relations, and taxonomies require a rule system to derive/use further information that cannot be captured by them [18].

The proposed rules consist of an antecedent (body) and a consequent (head), each of which consists of a set of atoms.

Learner Modeling Rules - This section describes some examples of inference rules. When a learner is logged in, a session is initiated based on learner specific learning style and sequence of lessons are recommended to him/her [10]. After selecting a lesson, from available the collection of Java tutorials, system chooses presentation method based on the preferred style. For the rest of the lesson, learners were free to switch between presentation methods by using the media experience bar [10]. When the learner completes the sequence of learning materials, the system evaluates the learner's knowledge degree for each lesson. Following rule updates learner model:

```
Learner(?x) ∧ Interaction(?y) ∧ hasInteraction(?x,?y) ∧
Concept(?c) ∧ conceptUsed(?y,?c) ∧ Performance(?p) ∧ ha-
sResult(?y,?p) ∧ asGrade(?p,?m) ∧ swrlb:greaterThan(?m,
1) → hasLearned(?x,?c) ∧ hasPerformance(?x,?p)
```

With the previous rule, Protus is using recorded results of learner's interaction, earned grade and data about used concepts to memorize learner's performance in the session. Variables *x, y, c, m* and *p* present *Learner, Interaction, Concept, Grade* and *Performance*. Concept presents a learning object which has been accessed by the learner in the current session. Meaning of the rule is: if in any time of the execution of Protus, exists learner which interacts with specific concept, and during that interaction he/she took the test and earned specific grade, than system should memorize that learner's performance and mark that concept as learned. Previous rule is executed when learner earn positive grade. If learner shows insufficient knowledge, next rule is executed:

```
Learner(?x) ∧ Interaction(?y) ∧ hasInteraction(?x,?y) ∧
Concept(?c) ∧ conceptUsed(?y,?c) ∧ Performance(?p) ∧ ha-
sResult(?y,?p) ∧hasGrade(?p,?m) ∧ swrlb:equal(?m, 1) →
hasExecuted(?x,?c) ∧ hasPerformance(?x,?p)
```

Previous rule marks concept as executed but learned status is still left negative, meaning that new concept that supports same learning object will be used in next iteration.

If learner does not provide required level of performance results within session with presentation method used for certain learning style category, his/her initial learning style category will be modified with following rule:

```
Learner(?x) ∧ hasLearningStyle(?x,verbal) ∧ Interac-
tion(?i) ∧ hasInteraction(?x,?i) ∧ Concept(?c) ∧ concep-
tUsed(?i,?c) ∧ ConceptRole(?r) ∧ hasRole(?c,?r) ∧ sup-
ports(?r, verbal) ∧ Performance(?p) ∧ hasResult(?i,?p) ∧
hasGrade(?p, grade) ∧ swrlb:lessThan(grade, required) →
hasLearningStyle(?x,visual)
```

Variables *x, i, c, r* and *p* present *Learner, Interaction, Concept, Concept role* and *Performance,* respectively. Meaning of the rule is: if in any time of the execution of Protus, exists learner with *Verbal* learning style which interacts with system and during that interaction he/she had accessed appropriate concept but not earned sufficient grade (required grade level is kept in global value *required*), than, learning style of that learner should be changed. Protus provides different presentation methods for 18 Java programming lessons, depending of learning style of particular learner. If initial learning style for learner was visual, than next rule would be executed:

```
Learner(?x) ∧ hasLearningStyle(?x, visual) ∧ Interac-
tion(?i) ∧ hasInteraction(?x,?i) ∧ Concept(?c) ∧ concep-
tUsed(?i,?c) ∧ ConceptRole(?r) ∧ hasRole(?c,?r) ∧ sup-
ports(?r, visual) ∧ Performance(?p) ∧ hasResult(?i,?p) ∧
hasGrade(?p, grade) ∧ swrlb:lessThan(grade, required) →
hasLearningStyle(?x,verbal)
```

Similar rules will be executed for other categories of learning styles (intuilar/sensing, global/sequential and active/reflective). The above SWRL rules can be executed using the Jess rules engine. After firing the rule engines, the inferred knowledge can be written back to the OWL repository as used to update the knowledge base. Whereas ontologies were used to increase interoperability and reusability of domain information, rules were employed to represent the adaptation logic in a way that teachers can inspect, understand and modify the rationales behind adaptive functionalities.

In our opinion the main achievements of our work are threefold:

- explicit representation of the rules, encouraging their understandability, maintainability and reusability,
- component-based definition of adaptive tutoring system that uses first-order logic to perform personalization,
- appropriate implementation of the rules in an adaptive tutoring system.

These rules represent good bases for further extension and modification in detailed modeling process. Also, the rules can be modified for specific learner modeling requirements.

6   Conclusion

Although some systems take a learner's characteristics (e.g. knowledge levels, learning styles, etc.) and needs into account, choice of right learning material or presentation method to the specific learner is especially important in order to reach the desired teaching effects. Hence, various pedagogical tactics are introduced in tutoring systems to perform personalized teaching. Intelligent pedagogical agents produce personalization based on data from learner models, teaching material, teaching methods etc.

In this paper we proposed usage of ontologies and rule languages for building learner model in Java tutoring system. Proposed architecture for building learner model completely relies on Semantic Web standards. The form of several learner model ontologies and SWRL rules for inferring and updating learner model has been presented. This ontology-based approach allows implementing adaptation customized to different requirements. The learner demand is derived from the knowledge contained in the ontology. Various conditions are captured in the body of SWRL rules. As a result of the firing of rules, updates, necessary for further adaptation to learner model had been performed.

Acknowledgements. This paper is part of the research project *Infrastructure for Technology Enhanced Learning in Serbia* supported by the Ministry of Education and Science of the Republic of Serbia [Project No. 47003].

References

1. Devedžić, V.: Semantic Web and Education. Springer Science, New York (2006)
2. Berners-Lee, T., Hendler, J., Lassila, O.: The Semantic Web. Scientific American 184(5), 34–43 (2001)
3. Mizoguchi, R., Bourdeau, J.: Using Ontological Engineering to Overcome AI-ED Problems. International Journal of Artificial Intelligence in Education 11(2), 107–121 (2001)
4. Jovanović, J., Rao, R., Gašević, D., Devedžić, V., Hatala, M.: Ontological Framework for Educational Feedback. In: SWEL Workshop of Ontologies and Semantic Web Services for IES, AIED, pp. 54–64 (2007)
5. Gascueña, J.M., Fernández-Caballero, A., González, P.: Domain Ontology for Personalized E-Learning in Educational Systems. In: The Sixth IEEE International Conference on Advanced Learning Technologies, pp. 456–458 (2006)
6. Carmagnola, F., Cena, F., Gena, C., Torre, I.: A semantic framework for adaptive web-based systems. In: Bouquet, P., Tummarello, G. (eds.) SWAP, vol. 166 of CEUR Workshop Proceedings. CEUR-WS.org (2005),
   http://www.ceur-ws.org/Vol-166/17.pdf
7. Henze, N., Dolog, P., Hejdl, W.: Reasoning and Ontologies for Personalized E-Learning in the Semantic Web. Educational Technology & Society 7(4), 82–97 (2004)
8. Kobsa, A., Koenemann, J., Pohl, W.: Personalized Hypermedia Presentation Techniques for Improving Online Customer Relationships. The Knowledge Engineering Review 16(2), 111–155 (2001)
9. Wang, F., Chen, D.: A.: Knowledge Integration Framework for Adaptive Learning Systems Based on Semantic Web Languages. In: Eighth IEEE International Conference on Advanced Learning Technologies, pp. 64–68 (2008)
10. Klašnja-Milićević, A., Vesin, B., Ivanović, M., Budimac, Z.: E-Learning Personalization Based on Hybrid Recommendation Strategy and Learning Style identification. Computers & Education 56, 885–899 (2011)
11. SWRL: A Semantic Web Rule Language Combining OWL and RuleML,
    http://www.w3.org/Submission/2004/SUBM-SWRL-20040521
12. Hee Lee, C., Hyun Seu, J., Evens, M.W.: Building an Ontology for CIRCSIM-Tutor. In: 13th Midwest AI and Cognitive Science Society Conference, Chicago, pp. 161–168 (2002)
13. Zhiping, L., Tianwei, X., Yu, S.: A Web-Based Personalized Intelligent Tutoring System. In: Proceedings of the 2008 International Conference on Computer Science and Software Engineering, vol. 05, pp. 446–449 (2008)
14. Yu, S., Zhiping, L.: Intelligent Pedagogical Agents for Intelligent Tutoring Systems. Computer Science and Software Engineering (1), 516–519 (2008)

15. Jaesoo, K., Shinn, Y.H.: An Instructional Strategy Selection Model Based on Agent and Ontology for an Intelligent Tutoring System. In: IEEE 24th International Conference on Advanced Information Networking and Applications Workshops, pp. 848–853 (2010)
16. Garcia, E., Romero, C., Ventura, S., de Castro, C.: An architecture for making recommendations to courseware authors through association rule mining and collaborative filtering. User Modeling and User-Adapted Interaction 19(1-2), 99–132 (2009)
17. Baishuang, Q., Wei, Z.: Student Model in Adaptive Learning System based on Semantic Web. In: First International Workshop on Education Technology and Computer Science, pp. 909–913 (2009)
18. Henze, N., Nejdl, W.: A Logical Characterization of Adaptive Educational Hypermedia. In: International Workshop on Adaptive Hypermedia and Adaptive Web-based Systems, vol. 10(1), pp. 77–113 (2004)
19. Brut, M., Asandului, L., Grigoras, G.: A Rule-Based Approach for Developing a Competency-Oriented User Model for E-Learning Systems. Internet and Web Applications and Services, 555–560 (2009)
20. Liu, H., Tang, S., Ma, L.: A Rule-Based Approach for Student Modeling. In: Fifth International Conference on Fuzzy Systems and Knowledge Discovery, vol. 04, pp. 526–530 (2008)
21. Zhiyong, L., Lei, L., Hui, K., Shaochun, Z., Bing, J.: An Ontology-Based Method of Adaptive Learning. In: Fifth International Joint Conference on INC, IMS and IDC, pp. 1586–1591 (2009)
22. Swartout, W., Tate, A.: Guest Editors' Introduction: Ontologies. IEEE Intelligent Systems 14(1), 18–19 (1999)
23. Tran, T., Cimiano, P., Ankolekar, A.: Rules for an Ontology-based Approach to Adaptation. In: First International Workshop on Semantic Media Adaptation and Personalization, pp. 49–54 (2006)
24. Sicilia, M.A., Lytras, M.D., Sances-Alonso, S., Garcia-Barriocanal, E., Zapata-Ros, M.: Modeling instructional-design theories with ontologies: Using methods to check, generate and search learning designs. Computers in Human Behavior 27(4), 1389–1398 (2011)
25. Papataxiarhis, V., Tsetsos, V., Karali, I., Stamatopoulos, P., Hadjiefthymiades, S.: Developing rule-based applications for the Web: Methodologies and Tools. Web Technologies: Concepts, Methodologies, Tools, and Applications 4, 456–477 (2010)
26. Protégé, http://protege.stanford.edu/
27. Jess (Java Expert System Shell), http://jessrules.com/
28. Ullrich, C.: Description of an Instructional Ontology and its Application in Web Services for education. In: Poster Proceedings of the 3rd International Semantic Web Conference, pp. 93–94 (2004)
29. Klašnja-Milićević, A., Vesin, B., Ivanović, M., Budimac, Z.: Integration of recommendations and adaptive hypermedia into Java tutoring system. Computer Science and Information Systems – ComSIS 8(1), 211–224 (2011)
30. Felder, R.M., Soloman, B.A.: Index of learning styles questionnaire (1996), http://www.engr.ncsu.edu/learningstyles/ilsweb.html (retrieved December 17, 2009)
31. Carmagnola, F., Cena, F., Gena, C., Torre, I.: MUSE: A Multidimensional Semantic Environment for Adaptive Hypermedia Systems. In: The Proceedings of ABIS 2005, pp. 14–19 (2005)

A Personalized Genetic Algorithm Approach for Test Sheet Assembling

Peipei Gu, Zhendong Niu, Xuting Chen, and Wei Chen

School of Computer Science, Beijing Institute of Technology, Beijing 100081, China
The Software Laboratory, Beijing Institute of Technology, Beijing 100081, China
Beijing Lab of Intelligent Information Technology, Beijing Institute of Technology,
Beijing 100081, China
{10812005,zniu,cxt,wchen}@bit.edu.cn

Abstract. In recent years, computer-aided test-sheet composition has become an effective method to evaluate students' learning level. To meet the needs of personalized test-sheet assembling for every student, a new test-sheet construction model is proposed. Based on the model, a personalized genetic algorithm (PGA) is proposed to assemble appropriate test sheets for individual students according to their different levels in mastered concepts of subjects. The proposed approach incorporates personalized information as preference gene bit into the crossover operator of genetic algorithm and fitness function, so as to select more non-mastered questions in the final test. In the experiments, the proposed algorithm was applied to assemble a series of items for students and the results demonstrate that the proposed approach is capable of effectively assembling personalized test sheets that meet the needs of different students and achieve good performance.

Keywords: test assembling, personalized genetic algorithm, computer-aided testing, online testing systems, test-sheet composition problem.

1 Background and Motivations

With the rapid development of information technology, computer-based testing is becoming an inevitable trend of education reform throughout the world [1]. Computer-based testing, which can provide an easy approach for instructors to evaluate students' learning level and for students to evaluate themselves, plays an important role in E-Learning systems and intelligent computer-aided instruction systems [2].

The quality of an assembled test depends on not only the quality of the item bank that is candidate set in which selecting items to compose final test sheet, but also the way how to construct the final sheet [3][6]. A test sheet is generated by manually or randomly selecting test items from item banks in many existing systems [4-5]. Those methods are inefficient and usually cannot satisfy multiple assessment requirements. To cope with this situation, intelligent test sheet generation which selects an appropriate set of items from the item bank according to multiple assessment constraints can be considered as the problem of constrained multi-objective optimization [5][7]. Hwang suggests

H. Leung et al. (Eds.): ICWL 2011, LNCS 7048, pp. 164–173, 2011.

utilizing the techniques of clustering and dynamic programming to facilitate the construction of a high quality test sheet in accordance with specified requirements [5]. Hwang *et al.* propose two enhanced genetic algorithms to compose test sheet under the constraints of specified number of test items and specified range of test item [4]. Yin *et al.* explore the use of particle swarm optimization (PSO) approach to improve the efficiency of assembling near optimal serial test sheets from large item bank for satisfying multiple assessment constraints in test sheet generation [8]. Hwang *et al.* propose Tabu search-based approach and two heuristic algorithms to get approximate test sheets [9]. Lee *et al.* propose an Immune Algorithm to improve the efficiency of generating near optimal test sheet [10]. Yang *et al.* explore a discrete differential evolution algorithm with discrete coding strategy to generate test-sheets [11]. All the above algorithms are based on Classical Test Theory (CTT). On the other hand, Item Response Theory is a different psychological and educational measurement theory which establishes some non-linear models between subjects' ability and item parameters such as difficulty and discrimination, and item parameters will not base on subject samples [12].

When a student prepares to attend public examination such as Public English Testing System (PETS) or College English Test (CET), he/she should learn related knowledge and take some quizzes. Moreover, he/she should practice simulate tests , which are of the same difficulty and discrimination degree as regular examinations and generated according to his/her learning level and preference information, before he/she takes regular examinations. The proportion of mastered items and non-mastered ones should be a variable, and varies around the selected value (percentage of mastered or non-mastered items in item sheet). The personalized simulated tests can help the student to explore his/her inner strengths and guide him/her to learn knowledge which he/she hasn't mastered.

However, the approaches proposed above which contain no users' personalized information could not construct appropriate personalized simulated tests for different students.

In this paper, we propose a model to formulate the personalized test generation problem of composing a test sheet from an item bank satisfying personalized requirements. Moreover, based on the model, we present a personalized genetic algorithm (PGA) which assembles appropriate test sheet for every student according to their different level of mastered concepts. PGA incorporates students' preference information as preference gene bits to the crossover operator of genetic algorithm (GA) and fitness function. Experiments and comparison are conducted to demonstrate efficiency of PGA.

The rest of the paper is organized as follows. Section 2 presents a model that formulates the personalized test sheet generation problem. Section 3 proposes a personalized genetic algorithm. Section 4 is the experiments and evaluation. Section 5 draws the conclusion of this paper and presents the future work.

2   Model of Personalized Test Sheet Generation Problem

In this section, the model that formulates the personalized test sheet generation (PTSG) problem for student *j* with multi-assessment constraints will be proposed. The purpose of personalized test sheet generation is to select a subset of n candidate test items Q_1, Q_2 ..., Q_n to compose a test sheet that satisfies specific requirements and levels of mastered concepts in subject for every student. In this model, each test item has three considerations including difficulty degree $diff_i$, $_{1 \leq i \leq n}$, discrimination degree dis_i, $_{1 \leq i \leq n}$ and preference information $pref_{ji}$, $_{1 \leq i \leq n}$. The specific constraints of personalized test sheet generation problem are item quantity p, expected difficulty degree $diff$ and expected discrimination degree dis.

In the PTSG problem, we assume that there are n items Q_1, Q_2 ..., Q_n in the item bank. And m concepts C_1, C_2 ..., C_m are involved in the test. The relationship of test item and concept is one-to-one. The relationship between concept and test item is one-to-many. The variables used in the formulated model are defined as follows:

- t_i, $_{1 \leq i \leq n}$: $t_i = 1$ represents that item Q_i is included in the test, and $t_i = 0$ otherwise.
- dis_i, $_{1 \leq i \leq n}$: degree of the discrimination of Q_i.
- $diff_i$, $_{1 \leq i \leq n}$: degree of the difficulty of Q_i.
- dis: the expected discrimination degree of the whole test.
- $diff$: the expected difficulty degree of the whole test.
- $pref_{ji}$, $_{1 \leq i \leq n}$: j student's preference information of Q_i, $pref_{ji}=0$ represents that student j master item Q_i, and $pref_{ji} = 1$ otherwise (detailed calculation process as (4) shown).
- $pf\%$: expected percentage of level of non-mastered concepts of subject in test.
- $Z(pref_{j1}, pref_{j2},..., pref_{ji},...pref_{jn})$: preference information for student j.

The objective function can be defined as follows:

$$\text{Min } f = \left(\sum_{i=1}^{n} |diff_i - diff| t_i + \sum_{i=1}^{n} |dis_i - dis| t_i \right) / (2 * \sum_{i=1}^{n} t_i) - Z(pref_{j1},...pref_{ji},...pref_{jn}) - 1 \quad (1)$$

where

$$Z(pref_{j1}, pref_{j2} \cdots pref_{ji},... pref_{jn}) = \begin{cases} 0.5, & \sum_{i=1}^{n} pref_{ji} t_i >= p * pf\% \\ -0.5, & \sum_{i=1}^{n} pref_{ji} t_i < p * pf\% \end{cases} \quad (2)$$

In (1), variable t_i indicates whether item Q_i is selected or not. In (2), $pref_{ji}$ indicates whether student j masters item Q_i or not, $\sum_{i=1}^{n} pref_{ji} t_i$ indicates the number of items in the test that are mastered by student j, and $p*pf\%$ represents the expected quantity of non-mastered items that should be selected in the final test sheet. When $\sum_{i=1}^{n} pref_{ji} t_i \geq p*pf\%$, $Z(pref_{j1}, pref_{j2},..., pref_{ji},...pref_{jn})=0.5$ will be in favor of (1) to optimize the genetic process to assemble more non-mastered items for student j in the test. The objective of this model is to select a subset of test items which contains the non-mastered items that amount to $pf\%$ of the subset and satisfy the expected difficulty and discrimination degree constraints.

3   Personalized Genetic Algorithm for Students

The conventional GA cannot generate appropriate personalized test sheet for every student based on the model of PTSG problem. To solve the personalized test sheet generating problem, we propose a personalized genetic algorithm named PGA which is an improved GA that incorporates students' preference information into crossover operator based on the model of the PTSG problem.

3.1   Analyzing Mastered Concepts and Questions Levels for Each Student

Preference information and learning level of the students may vary significantly. For example, student A learns very well for concept 1, 5, 6 in the subject, while student B learns very well for concept 3, 7, 8 in the subject, and concept 1, 5, 6, 3, 7, 8 has the same importance. If there is a final test just contains items correspond to concepts 1, 5, 6 and 7, B may get lower scores than A though maybe they have the same level in mastered subject.

Constructing a personalized test sheet for every student should consider the learning level and preference information. In this paper, we incorporate $pref_{jc_s, \ 1 \leq s \leq m}$, the level of mastered concept C_s for student j, into the procedure assembling personalized test sheet for student j. The definition of $pref_{jc_s, \ 1 \leq s \leq m}$ is as follows:

$$pref_{jc_s, \ 1 \leq s \leq m} = \begin{cases} 0 & , YanswerNum >= answerNum * Af\% \\ 1 & , YanswerNum < answerNum * Af\% \end{cases}. \qquad (3)$$

In (3), variable $YanswerNum$ indicates the numbers of answering the items which corresponding concept is C_s is right. Variable $answerNum$ indicates the answering items which corresponding concept is C_s numbers. Variable $Af\%$ is a percentage which indicates that when $Af\%$ items are answered right, the level of mastered concept C_s is 0 (0 represents student j has mastered the concept C_s, 1 is not).

The definition of $pref_{ji, \ 1 \leq i \leq n}$ for question Q_i which is corresponding to concept C_s is as follows:

$$pref_{ji, \ 1 \leq i \leq n} = \begin{cases} 0, & \text{if student } j \text{ answers } Q_i \text{ is right} \\ 1, & \text{if student } j \text{ answers } Q_i \text{ is wrong} \\ pref_{jc_s}, & \text{if student } j \text{ have not answered } Q_i \end{cases}. \qquad (4)$$

In (4), $pref_{ji}$ which represents the level of mastered question Q_i for student j is a preference gene bit that is incorporated into crossover operator in PGA processing.

3.2   PGA Processing

PGA processing incorporates $pref_{ji}$ in the crossover operation. The procedure of PGA is as follows:

Input: test items $Q_1, Q_2 ..., Q_n$, concepts $C_1, C_2 ..., C_m$, expected difficulty degree, expected discrimination degree, item quantity p and expected percentage of level of non-mastered concepts of subject in test $pf\%$.

a) Initialize the population $P(t_q)=\{ind_k/1 \leq k \leq ps\}, 0 \leq q \leq p_{end}$.
b) Compute fitness of $P(t_q)$ with (1).
c) Go to step *h)* if the termination criterion is satisfied.
d) Select ind_{mum} and ind_{dad} according to roulette algorithm for $P(t_q)$.
e) Crossover ind_{mum} and ind_{dad}.
   e.1) Decode ind_{mum} and ind_{dad}.
   e.2) Choose crossover situation cp randomly.
   e.3) Get question Q_i in cp of ind_{mum} and question Q_r in cp of ind_{dad}.
   e.4) Compare gene bit $pref_{ji}$ of Q_i and $pref_{jr}$ of Q_r.
   e.5) When $pref_{ji}(ind_{mum})=0$ and $pref_{jr}(ind_{dad})=1$, exchange Q_i and Q_r.
   e.6) Crossover situation cp move forward.
   e.7) If cp is the end of ind_{mum}, encode ind_{mum} and ind_{dad}, and then go to *f)*.
   e.8) Go to *e.3)*.
f) Mutate $P(t_q)$.
g) Go to *b)*.
h) Output the final item set of the test sheet.

In *a)*, ps represents the population size, p_{end} denotes maximum iterations of PGA, and q indicates the generation number of current iteration in PGA.

In the crossover operator, the exchange method between ind_{mum} and ind_{dad} plays an important role to optimize the genetic process in the personalized approach. The improved exchange pattern is in favor of assembling a student's personalized test sheet that meets the student's preference information and learning level.

The ind_k that consists of n genes is denoted as an n-bit binary string $[x_1, x_2 ..., x_n]$, where $x_i=1$ represents that the item is included and $x_i=0$ otherwise. An initial set of binary strings is randomly generated to indicate the status of each item, such as $X = [1, 0 ..., 1]$.

The genes length of every item in the ind_k depends on the bounds of the items quantity p. In *e.7)* of the improved *crossover* operator, ind_{mum} and ind_{dad} which have exchanged some questions should be encoding as binary coding scheme in order to process the next *mutate* and *select* operators.

4   Experiments and Evaluation

To evaluate the performance of the proposed PGA, a series of experiments are conducted by comparing it with conventional GA and mastered GA (MGA) in three aspects: execution time, final result quality, and final result distribution between mastered and non-mastered questions. Conventional GA which adopts the model of PTSG problem selects test items from the whole item bank to generate final test sheets. MGA that aims to generate test sheets which have good distribution in mastered and non-mastered questions conducts conventional GA in mastered question set and non-mastered question set separately. It divides into two parts: 1) select $\lceil p*pf\% \rceil$ items from non-mastered question set. 2) select $p-\lceil p*pf\% \rceil$ items from mastered question set. The objective function of MGA is

$$\text{Min} \quad f = \left(\sum_{i=1}^{n} \left| diff_i - diff \left| t_i + \sum_{i=1}^{n} \left| dis_i - dis \left| t_i \right. \right. \right) / (2 * \sum_{i=1}^{n} t_i) - 1 \right.^{\cdot} \tag{5}$$

There are totally 6000 test items and 30 concepts, which come from CETV-Web Evaluation Assessment System[1] that can evaluate students' ability, analyze students' interests and learning attitudes, used in the experiments. Degree of difficulty and discrimination of items contains 5 grades: 1.0-the lowest, 2.0-the lower, 3.0-normal, 4.0-the higher, and 5.0-the highest. The expected percentage of level of non-mastered concepts of subject in test is assumed to set to 60%, so amount of non-mastered items in the final test sheet should be approximated as 12.

There are five students in the experiments: Zhang, Wang, Wu, Li, and Chen. Moreover, the amount of mastered concepts for those students is 7, 15, 9, 21 and 25 separately. The experiments aim to compose test sheets which can satisfy the preference information and learning level of these students. Table 1 presents the distribution of difficulty and discrimination degree of items with every level. All algorithms used in the experiments are coded in Java Language conducted on a personal computer with Intel (R) Core (TM) 2 Duo CPU @ 2.53GHz and 1.93GB memory.

Table 1. Distribution Of difficulty and discrimination degree of items in every level

Difficulty / Discrimination	1.0	2.0	3.0	4.0	5.0
1.0	3.82%	4.32%	4.25%	3.97%	4.27%
2.0	3.09%	4.22%	3.8%	3.87%	3.83%
3.0	4.2%	3.72%	4.03%	3.83%	4.15%
4.0	3.87%	4.13%	4.25%	4.25%	3.88%
5.0	4.18%	3.82%	3.45%	4.07%	3.93%

Table 2. Experiment results of test assembling for Zhang

(diff, dis)	Conventional GA		MGA		PGA	
	(Diff, Dis)	V	(Diff, Dis)	V	(Diff, Dis)	V
(1.0, 1.0)	(2.55, 2.45)	1.5	(2.60, 1.69)	1.145	(2.65, 2.3)	1.475
(2.0, 2.0)	(2.3, 2.7)	0.5	(3.23, 2.67)	0.95	(2.3, 2.65)	0.475
(3.0, 3.0)	(3.4, 3.2)	0.3	(3.71, 3.46)	0.585	(3.45, 2.55)	0
(4.0, 4.0)	(3.4, 3.85)	-0.375	(3.62, 3.94)	-0.22	(3.55, 3.55)	-0.45
(5.0, 5.0)	(3.65, 3.95)	-1.2	(3.94, 3.73)	-1.165	(3.95, 3.15)	-1.45

---

[1] http://evaluate.guoshi.com/publishg/

Table 3. Experiment results of test assembling for Wang

(*diff* , *dis*)	Conventional GA		MGA		PGA	
	(Diff , Dis)	*V*	*(Diff , Dis)*	*V*	*(Diff , Dis)*	*V*
(1.0 , 1.0)	(2.4 , 2.5)	1.45	(2.44 , 1.79)	1.115	(2.75 , 2.25)	1.5
(2.0 , 2.0)	(2.55 , 2.4)	0.475	(2.90 , 3.04)	0.97	(2.45 , 2.45)	0.45
(3.0 , 3.0)	(3.25 , 3.35)	0.3	(3.5 , 3.73)	0.615	(3.5 , 3.3)	0.4
(4.0 , 4.0)	(3.75 , 3.6)	-0.325	(3.96 , 3.81)	-0.0115	(3.35 , 3.7)	-0.475
(5.0 , 5.0)	(3.45 , 3.6)	-1.475	(4.10 , 4.29)	-0.805	(3.35 , 3.8)	-1.425

Table 4. Experiment results of test assembling for Wu

(*diff* , *dis*)	Conventional GA		MGA		PGA	
	(Diff , Dis)	*V*	*(Diff , Dis)*	*V*	*(Diff , Dis)*	*V*
(1.0 , 1.0)	(2.4 , 2.45)	1.425	(2.42 , 1.81)	1.115	(2.4 , 2.4)	1.4
(2.0 , 2.0)	(2.55 , 2.4)	0.475	(3.23 , 2.71)	0.97	(2.3 , 2.4)	0.35
(3.0 , 3.0)	(3.2 , 3.4)	0.3	(3.48 , 3.81)	0.645	(3.5 , 2.6)	0.05
(4.0 , 4.0)	(3.8 , 3.6)	-0.3	(3.77 , 3.83)	-0.2	(3.55 , 3.55)	-0.45
(5.0 , 5.0)	(3.6 , 3.9)	-1.25	(4.48 , 4.10)	-0.71	(3.75 , 3.2)	-1.525

Table 5. Experiment results of test assembling for Li

(*diff* , *dis*)	Conventional GA		MGA		PGA	
	(Diff , Dis)	*V*	*(Diff , Dis)*	*V*	*(Diff , Dis)*	*V*
(1.0 , 1.0)	(2.55 , 2.5)	1.525	(2.40 , 1.77)	1.085	(2.65 , 2.4)	1.525
(2.0 , 2.0)	(2.4 , 2.5)	0.45	(2.85 , 3.10)	0.975	(2.5 , 2.4)	0.45
(3.0 , 3.0)	(3.35 , 3.2)	0.275	(3.46 , 3.75)	0.605	(2.85 , 3.7)	0.275
(4.0 , 4.0)	(4.0 , 3.1)	-0.45	(3.75 , 3.81)	-0.22	(3.6 , 3.55)	-0.425
(5.0 , 5.0)	(3.3 , 3.95)	-1.375	(4.10 , 4.31)	-0.795	(3.2 , 3.9)	-1.45

The experiments are conducted by applying conventional GA, MGA, and PGA 10 times for achieving best difficulty and discrimination degree when assembling item sheet contains 20 items for every student in every expected difficulty and discrimination level: Zhang, Wang, Wu, Li, and Chen. The initialized population size is set to 40. As Table 2, Table 3, Table 4, Table 5 and Table 6 shows, *(diff , dis)* indicates expected difficulty and discrimination level of the whole test, *(Diff , Dis)* demonstrates the best difficulty and discrimination level achieved by applying conventional GA, MGA and PGA for every student and V is average value of difference between *(Diff , Dis)* and *(diff , dis)*, that is,

$$V=(Diff+Dis-diff-dis)/2. \qquad (6)$$

The absolute value of V should be as small as possible. The *(Diff , Dis)* is best in applying three algorithms when absolute value of V is the smallest. All the experiments get bad efficiency that $V>1$ when generating test sheet which satisfy the constraints of *(diff , dis)* is (1.0 , 1.0). We assume MGA gets best *(Diff , Dis)*, conventional GA and PGA get medium *(Diff , Dis)* in experiments of selecting 20 items for Li when *(diff , dis)* are (2.0 , 2.0) as Table 5 shows. When *(diff , dis)* are (2.0 , 2.0), (3.0 , 3.0), (4.0 , 4.0) and (5.0 , 5.0), the grades distribution of *(Diff , Dis)* are: conventional GA achieves 4 best, 12 medium, and 2 worst, MGA achieves 8 best, 2 medium, and 8 worst, and PGA achieves 8 best, 4 medium and 6 worst. PGA gets more medium *(Diff , Dis)* than MGA though they get the same amount of best *(Diff , Dis)* which is twice the amount in applying conventional GA.

Table 6. Experiment results of test assembling for Chen

(*diff* , *dis*)	Conventional GA		MGA		PGA	
	(Diff , Dis)	*V*	*(Diff , Dis)*	*V*	*(Diff , Dis)*	*V*
(1.0 , 1.0)	(2.2 , 2.75)	1.475	(2.06 , 2.44)	1.25	(2.7 , 2.5)	1.6
(2.0 , 2.0)	(2.75 , 2.2)	0.475	(2.88 , 3.06)	0.97	(2.25 , 2.6)	0.425
(3.0 , 3.0)	(3.5 , 3.15)	0.325	(4.0 , 3.10)	0.55	(3.0 , 3.9)	0.45
(4.0 , 4.0)	(3.5 , 3.7)	-0.4	(4.0 , 3.58)	-0.21	(3.6 , 3.55)	-0.425
(5.0 , 5.0)	(4.05 , 3.2)	-1.375	(4.27 , 3.98)	-0.875	(3.7 , 3.75)	-1.275

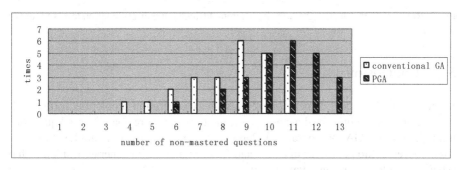

Fig. 1. Comparison of distribution of non-mastered questions assembled in a test sheet using conventional GA and PGA

The numbers of non-mastered items and mastered items are fixed in MGA (amount of non-mastered questions is 12 in these experiments). When using PGA, the amounts of non-mastered questions are more flexible (varying between 6 and 13) than MGA and more than conventional GA as Fig. 1 shows.

Fig. 2 presents the execution time using conventional GA, MGA and PGA with different difficulty and discrimination degrees of final test sheet when selecting 20 items for students. In all experiments, PGA achieves the shortest execution time satisfying all the constraints for one student. As shown, in experiments that applying conventional GA and PGA to assemble personalized test sheet for one student, improved crossover operator is proved to be effective for optimizing genetic process because that PGA can find satisfied test sheet for every student in very short time which is far less than the time consumption in conventional GA.

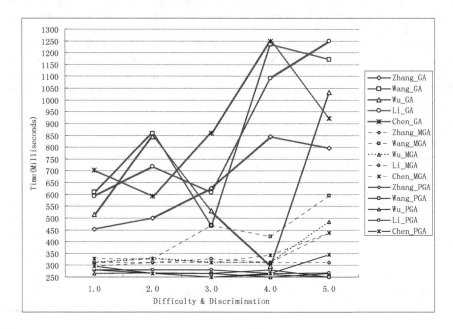

Fig. 2. Run time with selecting 20 items in different difficulty and discrimination levels for every student

5   Conclusion

In this paper, the model of personalized test sheet generation problem is formulated. And we propose an improved genetic algorithm to select more non-mastered questions in the final test. PGA incorporates students' preference information and level of mastered concepts into crossover operator and fitness function, to generate test sheet that satisfy multiple assessment requirements.

All the above experiment results show that PGA can effectively select personalized test sheet for a student, the execution time of PGA is the shortest one and the numbers of non-mastered items are flexible according to expected percentage of level of non-mastered concepts of subject.

In our future work, we will introduce some other constraints such as item score, testing time, and item type into personalized test sheet generation process. As large item banks is an inevitable trend of examination questions stock, study of generating personalized test sheet from large item banks is needed. PGA approach will be used in several normal tests which present many practice tests before official examinations.

Acknowledgements. This work was supported by Program for New Century Excellent Talents in University, China (grant no. NCET-06-0161, 1110012040112), Graduate Student Scientific and Technological Innovation Project of Beijing Institute of Technology (grant no.3070012240901), Key Foundation Research Projects of Beijing Institute of Technology (grant no.3070012231001), Graduate Students Research and Application Programs, Beijing Municipal Commission of Education (grant no.1320037010601) and the 111 Project of Beijing Institute of Technology.

References

1. Wang, F.R., Wang, W.H., Pan, Q.K., Zuo, F.C., Liang, J.J.: a Novel Online Test-sheet Composition Approach for Web-based Testing. In: IEEE International Symposium on IT in Medicine & Education, ITIME 2009, pp. 700–705. IEEE Press, Ji Nan (2009)
2. Chen, P., Meng, A.B., Zhao, C.H.: Particle Swarm Optimization in Multi-agent System for the Intelligent Generation of Test Papers. In: The 2008 IEEE World Congress on Evolutionary Computation, pp. 2158–2162. IEEE Press, Hong Kong (2008)
3. Hwang, G.J., Lin, B.M.T., Lin, T.L.: An Effective Approach for Test-sheet Composition from Large-scale Item Banks. Computers & Education 46(2), 122–139 (2006)
4. Hwang, G.J., Lin, B.M.T., Tseng, H.H., Lin, T.L.: On the Development of a Computer-assisted Testing System with Genetic Test Sheet-generating Approach. IEEE Transactions on Systems, Man, and Cybernetics. Part C 35(4), 590–594 (2005)
5. Hwang, G.J.: A Test-Sheet-Generating Algorithm for Multiple Assessment Requirements. IEEE Transactions on Education 329 – 337 (2003)
6. Tsai, K.H., Wang, T.I., Hsieh, T.C., Chiu, T.K., Lee, M.C.: Dynamic Computerized Testlet-based Test Generation System by Discrete PSO with Partial Course Ontology. Expert Systems with Applications 37(1), 774–786 (2010)
7. Cheng, S.C., Lin, Y.T., Huang, Y.M.: Dynamic Question Generation System for Web-based Testing Using Particle Swarm Optimization. Expert Systems with Applications 36(1), 616–624 (2009)
8. Yin, P.Y., Chang, K.C., Hwang, G.J., Hwang, G.H., Chan, Y.: A Particle Swarm Optimization Approach to Composing Serial Test Sheets for Multiple Assessment Criteria. Educational Technology & Society 9(3), 3–15 (2006)
9. Hwang, G.J., Yin, P.Y., Yeh, S.H.: A Tabu Search Approach to Generating Test Sheets for Multiple Assessment Criteria. IEEE Transactions on Education 49(1), 88–97 (2006)
10. Lee, C.-L., Huang, C.-H., Lin, C.-J.: Test-Sheet Composition Using Immune Algorithm for E-Learning Application. In: Okuno, H.G., Ali, M. (eds.) IEA/AIE 2007. LNCS (LNAI), vol. 4570, pp. 823–833. Springer, Heidelberg (2007)
11. Wang, F.R., Wang, W.H., Yang, H.Q., Pan, Q.K.: A Novel Discrete Differential Evolution Algorithm for Computer-Aided Test-Sheet Composition Problems. In: International Conference on Information Engineering and Computer Science, ICIECS 2009, pp. 1–4. IEEE Press, Wu Han (2009)
12. Wang, H., Ma, C.Q., Chen, N.N.: A Brief Review on Item Response Theory Models-based parameter Estimation Methods. In: The 5th International Conference on Computer Science & Education, ICCSE 2010, pp. 19–22. IEEE Press, He Fei (2010)

Fuzzy Cognitive Map Based Student Progress Indicators

Fan Yang[1], Frederick W.B. Li[1], and Rynson W.H. Lau[2]

[1] School of Engineering and Computing Sciences, University of Durham, United Kingdom
[2] Department of Computer Science, City University of Hong Kong, Hong Kong

Abstract. Student progress is critical for determining proper learning materials and their dissemination schedules in an e-learning system. However, existing work usually identifies student progress by scoring subject specific attributes or by determining status about task completion, which are too simple to suggest how teaching and learning strategies can be adjusted for improving student performance. To address this, we propose a set of student progress indicators based on the fuzzy cognitive map to comprehensively describe student progress on various aspects together with their causal relationships. These indicators are built on top of a student attribute matrix that models both performance and non-performance based student attributes, and a progress potential function that evaluates student achievement and development of such attributes. We have illustrated our method by using real academic performance data collected from 60 high school students. Experimental results show that our work can offer both teachers and students a better understanding on student progress.

Keywords: learning progress, student modeling, fuzzy cognitive maps.

1   Introduction

Teachers often need to provide students various feedbacks, including scores and breakdowns, description on what went good/wrong, and suggestions for further improvement. Most of this information can be expressed numerically and consolidated to form inputs to the e-learning systems [Li08] for generating adaptive courses. They may also form meaningful feedbacks to help teachers and students make various enhancements. However, existing work has not exploited such information well. Our paper addresses this issue. The main contributions are:

1. Proposing student attribute descriptors to mathematically model the casual relationship and the changes of both performance and non-performance based attributes of students. This sets the foundation to support student progress analysis.
2. Proposing student progress indicators to pedagogically depict student progress and development in terms of individual student and various groupings, and against teacher expectations.

The rest of this paper is organized as follows. Section 2 summarizes existing work. Section 3 presents our modeling on student progress and development. Section 4

H. Leung et al. (Eds.): ICWL 2011, LNCS 7048, pp. 174–187, 2011.

presents experimental results and discussions. Section 5 shows an evaluation of our work. Finally, Section 6 concludes this paper.

2   Related Work

Student assessment measures the level of student achievement on knowledge and abilities. The form of student assessment can be summative or formative [Osca11]. Information about student progress needs to be collected before, during and after certain learning activities [Feng09, Osca11]. Student progress can be expressed as growth rate [Stec08, Bete09] and overall improvement [Pets11]. In addition, prediction on student's future performance [Hanu05, Wiel10] can also be done. A teacher may review and enhance teaching strategy based on student progress [Stec05, Stec08].

To model student learning state, *subject specific* and *general attributes* can be considered. By considering subject specific attributes, [Chen05] evaluates how students make progress on their understanding of certain learning materials. The method runs maximum likelihood estimation on the level of understanding claimed by students against the difficulty of learning materials. [Mitr01] investigates self-assessment skills of students by identifying the reasons for a student to give up solving a problem and the ability of the student to identify the types of problems to work on. The method collects student progress based on mainly two attributes: the difficulty level and the type of problem. [Guzm07] studies the use of self-assessment tests to improve student's examination performance; the tests generate questions adaptively based on student's answers to each previous question. The method applies item response theory (IRT) to predict student's probability of correctly answering questions based on a student's knowledge level. A student is assessed based on the correctness of the answers and the probability distribution, i.e., the probability of the corresponding knowledge level, associated with each concept. Besides subject specific attributes, there are also non-subject related attributes governing student learning progress, which are referred to as general attributes. [Yang10B] studies how students learn through peer assessment. Students are asked to qualitatively assess their peers based on feasibility, creativity and knowledge, where the first two are general attributes, which respectively represent the ability to identify appropriate learning material and to come up with original ideas. [Gres10] investigates the minimal set of social behavior to be included in the brief behavior rating scale (BBRS), forming a compact progress monitoring tool for efficiently identifying the change in student's social behavior. [Limo09] shows that learning styles are critical to student learning and can help identify adaptive learning materials to students. In addition, learning styles can be evolved over time. As shown above, existing work model student learning state using a few specific types and numbers of attributes. They give students feedback on certain aspects but can hardly provide students a global picture showing how improvement can be made across different subjects or learning activities, as they do not consider that student learning progress can be governed by students' performance and development in both subject specific and general attributes as well as the causal relationships among such attributes.

To evaluate student learning progress, existing work has developed ways to collectively model knowledge and skill sets of students. For instance, [Chen01] uses attributed concept maps to represent both knowledge gained by a student after a learning activity and the teacher's prototypical knowledge. A fuzzy map matching process is then used to compare both maps to determine how well the student has progressed in the learning. [Feng09] proposes to use a fine-grained skill model to represent a set of skills hierarchically. A generalized linear mixed effects model is then applied to generate statistic information to describe the student progress on different skills. [Stec05] proposes curriculum-based measurements to intuitively monitor student progress. It monitors student knowledge and skills frequently and depicts the results graphically in order to show what progress a student has made globally over a period of time and locally among each piece of knowledge/skill, and whether such progress meets the teacher expectation. Existing work mainly identify student progress as a set of state changes made by a student regarding certain learning attributes and whether they match with the teacher expectations. However, such progress information is quite primitive. It is not sufficient to form indicators helping students and teachers make improvement on learning and teaching, unless they pay extra cognitive effort to manually extract more comprehensive progress information from the feedback. It is because learning attributes are not independent but may have certain causal relationships among each others, which can also be dynamically changed over time. In addition, at different learning stages, student progress may be governed by a different set of learning attributes. For example, a student may be expected to mainly train up with concept memorization at an initial stage rather than focusing on the ability of applying knowledge. But the situation will become in the opposite when a student is going through a mature learning stage. On the other hand, a teacher may need a higher level of student progress information, such as the performance distribution within a cohort, the portion of students meeting the teacher expectations, or whether a student or a group of students is developing certain learning skills, to support teaching strategies adjustment. Our work is developed to provide a comprehensive solution to address such complicated needs.

3   Student Progress and Development

Analyzing student progress is not trivial. Different subjects (or learning activities (LAs) [Yang10]) have different assessment criteria, where some are subject specific but some are shared among subjects. On the other hand, student learning styles and learning modes also play significant roles on how a student perform and make development in different assessment criteria. We have developed the student attribute descriptors to provide a more complete picture on student's progress and development.

3.1   Modeling of Student Attribute Descriptors

3.1.1   Student Attribute Matrix
We propose a student attribute model (SAM) (Eqs. 1-2) to incorporate both performance (PA) and non-performance (NPA) based learning attributes, forming a

unified representation to support student progress and development analysis. SAM is the foundation of student attribute descriptors. It comprises subject-related and generic outcome attributes from Bloom's Taxonomy [Bloo56] (Table 1), learning style attributes from Felder-Silverman's model [Feld88] and learning mode attributes describing whether a learning activity is an individual or a collaborative one [Gokh95] (Table 2). We have adopted these well-established models to describe student attributes as they have been widely used and verified. In practice, teachers can use only a subset of attributes to model their teaching subjects (or LAs), forming a *local measurement*, and optionally annotate attributes with subject specific names if needed. Teachers can also put together local measurements to reveal a bigger picture on the all-round performance and development of a student, forming a *global measurement*.

SAM is modeled as a dot product of the attribute criteria matrix C, which comprises criteria for PAs (C_{PA}) and NPAs (C_{NPA}), and the score matrix, which comprises scores α_{ij}. As shown in Eq. 1, each criterion is modeled as a row vector A_i, which comprises a set of a_{ij} to model the different aspects of an attribute. For attributes from Bloom's Taxonomy, each aspect corresponds to a level of complexity, while for attributes regarding learning styles and learning modes, each aspect corresponds to a characteristic of each learning style or learning mode. An aspect is modeled by a real number between 0 and 1 to represent its importance in a subject (or LA), where an aspect is set to be 0 if it is not being assessed. *To* model student learning state and teacher expectation of a subject (or LA), as shown in Eq. 2, we define a score matrix to comprise scores α_{ij}, where each score represents the level of achievement (or required effort) of an aspect of a PA (or NPA). In an e-learning system, each subject (or LA) will associate with a SAM to define the teacher expectation, while each student studying the subject (or LA) will be assigned with a SAM that is constructed by the same C to maintain his/her learning state.

Table 1. Attributes from Bloom's Taxonomy

Level of Complexity	Cognitive (Knowledge)	Affective (Attitude)	Psychomotor (Skill)
1	Knowledge	Receiving	Perception
2	Comprehension	Responding	Mind Set
3	Application	Valuing	Guided Response
4	Analysis	Organizing	Mechanism
5	Synthesis	Characterizing by value or value concept	Complex Overt Response
6	Evaluation	/	Adaptation
7	/	/	Origination

Table 2. Attributes regarding learning styles and learning modes

Learning Mode	Perception	Input	Organization	Processing	Understanding
Collaborative	Concrete	Visual	Inductive	Deductive	Sequential
Individual	Abstract	Verbal	Deductive	Passive	Global

$$C = \begin{bmatrix} C_{PA} \\ C_{NPA} \end{bmatrix} = [A_1, \cdots, A_i, \cdots, A_n]^T = \begin{bmatrix} a_{11} & \cdots & a_{1m} \\ \vdots & \ddots & \vdots \\ a_{nPA,1} & \cdots & a_{nPA,m} \\ a_{nPA+1,1} & \cdots & a_{nPA+1,m} \\ \vdots & \ddots & \vdots \\ a_{n1} & \cdots & a_{nm} \end{bmatrix} \quad (1)$$

$$SAM = \left\langle \begin{bmatrix} \alpha_{11} & \cdots & \alpha_{1m} \\ \vdots & \ddots & \vdots \\ \alpha_{n1} & \cdots & \alpha_{nm} \end{bmatrix}, C \right\rangle = \begin{bmatrix} \alpha_{11} \cdot a_{11} & \cdots & \alpha_{1m} \cdot a_{1m} \\ \vdots & \ddots & \vdots \\ \alpha_{n1} \cdot a_{n1} & \cdots & \alpha_{nm} \cdot a_{nm} \end{bmatrix} = \begin{bmatrix} sa_{11} & \cdots & sa_{1m} \\ \vdots & \ddots & \vdots \\ sa_{n1} & \cdots & sa_{nm} \end{bmatrix} \quad (2)$$

Because a student will perform independently among different aspects of the attributes, each aspect could then be considered as a random variable, which follows the normal distribution $sa_{ij} \sim N(\theta, \sigma^2)$ as shown in Eq. 3.

$$p(sa_{ij}; \theta) = \frac{1}{\sqrt{2\pi}\sigma} e^{-\frac{(sa_{ij}-\theta)^2}{2\sigma^2}} \quad (3)$$

where $p(\cdot)$ is the probability distribution function of sa_{ij}; θ is the estimation value of sa_{ij}; σ^2 measures the width of the distribution. We use *Maximum Likelihood Estimation* [Kay93] to estimate θ, where the largest probability happens when sa_{ij} equals to θ, which is proved as a correct expectation of the observed data of sa_{ij}. So *SAM* could be dynamically updated by the mean value of all previous SAMs (Eq. 4).

$$SAM(t) = \frac{1}{t} \sum_{i=1}^{t} SAM_i \quad (4)$$

where SAM_i only expresses the learning state for the ith LA. $SAM(t)$ records the overall learning state of a student after learning t LAs. Because the change between $SAM(t)$ and $SAM(t-1)$ may be perturbed by some uncertain factors and may not reflect the real student performance, we consider averaging all previous student performance to be the latest learning state of a student to reduce such an error.

3.1.2 Progress Potential Function (PPF)
To analyze the potential of a student for making progress in learning performance and for developing skills in non-performance based attributes, we have developed a PPF to form a student achievement descriptor (Eq. 5).

$$P = f(L_{PAs}, L_{NPAs}) \quad (5)$$

where $f(\cdot)$ is the PPF, P is student progress, L_{PAs} and L_{NPAs} , as shown in Eqs. 6-7, are student performance in *PAs* and the degree of balance of a student's development in *NPAs*, respectively. A student has a higher potential to achieve more if he/she can perform better in PAs and/or has a more balanced development in *NPAs*.

$$L_{PAs} = \sum_{i=1}^{nPA} \sum_{j=1}^{m_i} sa_{ij} \quad (6)$$

$$L_{NPAs} = \frac{1}{nNPA \times \sum_{i=1+nPA}^{n} m_i} \sum_{i=1+nPA}^{n} \sum_{j=1}^{m_i} \left(sa_{ij} - \frac{1}{m_i} \right)^2 \qquad (7)$$

where m_i is the number of non-zero aspects for each attribute, N_{PA} is the number of PAs, N_{NPA} is the number of NPAs, and n is the number of attributes. $1/m_i$ is the perfect probability if NPAs can be developed evenly. We normalize the values of all L_{PAs} and L_{NPAs} to be within [0,1] to allow them to be processed in a unified way. In the end, $f(\cdot)$ is given by $P = L_{PAs} + (L_{NPAs})^{-1}$.

3.1.3   Fuzzy Cognitive Map (FCM)

Existing work evaluate students' progress mainly by their subject performance (PAs). However, student learning is a complicated process. Student performance can also be affected by NPAs, e.g. an active learner tends to have better communication skills than a passive learner. In addition, both PAs and NPAs may affect among each others. To model such complicated relationships and infer changes among the attributes, we apply Fuzzy Cognitive Map (FCM), which is formulated by Eqs. 8-10, to analyze changes of SAMs and infer the causal relationship among the attributes in a SAM.

$$F_j = f\left(\sum_{\substack{i=1 \\ i \neq j}}^{n} F_i f_{ij} \right) \qquad (8)$$

where F_j and F_i are the state values of a pair of a starting attribute A_j and an ending attribute A_i, respectively. There are n attributes in total. The value of state F_j indicates the existent degree of a FCM node (i.e. an attribute). In our model, F_j reflects the overall strength of impact of an attribute on all the others, which can be formulated by:

$$F_j(t) = \sum_{\substack{i=1 \\ i \neq j}}^{n} F_i(t-1) \cdot f_{ij}(t) \qquad (9)$$

where $F_j(t)$ is the status value of attribute A_j after finished the tth LA. It is updated by the current causal weights f_{ij} from all the other attributes to attribute A_j together with the previous status values of all the other attributes. We assume all attributes having the same impact on each other at the beginning and set their initial state values to '1'. Note that f_{ij} is represented by a real number within [-1, 1] as it reflects the fuzzy meaning showing the impact degree from a starting attribute to an ending attribute, where $f_{ij} > 0$ (or $f_{ij} < 0$) implies increasing (decreasing) in the state value of a starting attribute will lead to an increase (decrease) in the state value of ending attribute. Otherwise, $f_{ij} = 0$ implies no causal relation existing between a starting and an ending attribute. The matrix of the causal weights forming the FCM is shown as follows:

$$FCM = \begin{bmatrix} 0 & f_{12} & \cdots & f_{1n} \\ f_{21} & 0 & \cdots & f_{2n} \\ \vdots & \vdots & \ddots & \vdots \\ f_{n1} & f_{n2} & \cdots & 0 \end{bmatrix} \qquad (10)$$

After a student finished the current LA, the causal relationships among attributes are re-evaluated by taking mean of the Mahalanobis distances between the current and each of all previous SAMs, which essentially captures the changes of attributes of the SAMs. Hence, the causal weights f_{ij} of FCM can then be dynamically updated. Such calculations are shown by Eqs 11-13.

$$f_{ij}(t) = \begin{cases} \frac{t-2}{t}f_{ij}(t-1) + \frac{2}{t(t-1)}\sum_{k=1}^{t-1}y_{ij}(k,t) & i \neq j \\ 0 & i = j \end{cases} \quad (11)$$

$$y_{ij}(x,t) = \frac{Sign_i \cdot d_i(SAM_k,SAM_t)}{Sign_j \cdot d_j(SAM_k,SAM_t)} \quad (12)$$

$$Sign_i = sign\left(\sum_{level=1}^{num\ of\ levels}(SA_{i,k} - SA_{i,t})\right) = \begin{cases} 1 & progress \\ -1 & regress \end{cases} \quad (13)$$

where $f_{ij}(t)$ expresses a causal weight after a student finished the tth LA and $k \in [1, t-1]$ is the index of previous t-1 activities. Since the changes of attributes are measured between the current SAM and each of the previous SAMs, after a student finished studying a new LA (i.e. a new SAM is generated), there will be $\frac{(t-1)t}{2}$ times comparisons in total. $y_{ij}(k,t)$ models how much A_j will change relative to the change of A_i between SAMs obtained at the tth and the kth LAs, where $d_i(SAM_k, SAM_t)$ is the Mahalanobis distance of these SAMs. $Sign_i$ equals to 1 if the student makes progress, otherwise it equals to -1.

3.2   Student Progress Indicators

3.2.1   Learning Attribute and Student Groups

To analyze student progress and development, we need different kinds of groupings, namely *learning attribute groups (LAGs)* and *student groups (SGs)*. LAGs are formed to support local measurement. They comprise groups to maintain subsets of learning attributes. These groups are:

- **Subject Group:** to assess subject (or LA) specific knowledge or skills. In our experiments, we maintain groups for Arts, Science and all subjects.
- **Learning Stage Group:** to assess students at appropriate cognitive levels during different stages, e.g. during an early (mature) learning stage, students are usually assessed by attributes of lower (higher) cognitive levels.

SGs are formed to support a more holistic analysis. They can be constructed manually or automatically, which include:

- **Study Group:** to divide students based on subject of study, e.g. Arts and Sciences. We also consider individual or all students as general groups. All these groups are manually pre-defined.
- **Performance Group:** to divide students based on their performance. Teachers are expected to apply their experience to define groups of best, good, satisfactory, below average, and disqualified students, which form *performance metrics* describing teacher expectations on students with different performance.

Such metrics may also be automatically generated by applying performance information from former cohorts. When analyze students' actual performance, we apply the Fuzzy C-mean clustering method [Bezd81] to divide students into groups based on their SAMs, where the student performance metrics defined by teachers form the representatives of the clusters.

3.2.2   Formulation of Student Progress Indicators

Student progress indicators are functions developed to produce information for pedagogically depicting student progress and development. There are three indicators:

- **Knowledge Construction Indicator (KCI):** Inputs of KCI are PAs, NPAs based on selected LAGs. It produces the learning status of a student with respect to certain learning stage by evaluating the updated SAM and FCM, followed by classifying the student into a proper performance group. KCI offers comprehensive information describing how a student performs.
- **Teacher Expectation Indicator (TEI):** Inputs of TEI are a set of KCI based on selected LAGs and SGs, i.e. collective information indicates the learning progress and development from a group of students. Based on the performance metrics, TEI produces a picture on how a selected group of students make progress against the teacher expectation. For instance, showing whether there are too many students perform significantly better than what a teacher expected. In such a case, the teacher may conclude the course is too easy.
- **Student Growth Indicator (SGI):** Inputs of SGI are a number of sets of PAs and NPAs of a student or a group of students from certain series of learning stages, i.e. the progress and development made by certain student(s) over a period of time. SGI evaluates PPF based on the inputs to indicate whether certain student(s) make progress or regress over time.

4   Experimental Results and Discussions

We conducted experiments with our method by evaluating the progress of 60 students from No. 83 High school of Xi'an, China. Results are collected from 4 assessments conducted on the students over last year. All students studied the same 6 subjects, including Math, English, Physics, Chemistry, Political economy, and History. Math, Physics, and Chemistry are considered as Science subjects, while the other ones are Arts subjects. Requirements of PAs and NPAs of each subject are set by the corresponding subject teachers.

4.1   Progress and Development in Different Stages

We select student S2 to demonstrate how we depict the progress and development of a student at different stages. During the *early stage*, S2 was assessed by the lower level (level 1 to 3) attributes of Bloom's cognitive domain (Fig. 1). During the *interim stage*, S2 was mainly assessed by non-subject specific attributes with a formative

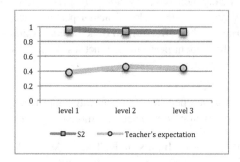 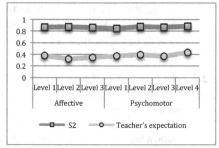

Fig. 1. Early stage performance of S2   **Fig. 2.** Interim stage performance of S2

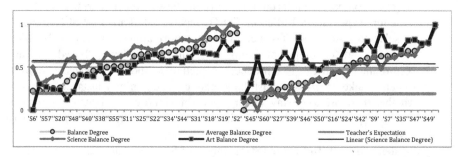

Fig. 3. Students' development in NPAs during the interim stage

assessment (Fig. 2). Such attributes included those of the first 3 levels of the affective domain and the first 4 levels of psychomotor domain of Bloom's Taxonomy. Results show that S2 performed much better than the teacher expectation in both stages. This suggests that S2 had developed the required set of learning skills very well.

Fig. 3 depicts the balance degree of NPAs of all students. The left half of the figure shows the balance degree for Science students, while the right half is for Arts students. We sorted the results based on the balance degree within each subject major for sake of readability. S2 has a more balanced development in NPAs comparing to other students. Such a balance degree is significantly above the teacher's expectation. In addition, S2 has developed a higher balance degree in Science subjects than Arts subjects. Overall, the teacher expected that S2 would not have any major problem when moving forward to later stages, and encouraged S2 to keep on studying in this way.

During the *mature stage*, the students were mainly assessed by the high levels of attributes to examine whether they had properly developed more advanced skills to handle more complicated parts of the study. Fig. 4 shows S2 had continuously performed better than the teacher's expectation. Part of the reason was S2 had built up a solid foundation during earlier stages. Fig. 5 shows S2 had scored very high from PPF, i.e. S2 had both a high progress potential in PAs and high degree of balance in NPAs. Hence, the student had developed advanced skills very well. Although scores from PPF of S2 was lower in Arts subjects than Science subjects, the scores were above average, which means S2 would likely to perform better than average students.

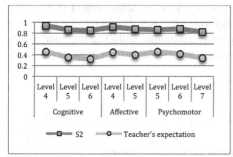

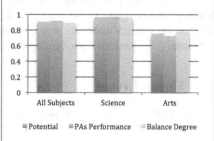

Fig. 4. Mature stage performance of S2

Fig. 5. PPF scores of S2

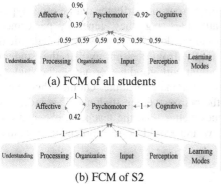

(a) FCM of all students

(b) FCM of S2

Fig. 6. Attributes causal relationships

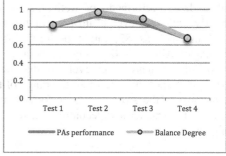

Fig. 7. Continual progress made by S2

We also construct FCM for the students to examine the causal relationships among attributes to suggest students the ways for improvement. Fig. 6(a) and 6(b) shows the FCM for all students and S2, respectively. The FCM was constructed using the high-level Bloom's attributes (i.e. domains) and the attributes from learning styles and learning modes. As shown in Fig. 6(a), if a student could make more balance development on each learning styles and learning modes, the psychomotor domain skills of the student could get improved, due to the positive causal relationships (all weights = 0.59). Once the psychomotor domain skills were improved, the student would significantly improve the cognitive domain performance (weight = 0.92) and slightly improve the affective domain skills (weight = 0.39). If the student improved the affective domain skills, the psychomotor domain skills would be significantly improved (weight = 0.96). As shown in Fig. 6(b), the FCM of S2 also had similar causal relationships among attributes, except the weights were much stronger. This means that S2 could make all-round improvement more easily than the other students in average.

Finally, we examine the continual progress and development made by S2. Four tests were conducted on S2 during the year of study. As shown in Fig. 7, S2 made similar performance and development on PAs and NPAs, respectively. Until taking test 2, S2 had been improving and had a very high level of achievement in progress. However, the progress of S2 started to deteriorate after test 2. It might be due to the fact that the subject materials were getting more complicated during the later stages. Fortunately, S2 were still performing by making an above-average progress.

4.2   Student Groups

We examine the progress and development of all students by all Bloom's attributes (Fig. 8). We classify students into different performance groups by running Fuzzy C-mean on the student attributes against teacher's performance metrics.

Each student group is depicted with a different color. We also show the number of students in each group in the legends of the figures. Fig. 8(a) and 8(b) present the results from Science, and Arts students, respectively. We mainly discuss Fig. 8(b), while Fig. 8(a) can be interpreted in a similar way. As shown in Fig. 8(b), students of the "best" and "good" types performed evenly across all attributes, while other types of students performed not well in some attributes, e.g. they generally performed poorly with the level 5 attribute of the affective domain. However, an individual student, such as S2, might perform differently from the group that the student belonged. Although S2 was classified as a student with good performance, the student also had weakness in the level 5 of the affective domain attribute. On the other hand, teacher's expectation fell into the range of the below average students. This indicates that most of the Art students performed much better than the teacher's expectation. Hence, the teacher's expectation was too low and would be recommended to adjust higher.

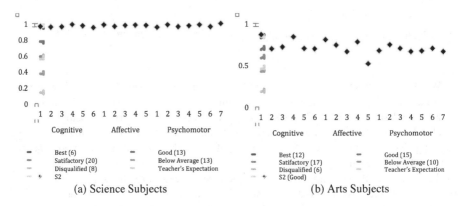

(a) Science Subjects   (b) Arts Subjects

Fig. 8. Student grouping results

5   Evaluations

Besides involved in our experiments, the teachers and students also helped evaluate our method by answering questionnaires. We have asked them opinions on our 6 parts of experiments (P1 – P6). P1, P2 and P3 concerns results describing the early, interim and mature stages of study. P4 concerns student progress over time. P5 concerns student grouping. Finally, P6 concerns the strength of impact of each attribute for different groups of students. We respectively asked opinions from teachers and students about how accurate our experiment results explain student performance and how good our results in helping students understand their performance and make improvement. We used a Likert-type scale with scores from 1 to 5 in each of the questions P1 – P6. Scores 1 – 5 means totally disagree, agree with a small part, agree with half of the experiment results, mostly agree, and totally agree, respectively. Based on the scores obtained, we normalized them within the range of [0, 1] as shown in Fig. 9 to intuitively illustrate the level of agreement by teachers and students. As shown in Fig. 9(a), the average score 0.74 shows teachers mostly agree our results explain student performance accurately. Specifically, as shown in Fig. 9(b), such level of agreement applied to both teachers of the Science and Arts subjects as they got almost the same scores. Fig. 9(c) shows opinion from students. Results show that students had a very high level of agreement (scored 0.86 in average and scores of P2 and P6 >= 0.9) that our results well depicted their performance and could help them to make improvement.

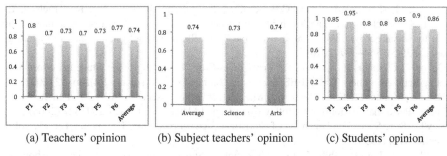

(a) Teachers' opinion   (b) Subject teachers' opinion   (c) Students' opinion

Fig. 9. Evaluation results

6   Conclusion

We have developed student descriptors, which are formed by SAM, PPF and FCM to mathematically model both students' PAs and NPAs, the changes of these attributes over time and their causal relationship. This supports comprehensive student progress analysis. We have also developed student progress indicators to pedagogically depict student progress and development in both individual and group of students setting, and also show such information against the teacher expectation. We have conducted experiments with 60 students and have disseminated information on student progress and development based on our method. Our evaluation shows that both the teachers and the students mostly agree that our method can well explain student progress and development, and the information that we depicted can clearly illustrate how a student can make improvement. As a future work, we are now working on visualization methods to help disseminate student progress and development in a more intuitive way.

References

[Bete09] Betebenner, D.: Norm- and Criterion-Referenced Student Growth. Educational Measurement: Issues and Practice 28(4), 42–51 (2009)

[Bezd81] Bezdek, J.C.: Pattern Recognition with Fuzzy Objective Functional Algorithms. Plenum Press, New York (1981)

[Bloo56] Bloom, B., Englehart, M., Furst, E., Hill, W., Krathwohl, D.: Taxonomy of Educational Objectives: Handbook I: The Cognitive Domain. David McKay & Co., Inc. (1956)

[Brus05] Brusilovsky, P., Sosnovsky, S.: Individualized Exercises for Self-Assessment of Programming Knolwedge: An Evaluation of QuizPACK. ACM Journal of Educational Resources in Computing 5(3), 1–22 (2004)

[Chen01] Chen, S.W., Lin, S.C., Chang, K.E.: Attributed Concept Maps: Fuzzy Integration and Fuzzy Matching. IEEE Transaction on Systems 31(5), 842–852 (2001)

[Feng09] Feng, M., Heffernan, N.T., Heffernan, C., Mani, M.: Using Mixed-Effects Modeling to Analyze Different Grain-Sized Skill Models in an Intelligent Tutoring System. IEEE Transactions on Learning Technologies 2(2), 79–92 (2009)

[Feld88] Felder, R.M.: Learning and Teaching Styles in Engineering Education. Engr. Education 78(7), 674–681 (1988)

[Gres10] Gresham, F.M., Cook, C.R., Collins, T., Dart, E., Rasetshwane, K., Truelson, E., Grant, S.: Developing a change-sensitive brief behavior rating scale as a progress monitoring tool for social behavior An example using the Social Skills Rating System. School Psychology Review 39(3), 364–379 (2010)

[Guzm07] Guzman, E., Conejo, R., Perez-de-la-Cruz, J.-L.: Improving Student Performance Using Self-Assessment Tests. IEEE Transaction on Intelligent Systems 22(4), 46–52 (2007)

[Hanu05] Hanushek, E.A., Raymond, M.E.: Does School Accountability Lead to Improved Student Performance? Journal of Policy Analysis and Management 24(2), 297–327 (2005)

[Kay93] Kay, S.M.: Fundamentals of Statistical Signal Processing: Estimation Theory, vol. I. Prentice-Hall (1993)

[Li08] Li, Q., Lau, R., Shih, T., Li, F.: Technology Supports for Distributed and Collaborative Learning over the Internet. ACM Trans. on Internet Technology 8(2), Article No. 5 (2008)

[Limo09] Limongelli, C., Sciarrone, F., Temperini, M., Vaste, G.: Adaptive Learning with the LS-Plan System. IEEE Transaction on Learning Technologies 2(3), 203–215 (2009)

[Mart95] Martin, J., Vanlen, K.: Student assessment using Bayesian nets. International Journal of Human-Computer Studies 42, 575–591 (1995)

[Mart07] Paek, J.P., Keene, J., Hirsch, T.: Integrated, Comprehensive Alignment as a Foundation for Measuring Student Progress. Educational Measurement: Issues and Practice 26(1), 28–35 (2007)

[Mitr01] Mitrović, A.: Investigating Students' Self-Assessment Skills. In: Bauer, M., Gmytrasiewicz, P.J., Vassileva, J. (eds.) UM 2001. LNCS (LNAI), vol. 2109, pp. 247–250. Springer, Heidelberg (2001)

[Osca11] Oscarson, M., Apelgren, B.M.: Mapping language teachers' conceptions of student assessment procedures in relation to grading: A two-stage empirical inquiry. Journal of System 39(1), 2–16 (2011)

[Pets11] Pets, Y.: A Simulation Study on the Performance of the Simple Difference and Covariance-Adjusted Scores in Randomized Experimental Designs. Journal of Educational Measurement 48(1), 31–43 (2011)

[Stec05] Stecker, P.M., Fuchs, L.S., Fuchs, D.: Using Curriculum-Based Measurement to Improve Student Achievement: Review Of Research. Psychology in the Schools 42(8), 795–819 (2005)

[Stec08] Stecker, P.M., Lembke, E.S., Foegen, A.: Using Progress-Monitoring Data to Improve Instructional Decision Making. Preventing School Failure 52(2), 48–58 (2008)

[Wiel10] Wieling, M.B., Hofman, W.H.A.: The Impact of online video lecture recordings and automated feedback on student performance. Compertes & Education 54(4), 992–998 (2010)

[Yang10] Yang, F., Li, F., Lau, R.: An Open Model for Learning Path Construction. In: Proceedings of International Conference on Web-based Learning (December 2010)

[Yang10B] Yang, Y.F., Tsai, C.C.: Conceptions of and approaches to learning through online peer assessment. Learning and Instruction 20, 72–83 (2010)

Evaluating the Student Activity Meter: Two Case Studies

Sten Govaerts, Katrien Verbert, and Erik Duval

Katholieke Universiteit Leuven
Dept. Computer Science
Celestijnenlaan 200A, 3001 Heverlee, Belgium
{sten.govaerts,katrien.verbert,erik.duval}@cs.kuleuven.be
http://hci.cs.kuleuven.be/

Abstract. In the Technology Enhanced Learning (TEL) domain, visualizations are attracting increased interest. In this paper, we present the Student Activity Meter that visualizes learner activities within online learning environments for learners and teachers to help increase awareness and to support self-reflection. We present evaluation results of two case studies with teachers, learning analytics students and experts. Results from teachers show that the visualizations can assist in creating awareness, understanding of student resource use and student time spending behavior. SAM's three visualizations were perceived as equally useful, but for different tasks. The evaluation participants also identified new metrics to extend our current set and prioritized new visualization ideas.

Keywords: Visualization, Self-reflection, Awareness, Case Study.

1 Introduction

With co-located learning in a physical classroom, learners interact directly with teachers and learners. In a digital environment, learners often struggle to position their work and to assess if it matches the teacher's expectation [3]. Teachers experience similar problems online, e.g. tracking progress and detecting learners in need. In recent years, research on learning analytics [3,1] evolved and describes measurement, tracking, analysis and visualization of data about learners. Capturing user activities is often a basis to analyze student behavior [2] and can be modeled with e.g. CAM [17] and UICO [11].

Visual analysis is a key enabler to gain insights into the learning process and provides a basis to support self-reflection, awareness and collaboration among learners or teachers [15]. Studies have shown that visualizations enable understanding [16] and discovery of patterns [2]. Our tool, SAM (Student Activity Meter), visualizes time spent on learning activities and resource use in online learning environments. An earlier study of SAM [5] with students evaluated its usability. This paper presents two case studies of SAM in real teaching and learning scenarios. We identify requirements and preferences of users and evaluate how and for which purposes they would use SAM. The first case study evaluates the usefulness for teachers. A second case study assessed the perceived usefulness of participants of a learning analytics course. Their visualization expertise provides useful feedback and the evaluation results will be used to improve SAM.

The paper is organized as follows: we first present related research, then the objectives and the design of SAM. Section 4 describes two case studies, the evaluation methodologies and results. Conclusions and future work are outlined in Section 5.

H. Leung et al. (Eds.): ICWL 2011, LNCS 7048, pp. 188–197, 2011.

2   Related Work

Soller et al. [15] identify categories of visualizations that support self-reflection, aware-ness and collaboration among learners. A first category includes systems that improve awareness of resource use, e.g. along a time-line. The second class aggregates data into high-level indicators, e.g. participation rates based on word counts, and relates this to a model. SAM visualizes and allows analysis of activities and resource use over time. Hence, it situates itself in the first, because it shows student activities over time, and partly in the second category through simple statistics on time spent and document use.

Several other systems visualize learner activities to support awareness and self-reflection. CAMera [12] is an application that visualizes user activities and simple metrics of events, e.g. mouse clicks. The system relies on the CAM schema [17] that captures user interactions with tools and resources. SAM also uses CAM data, but fo-cuses on higher-level indicators, e.g. the time spent on learning activities. Moodog [18], a Moodle plug-in, visualizes activity logs to enable learners to compare their progress and provide teachers with insights. The statistics per user or resource are presented in a table of numbers combined with bars for visual comparison. We use similar metrics as Moodog (e.g. total views and total time), but with more advanced visualizations.

Other applications visualize communication and collaboration between learners. The Participation Tool [7] uses the communication between learners to increase motivation. The Social Networks Adapting Pedagogical Practice tool, SNAPP [4], visualizes learner social networks and their interactions, in order to understand the participation and per-formance. Larusson et al. [10] visualize blogging activity, e.g. conversations.

Although systems mentioned above use visualizations to support awareness, self-reflection and collaboration, only a few studies have been conducted that assess the usefulness of visualizations for teachers and learners in real-life scenarios. In this paper, we present case studies that present first insights into how and why teachers and learners would use visual analysis systems in real-life to increase awareness and self-reflection.

3   Objectives and Design

3.1   Objectives

SAM can be used by both teachers and learners in personal learning environments (PLE) [6], which are user customizable learning environments that allow creation and mashup of resources and tools. PLEs are often used in self-regulated learning where self-monitoring and self-reflection is important [19].

First, we describe briefly the teacher objectives of SAM, which are important for both case studies of Section 4.1. Then, we discuss learner goals, which are assessed in the learning and knowledge analytics (LAK) course case study (see Section 4.2).

Teacher goals. SAM provides support for the following teacher objectives:

- *Awareness for teachers* of what and how learners are doing is important to assess learner progress. This is difficult in online and distant courses due to lack of face-to-face communication. SAM provides visual overviews of the time learners spent

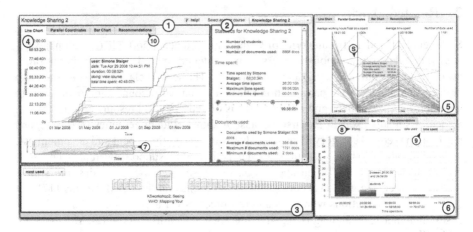

Fig. 1. The user interface with the three different visualizations

and the resources they use. Both are good indicators for awareness [8]. The visualizations can be used by teachers to find patterns and spot potential problems.

- *Time tracking* information allows teachers to assess their initial time estimates with the real time spending of students and find the exercises that consume most time.
- *The resource usage* can show the popular learning materials and enables resource discovery, through a list of most used or most time spent on resources in SAM.

Learner goals. SAM targets the following objectives for learners:

- *Self-monitoring* can provide self-reflection and awareness. SAM visualizes when, on which resources and how long learners have been working in comparison to their peers. Discovery of averages and trends in the monitoring data is also possible.
- *Time tracking* can help the learner to understand his time allocation compared to his peers and assist sometimes to report time spending to the teacher.
- *Resource recommendation* provides related interesting learning material used by their peers. This can be especially useful in self-regulated learning.

3.2 Visualizations and Design

Fig. 1 shows the visualizations that SAM provides in teacher mode (see box 1). In learner mode, the user is highlighted in green for fast lookup. Three visualizations were iteratively designed using paper mockups. SAM is a fully implemented web application and is independent of a learning environment. SAM relies on CAM [17] data for interoperability. For both case studies[1] CAM data was generated from Moodle logs.

---

[1] The tool is available at http://ariadne.cs.kuleuven.be/
monitorwidget-cgiar for the CGIAR case study and at
http://ariadne.cs.kuleuven.be/
monitorwidget-lak11 for the LAK case study.

The statistics of global time spent and document use are shown in box 2 in Fig. 1. Next to the actual numbers, a graphical view is presented with color-coding.

The recommendation pane presents a list of the top most used resources or those on which the most time was spent (box 3). The 'Recommendations' tab (see label 10) contains an animated tag cloud of the recommendations. We opted for a tag cloud, because the information-seeking task is not clearly defined and exploratory [14].

The line chart (vis. 4) shows a line for every student, connecting all the timestamps with the cumulative amount of time spent. The horizontal axis shows the date and the vertical axis the total time spent. The inclination of the line shows the student's effort. A steep line means an intensive working period. A flat line shows inactivity. The selected student (in red) has been working hard from March to May 2008, then idled until September, when he re-started again. For more details, a specific period can be selected the small chart below (see label 7). The chart enables teachers and learners to compare with similar learners and to find out on what activities or resources they spent their time.

Parallel coordinates [13] (vis. 5) are a common way to visualize high dimensional data. The vertical axes represent: the median of the time of day that students work, the total time spent on the course, the average time spent on a resource and the number of resources used. A learner is shown as a polyline where the vertex on the ith axis corresponds to the ith data point. The yellow line shows a calculated average student for comparison. The selected student, S, works preferably in the afternoon, spends the 2nd most time in total and uses many resources for a bit above average time. This is a more advanced visualization that can provide an overview of the tendencies.

The bar chart (vis. 6) shows the student distribution for the total time spent and the resources used. The bar chart allows grouping of students and provides a visual impression of the distribution. One can drill down in the data by clicking on a specific bar. The slider (see label 8) and the drop-down list (see label 9) at the top right allow to change respectively the number of bins and the metric. The bar chart allows to better understand the distributions, group the learners and to grasp the overall course state.

4 Case Studies and Evaluation

Two case studies are presented: the agroforestry courses of CGIAR[2] and the open online course of Learning and Knowledge Analytics (LAK)[3].

4.1 The CGIAR Case Study

In this case study, we applied the design based research methodology [9]. We presented SAM to teachers to evaluate whether SAM could assist teachers with their teaching tasks and whether the functionalities of SAM would be useful for them.

Evaluation Setup and Demographics. Nineteen CGIAR teachers, teaching different agroforestry and science related courses on the same Moodle[4] system, were contacted.

---

[2] CGIAR - Consultative Group on International Agricultural Research, http://cgiar.org

[3] LAK course, http://scope.bccampus.ca/course/view.php?id=365

[4] Moodle, http://www.moodle.org

Table 1. Table of the Likert scale analysis of the teaching issues and the issues addressed by the tool (IQR=InterQuartile Range)

(a) The CGIAR case study

	Issues				Addressed by tool			
	Mode	Median	Range	IQR	Mode	Median	Range	IQR
Provide feedback to the students	5	5	3	1	4	3	4	2
Being aware of what the students are doing	4	4	3	1	4	4	2	1
Knowing about collaboration and communication *	3	4	3	2	1	2	3	2
Knowing which documents are used and how much	4	4	3	1	4	4	3	1,25
Knowing how and when online tools have been used	3	3	4	1,25	4	4	4	1
Finding the students who are not doing well	4	4	4	1	3	3,5	4	1
Finding the best students	4	3	4	2	4	3	4	2
Knowing how much time students spent	4	3	4	2	5	5	3	1
Knowing if external learning resources are used	4	4	4	2	3	3	4	0

(b) The LAK case study

	Issues				Addressed by tool			
	Mode	Median	Range	IQR	Mode	Median	Range	IQR
Provide feedback to the students	5	5	0	0	4	4	1	0
Being aware of what the students are doing	4	4	2	0,75	3	3	3	0,75
Knowing about collaboration and communication *	4	4,5	1	1	2	2,5	3	1,75
Knowing which documents are used and how much	5	4	4	1,5	3	2,5	3	1
Knowing how and when online tools have been used	1	2	3	2,75	4	3,5	4	2,5
Finding the students who are not doing well	5	5	2	0,75	4	3	3	1,5
Finding the best students	3	3	3	0,75	1	2,5	3	1,75
Knowing how much time students spent	4	3,5	4	1	5	3,5	4	1,75
Knowing if external learning resources are used	4	3,5	3	1	3	3	3	1,5

Due to low availability and bad Internet connection in third world countries, only three teachers responded. To increase participation, we contacted computer science (CS) and law professors and teaching assistants (TA). These teachers were not involved in the visualized courses, but as teachers they could still provide valuable feedback. In total, 20 persons participated: 3 agricultural, 2 law, 8 CS teachers and 7 CS TA's, of which 6 females and 14 males, between 24 to 66 years old. Nine teach less than 5 years.

The online survey inquired about the usefulness through a detailed study with Likert items, eight open free-text questions and multiple yes/no-questions on usage intentions. Although many usability surveys are available, we designed our own survey to enable a qualitative study on how teachers use SAM and it assists them.

Evaluation Results. With Google Analytics[5] the use of SAM was tracked. The 20 users visited SAM 48 times, spending 40 minutes on average. When removing two outliers, who probably kept their browser open, the average time spent is 29.5 minutes. First, the respondents rated 9 5-scale Likert items about teaching issues (*'1 - not relevant'* to *'5 - very important'*). Afterwards, we asked to rate whether the same issues could be addressed by the tool (*'1 - impossible'* to *'5 - definitely'*). This way the real needs of the teachers can relate back to how they perceive SAM addresses these problems.

Table 1a shows the Likert scales on teaching needs and the needs SAM addresses according to the teachers. The most important issue for teachers is to provide feedback. They also grade 'being aware of what students do' and 'knowing which documents are used and how much' as important, followed closely by 'finding students who are not doing well'. The questions on resource use are rated equally important to finding students

---

[5] Google Analytics, http://analytics.google.com

Table 2. Table of the Likert scale analysis of usefulness of the visualizations of the CGIAR and LAK case study (IQR=InterQuartile Range)

	CGIAR				LAK			
	Mode	Median	Range	IQ R	Mode	Median	Range	IQ R
Line Chart	4	4	3	0,25	3	3,5	3	1
Parallel Coordinates	4	4	4	1	3	3	3	1
Bar Chart	4	4	3	1	3	3	4	1,25

in trouble. 'Finding the best students' and 'Knowing how much time is spent' is less important, but still above average. The usage of online tools is only rated as moderately interesting. 'Knowing about collaboration and communication' (the 3rd row with *) is something that we think cannot be solved by SAM, but is added to check a possible bias. The difference in responses from teachers and TA's has been statistically tested with Mann-Whitney's U tests. This uncovered that giving feedback is more important for teachers than for TA's (mean ranks of teachers = 12.19 and TA's = 7.36; U = 23.5, Z = -2.16, p = 0.02, r = 0.48). TA's find collaboration significantly less important than teachers (mean ranks of teachers = 12.73 and TA's = 6.36; U = 16.5, Z = -2.40, p = 0.01, r = 0.54). The results show that the awareness goal (see Section 3.1) (through 'provide feedback to students' and 'being aware of what students are doing') and resource use (through 'knowing which documents are used' and 'knowing if external resources are used') are rated as important. Time tracking is less important, but still above average.

From the addressed issues in Table 1a, the collaboration issue (the 3rd row with *), used to check a bias, is rated the lowest as expected. However, the participants did not fully agree (high range and IQR). The highest rated was 'knowing how much time students spent', which is easily derived from the statistics window. 'Awareness of what students are doing' was also rated as high. 'Providing feedback to the students' scores a bit lower (mode = 4, median = 3, high range & IQR), potentially because it often requires more performance details, such as grades. For resource use, 'knowing which documents are used and how much' is rated quite high, as well as for the online tools, although the range is high. The external resource usage is indecisive. Finding students in trouble and the best students was also rated rather low. Some participants argued that time spending and resource usage is insufficient and that in most cases quantitative data does not demonstrate that students learned. Currently SAM provides only basic insights and can be improved by richer data, if available (e.g. grades), and additional visualizations. Comparing the results to the teacher goals, SAM handles the time tracking goal. The highly rated awareness goal has been partially met through 'Awareness of what students are doing', but can be improved. The resource use goal has been mostly met, but can be improved by differentiating external resources.

Table 2 assesses the usefulness of each visualization using 5-scale Likert items ('*1 - not useful at all*' to '*5 - very useful*'). The line chart scores highest, than the bar chart and than the parallel coordinates. Two participants rated parallel coordinates as useless.

We also inquired why participants would use the different charts with open questions. They indicated that the time spending patterns are important to control the workload evolution during the course and to see when students really start working. Six persons use it to detect outliers for assistance. Three teachers look for dropouts and three use the line chart to learn about the behavior and progress. Most of the use of the line chart is related to the awareness, finding students in trouble and time tracking issue. The parallel coordinates are used by eight users to obtain a quick course overview and to compare students with more parameters than time only. Four persons like to compare students with the average student. Teachers also mentioned that it could be used for finding outliers, finding patterns and gaining a clearer overview on the student distributions per metric. The parallel coordinates are apparently more used to get a course overview and some teachers can detect students who need assistance. The bar chart is used by eight persons to check the student distribution and get a course overview. Six users use the bar chart to find outliers. Some teachers indicate uncertainty whether the outliers are really doing well or experiencing problems. The bar chart is also used for a course overview and awareness, but also for resource use. Only 5 teachers found the current resource recommendations useful. Teachers want to understand the resource use and are not interested in recommendations as such. The tag cloud was not always clear and some would prefer a list combined with statistics. Two stated that the recommendations might be more useful for students and 14 want to give SAM to their students.

The participants also proposed new features to improve SAM in another open question. Drilling down in the data (e.g. to obtain a list of students or documents in a bin in the bar chart) and to have more search capabilities (e.g. find a specific student) would be welcome. They also requested a wider range of metrics (e.g. the number of times a student works on the course was proposed) in the bar chart and parallel coordinates. The latter would also benefit from configurable axes (which we implemented for the LAK case study, see Section 4.2). Teachers want to access the details of every student.

When asked what insights they gained from SAM, three said that time spent was a good indicator for effort. Three understood the course workload and usage better, and two would like to use SAM for course design optimization. Three teachers understood the student distributions and found outliers. Eight participants would want to use it to increase awareness and obtain a course overview. Four would use it for statistical analysis and two for a course evaluation. 18 out of 20 would like to use it in their own courses and three requested to obtain the tool. From the teachers' eagerness to use SAM in their own courses, we can conclude that they perceive the added value for them.

4.2   The Learning and Knowledge Analytics Case Study

We also applied SAM in a large online open course on learning analytics. This way an audience active in the learning analytics domain can give feedback on SAM.

Evaluation Setup and Demographics. The Learning and Knowledge Analytics (LAK) online course was organized in collaboration with the International Conference on Learning Analytics and Knowledge [1]. Moodle was used extensively for communication and collaborations via forums. We visualized the user activities of the Moodle system in SAM. 270 participants registered for the course. The participants are researchers active in the learning analytics field and/or teachers interested in learning analytics. Evaluating SAM in this diverse test bed triggered interesting discussions[6].

We again used an online survey but with two paths: one for all users and one for teachers. The path for teachers is identical to the CGIAR case study to allow comparison. Some additional questions were added. In this case study we wanted to get more details on the use of SAM in a large course and the perceived usefulness of SAM by learning analytics experts. Twelve people, between 27 and 62 years old, completed our survey. Six of them are teaching courses and five for more than 10 years.

Evaluation Results. We first discuss the results of the teachers. Six teachers rated the relevancy of the same 9 teaching issues as in the CGIAR case study in Section 4.1. Table 1b shows that LAK teachers perceive teaching issues slightly different than the CGIAR teachers. The most important issue is again 'providing feedback to students'. The LAK teachers are very interested in finding students who are not doing well. Finding the best students is less important than in the CGIAR case. Both LAK and CGIAR teachers want to understand the document use. 'Knowing how and when online tools have been used' and 'knowing if external resources are used' is rated a bit lower. So they are probably more interested in the document use within Moodle. 'Student awareness' is also rated high. Collaboration and communication is more important for LAK teachers. The time tracking issue is almost rated the same. Comparing with the teacher goals (see Section 3.1), we see that awareness and resource is again the most important.

Table 1b depicts that LAK teachers are more convinced that SAM addresses the 'providing feedback to students' issue. This might be related to their expertise in visual analytics. The time spending issue is scoring the second best, but this is less convincing as in the CGIAR case. On most other issues the teachers are indecisive (most medians about 3). The second part of the survey was targeted at both teachers and learners. When asked to assess the contribution of each visualizations, indecisive answers came out as well (all mode & median around 3), see Table 2. There is no statistical evidence that teachers and learners would rate the visualizations differently.

The open questions on how to apply each of the visualizations gave better insights on the use of SAM. One teacher would use the line chart to detect the participation intensity and tendency. Another teacher can learn about 'chronological course dwell time'. The line chart can also be used to verify the classroom activity status. The teacher would expect it to be normal if few students participate much and few participate very little, while most are in the center. A student uses it for comparison with his peers. Three students use the parallel coordinates for comparison with the rest of the class for self-reflection, to measure progress and to increase motivation. One person did not understand how the parallel coordinates worked. He liked the bar chart to find the group where he fits in. The bar chart was perceived as a bit redundant by one teacher, maybe due to the addition of the histograms on the parallel coordinates.

Seven out of nine users find the recommendations useful. Eight want to continue using SAM and four are unsure. In an open question on what they liked about SAM, three mentioned its simplicity and the multitude they can observe. Two enjoyed the tool's speed. Two participants liked the accurate, detailed time information and the insight

---

[6] http://scope.bccampus.ca/mod/forum/discuss.php?d=16525

and motivation it provides. Although results of Table 1b and 2 are hard to interpret, we can derive from the open questions and willingness to continue using SAM that most LAK users, perceive it as useful for different tasks. The study was affected by the incomplete user activity data of some users, who studied outside of the Moodle system.

Two learning analytics experts requested more details on forum use (e.g. comments in a time period), maybe due to the course's extensive forum use. Next, we asked them to prioritize visualization ideas from the CGIAR case study. From most desired to least, these are the results: (1) visualization on content creation by students, (2) used resource types visualization, (3) detailed statistics of used resources, (4) comparison of the actions of two students and (5) detailed student information. Some ideas can be embedded in the parallel coordinates, e.g. metrics on content creation and resource types.

5   Conclusion and Future Work

We presented SAM, a visualization tool to provide an overview of activities in a virtual classroom and to enable both students and teachers to explore user activities and find patterns, contributing to awareness and self-monitoring. We evaluated the effectiveness of SAM to assess what works well in two real-world settings. The CGIAR case study shows that SAM contributes to creating awareness for teachers, as evidenced by the survey results. SAM meets the time tracking goal. The resource use can be improved by differentiating internal and online resources. Overall, teachers would like more statistics. Currently, we focus on resource access and time spent [8], but other metrics can be easily added. In both case studies, test subjects reported various strategies to become aware of student activities, e.g. the parallel coordinates are used to get an overview and the line chart is used to detect outliers. SAM's three visualizations were perceived as useful in the CGIAR case and 18 out of 20 teachers would like to use SAM in their own courses. This confirms that SAM provides useful functionality for teachers.

The results from the Likert scales in the LAK case study are indecisive. From the open questions, we learned that the LAK participants employed SAM to come to similar conclusions, e.g. find outliers. Generally, they also perceived SAM as useful for various tasks. Missing data for learners who spent most of their time offline also affected the results. The learning analytics experts provided new ideas, e.g. statistics on content creation. The users of the CGIAR case also proposed new features related to finding students and drilling down in the data. They also requested additional metrics to improve awareness, which can be easily added to the parallel coordinates and bar chart.

After extending SAM, we want to re-evaluate it with teachers. A large evaluation with students allowing the effects of SAM over time is also planned in an engineering course. Several institutes requested to use SAM in the LAK course. Tallinn University[7] would like to use SAM to visualize all their Moodle courses for teachers. In this way, we are confident that we will be able to carry out larger scale evaluations in the future.

Acknowledgements. This research is funded by the European Commission's Seventh Framework Programme (FP7/2007-2013) under grant agreement no 231396 (ROLE). Katrien Verbert is a Postdoctoral Fellow of the Research Foundation - Flanders (FWO).

---

[7] Tallinn University, http://www.tlu.ee/

References

1. 1st International Conference on Learning Analytics and Knowledge 2011 (February 2011), https://tekri.athabascau.ca/analytics/
2. Allendoerfer, K.R.: How information visualization systems change users' understandings of complex data. Ph.D. thesis, Drexel University (2010)
3. Blakelock, J., Smith, T.E.: Distance learning: From multiple snapshots, a composite portrait. Computers and Composition 23(1), 139–161 (2006)
4. Dawson, S., Bakharia, A., Heathcote, E.: Snapp: Realising the affordances of real-time SNA within networked learning environments. In: Proceedings of the 7th International Conference on Networked Learning 2010, pp. 125–133 (2010)
5. Govaerts, S., Verbert, K., Klerkx, J., Duval, E.: Visualizing Activities for Self-Reflection and Awareness. In: Luo, X., Spaniol, M., Wang, L., Li, Q., Nejdl, W., Zhang, W. (eds.) ICWL 2010. LNCS, vol. 6483, pp. 91–100. Springer, Heidelberg (2010)
6. van Harmelen, M.: Personal learning environments. In: ICALT 2006: Proc. of the 6th IEEE Int. Conf. on Advanced Learning Technologies, pp. 815–816. IEEE Computer Society (2006)
7. Janssen, J., Erkens, G., Kanselaar, G., Jaspers, J.G.M.: Visualization of participation: Does it contribute to successful computer-supported collaborative learning? Computers & Education 49(4), 1037–1065 (2007)
8. Keith, T.Z.: Time spent on homework and high school grades: A large-sample path analysis. Journal of Educational Psychology 74(2), 248–253 (1982)
9. Kelly, A.: Design research in education: Yes, but is it methodological? Journal of the Learning Sciences 13(1), 115–128 (2004)
10. Larusson, J.A., Alterman, R.: Visualizing student activity in a wiki-mediated co-blogging exercise. In: CHI 2009: Proceedings of 27th International Conference on Human Factors in Computing Systems, pp. 4093–4098. ACM (2009)
11. Rath, A.S., Devaurs, D., Lindstaedt, S.N.: UICO: an ontology-based user interaction context model for automatic task detection on the computer desktop. In: Proc. of the 1st Workshop on Context, Information and Ontologies, CIAO 2009, pp. 8:1–8:10. ACM (2009)
12. Schmitz, H.-C., Scheffel, M., Friedrich, M., Jahn, M., Niemann, K., Wolpers, M.: CAMera for PLE. In: Cress, U., Dimitrova, V., Specht, M. (eds.) EC-TEL 2009. LNCS, vol. 5794, pp. 507–520. Springer, Heidelberg (2009)
13. Siirtola, H., Laivo, T., Heimonen, T., Raiha, K.-J.: Visual perception of parallel coordinate visualizations. In: IV 2009: Proc. of 13th Int. Conf. of Info. Visual, pp. 3–9. IEEE (2009)
14. Sinclair, J., Cardew-Hall, M.: The folksonomy tag cloud: when is it useful? Journal of Information Science 34, 15–29 (2008)
15. Soller, A., Martínez-Monés, A., Jermann, P., Muehlenbrock, M.: From mirroring to guiding: A review of state of the art technology for supporting collaborative learning. I. J. Artificial Intelligence in Education 15(4), 261–290 (2005)
16. Thomas, J.J., Cook, K.A.: Illuminating the Path: The Research and Development Agenda for Visual Analytics. National Visualization and Analytics Ctr (2005)
17. Wolpers, M., Martin, G., Najjar, J., Duval, E.: Attention metadata in knowledge and learning management. In: Proceedings of I-Know 2006: 6th International Conference on Knowledge Management, pp. 1–8 (2006)
18. Zhang, H., Almeroth, K., Knight, A., Bulger, M., Mayer, R.: Moodog: Tracking students' online learning activities. In: Proc. of World Conf. on Educational Multimedia, Hypermedia and Telecomm. 2007, pp. 4415–4422. AACE, Vancouver (2007)
19. Zimmerman, B.J.: Becoming a self-regulated learner: An overview. Theory Into Practice 41(2), 65–70 (2002)

Antecedents of Students' Intent to Watch Online Theory Videos as Part of an Online Learning Platform

Frank Geert Goethals, Loïc Plé, and Maxime Taisne

IESEG School of Management (LEM-CNRS), 3 Rue de la Digue, 59000 Lille, France
{f.goethals,l.ple,m.taisne}@ieseg.fr

Abstract. Our research project identifies antecedents of students' intention to voluntarily watch online theory videos available through an online learning platform. This paper extends the classic UTAUT by introducing the student year in the model next to three constructs that were derived from literature on student satisfaction with classic (offline) classes: perceived content usefulness, perceived e-learning enjoyment and facilitating conditions. Statistical tests (on a dataset of 766 students in three different years) show these four new constructs are statistically significant antecedents of the students' intent to use the new feature. The *perceived content usefulness* and *perceived e-learning enjoyment* seem as important as the main UTAUT constructs *performance expectancy* and *effort expectancy*. The R^2 of our model is considerably higher than that of the UTAUT when applied to our dataset. We also detect moderating effects.

Keywords: UTAUT, perceived content usefulness, e-learning enjoyment.

1   Introduction

Over the last few years educational institutions have faced the rise of a so-called "Virtual Generation" (V-Gen) [1]. Institutions and thus professors have increasingly adapted their curricula and teaching modes to align with strong evolutions in the students' learning behavior. This resulted in relying more and more on technologies in the way that courses are delivered. However, many studies have shown counter-intuitive results. Students do not systematically use virtual learning systems (including online learning platforms, podcasts, online videos, etc.) when these are put at their disposal [2]. Students may even present high resistance to the implementation of such technologies in their courses, which is quite paradoxical given the macro-environment that they are evolving in (daily and usually heavy use of online services such as YouTube, Facebook, etc.) [3]. Scholars underline that many factors may affect the students' motivation to use such systems, and call for exploring motivational antecedents in greater depth.

This paper aims to contribute to this debate by investigating the antecedents of student's motivation to watch online theory videos. Here, we draw specifically on the Unified Theory of Acceptance and Use of Technology (UTAUT) to build a new model that includes new antecedents of the intention to use the system. Contrary to

H. Leung et al. (Eds.): ICWL 2011, LNCS 7048, pp. 198–208, 2011.

previous research, our adapted model integrates knowledge from (non-IS) literature on student satisfaction with traditional (offline) classes, since we argue that the constructs developed in this literature are valuable in explaining students' intent to use online theory video considered as features of an online learning platform.

Our study focuses on a French school of management that introduced a new Online Learning Platform (OLP) in September 2010, which made it possible to include online theory videos in the courses from that moment. The results show an elevation of the R^2 of the UTAUT, and accordingly enable to identify guidelines for the development of online theory videos as part of an OLP. In a broader way, they also provided hints to enhance some teaching methods and contents, improve change management practices and to better evaluate professors who use such systems.

Given the page limitations and our will to focus on new findings, the literature review is integrated with the hypotheses-building section.

2   Research Model and Hypotheses

The Unified Theory of Acceptance and Use of Technology (UTAUT) developed by Venkatesh et al. [4] builds upon the TAM (Technology Acceptance Model) and many other theories (such as the Theory of Planned Behavior [5]) and is considered in modern literature as a more complete model. The UTAUT unifies the general determinants of system appreciation (e.g. performance expectancy, facilitating conditions and effort expectancy) with individual-related variables such as gender, age or experience using the system and social influences. Given the fact that prior research on the UTAUT showed a clear postive relation between behavior intention and actual use behavior [4], our goal is to get more insight into antecedents of intention to use.

Figure 1 shows the research model. Hypotheses H1 till H9 are directly derived from the UTAUT. They involve well known constructs such as performance expectancy (PE), effort expectancy (EE) and social influence (SI) and the moderating effects of gender and voluntariness. These are considered to be well known antecedents of behavioral intention (BI). Hence, we will not explain these hypotheses in this paper. We here turn to the shortcomings of the UTAUT identified on the basis of a literature study outside the IS field, namely from theory on antecedents of students' satisfaction with (traditional offline) classes. We here investigate whether variables that lead to high satisfaction with a class have online equivalents leading to a higher intent to use a system that supports a class.

First, the UTAUT contains a variable that measures the usefulness of the system via the Effort Expectancy construct, but that construct only measures the usefulness of the system, not of the movies' content. The perceived usefulness of offline training has a major impact on the satisfaction with training [7]. This refers to the extent to which participants believe the training provides them with skills and knowledge that are useful for their (future) job [8, 9, 10]. We therefore introduce a new construct, the *perceived content usefulness* (PCU) and hypothesize:

H.10: The higher the perceived content usefulness, the higher the intention to use the system.

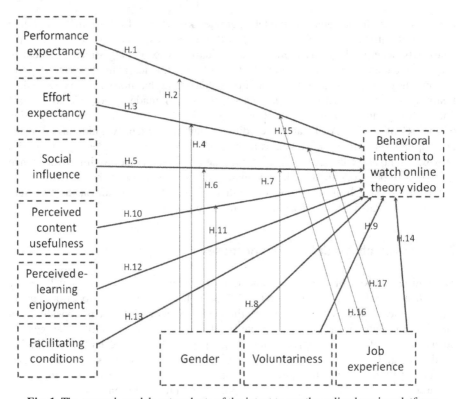

Fig. 1. The research model: antecedents of the intent to use the online learning platform

Previous research pointed out that females tend to be less task-oriented than males [11]. Hence, we hypothesize that the relationship between perceived content usefulness and behavioral intent will be moderated by gender:

H.11: Gender will moderate the relationship between PCU and BI so that the positive relationship between PCU and BI will be stronger for male students.

A second factor that influences a trainee's reactions to training concerns the trainees' perceptions of the trainer's performance [12, 13]. The perceived trainer performance has been measured through aspects such as the teacher's ability to create a good course atmosphere and dynamic and convincing teaching styles. Therefore, we include *perceived e-learning enjoyment* as an antecedent of BI in our model:

H.12: The higher the perceived e-learning enjoyment associated with an OLP feature, the higher the intention to use that feature of the OLP.

Thirdly, the perceived training efficiency is a significant antecedent of trainee satisfaction [15]. Perceived training efficiency concerns aspects such as the physical location of the course, whether the location can be easily reached, whether it is suitably equipped, etc. [16]. Other resources are also considered, such as the quantity and quality of the teaching materials [17]. Another aspect is the course planning in terms of number of sessions and the scheduling of the sessions [18]. The UTAUT contains a very similar construct to the perceived training efficiency, being the facilitating conditions. Still, in the UTAUT facilitating conditions are not regarded as an antecedent of behavioral intentions, but as a direct antecedent of real use behavior. We here hypothesize that the quality of the facilities also influences the intent to use the system:

H.13: The more positive the perception that the facilities support a feature of the OLP, the higher the intention to use the OLPs feature.

Finally, an important control variable is presumably missing in the UTAUT. *Experience using the system* is included in the UTAUT, but the user's *experience on the job* before the system was implemented is not included. Nevertheless, 'job experience', being the number of years someone studied in higher education, is likely to be a determinant of the flexibility of a person. For first bachelor students there is no fixed image yet of how classes should look like and students are still flexible in terms of accepting a new system. For elder students it might be unclear why new features are added if they were happy with the old system. Besides, students in higher years have proven already they are able to pass classes and are less motivated to work hard during the year than freshmen that have a hard time to estimate what it takes to pass. The latter are willing to work hard to improve their (unknown) chances of succeeding. We then hypothesize:

H.14: The longer the job experience the lower the intention to use a new feature of the OLP.

Job experience is likely to have a moderating effect on the UTAUT's key variables. For more mature students to accept the system, professors will have to justify to what extent this will actually help them to increase their learning performance. For younger students *everything* is new and there is no reason why new students would object exactly to the new feature on the OLP. Therefore we hypothesize:

H.15: Job experience will moderate the relationship between PE and BI so that the positive relationship between PE and BI will be stronger for students in higher years.

Secondly, senior students used other OLP features in the past. While it may not be clear to them why a new feature is introduced (leading to H.15), they already know about using OLPs and they need little effort to learn to work with new features. For new students the entire way of working is new so they can be expected to have to do more effort to use features of the OLP. Assuming a higher score on effort expectancy means the system is easier to use, we hypothesize:

H.16: Job experience will moderate the relationship between EE and BI so that the positive relationship between EE and BI will be less strong for students in higher years.

Finally, students in higher year presumably discuss less with each other what they need to do to pass, because they know better than in first year what the actual workload and the capacities of their peers are. Most of these scarce discussions are with people whose opinion they deem valuable. The impact of such scarce discussions on the behavioral intent is then likely to be higher.

H.17: Job experience will moderate the relationship between SI and BI so that the positive relationship between SI and BI will be stronger for students in higher years.

3   Research Setting and Method

The research model was tested in a French management school, relying on 3 courses delivered at the Bachelor level. One course is an introductory course in business and management (1st year of the Bachelor), another is a class on Sales Techniques (2nd year of the Bachelor), and the last one is a course of Management of Information Systems (3rd year of the Bachelor). For the academic year 2010-2011, the professors of the two first courses changed the way that they relied on online theory videos insofar as they benefited from the implementation of an OLP where they could store them and where the students could easily access them. As for the professor of the Management of Information System, he redesigned a class by moving theory lessons online. This way, students can study theory at their own speed and more contact hours are available to help students doing exercises. During those lessons, students were asked by their respective professors to watch movies before almost every session. The movies generally ranged from 25 minutes to 50 minutes. Professors gave instructions at the end of each class and highly recommended to use the system as a complement to the course. For example, one movie in the MIS class explained the creation of Entity-Relationship diagrams. The professor than stated in class (in session 4) that the next session (session 5) would be devoted entirely to making exercises on Entitity-Relationship diagrams. Watching the movies would make the offline sessions much more valuable to the students, giving the movies a mandatory character. Still, students who had not watched the movie were not denied access to the class.

At the end of the semester, students were asked to fill out a survey on paper. 766 of the 903 students responded (=85%). Questions were based on prior questionnaires and adapted to our setting. We used a seven-point Likert scale to measure all constructs. We primarily used items from Venkatesh et al. [4] to measure behavioral intention (Cronbach's alpha of 0.941). The independent variables, the performance expectancy, effort expectancy, social influence and facilitating conditions scales were also adapted from Venkatesh et al. [4]. After testing for Cronbach's alpha, six items were retained to measure performance expectancy (alpha = 0.844) and for effort expectancy (alpha = 0.826), five items were retained to measure facilitating conditions (alpha = 0.724) and four items to calculate the social influence (alpha = 0.732). Furthermore six items were used to measure perceived e-learning enjoyment (alpha = 0.801) and five items to measure perceived content usefulness (alpha = 0.815). The items for the latter two constructs were mainly derived from Giangreco et al.'s research on training evaluations [14]. All internal reliability coefficients were thus well above the 0.70 threshold. To enable the reader to interpret the statistical results presented below, we clarify a higher score on some construct means the system is perceived as more useful (performance expectancy), the system is easier to use (effort expectancy), facilitating conditions are satisfied, more social pressure is perceived to use the system, the system is more enjoyable (e-learning enjoyment), and the content is perceived as more useful.

Gender was coded as 1 for males and 2 for females. The 'job experience' in this case was measured through the year in which the student is enrolled. It should be noted that the success rate of students at the school is around 90% (thanks to severe entrance exams) so that there are very few students that retake the year. The student year is thus a very good proxy of the job experience. The survey instrument was pretested with two students from each year. Only minor changes were needed after the pretest.

4   Research Results

The research results are shown in Table 1. Model A shows the base model, being the constructs that could be used from the UTAUT in our setting. The R^2 of the base model is 0.37. (That is, 37% of the variability in the intent to watch videos is explained by the variables in the base model.) As this R^2 is rather low, the goal of our study, to significantly improve the R^2, is even more important. All direct antecedents in the base model are significant and show a positive relation with the intent to watch online movies. Only one moderating effect is significant: the more a class is perceived as mandatory, the lower is the impact of social influence on the intent.

Model B shows the test results for our model. The R^2 improved considerable to 0.45. Moreover all new constructs are significant at the p<0.05 level. The student year has a negative impact, confirming the rigidity in the students' learning style and a lower willingness to work during the year (H14). E-learning enjoyment and perceived content usefulness are statistically significant antecedents of behavioral intention (confirming H10 and H12), with the size of the betas being of the same order as the betas of PE and EE. The positive relation between facilitating conditions and BI is also significant, confirming H13. Furthermore, while gender has no impact on the effect of PE on BI (what would be hypothesized in line with the UTAUT's hypotheses [4]) it does have the hypothesized effect on the impact of the PCU on BI (confirming H11). Also as hypothesized, the higher the student year, the bigger the impact of an increase in performance expectancy upon BI (confirming H15) and the bigger the impact of an increase in perceived social influence upon BI (confirming H17). Finally, H16 is also confirmed as the impact of an increase in effort expectancy (i.e., making the system easier to use) upon BI is bigger for students in lower years.

5   Discussion

All hypotheses that were put forward were confirmed at $p < 0.05$ and the R^2 of the model increased significantly from 0.37 to 0.45. Hence, the model extensions make much sense from a statistical viewpoint. Let us now turn to the consequences of the significance of each of the variables.

Table 1. Linear regression results; dependent variable: intent to use the online movie system

	Model A: Original UTAUT		Model B: Our model	
R²	0,373		0,450	
R² adjusted	0,367		0,439	
	β	p-value	β	p-value
Performance Expectancy (PE)	0,268	0,000	0,160	0,000
Effort Expectancy (EE)	0,314	0,000	0,156	0,000
Social Influence (SI)	0,101	0,001	0,052	0,076
Gender	0,058	0,032	0,052	0,043
Voluntariness	0,109	0,000	0,065	0,016
MF voluntariness X SI	-0,070	0,012	-0,065	0,013
MF gender X SI	-0,051	0,085	-0,052	0,075
MF gender X PE	-0,011	0,739	0,023	0,496
MF gender X EE	0,007	0,824	0,033	0,304
year			-0,102	0,000
MF year X PE			0,067	0,032
MF year X EE			-0,060	0,048
MF year X SI			0,061	0,028
E-learning enjoyment			0,165	0,000
Perceived Content Usefulness (PCU)			0,150	0,000
MF gender X PCU			-0,077	0,019
Facilitating Conditions			0,125	0,000

As hypothesized, job experience (i.e., the number of years one has been a student) has a negative relation with the intent to use the new feature of the online learning platform. Hence, change management is more important in higher years and seasoned students need more stimulus to use new features. Our research shows that job experience moderates the effect of the antecedents that were already identified in the UTAUT (performance expectancy, effort expectancy and social influence). While performance expectancy has already a high impact for first year students (beta = 0.160), the importance given to this variable only increases over the student years (shown by the significant, positive interaction effect, beta = 0.067). The higher the year of the student, the higher should the performance expectancy be for students to intend to use the new feature. This is important from a change management viewpoint in that features that may be perceived as less useful to a student (but which may be useful to the school), might be better introduced gradually, starting in first bachelor and being introduced in subsequent bachelor years as students move from one year to the other. Also, the evaluation of the use of a general, new feature can happen better on basis of 1st bachelor data than 3rd Bachelor data, although a longitudinal study has to confirm this suggestion by checking whether the use of the new feature persists. Still, more complex features may be better introduced and tested first in higher years because effort expectancy is highly significant for first year students (beta = 0.156), and more seasoned students are less bothered with the effort that is needed to learn to work with a new feature (a significant, negative interaction effect: beta = -0.06).

Perceived content usefulness was shown to have a significant, positive relation with the intent to use the system (beta = 0.15; p =0.000). While prior research on system acceptance had investigated to a big extent the usefulness of the system to do a job, the usefulness of the job in itself was neglected in important models such as the TAM [5] and the UTAUT [4]. Our research shows that students have a higher intent to watch movies if they think the contents of the movies will be useful to them for a better understanding of the course content, for getting a better grade, or for their future career, the contents was interesting and it seemed to fit within the entire school's curriculum. This has consequences for evaluating the success of the movie system. Students tend to perceive some classes as more interesting than others and the students' intention to watch movies that are embedded in such classes is higher. While this finding seems logical (and questions arise why a similar construct was not included in the TAM and UTAUT), students also have to pass classes that seem less interesting if they want to obtain their degree and students may be assumed to watch all movies. Thus, for the evaluation of a new feature of an online learning platform, it is important to take into account whether that feature is used for a class in which students are generally very interested or not. It may be appropriate to test new features first in classes in which students are highly interested, to increase the general adoption rate of the new feature. Furthermore, it has to be noticed that the importance of PCU is higher for male students than for female students. Consequently, also the class' gender composition (percentage of males vs. females) has to be taken into account when evaluating the use of the new feature on the online learning platform. Increasing the PCU will have a bigger impact upon the intent to use the system for a male student population than for female students.

E-learning enjoyment has a very significant, positive relation with the intent to use the system (p=0.000). Students are more motivated to watch movies if they are presented in a more dynamic and convincing way, involve the student, motivate the student to learn, etcetera. Hence, the fact that watching the movies is important for students to get most out of the class is not enough to motivate students to watch movies: the movies also have to be perceived as giving enjoyment, mainly through great designs and through interactions with the course video content. This implies that making movies more dynamic and motivating is not optional, but something professors *have to* take into account. We noticed that creating the movies is a big effort for professors and that they usually tend to focus more on "getting the content right", given their technical stance on their subject. Yet, as stated above (see the discussion on PCU), it is indeed important to pay attention to the perceived usefulness of the content, but we now notice that the beta of e-learning enjoyment is even bigger than that of PCU. When talking to the professors that were involved, it became clear that only one had actually taken into account this dimension. The two others had underestimated it, since they focused more on what content to put online and what content to keep in offline classes. They were also trying to understand the functioning of the new online system. The same two professors seem to have focused first on the features that seem useful (how can I show my content?), and put the enjoyment contained in the online theory videos (e.g. adding animations and interactive quizzes) in the background.   Accordingly, future research should not only focus on the adoption of features of the platform by students, but also upon features adopted by professors. This is all the more important as most professors don't have an IS background and often have difficulties to get most out of a new system.

A higher score on facilitating conditions is positively related to a higher intent to watch the movies (beta = 0.125, p = 0.000). Professors have control over a number of the facilitating conditions: they have to choose upon an appropriate frequency to watch movies, an appropriate duration of the movies (as it was often heard that the movies are actually too long) and the structure of the movies. Other elements are under the control of the IT department: the movie system has to be compatible with the systems the students normally use (in terms of browsers, operating systems, etc.) and the necessary resources have to be available to watch the movies (e.g. fast internet connections). The school under consideration has several computer labs that allow students to watch movies, and is also equipped with wireless internet connection so that the students can watch the videos on their laptop. Finally, students can also watch the movies at home. All the last elements fall outside the power of the professor and sometimes even outside the control of the school. The facilitating conditions should be taken into account when evaluating the acceptance of the new feature of the online learning platform. For instance, the school moved from one internet provider to another during the year, which generated issues with the wireless connections, which in a way demotivated the students and obliged the professor to emphasize that this was not a shortcoming of the new feature, but of the available infrastructure. This prevented the students from dropping the movie system.

The school has acted upon the findings in this paper. First, professors have been advised to pay more attention to the enjoyment dimension of their movies. Second, it was suggested to generalize a practice that already existed in one of the 3 courses studied, that is to say starting the offline class with a quiz, in order to motivated the students (especially those in higher years) to watch the movies. Furthermore, actions are being taken to improve the supporting facilities.

Our future research will investigate how the intent to use OLP features depends upon the student's intent to use computer systems in general. Also, the social influence construct will be measured in a different way, by investigating the social networks that really exist between students. Further research has to investigate whether our findings are also applicable in the context of pure online classes and in cases where the students are employees who take additional classes. Finally, we stress the fact that our research was conducted in a single country and that the research needs to be replicated in other countries to guarantee the external validity.

6   Conclusions

This paper identified four new antecedents of the intent to watch online theory videos: the student year, the perceived content usefulness, the perceived e-learning enjoyment and the facilitating conditions. We also detected moderating effects: student year influences the impact of the classic UTAUT variables (effort expectancy, performance expectancy and social influence) upon the behavioral intention.

References

1. Proserpio, L., Dennis, A.G.: Teaching the Virtual Generation. Academy of Management Learning and Education 6(1), 69–80 (2007)
2. De Lange, P., Suwardy, T., Mavondo, F.: Integrating a Virtual Learning Environment into an Introductory Accounting Course: Determinants of Student Motivation. Accounting Education 12(1), 1–14 (2003)
3. Marriott, N., Marriott, P., Selwyn, N.: Accounting Undergraduates' Changing Use of Ict and Their Views on Using the Internet in Higher Education - a Research Note. Accounting Education 13(1), 117–130 (2004)
4. Venkatesh, V., Morris, M.G., Davis, G.B., David, F.D.: User Acceptance of Information Technology: Toward a Unified View. MIS Quarterly 3(27), 425–478 (2003)
5. Davis, F.: Perceived Usefulness, Perceived Ease of Use, and User Acceptance of Information. MIS Quarterly 3(13), 319–339 (1989)
6. Taylor, S., Todd, P.A.: Understanding information technology usage: a test of competing models. Information Systems Research 6(4), 144–176 (1995)
7. Warr, P., Allan, C., Birdi, K.: Predicting Three Levels of Training Outcome. Journal of Occupational and Organizational Psychology 72, 351–375 (1999)
8. Webster, J., Martocchio, J.J.: The Differential Effects of Software Training Previews on Training Outcomes. Journal of Management 21(4), 757–787 (1995)
9. Noe, R.A.: Trainees' Attributes and Attitudes: Neglected Influences on Training Effectiveness. The Academy of Management Review 11(4), 736–749 (1986)
10. Lipari, D.: Logiche di Azione Formativa nelle Organizzazioni. Franco Angeli, Milan (2002)
11. Minton, H.L., Schneider, F.W.: Differential Psychology Prospect Heights. Waveland Press, IL (1980)
12. Morgan, R.B., Casper, W.J.: Examining the Factor Structure of Participant Reactions to Training: A Multidimensional Approach. Human Resources Development Quarterly 11(3), 301–317 (2000)
13. Russ-Eft, D.F., Dickinson, P.D., Levine, R.: Instructor Quality Affecting Emergency Medical Technician (EMT) Preparedness: a LEADS Project. International Journal of Training and Development 9(4), 256–270 (2005)
14. Giangreco, A., Carugati, A., Sebastiano, A., Della Bella, D.: Trainees' reactions to training : shaping groups and courses for happier trainees. International Journal of Human Resource Management 21(13), 2468–2487 (2010)

15. Giangreco, A., Sebastiano, A., Peccei, R.: Trainees' reactions to training: an analysis of the factors affecting overall satisfaction with training. International Journal of Human Resource Management 20(1), 96–111 (2009)
16. Lee, S.H., Pershing, J.A.: Dimensions and Design Criteria for Developing Training Reactions Evaluations. Human Resources Development International 5(2), 175–197 (2002)
17. Kidder, P.J., Rouiller, J.Z.: Evaluating the Success of a Large–Scale Training Effort. National Productivity Review, 79–89 (Spring 1997)
18. Amietta, P.: I Luoghi dell'Apprendimento: Metodi, Strumenti e Casi di Eccellenza. FrancoAngeli, Milan (2000)

Measuring Student E-Learning Readiness:
A Case about the Subject of Electricity
in Higher Education Institutions in Turkey

Dursun Akaslan and Effie L.-C. Law

Department of Computer Science, University of Leicester, United Kingdom
{info@dursunakaslan,elaw@mcs}.le.ac.uk

Abstract. Today e-learning is embraced for delivering education and training as it offers various potential benefits. However, successful uptake of e-learning depends on a cluster of personal, technological, institutional and domain-specific (content) factors. Based on our literature review and empirical results of our previous work, we have identified specific attributes subsumed by each of these factors and integrated them into our model of student e-learning readiness. To validate the model, we have conducted a web-based survey to investigate the extent to which students in the Higher Education Institutions (HEIs) in Turkey offering the subject of electricity are ready for e-learning. 704 responses from the students of 417 departments in the related HEIs have been collected; 425 were complete responses. Whilst the findings revealed that the students were sufficiently ready for e-learning, training for e-learning is considered essential for enhancing student e-learning readiness.

Keywords: E-learning readiness, electricity, higher education.

1   Introduction

Today many organizations and individuals embrace e-learning for delivering education and training as it potentially offers different benefits. However, successful integration of e-learning into an organization, be it academic or industrial, is deemed challenging. An ever-increasing number of research studies have investigated factors pertaining to the integration of e-learning in academic institutions in developing countries. The aim of the paper is to understand whether students in the Higher Education Institutions (HEIs) offering the subject of electricity (e.g. departments of electrical and electronic engineering) in Turkey are ready for e-learning in terms of successful integration. To meet this aim, we investigated the extent to which students believe that e-learning would be free of effort and would enhance their learning. This is important to understand the needs of students before embarking on e-learning. We addressed these issues by adapting the conceptual model we had previously developed for measuring teachers' e-learning readiness [2]. The adapted model has then been validated with students from some of the HEIs which had been involved in the corresponding survey with their teachers.

H. Leung et al. (Eds.): ICWL 2011, LNCS 7048, pp. 209–218, 2011.

2   Literature Review

E-learning offers many benefits for individuals and organizations First, organizations can save their training budget [6]. Second, it provides flexibility for delivering education and training from anywhere and at anytime. Third, the cost of commuting from residences to colleges may be reduced [1]). Another obvious importance of e-learning is that students can study at their own pace in their own preferable environment, given that students do not have to be together with their teachers [8]. A number of papers have described the benefits of e-learning in detail. Specifically, Akaslan, Law & Taşkın [3] conducted in-depth interviews with a number of academic staff to identify issues for applying e-learning to the subject of electricity in Turkey. The results indicate that e-learning is perceived as a solution for some of the issues and is deemed useful for enhancing education and training in the institutions surveyed.

Akaslan and Law [2] argue that e-learning may not have the same effect for every individual, institution, organization or country. To ensure that the actual benefit of e-learning is valid in different situations, there is a need to measure organizations' or individuals' readiness for e-learning appropriately. E-learning readiness is defined as the ability of an organization or individual to take advantage of e-learning [13]. Furthermore, it is the mental and physical preparedness of users to gain some learning experience or action [5]. It is therefore important to investigate whether individuals and organizations are ready to succeed in e-learning [7, 11,12]. Besides, it is deemed relevant to analyse the factors that may affect the readiness of organizations and individuals for e-learning. Such factors should be included in a structural model describing their relationships.

The often-cited model of e-learning readiness is Chapnick's, which informed the development of items for measuring e-learning readiness [7]. Chapnick defined measuring e-learning readiness as a process for determining the gap between what students know and what they need to know. She grouped different factors identified into eight categories (i.e. psychological, sociological, environmental, human resource, financial, equipment, content and technical skill readiness), thereby enabling practitioners to use the same process to assess different types of stakeholders. Besides, there are other models of e-learning readiness for some general as well as specific situations [2, 4,7, 12].

3   A Model for Measuring Readiness for E-Learning

Akaslan and Law [2] developed a model to measure teachers' readiness for e-learning in HEIs offering the subject of electricity in Turkey (Fig. 1, the underlined factor 'Traditional Skills' is only included in the model for students' e-learning readiness). This model is basically appropriate for measuring students' e-learning readiness, because the core factors and their subsuming attributes (or sub-factors) remain relevant. Presumably the model is generalizable for assessing e-learning readiness in developing countries such as Turkey, albeit some fine-tuning may be required for specific socioeconomic attributes.

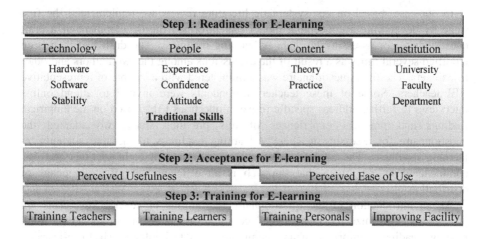

Fig. 1. A Model for Measuring Students' Readiness for E-learning

In comparing with the model for measuring teachers' e-learning readiness, the model for students has been further refined by adding a new factor to investigate students' traditional skills (e.g. self motivation, self-responsibility, and time management skills). One of the key factors of the teacher model in Fig. 1 is "People". This factor subsumes three attributes, namely, *attitude*, *confidence* and *experience*. Students' experiences and confidence in the use of various ICT and their attitudes towards e-learning are critical success factors for e-learning. However, the factor 'People' should be refined by measuring students' traditional skills (e.g. self-motivation, time management skills). Clarke [9] argued that e-students need a foundation of traditional skills on which to build their e-learning skills to succeed in e-learning. Dabbagh [15] and Dray et al. [14] also believed that characteristics of students that make them successful in traditional learning can contribute to their success to e-learning. Chapnick [7] pointed out that the individual's state of mind is an important factor influencing the outcome of e-learning initiative.

4   Methodology

4.1   Questionnaire Design

To conduct a survey with a validated instrument, Dray et. al. [14] suggest a two-stage approach: first, an initial questionnaire is to be developed with respect to the constructs specified in a conceptual model, which should be grounded in the related literature and should also address the objectives of a research study; discussions among researchers and subject matter experts are to refine the items in the questionnaire. Second, focus groups and interviews are to be conducted to explore prospective respondents' interpretations of the meaning of individual item in the questionnaire.

In our case, based on our systematic literature review we implemented the first stage by developing a conceptual model that informed the development of a draft questionnaire for assessing teachers' e-learning readiness. The draft had then been modified several times as a result of the discussions among the two authors and other researchers. The final questionnaire was administered with a sample of representative HEI teachers. Some of these teacher respondents were invited to attend online interviews to further address specific research questions [3]. Based on the empirical findings and practical experiences of this previous study, we adapted the questionnaire for assessing teachers' e-learning readiness to measure students' e-learning readiness. The adapted questionnaire consisted of eight sections and was administered online, given that the web is an efficient and effective means of distribution.

As an introduction of the questionnaire, definitions of several key terms are provided to maximize the respondents' common understanding of the items used, namely: readiness, information and communication technologies (ICT), e-learning and readiness for e-learning. The first section consisted of several items to gather demographic data of the students, including their age, gender, education level, academic year, and affiliated institution. Section 2, 3, 4, 5, and 6 of the questionnaire were designed to measure the extent to which the students and their affiliated institutions are ready for e-learning by considering five main factors and several sub-factors (or attributes): technology, people, institution and content. Section 7 of the survey was designed to understand the extent to which students believe that e-learning would be free of effort and would enhance learning. Section 8 was also developed to evaluate whether the respondents in the respective institutions need training for e-learning before its integration. Furthermore, all the items are measured with either a binary option or a five-point Likert scale (Section 4.3), and most of them are supplemented with a free text box for the respondents to elaborate their choice or rating. There were altogether 78 items in the questionnaire, which were divided into three parts to investigate self-reported perceptions of respondents on different aspects of e-learning. These items are explained in Section 5. Additionally, the respondents were invited to be interviewed to discuss four main questions: current issues in their institutions; their perceptions towards e-learning; the advantages and disadvantages of e-learning as a solution for the current issues; their scenarios for the implementation of e-learning. Due to the space constraint, findings of the interviews will not be reported here.

4.2   Sampling of Participants and Response Rate

417 departments in HEIs in Turkey were selected for the study. The participating institutions were screened by considering whether they offer the subject of electricity, according to the official data in 2010 provided by the OYSM, which stands for the Student Selection and Placement Centre in Turkey. Individuals who pursue undergraduate, master or PhD degree in those institutions were chosen as respondents who can provide data regarding their institutions' and their own readiness for e-learning. A personalized invitation and reminders were sent to the teachers of those

students and faculty/high school secretaries to notify their students to participate in the survey. Until the deadline of the survey, 811 students showed interest to participate in the survey. 704 responses were valid, but only 425 of them were complete.

4.3   Procedure

After the preparation of the questionnaire, the open source lime-survey software was used to convert the questionnaire into the web-based format. Active students in the HEIs offering the subject of electricity in Turkey were invited to participate in the survey by notifying the teachers (1672 invitations) and secretaries in the respective institutions (125 invitations). The web-based survey was launched on 9th January 2011 and closed on 20th April 2011. Table 1 illustrates the distribution of the respondents for each group. The majority of the respondents are male (626; 88.9 %); a distinct contrast to the number of female (78; 11.1%). However, a similar proportion between female and male exists in the targeted population as the subject of electricity is not usually preferred by females in Turkey. The age groups of the respondents reveal that 90% of the respondents are less than 27 years old. Another variable is the respondents' educational level: 92.8 % are currently studying an undergraduate degree and the rest are taking a postgraduate degree. Besides, the respondents were also classified according to their university affiliation: 15.5 % private universities and 84.5 % public universities. Furthermore, the majority of the students are studying in departments of electrical and electrics engineering (59.8%) and some are in the study programmes related to electricity (25.3%) across Turkey.

Table 1. The frequencies and percentage of research groups

Gender	N	%	University	N	%
Female	78	11.1	Private	109	15.5
Male	626	88.9	Public	595	84.5
Degree programme	**N**	**%**	**Age Groups**	**N**	**%**
Associate	223	31.7	Less than 21	348	49.4
Bachelor	430	61.1	Between 22 - 26	286	40.6
Course-based Postgraduate	31	4.4	Between 27 - 31	31	4.4
Research Postgraduate	20	2.8	More than 32	39	5.5

4.4   Assessment Method

There are 78 items in the questionnaire with different types, namely binary (7 items), categorical (3 items) and a five-point Likert-scale with the leftmost and rightmost anchors being "Strongly Disagree" and "Strongly Agree". The Likert-scale questions were coded with 1 indicating the lowest readiness and 5 the highest. As the choices were coded as 1, 2, 3, 4 or 5, it is suggested that the mean score of 3.40 can be identified as the expected level of readiness for e-learning. It is because a five-point scale contains 4 intervals and 5 categories with the ratio 4 / 5 being equal to 0.8 [10] (Fig. 2).

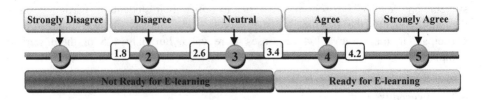

Fig. 2. An Assessment Model for Measuring Readiness for E-learning [10]

5   Results and Discussion

In this section we aim to analyse the responses of the respondents under six parts: the first four parts analyse the extent to which the student respondents are ready for e-learning; the fifth part reports the extent to which student respondents believe that e-learning would be free of effort and would enhance their learning; the sixth one discusses whether students need training for e-learning before embarking on it. Independent-sample t-test and one-way ANOVA were also used to verify statistical significance of differences in the mean scores of various variables (e.g. between male and female, between public and private universities).

5.1   Findings in the Factor 'Technology'

The respondents were asked about their access to a desktop or laptop computer connected to the internet at their residence (I6) and at university (I9). The majority of the respondents reported that they have access to the Internet at their residence (576; 83.8 %) and at university (550; 80.1 %). Table 2 shows the mean scores for the items associated with students' access to the internet. According to this table, the speed of the internet that the students use at the place they live (I8) and at university (I11) are not sufficient because the mean scores of these items are lower than the expected level of readiness ($M_0 = 3.40$). This indicates that there is a lack of infrastructure in the respective HEIs. This result can be interpreted that students' access to the internet are not sufficient for e-learning and must be improved before embarking on e-learning. Therefore, the HEIs should identify proper strategies to ensure that e-learning is accessible to all in case they are interested in e-learning,

Table 2. Statistics for the items related to technology factor

	Items and their contents	N	M
I7	I am satisfied with the Stability of the Internet access at the place I live	568	3.56
I8	I am satisfied with the Speed of the Internet access at the place I live.	571	3.26
I10	I am satisfied with the Stability of the Internet access at university.	524	3.43
I11	I am satisfied with the Speed of the Internet access at university.	530	3.32

An independent-sample t-test was used to verify whether there is a significant difference in the stability of the internet access at their university (I10) between the student respondents who study in private and public universities. A significant difference (t (702) = 1.865, p = 0.063) was not found between private (M_{I10}=3.63) and public (M_{I10}=3.38) universities. However, the mean score of the students in public universities is slightly lower than the expected level of readiness for e-learning (M_0= 3.40). Therefore, it seems more urgent for the public universities than the private ones across Turkey to improve the internet access before embarking on e-learning. Furthermore, we found that the mean scores of the respondents on the stability and speed of the internet access at their home and at the university reduce when the their educational degrees are lower. That is to say, doctorate and master students are more satisfied with their internet access than bachelor and associate students.

5.2   Findings in the Factor 'People'

The respondents' experiences and confidences in the usage of different ICT for their study, their attitudes towards e-learning and their traditional skills were investigated to find out the extent to which they are ready for e-learning. Given the space limit, only the overall mean scores of all the related items are given in Table 3.

Table 3. Statistics for the items related to people factor

Items and their contents		N	M
I12 - I17	Students' experiences in the usage of different ICT for their study: internet (I12), e-mail (I13), office software (I14), social network sites (I15), instant messaging software (I16) and engineering software (I17)	644-654	3.90
I18 – I22	Students' confidences in different ICT usage: computers (I18), web browsers (I19), search engines (I20), digital file management tools (I21) and authoring tools to create learning materials (I22)	619-611	4.19
I23 – I34	Students' attitudes toward e-learning: information about e-learning (I23, I29, I30), ICT competencies for e-learning (I24), feeling ready for e-learning (I25), having enough time for e-learning (I26), supporting e-learning (I27, I31, 32) and liking e-learning (I28, I33, I34)	590-498	3.50
I35 - I58	Students' traditional skills: writing skills (I35-37), note-taking skills (I38-I40), collaboration skills (I41-43), reading skills (I44-46), attendance to classrooms (I47-49), time management skills (I50-52), self-directed skills (I53-55) and self-motivation (I56-58)	542-488	3.62

As shown in Table 3, the mean scores of all the items related to the factor 'People' are higher than the expected level of readiness. Although the mean scores of the items related to students' attitudes towards e-learning are higher than the expected level of readiness, they are the lowest scores among the factor 'People'. Therefore, informing the students about basic characteristics of e-learning is significant. With the better understanding, their attitudes towards e-learning may improve.

5.3   Findings in the Factor 'Institution'

The respondents were also asked whether e-learning is currently implemented in their own institution at three levels: department, faculty, and university. Data provided by the respondents show that 24.0 % of their universities (I59), 20.2 % of their faculties (I60) and 20.0 % of their own departments (I61) currently implement e-learning officially or with personal efforts of their teachers. This finding can be interpreted that the majority of the HEIs are not familiar with e-learning and thus it is important to train academic as well as non-academic staff how to succeed in e-learning before embarking on it.

5.4   Findings in the Factor 'Content'

Table 4 provides the mean scores and number of the respondents for each item related to the factor 'Content'. The respondents were asked to what extent they agree that e-learning can enhance the quality of the theoretical and practical parts of the subject of electricity and can be applied to the two parts. As shown in Table 4, it can be easily observed that the mean scores of all the items related to the factor 'Content' is higher than the expected level of readiness ($M_0 = 3.40$). This implies that the respondents consider that e-learning can be integrated into theory and practice to enhance the quality of the courses on the subject of electricity.

Table 4. Statistics for the items related to content factor

Items and their contents		N	M
I62	E-learning can be applied to the theoretical part of the subject of electricity.	454	3.88
I63	E-learning can enhance the quality of the theoretical part of the electricity.	451	3.88
I64	E-learning can be applied to the practical part of the subject of electricity.	452	3.46
I65	E-learning can enhance the quality of the practical part of the electricity.	452	3.56

Results of one-way ANOVA indicated significance differences in the scores of I64 (F_{I64} (3, 448) = 5.759, $p < 0.01$) and I65 (F_{I65} (3, 448) = 2.864, $p < 0.05$) among the respondents studying for the associate ($M_{I64}= 3.79$, $M_{I65}= 3.79$), bachelor ($M_{I64}= 3.28$, $M_{I65}= 3.43$), master ($M_{I64}= 3.36$, $M_{I65}= 3.43$) and doctorate ($M_{I64}= 3.73$, $M_{I65}= 3.64$) degree.

5.5   Findings in the Factor 'Acceptance'

The respondents were asked to opine for 8 items to measure their acceptance for e-learning (i.e. items I66 to I73). Table 5 shows the overall mean scores of all the items related to the factor 'Acceptance'. It can be easily interpreted that the respondents hold positive attitudes towards e-learning because their responses show that they believe e-learning would be free of effort and would enhance their learning.

Table 5. Statistics for the items related to the factor 'Acceptance'

Items and their contents		N	M
I66 – I70	The items related to the perceived usefulness: e-learning will improve students' learning experiences (I66), learning outcomes (I67), increase their productivity (I68), be useful their studies (I69) and be better than face-to-face learning (I70)	450-443	3.77
I71 – I73	The items related to the perceived ease of use: e-learning will be easy for students (I72), for their peers (I73) and for their teachers (I74)	442-434	3.83

5.6   Findings in the Factor 'Training'

The respondents were asked to answer five questions to find out whether there is a need of training for e-learning before it is implemented (items I74 to I78). Table 6 indicates that the respondents, their peers and teachers highly need training for e-learning and their institutions do not have sufficient facilities to implement e-learning (I78). Therefore, there is a need to ensure a clear understanding of e-learning through the respective HEIs. This should include understanding the potential benefits of e-learning and how it can enhance students to learn more effectively and efficiently.

Table 6. Statistics for the items related to the factor 'Training'

	Items and their contents	N	M
I74	I do not need training on e-learning.	457	2.46
I75	My teachers do not need training on e-learning.	419	2.35
I76	My peers do not need training on e-learning.	430	2.29
I77	Technical and administrative personals do not need training on e-learning.	415	2.22
I78	The facilities of university are sufficient for e-learning.	425	2.80

6   Conclusion

This study focused on measuring students' readiness for e-learning in three steps: readiness, acceptance and training for e-learning. 417 departments in HEIs offering the subject of electricity were selected for getting involved in our web-based survey. Undergraduates and postgraduates of those HEIs were eligible to participate in the survey. Personalized invitations and reminders were sent to their teachers and related institutions. In summary, there are many factors we need to consider before integrating e-learning into the respective HEIs. First, according to students' responses, teachers, students, and personals should be trained for e-learning and the facilities of the universities should be strengthened before embarking on it. Without this training, there is a high risk to end up with failure. The training of individuals for e-learning will also help students and teachers to have enough information about e-learning and thus to enhance their attitudes towards e-learning. Besides, our detailed analyses show that students do not integrate ICT effectively into their studies. This inadequacy may aggravate the problem of integrating e-learning into the respective HEIs. Results of the research may also help students assess their own e-learning readiness and enable us to determine how to implement e-learning in the researched HEIs in Turkey.

References

1. Akaslan, D., Law, E.L.-C.: E-learning in the Science of Electricity in Higher Education in Turkey in terms of Environment and Energy. In: Proceedings of Postgraduate Research Student Conference 2010: Perspectives in Society. EMUA, Nottingham (2010)
2. Akaslan, D., Law, E.L.-C.: Measuring Teachers' Readiness for E-learning in Higher Education Institutions associated with the Subject of Electricity in Turkey. In: Proceedings of 2011 IEEE Global Engineering Education Conference: Learning Environments and Ecosystems in Engineering Education, Amman, Jordan, pp. 481–490 (2011)
3. Akaslan, D., Law, E.L.-C., Taşkın, S.: Analysing Issues for Applying E-learning to the Subject of Electricity in Higher Education in Turkey. In: Proceedings of the International Conference on Engineering Education: Engineering Sustainability for a Global Economy. ICEE, Belfast (2011)
4. Anderson, T.: Is e-learning right for your organization? (2002), http://www.astd.org/LC/2002/0102_anderson.htm (retrieved June 29, 2011)
5. Borotis, S.A., Poulymenakou, A.: E-learning Readiness Factors. In: Proceedings of World Conference in E-learning in Cooperate, Government, Healthcare and Higher Education, Washington, D. C (2004)
6. Baradyana, J.S.: Readiness factors for e-learning in higher education institutions in Tanzania: Option of academic member of staff. Business Management Review 9(1) (2009)
7. Chapnick, S.: Are You Ready for E-Learning? from ASTD (2000), http://www.astd.org/LC/2000/1100_chapnick.htm (retrieved February 20, 2010)
8. Srichanyachon, N.: Key factors of e-learning readiness (2009), http://www.bu.ac.th/knowledgecenter/epaper/jan_june2010/pdf/Page_56.pdf (retrieved August 19, 2010)
9. Clarke, A.: E-Learning Skills. Palgrave Study Guides, London (2004)
10. Aydin, C.H., Tasci, D.: Measuring readiness for e-learning. Educational Technology and Society, 244–257 (2005)
11. Guglielmino, P., Guglielmino, L.: Are your students ready for e-learning? In: Piskurich, G. (ed.) The AMA Handbook of e-Learning. American Management Association, New York (2003)
12. Kapp, K. M.: Are you ready for e-learning? from ASTD (2005), http://www.astd.org/LC/2005/0405_kapp.htm (retrieved February 20, 2010)
13. Lopes, C.T.: Evaluating e-learning readiness in a health sciences higher education institution. In: Proceedings of IADIS International Conference of E-learning, Porto (2007)
14. Dray, B.J., Lowenthal, P.R., Miszkiewicz, M.J., Ruiz-Primo, M.A., Marczynski, K.: Developing an instrument to assess student readiness for online learning: a validation study. Distance Education 32(1), 29–47 (2011)
15. Dabbagh, N.: The online learner: Characteristics and pedagogical implications. Contemporary Issues in Technology and Teacher. Education 7(3), 217–226 (2007)

Dynamical User Networking and Profiling Based on Activity Streams for Enhanced Social Learning

Xiaokang Zhou and Qun Jin

Graduate School of Human Sciences, Waseda University,
2-579-15 Mikajima, Tokorozawa-shi, Saitama, Japan
{xkzhou@ruri.,jin@}waseda.jp

Abstract. Recently, social media enhanced learning has become more and more popular. It is featured as learning through interaction and collaboration in a community or across a social network, which can be considered as a kind of social learning. In this study, we integrate SNS (such as twitter) into the web-based learning process and further delve into the discovery of potential information from the reorganized stream data. We propose a Dynamical Socialized User Networking (DSUN) model which represents users' profiling and dynamical relationship by a set of measures. Finally, we show an application scenario of the DSUN model to assist the learning process and enhance the learning efficiency in web-based environments.

Keywords: Social Stream, Social Learning, User Model, Stream Metaphor, SNS.

1 Introduction

Nowadays, SNS (Social Network Service), such as facebook, twitter, has become increasingly popular. Through them, we can post our feeling, experience and knowledge to share with each other at any time. Either these stream data in the cyber world or lifelog data from the physical world represent different aspects of people's information behaviors and social activities, which we call social streams. With the development of web-based learning, web2.0 technology has attracted more faculty members to look for ways to engage and motivate their students to be more active learners [1]. A variety of social media tools that contain a tremendous amount of social streams have aroused the interest in integrating them into learning process [2]. Since people are increasingly accustomed to sharing their feelings with others on Internet, learning through a variety of social media has become more and more popular, which can be called as social learning. Social learning focuses on the learning that occurs within a social context, including such concepts as observational learning, imitation, and modeling [3].That is, people can learn by observing the behavior of others and the outcomes of those behaviors [4]. Furthermore, sharing learning activities and a learning process could also be enhanced and facilitated with social media. In this study, we try to utilize these stream data to assist learning process.

H. Leung et al. (Eds.): ICWL 2011, LNCS 7048, pp. 219–225, 2011.
© Springer-Verlag Berlin Heidelberg 2011

In our previous study [5], we have introduced a set of metaphors to represent a variety of social stream data which include different aspects of people's information behaviors and social activities. We further defined two new metaphors: Heuristic Stone and Associative Ripple to assist users' information seeking that can best fit users' current needs and interests with two algorithms [6]. In this study, to assist web-based learning, we integrate SNS (such as twitter) into the social learning process We build a Dynamical Socialized User Networking Model to represent users' profiling and relationship which are described by a set of measures and concepts in both subjective and objective ways, in order to provide recommendations to benefit the mobilization of learning interaction and the improvement of teaching quality.

2   Related Work

There are a host of applications of SNS in learning process. Analysis of twitter communications in [7] showed the experimental evidence that twitter can be used as an educational tool to help engage students and to mobilize faculty into a more active and participatory role. A study addressed in [8] examined the impact of posting social, scholarly, or a combination of social and scholarly information to twitter on the perceived credibility of the instructor, which may have implications for both teaching and learning. Soller et al. analyzed and assessed online knowledge sharing conversations during collaborative learning activities, and concluded that their approach can improve the effectiveness of knowledge sharing [9]. Huang et al. proposed a prompt response monitoring system to support collaborative learning activities [10]. Activity streams provide us an opportunity to share learning activity cross different systems to create advanced reuse of learning process information to deal with the questions in various learning systems [11].

There are a variety of researches on information recommendation. A new document representation model was presented in [12], which is based on implicit users' feedback to achieve better results in organizing web documents, such as clustering and labeling. LinkSelector [13] is a web mining approach focusing on structure and usage. By this approach, hyperlinks-structural relationships were extracted from existing web sites and theirs access logs.

3   Dynamical Socialized User Networking Model

3.1   Construction of LONET

In our previous study, social streams have been defined as an abstract class with various sources of stream data [5]. To assist learning, learning actions and learning activities occurred in a learning system can be viewed as stream data. In this section, we first introduce a set of metaphors to represent these kinds of data streams in the e-learning environment with a hierarchical structure.

Drop: a minimum unit of learning action streams, such as a learning action in a learning system.

Stream: a collection of drops in timeline, which contains the messages, activities and actions of a learner.

River: a confluence of streams from different learners. Streams can be reorganized and reused in this level. For example, to generate associative ripples.

Ocean: a combination of all the streams.

A learning action such as a learning message generated by each learner in a learning system can be viewed as a drop, and the drops come from one learner converge together to form a stream. Then the streams of the learner and his/her companies form the river. Finally, all the streams come together to form the ocean.

In this study, we introduce a Dynamical Socialized User Networking (DSUN) model, which can be defined as G (V, R), where

V= {V_1, V_2, V_3, ..., V_n}: a non-empty set of vertexes in the network, each of which indicates a user in the system.

R= {<u, v> | u, v ∈V}: the collection of edges in the network, which represent all the relationships between each vertex.

The vertex and the edge are defined as follows.

Vertex (id, heuristic stone): we store a user's information in each vertex, such as the user's id, user's interest or need represented as the heuristic stone.

Edge<u, w, v>: vertex *u* is the head of this edge, which indicates the user who has been recommended the information in the system; *v* is the tail of this edge, which indicates the user who is the origin of the information in the system; *w* is the relationship weight between these two users, which can be calculated from the associative ripple.

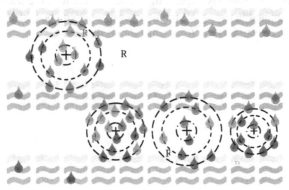

Fig. 1. Associative ripples in a learning river

To build the DSUN model for a learning system to support the learning process, we employ the definitions: heuristic stone and associative ripple previously defined in [6] to extract the reorganized social streams in accordance with a learner's current interests and needs. Figure 1 shows the ripples generated by the heuristic stone in the river. The drops cluster to the cluster center in different circles to form an associative ripple, which represents the messages that are related to the corresponding interest center in various degrees. Based on these, we can calculate the weight w_{ij} which will then be used as a determining factor in the user network building process. Finally, each collected w_{ij} can be stored in each corresponding edge of the DSUN model for the further process.

To build a DSUN model, firstly, the sample space is defined as (Z_s, W_s, E_s, Q, $G(V, R)$), where

$Z_s = \{Z_1, Z_2, Z_3, ..., Z_n\}$: a non-empty set of input users, which will finally become all the vertex in the network.

$W_s = \{W_1, W_2, W_3, ..., W_n\}$: a set of input weight sets for users, which have been calculated from the associative ripples. For each W_i, $W_i = \{w_1, w_2, w_3, ..., w_{n-1}\}$.

$E_s = \{<Z_i, Z_k>| Z_i, Z_k \in Z_s\}$: a set of user pairs, if there exists a calculated weight between two specific users, there is a pair of them.

$Q(Z_i, W_i) \rightarrow E_j \in R$: a matching function which is used to determine whether Z_i and E_j should be added into the network.

$G(V, R)$: the final network built based on the ripples.

Figure 2 shows a simple DSUN model which has been built based on the algorithm, which is described as follows.

1) Take any Z_i of Z_s, for instance Z_1, add it into the set V, which means to create the first vertex for this element.
2) Take Z_1 and W_i into the matching function, and compare each w_i with a threshold by Q. The comparing result should always be 0 or 1. If the comparing result is 1, the corresponding E_j should be added into the set R, as well as the corresponding Z_k into the set V.
3) Repeat this process: using the matching function Q to calculate all the Z_i with their W_i, and continuously expanding the sets V and R in the network G, until all the Z_i is contained in the set V and no other edge E_j can be added into the set R.
4) Finally, the collection $G(V, R)$ is what we need.

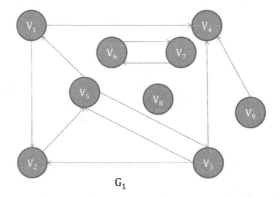

G_1

Fig. 2. An example of a DSUN model

As an example shown in Figure 2, $G_1 = \{V_1, R_1\}$, where,

$V_1 = \{v_1, v_2, v_3, v_4, v_5, v_6, v_7, v_8, v_9\}$

$R_1 = \{<v_1, v_2>, <v_1, v_4>, <v_2, v_5>, <v_3, v_2>, <v_3, v_4>, <v_3, v_5>, <v_5, v_1>, <v_5, v_3>, <v_6, v_7>, <v_7, v_6>, <v_9, v_4>,\}$

That is, G_1 consists of nine vertexes and eleven edges, which means in this learning system represented by G_1, there are nine users in this system and there are eleven relationships calculated based on the interaction(such as posting a message) among them.

The DSUN model is built timely and dynamically based on the users' current and personal interests or needs. In other words, this adaptive model will change dynamically in different periods to best fit users' requirements, which can finally support the learning process.

To describe our DSUN model, we introduce two measures and one concept as follows.

Interest degree: Interest degree is the out-degree of each vertex. That is, the interest degree of each vertex is the number of the arcs that take this vertex as the tail, which can be recorded as $ID(v)$.

The interest degree of a specific vertex indicates the number of other users from whom this user may get helpful information related to his/her current interests or needs. The higher interest degree is, the more extensive interests this user may have.

Popularity degree: Popularity degree is the in-degree of each vertex. That is, the popularity degree of each vertex is the number of the arcs that take this vertex as the head, which can be recorded as $PD(v)$.

The popularity degree of a specific vertex indicates the number of other users who may get information related to his/her current interests or needs from this user. The higher popularity degree is, the more contribution this user may have.

Tie: tie indicates a relationship among a series of vertexes, which may have several types.

There may be a variety of ties in a DSUM model. One tie in the model may contain different amount of vertexes, from one vertex to all vertexes. For instance, in a special situation, a tie that contains only one vertex is a weakest tie, which means this isolated user may have no similarity with other users. On the other hand, a tie that contains all the vertexes in the model is a super strong tie, which means all users communicate well in this learning system represented by the model.

Take the DSUN model G_1 for example again.

The interest degree of each vertex is: $ID(v_1)=2$, $ID(v_2)=1$, $ID(v_3)=3$, $ID(v_4)=0$, $ID(v_5)=2$, $ID(v_6)=1$, $ID(v_7)=1$, $ID(v_8)=0$, $ID(v_9)=1$.

The popularity degree of each vertex is: $PD(v_1)=1$, $PD(v_2)=2$, $PD(v_3)=1$, $PD(v_4)=3$, $PD(v_5)=2$, $PD(v_6)=1$, $PD(v_7)=1$, $PD(v_8)=0$, $PD(v_9)=0$.

There are also several ties in this graph, but no tie contains all the vertexes. Thus, G_1 is not strongly connected.

4   Application Scenario of the DSUN Model for Enhanced Social Learning

We assume a class with 30 students, where the professor requires these students to use microblog (we are using StatusNet[1] as a test bed for a lecture called *Introduction to Information Systems*) to publish messages, to raise questions, and discuss with the

---

[1] http://nislab.human.waseda.ac.jp/statusnet/

professor and/or other students. This will show if they understand the lecture and help the professor to monitor and regulate the progress of learning activity.

Each drop means a message from one student comes together to form a stream. In this case, the professor follows 30 students' streams. Take a 90 minutes class for example, this class can be divided into several sessions, at any time in each session, we can build a DSUN model dynamically based on the associative ripples generated by each student using his/her own heuristic stones. In the network, the interest degree of each vertex can tell the corresponding student that who has the most similar questions or interests with him/her, so that he/she can decide whom he/she should share his/her idea with; The popularity degree of each vertex can tell the professor that who gives the most contributions to a discussing topic. Considering the connectivity, the more strongly the DSUN model is connected, the more effective the discussion in the class will have. Therefore, based on the connectivity of the network, the professor can decide whether he/she should change his/her teaching style, or what he/she should talk about in next session timely to make the discussion more effective and enhance the quality of teaching.

Students can also be divided into several discussion groups according to the various ties. Users in ties may have some points of similarity, because they may have several same interests or needs. Thus, for the students, in this learning course we mentioned above, for each session or each class, students can be dynamically and timely divided into a series of groups based on the DSUN model, in which they can share information that best fits others' needs or more related to their interests. On the other hand, for the professor, he/she can change his/her teaching style or add some more topics momentarily based on the network so that the whole network could become a strong connected network, which means the learning interaction and teaching efficiency have been enhanced to a higher level.

5   Conclusions

In this paper, we have proposed a Dynamical Socialized User Networking (DSUN) model, which can represent users' current profiling and dynamical relationship based on their current interests and needs with those related information calculated from social streams in web-based learning environments. We have introduced a set of metaphors to describe social streams in the e-learning environment with a hierarchical structure. We have given the definitions and structure of our DSUN model with a set of measures and concepts. We have further developed a mechanism to build a DSUN model with social streams. Based on these, we have finally showed an application scenario of the DSUN model to provide both teachers and students with potential information, which can enhance the learning efficiency to assist social learning process in web-based learning environments.

As for future work, we will try to create a relationship spanning tree for each user in the DSUN model, which can seek relationships best fitting his/her personal and current needs. We will further consider more efficient approaches to avoid problems such as combinatorial explosion.

Acknowledgments. The work has been partly supported by 2011 Waseda University Grants for Special Research Project No. 2011B-259 and 2010–2012 Waseda University Advanced Research Center for Human Sciences Project "Distributed Collaborative Knowledge Information Sharing Systems for Growing Campus."

References

1. Hughes, A.: Higher education in a Web 2.0 world. JISC Report (2009),
   http://www.jisc.ac.uk/media/documents/publications/heweb20rp
   tv1.pdf
2. Grosseck, G., Holotescu, C.: Can we use Twitter for educational activities? In: 4th International Scientific Conference: eLearning and Software for Education, Bucharest, Romania (2008)
3. Ormrod, J.E.: Human learning, 3rd edn. Prentice-Hall, Upper Saddle River (1999)
4. Social Learning Theory,
   http://teachnet.edb.utexas.edu/~Lynda_abbot/Social.html
5. Chen, H., Zhou, X.K., Man, H.F., Wu, Y., Ahmed, A.U., Jin, Q.: A Framework of Organic Streams: Integrating Dynamically Diversified Contents into Ubiquitous Personal Study. In: 2010 Symposia and Workshops on Ubiquitous, Autonomic and Trusted Computing, Xi'an, China (2010)
6. Zhou, X.K., Chen, H., Jin, Q., Yong, J.M.: Generating Associative Ripples of Relevant Information from a Variety of Data Streams by Throwing a Heuristic Stone. In: ACM ICUIMC 2011 (5th International Conference on Ubiquitous Information Management and Communication), Seoul, Korea (2011)
7. Junco, R., Heiberger, G., Loken, E.: The effect of Twitter on college student engagement and grades. Journal of Computer Assisted Learning 27(2), 119–132 (2011)
8. Johnson, K.A.: The effect of Twitter posts on students' perceptions of instructor credibility. Learning Media and Technology 36(1), 21–38 (2011)
9. Soller, A., Wiebe, J., Lesgold, A.: A Machine Learning Approach to Assessing Knowledge Sharing During Collaborative Learning Activities. In: Proc. CSCL 2002, Colorado, USA, pp. 128–137 (2002)
10. Huang, L.H., Dow, C.R., Li, Y.H., Hsuan, P., Koo, W.L.: A Prompt Response Monitoring System for the Guiding Support of Learning Activities. In: Proc. ICIT 2010, Las Vegas, USA, pp. 1080–1085 (2010)
11. Man, H.F., Chen, H., Jin, Q.: Open Learning: A Framework for Sharable Learning Activities. In: 9th International Conference on Web-based Learning, Shanghai, China, pp. 387–392 (2010)
12. Poblete, B., Baeza-Yates, R.: Query-Sets: Using Implicit Feedback and Query Patterns to Organize Web Documents. In: Proc. WWW 2008, Beijing, China, pp. 41–48 (2008)
13. Fang, X., Liu Sheng, O.R.: LinkSelector: A Web Mining Approach to Hyperlink Selection for Web Portals. ACM Transactions on Internet Technology 4(2), 209–237 (2004)

Stage Predicting Student Stay Time Length on Webpage of Online Course Based on Grey Models

Qingsheng Zhang[1], Kinshuk[1], Sabine Graf[1], and Ting-wen Chang[2]

[1] Faculty of Science and Technology, Athabasca Univeristy, Canada
[2] National Chung Cheng University, Taiwan
{qzhang,kinshuk,sabineg}@athabascau.ca, lctw@cs.ccu.edu.tw

Abstract. To provide adaptive learning, an e-learning system needs to gather information about what student state is while the student learns online course. A student state index is the length of time the student stays on a webpage of online course. By predicting student's stay time length, the e-learning system has potential to dynamically tailor the learning content to the students. A literature review is conducted on power law of learning and knowledge component. We assume that online course consists of knowledge components. A knowledge component crosses several successive web pages. Accordingly, an initial prediction method is proposed based on the two learning curve modes and the grey models. Based on the experimental result of this initial prediction method, construction method of grey models is modified. The results produced by the grey models based on the two construction methods are then compared and analyzed. The results show that prediction of stay time length is possible to certain degree while the students learn knowledge on web pages.

Keywords: Stage Prediction, Learning Curve Mode, Knowledge Component, Power Law, Grey Model.

1   Introduction

In e-learning, students' various characteristics, such as learning style, as proposed by [1], can be modeled for adaptive learning. In this paper, stay time length is considered for adaptive learning. Stay time length is the time period that a student stays on a webpage of online course. It is affected by instructional organization of knowledge on web pages, the knowledge level and the cognitive ability of student. We explore if stay time length can be predicted based on the most recent history data of students' stay time length. However, in the context of e-learning, stay time length does not always mean that students are actually learning while they are on a webpage. Such duration is processed as noise. If the proposed method is able to predict stay time length, detailed research can be conducted in future about filtering noise.

The phenomena of power law are pervasive in the physical world and social environments. One of the earlier observations of the phenomena of power law in learning process is by [2]. Power law of learning states that to learn a skill, the learning performance and learning opportunities follow the distribution of power law.

H. Leung et al. (Eds.): ICWL 2011, LNCS 7048, pp. 226–232, 2011.

The power law of learning ranges from short term perceptual tasks to team-based longer term tasks [3]. Studies have also shown that the power law relationship between practice and performance may not always be readily evident in the practice of complex skills [4], but by decomposing the skill required in practicing each of the underlying rules, a clear power law relationship can be seen between practice and performance. If complex knowledge is decomposed into basic units, the fine grained analysis shows that learning curves of these basic units follow power law [5]. This kind of basic unit is named as knowledge component (KC). KC refers to the abstract knowledge unit containing concepts, principles, rules, declarative knowledge and schemata. In this paper, it is assumed that online course consists of KCs, and a KC crosses several successive web pages.

The rest of paper is organized as follows. The learning curve modes, power law and two grey models are introduced in section 2 in order to understand how to forecast stay time length. Lastly, the paper is concluded with a summary of the findings and discussion on future direction.

2   Learning Curve Modes, Power Law and Grey Models

A power law can be viewed as a probability distribution function in which the production of probability that a random variable takes a value is proportional to a negative power of this value. It is described by formula 1:

$$P(x) = c * x^{-k} \qquad\qquad c > 0, k > 0 \tag{1}$$

In the context of power law of learning, p is performance in formula 1, x is practice opportunities, c is performance on the first opportunity, and $-k$ is learning rate. With an increase in the practice opportunities, the performance decreases greatly at the beginning, and after some opportunities, the performance arrives at a stable state. Based on the assumption in section 1, we investigate if power law of learning exists in the log data of online course. Fig. 1 shows the stay time length curves of the learning of two students over two days. Curves in Fig. 1 show that fluctuations in stay time length varied greatly.

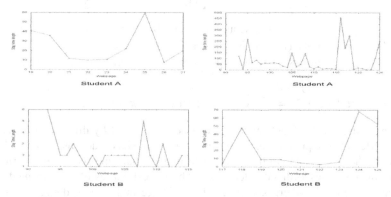

Fig. 1. Stay time length curves of two students learning in two days

In Fig. 1, y axis is stay time length on a webpage, and x axis is the index of web pages. Each diagram in Fig. 1 displays the record of stay time length in one day for the students A and B. The overall trend of stay time length in each curve is totally different from power law curve. But some parts of each curve in Fig. 1 are similar to power law curve to some degree. We also observe that other parts of each curve in Fig. 1 cannot be described by formula 1. However, the stay time length of these parts roughly follows another power law while the index k in formula 1 becomes negative. Therefore, we proposed two possible learning curve modes and their variants (broken line) as shown in Fig. 2, where k is webpage index, and y axis is stay time length.

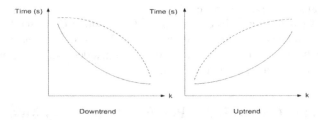

Fig. 2. Two learning curve modes and their variants

As proposed by [2], power law may be an artifact arising from averaging and that the exponential function may be the best fit when individual subjects employing a single strategy are considered. We substitute formula 2 for formula 1.

$$T(x) = c * e^{-mx} \qquad c > 0, m > 0 \qquad (2)$$

The trend of power law in the parts of curve in Fig. 1 is not evident. To predict stay time length, the grey models [6] is used. Advantage of using grey models is that they only require a few of history data for prediction. The accumulated generating operation (AGO) of grey models can make the unobvious trend of power law in the parts of curve in Fig. 1 evident. The AGO is defined as follows. Let $L^{(0)}$ be the original non negative sequence and $l^{(0)}$ be an element in the sequence. The AGO sequence $L^{(1)}$ can be presented as follows:

$$l^{(1)}(k) = \sum_{i=1}^{k} l^{(0)}(i) \qquad k = 1, 2, ..., n \qquad (3)$$

where $l^{(1)}$ is an element in the sequence $L^{(1)}$. To bring the data back to the original state, the inverse AGO (IAGO) is applied to the current data sequence. AGO and IAGO are a pair of inverse sequence operators. IAGO operation is defined as follows:

$$l^{(0)}(1) = l^{(1)}(1)$$
$$l^{(0)}(k + 1) = l^{(1)}(k + 1) - l^{(1)}(k) \qquad k = 1, 2, ..., n \qquad (4)$$

The curves used to fit AGO sequences can be represented by differential equations. These differential equations are referred as grey models, such as GM (1, 1) and Verhulst. The GM (1, 1) is often used to fit exponential type sequences. Verhulst is used to fit sequences with saturated trend. The typical curves of the two models are illustrated in Fig. 3, where k denotes the webpage and $l^{(0)}(k)$ denotes stay time length.

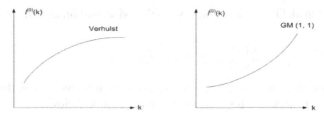

Fig. 3. Curves of model GM (1, 1) and Verhulst

Only using GM (1, 1) may not appropriately predict the stay time length. Therefore, we also use Verhulst model to predict stay time length. Now, we see that two grey models can only fit the learning curve mode of right side in Fig. 2. For the learning curve mode of left side in Fig. 2, we use the technique of curve flip to convert original curve into the curve which can be used by the two grey models. GM (1, 1) means grey model with single variable in first order equation. A type of single variable and first order linear dynamic differential equation is shown as follows:

$$\frac{dL^{(1)}}{dt} + a * L^{(1)} = b \tag{5}$$

where $L^{(1)}$ is the AGO sequence of the original sequence, and the parameters a and b are referred as the development coefficient and grey action quantity respectively, which can be acquired as follows:

$$\hat{a} = \begin{bmatrix} a \\ b \end{bmatrix} = (B^T B)^{-1} B^T Y_N \tag{6}$$

where

$$B = \begin{bmatrix} -z^{(1)}(2) & 1 \\ -z^{(1)}(3) & 1 \\ ... & ... \\ -z^{(1)}(n) & 1 \end{bmatrix} \tag{7}$$

$$Y_N = \begin{bmatrix} l^{(0)}(2) \\ l^{(0)}(3) \\ ... \\ l^{(0)}(n) \end{bmatrix} \tag{8}$$

and

$$z^{(1)}(k) = \frac{l^{(1)}(k) + l^{(1)}(k-1)}{2} \qquad k = 2, 3, ..., n \tag{9}$$

Then, the time response sequence of GM (1, 1) can be written as follows:

$$\hat{l}^{(1)}(k + 1) = (l^{(0)}(1) - \frac{b}{a}) e^{-ak} + \frac{b}{a} \qquad k = 1, 2, ..., n \tag{10}$$

where $\hat{l}$ is the predicated l. $\hat{l}^{(0)}(k + 1)$ can be acquired by IAGO as follows:

$$\hat{l}^{(0)}(k + 1) = \hat{l}^{(1)}(k + 1) - \hat{l}^{(1)}(k) \qquad k = 1, 2, ..., n \tag{11}$$

The Verhulst model is a type of single variable and second order differential equation, as follows:

$$\frac{dL^{(1)}}{dt} + a * L^{(1)} = b * (L^{(1)})^2 \tag{12}$$

where a and b are also acquired with formula 6. Y_N in formula 6 for Verhulst model is the same to formula 8, and B in formula 6 can acquired as follows:

$$B = \begin{bmatrix} -z^{(1)}(2) & (z^{(1)}(2))^2 \\ -z^{(1)}(3) & (z^{(1)}(3))^2 \\ \cdots & \cdots \\ -z^{(1)}(n) & (z^{(1)}(n))^2 \end{bmatrix} \tag{13}$$

$z^{(1)}$ in formula 13 is the same to formula 9. For Verhulst model, its time response sequence can be presented as follows:

$$\hat{l}^{(1)}(k+1) = \frac{a * l^{(1)}(0)}{b * l^{(1)}(0) + (a - b * l^{(1)}(0))e^{ak}}$$

$$k = 1, 2, \ldots, n \tag{14}$$

As saturated sequence already has some degree of exponential form, so the original sequence can be regarded as $L^{(1)}$ directly. $L^{(0)}$ in equation (8) should be the IAGO sequence of the original sequence. For Verhulst model, the predicted values of the original sequence can be acquired from equation (14). The two grey models are used to predict stay time length based on most recent three history data items. First, an extracted subsequence in raw sequence is evaluated for its curve type, and chooses a grey model for prediction. Then, we shift the subsequence window in the sequence to next data for new subsequence. A chosen grey model is used for next step prediction. This process is repeated until the last subsequence. As the abovementioned, we call our prediction method as stage prediction.

3   Experiment Analysis and Conclusion

Based on the prediction models in section 2, only data from the instructional unit lesson of online course are used, with learning events 91,084 from 459 students. Noisy low value (NLV) is set to less than or equal to 2 seconds. Noisy high value (NHV) is set to larger than or equal to 300, 1200 and 5400 seconds respectively. More than 50,000 learning events are used for testing while noise is filtered. For each prediction, we compare the predicted value with the original value to obtain the evaluation result. Here, we use the mean magnitude of relative error for all students (AMMRE) as evaluation measure. By averaging magnitude of relative error over number of predictions n in all days per student and all students m, AMMRE is obtained from the following formula:

$$\text{AMMRE} = \frac{1}{m}\sum_{j=1}^{m}\left(\frac{1}{n}\sum_{i=1}^{n}\left|\frac{p_i - \hat{p}_i}{p_i}\right|\right)_j \tag{15}$$

where $\hat{p}_i$ is the predicted value of original value p_i.

Table 1 shows the AMMRE in different NHVs. The higher value in the column AMMRE means the lower prediction accuracy. NHV takes serious effect for prediction. We also inspect prediction results in detail as we use the method of one-step-subsequence to construct the grey models. The underlying assumption is that it can dynamically fit the change trend of stay time length.

Table 1. AMMRE of prediction for different NHVs

NLV(s)	NHV(s)	AMMRE (%)	Predicted Learning Events
2	300	459.89	51,055
2	1200	997.37	57,060
2	5400	2169.89	59,231

One KC crosses several successive web pages. If a student does not know this KC, the student spends more time at the beginning. The stay time length would decrease for the subsequent web pages once the student has acquired the basic understanding. After the student finishes this KC on these web pages, the subsequent web pages may start another KC. It can drastically change the trend of stay time length. Therefore, the prediction is significantly affected. It reveals that the method of one-step-subsequence cannot dynamically reflect the occurrence of a new KC. Therefore, the proposed modified method observes the ratio between the predicted value and the original value. If the ratio exceeds the predefined value, the prediction models are built with stay time length from new KC. For the modified method, AMMRE changes from 37.45% to 121.06% in different NHVs. The value of AMMRE mainly depends on the ratio. The predicted learning events are 105, 4355, 5622, 5961, 5916, 5828 and 5706 as the ratio changes from 1 to 7 while NHV is 5400. As three most recent history data are used for prediction, in the worst situation, about 10 percent predicted learning events in Table 1 are used. In the best situation, we construct model for each predicted learning event, which means that about 30 percent predicted learning events in Table 1 are used besides ratio 1.

In this paper, we propose a stage prediction method about stay time length according to the learning curve modes and grey models. The initial prediction method is tested. Then, based on the experimental analysis, the analysis shows that the construction method of grey models is not robust to fit the change trend while a new knowledge component occurs. Therefore, we modify the construction method. The results show that AMMRE does not have strong effect from NHVs. It is dependent on the predefined ratio. In this paper, we consider only stay time length. Other factors, such as the length of webpage, may be used in future to model the stay time length. Additionally, we explore whether alternative learning curve modes exist in the dataset.

Acknowledgement. The authors acknowledge the support of NSERC, iCORE, Xerox, and the research-related gift funding by Mr. A. Markin.

References

1. Peter, B.: Adaptive Hypermedia. User Modeling and User-Adapted Interaction 11(1/2), 87–110 (2001)
2. Seibel, R.: Discrimination reaction time for a 1,023 alternative task. Journal of Experimental Psychology 66(3), 215–226 (1963)
3. Ritter, F.E., Schooler, L.J.: The learning curve. In: Kintch, W., Smelser, N., Baltes, P. (eds.) International Encyclopedia of the Social and Behavioral Sciences, pp. 8602–8605. Pergamon, Oxford (2001)
4. Kenneth, R.K., Santosh, M.: Distinguishing Qualitatively Different Kinds of Learning Using Log Files and Learning Curves. In: ITS 2004 Log Analysis Workshop, Maceio, Brazil, pp. 39–46 (2004)
5. Hausmann, R., VanLehn, K.: Self-explaining in the classroom: Learning curve evidence. In: McNamara, Trafton (eds.) The 29th Annual Cognitive Science Society, pp. 1067–1072. Cognitive Science Society, Austin (2007)
6. Sifeng, L.: The Grey System Theory and Applications (in Chinese). Science Press, Beijing (2005)

Enabling Open Learning Process with Learning Activity Streams: Model, Metaphor and Specification

Haifeng Man, Hong Chen, Jian Chen, Xiaokang Zhou, Yan Wu, and Qun Jin

Graduate School of Human Sciences, Waseda University,
2-579-15 Mikajima, Tokorozawa 359-1192, Japan
{manhaifeng@fuji.,chen@fuji.,wecan_chen@fuji.,
xkzhou@ruri.,yanwu@akane.,jin@}waseda.jp

Abstract. Sharing learning activity in and cross various systems is a prospective approach to implement OLP (Open Learning Process), a paradigm to share the knowledge generated in the learning process. The question is that the systems supporting teaching and learning are always separated and isolated. To implement OLP, firstly a uniform description of learning activity and a protocol to share learning activity in and cross systems are necessary. Secondly, a systematic framework to support learning activity description is also important. In this research, first, we show our vision of OLP by introducing metaphors such as a drop or an ocean of learning activity. Then based on the analysis of web based learning activity through Activity Theory, we propose a learning activity model to describe learning activity. Moreover, a specification of learning activity streams based on Activity Streams specification is introduced. Finally, a prototype system supporting learning activity streams is implemented based on UPS (Ubiquitous Personal Study) platform.

Keywords: Open Learning Process, Activity Streams, Learning Activity Streams, Learning activity, learning action, learning process.

1 Introduction

OLP (Open Learning Process) means sharing the learning process information in and cross systems to improve teaching, learning and other related educational activities. OLP can be achieved by some commonly used approaches, such as sharing user learning behavior, portfolio and other user generated information. Sharing user learning activity is one of the approaches to implement OLP. Comparing with learning design set by instructor, user learning activity can be thought as an artifact generated in the real course implementation process which can show us a real learning process containing more personalized characters than the original learning design by a teacher.

In order to share user learning activity in and cross systems, one issue to be solved is giving a uniform learning activity specification, with which the data of learning activity is capable of being interpreted in different systems. In addition, the syndication mechanism of learning activity information in various systems should be

H. Leung et al. (Eds.): ICWL 2011, LNCS 7048, pp. 233–242, 2011.

considered. This can be implemented with various communication protocols. Furthermore, such issues as storage, transmission, retrieval and reuse of the learning activity information are also the preconditions of the OLP implementation. This study focuses on the basic works of learning activity based OLP, including learning activity model, learning activity stream metaphor and learning activity specification.

The other parts of this paper are organized as follows. In Section 2, we review some existed works related to learning activity description and activity streams. In Section 3, the analysis of learning activity based on Activity Theory is described, and a learning activity model is presented. Learning activity stream metaphors and LAS (Learning Activity Streams) specification are introduced in Section 4. The implementation of LAS in a prototype system based on the UPS platform is illustrated in Section 5. Finally, in Section 6, we conclude this study, and highlight some future works.

2   Related Work

2.1   Learning Activity in a Web Based Learning System

In practice, the term, learning activity, is very flexible by its meaning. For example, a learning activity could be a learning activity happened on a small content unit or an aggregated one with some sub activities happened in many lessons covering a large time span. A learning activity could have clear teaching and learning objectives or just some not so clear objectives. This complexity of learning activity should be considered when trying to describe learning activity in a uniform way in a web based learning system.

IMS Simple Sequencing specification tries to a standard solution to describe learning activity in a learning system, where "a learning activity may be loosely described as an instructional event or events embedded in a content resource, or as an aggregation of activities that eventually resolve to discreet content resources with their contained instructional events. [1]" This descriptive definition of learning activity shows us the complexity of learning activity as well. But in practice, it just "maps the concept of a learning activity to an *item* element or a collection of *item* elements within an *organization* element [1]." This method is simple for system designers to describe a learning activity or an aggregation learning activities. In Moodle, the same approach is taken to describe learning activity; learning activity is mapped to a specific learning resource in a one-to-one style, namely one kind of resource can produce one kind of learning activity. We think a more detailed and learner centered description of learning activity could be of more potential to promote the reuse of learning activity information than the simple mapping learning content to learning activity. Moreover the description of learning activity should be capable of giving us enough information to support its more effective or potential reusing.

2.2   Activity Streams

Activity Streams [2] is an extension of the Atom feed specification. Among the various RSS/ATOM based protocols, it is able to describe not only the content, but also the activity and action in a system by adding activity related items. This draft works as an activity stream protocol to syndicate activities in various social web applications. It can describe users' activity with the items such as actors, verbs, objects and target elements, and has been adopted in Facebook, Google Buzz and MySpace. Activity streams provide us an opportunity to share learning activity cross different systems to create advanced reuse of learning process information to deal with the questions in various learning systems, such as learning management system, social network, etc [3]. Since learning activity is different with the common social activity conducted in the social networks, a specification for the description of learning activity does not exist yet.

Action Streams is a further extension to Activity Streams targeting to " permit posts not only to share activity updates across social networks, but to enable action within and around those posts also" [4]. Kirkpatrick [5] argued that the implementation of activity with actions would mean not only that you could operate the system from other networks. Action streams show us a bigger vision of connecting learners distributed in various learning systems to provide more influent learning experience.

3   An analytic Framework Based on Activity Theory

3.1   Analysis of Learning Activity Based on Activity Theory

Activity theory is a framework to analyze various human activities, which was first developed by the Russian psychologists L. Vygotsky, S. Rubinshtein, A. Leontiev, and others [6] and provides us a framework to analyze human activity in social and cultural context. A human activity can be a subject (human) with some motivation, mediated with some instruments (tools) to achieve his/her object (goal). And this structure includes more context information than the original framework, such as rules, community and division of labor. The community component is about people who share the same objective with the subject. Rules regulate actions and interactions within the activity system. The division of labor is about the type of the work between community members. According to the research of Allen, etc. [7], Engestrom [8] sought to call attention to the larger social context by adding in the community as a separate component.

The context information is important to understand and reuse a human activity. A learning activity is one kind of human activity, which happens in a teaching and learning environment, reflecting the interaction in the system at some instant in time, and must be explained based on his context information.

Learning activity is "an interaction between a learner or learners and an environment (optionally including content resources, tools and instruments, computer systems and services, 'real world' events and objects) that is carried out in response to a task with an intended learning outcome [9]. Activity theory can be used to analyze various learning activity, such as mobile learning activity [10]. Fig. 1 shows a learning activity system for the web based learning. A web based learning activity is trigged by the motivation of a subject, and mediated by some learning resources, such as learning objects, social tools, LMS and related devices, directed by the object (goal), such as knowledge, practice, etc. And the rules, community and division of labor component introduce more context information about this learning activity.

Learning activity must be explained in its related learning environment. For example, an activity, "Tom viewed a cat picture", if in Facebook, can be explained as "Tom is my friend followed by me, and he viewed a picture of his friend". If in a learning process, "Tom is learning something about animal by viewing a picture, which this is provided by his teacher".

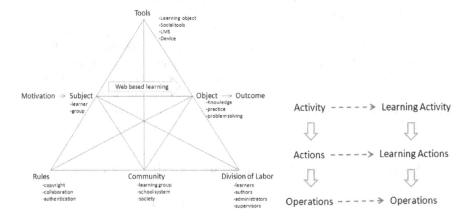

Fig. 1. Learning activity system   **Fig. 2.** Three levels of learning activity

Kuutti [11] reinterprets the three levels of activity as motive (activity), goal (action) and condition (operation), and shows us a vertical structure of learning activity. Accordingly, we propose a three level learning activity structure (as shown in Fig.2), in which: learning activity is implemented by a serious of learning actions, and learning actions can be implemented by some user and system behavior. Operation is the most granular description of user learning activity in this three layer architecture, which can also be reused to promote teaching and learning, however the tiny granularity of operation makes it not a suitable way to transmit on the web. Therefore operation is not considered in this research.

3.2   Learning Activity Model

In consideration of the component mentioned in the learning activity system, we proposed a learning activity model, and its subcomponent action model. And the operational layer of learning activity is not implemented in this model, since the operation information of users is difficult to capture without additional devices and the operation information of system is easy but difficult to be captured, processed and transmitted on the web.

As shown in Fig. 3, activity has six basic attributes. **ID** is identification for the model. **Time** attribute is the time at which the learning activity happened. Since time is always a period, this is always the start time of this description created. **Actor** attribute is about the learner or the person who triggered the activity to happen. **Task** (course) attribute represents the context under which the activity occurs. **Service** attribute shows where the action happened, pointing to a learning service system or system component. **Action** is the subcomponent of activity, which has much smaller granularity of learning process description. Learning activity can be regarded as the action collection happened in a course. Then the activity can be analyzed by a teacher for more effective instructional design based on the user learning actions, and for a user to follow the actions to finish his/her study.

Fig. 3. Learning activity model   **Fig. 4.** Learning action model

This simple model can be extended to include more information needed by the application in a specific learning system. The attribute set is only some basic perspectives generally needed to describe a learning activity. The outcome of the learning activity should be considered, which has not been represented in the learning activity model, but included in the learning action model to be described in the next sub-section.

3.3 Learning Action Model

Action is a subcomponent of learning activity, which represents more granular learner activity. It can be thought as a behavior or interaction happened between a learner and learning resource.

A typical learning action should have six basic attributes (as shown in Fig.4).

Time is the time of the action happened, which is a time point. **Actor** is the same with the learning activity actor attribute when the action aroused by that same actor (not by other actor). In this paper, we don't consider the complex action such as a learning action aroused by other actors. **Service** attribute contain the information about the system or system component. **Verb** is the uniform action description. **Target** is the object on which the verb happened. **Outcome** is the output of the user learning action, such as homework, a post. Outcome can be used to assess the related learning action, learning activity, and even the whole learning process.

4   Learning Activity Streams: Metaphor and Specification

4.1   Learning Activity Streams Metaphors

Streams metaphor is a convenient way to depict the dynamic characters of sequence data. In this study, a set of metaphors are adopted to represent learning activity streams. Fig.5 shows the related stream metaphors from a single drop generated in a system to the learning activity ocean composed by the learning activity information aggregated from various users and systems. This work is mainly based on the work of Chen et al. [12], in which the stream related metaphors have been introduced and defined. In this study, a learning activity pool metaphor is further introduced to represent the smaller functional learning activity set.

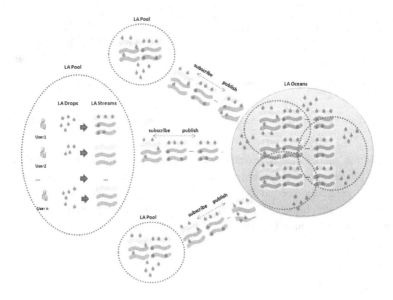

Fig. 5. Learning activity streams metaphor

The related metaphors are explained as follows (LA is the abbreviation of learning activity). **LA Drop**: Drop is a minimum unit of learning activity streams, such as a learning activity from a learning system. The LA Drops generated in a learning process can be shared with other systems through the publishing mechanism of the system. **LA Stream**: Stream is a set of LA drops in timeline, which contains the activities of a user or user group, and can show us the personalized user or group learning path. **LA Pool**: Pool is a repository of learning activities belonging to a system, such as Moodle. LA pool can provide users with some learning services. The aggregation and publishing of learning activity could be the two basic functions of the system. The reuse of learning activity streams is also implemented in the LA pool. **LA Ocean**: Ocean is a repository for storing large quantity of learning activity information, and provides the basic search service and other additional services to reuse learning activity information.

4.2   LAS Specification

LAS specification is based on the activity streams specification, aiming to describe the learning activity generated in the user learning process. This approach has some merits. For example, if a system supports Atom standard, we can easily upgrade the system to support learning activity standard; and if an existed system only supports ATOM protocol, it can also import learning activity information as well. Fig. 6 shows the item set used in the learning activity streams specification. Parts of them are from ATOM specification and activity streams specification.

Since context information is necessary to understand and reuse learning activity, we include some course related items in the specification, such as course name, summary, detail, link, which can provide us the context of the learning activity. Task item is also about the learning activity context, used to describe the user current learning task.

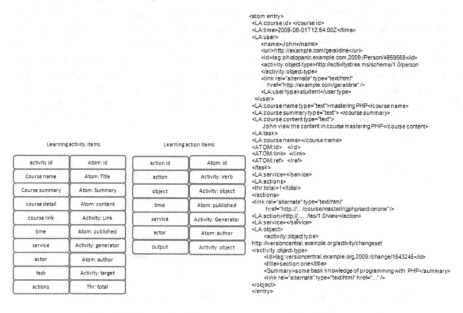

Fig. 6. LAS specification   **Fig. 7.** An example

Service is the metadata set about the system. A URI item records the link to the system or the system component, which can be used to show where the learning activity happened and what kinds of services can be used to implement this learning activity. Learning action is the basic component of the learning activity, with which the personalized user learning behavior can be captured. Verb (action) is used to describe the user behavior, such as "view", "post", etc., and include the description of the learning outcome. This is meaningful when we want to describe user learning activity and action, which can show us a sequence of user generated information in the learning process.

Fig. 7 shows an example, which is revised from the activity streams example. It is a description of an activity in a course, in which the actor "John" "viewed" the learning content of "section one" in course "Mastering PHP". This is a simple entry in which one action happened in the learning activity. A complex learning activity can include more than one action and more users and objects as well.

5   System Implementation

5.1   System Architecture

UPS (Ubiquitous Personal Study) [12] [13] platform can collect individual information together by organizing individual identity and personal information. A number of UPSs can also connect with each other by the XSNS (Cross Social Network Services) module to build a distributed UPS community. Fig. 8 shows an overall system architecture based on UPS, in which learning activity collected and stored in various learning pools can be published to the LA (Learning Activity) Ocean Cloud, and then can be retrieved and reused by other local learning systems to support teaching and learning.

Since learning activity is the relation between learner and learning resource, the description of related entities in the learning environment should be kept in the LA Ocean Cloud. An identity should be identified by IRI (Internationalized Resource Identifier) or URI (Uniform Resource Identifier) to facilitate the searching and retrieval of the learning activities.

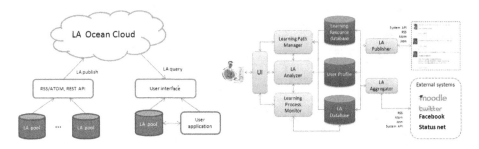

Fig. 8. Overall system architecture   **Fig. 9.** Local system architecture

Fig. 9 shows the architecture of a local system supporting learning activity streams. This system can share or reuse learning activity, or both of them to enhance teaching and learning. **Learning Process Monitor** is a basic function module of this system to monitor the user learning activity. **LA Publisher** is responsible for publishing the learning activity information in a uniform format that can be decoded effectively by other systems. **LA Aggregator** is used to aggregate learning activity information from various external systems conforming to activity streams specification, such as Moodle and some prevalent social software system, such as Twitter, Facebook, etc. **LA Analyzer** processes the learning activities and provides users with the related information to support their educational activities, such as teaching, learning, etc. **Learning Path Manager** is a common component of LMS (Learning Management System) to manage user learning path.

5.2   System UI

Fig. 10 shows the user interface of the prototype system. The actions from the users including teachers and students can be exposed to others and viewed and deleted and even followed by other users. With this kind of mechanism users can share their learning activity in a system and among systems. The activities from different users and system can be viewed in the information pool as shown in Fig. 11.

Fig. 10. The frontpage of the system   **Fig. 11.** LAS in a course

6   Conclusion

In this paper, first, we have given an analysis of learning activity based on Activity Theory, which is a framework to analyze human activity in the social and cultural perspective. According to the human activity analysis framework, web based learning activity should be explained with its related context information and have a three-layer architecture. And a learning activity model has been introduced in detail. Second, a set of stream metaphors for learning activity were introduced to show the dynamic character of shared learning activity. A specification based on Activity Streams specification has been presented as well. Finally, we implemented a prototype system based on the UPS (Ubiquitous Personal Study) platform, which provides a solution to implement the learning activity streams metaphors.

Some concluding remarks can be made as follows. First, learning activity should be explained in its learning environment, and rich context information set of learning activity is necessary. And current information technologies and services provide us more possibility to capture the learning activity related information, with which advanced applications can be created. Second, sharing learning activity is a practical and feasible way to connect users or systems to implement OLP (Open Learning Process). Third, LAS is a promising approach to share user knowledge, especially the tacit knowledge. Some of the challenges of Open Education can be met by the implementation of LAS in the current learning systems.

Our future works mainly include (1) Creating learning activity streams based applications to promote teaching and learning, such as learning activity recommendation service to support the design and use of learning resource. (2) Connecting formal and informal learning with learning activity based system, such as importing social activity as a reference resource to the formal learning activity, learning activity based recommendation, etc.

Acknowledgments. The work has been partly supported by 2011 Waseda University Grants for Special Research Project No. 2011B-259 and 2010–2012 Waseda University Advanced Research Center for Human Sciences Project "Distributed Collaborative Knowledge Information Sharing Systems for Growing Campus."

References

1. IMS: Simple Sequencing Information and Behavior Model (2003),
   `http://www.imsglobal.org/simplesequencing/ssv1p0/imsss_infov`
   `1p0.html`
2. Atkins, M., Media, S., Norris, W., Google, Messina, C., Citizen Agency, G., et al.: Atom Activity Streams 1.0., http://activitystrea.ms/specs/atom/1.0/
3. Man, H., Chen, H., Jin, Q.: Open Learning: A Framework for Sharable Learning Activities. In: Luo, X., Spaniol, M., Wang, L., Li, Q., Nejdl, W., Zhang, W. (eds.) ICWL 2010. LNCS, vol. 6483, pp. 387–392. Springer, Heidelberg (2010)
4. Chan, A.: Action streams: a blue sky proposal (2011),
   `http://www.gravity7.com/blog/media/2010/02/action-streams-`
   `blue-sky-proposal.html`
5. Kirkpatrick, M.: Action Streams: A New Idea for Social Networks (2011),
   `http://www.readwriteweb.com/archives/action_streams_a_new_id`
   `ea_for_social_networks.php`
6. Kaptelinin, V., Kuutti, K., Bannon, L.: Activity theory: Basic concepts and applications. Human-Computer Interaction (1995)
7. Allen, D., Karanasios, S., Slavova, M.: Working with Activity Theory: Context, Technology, and Information Behavior. Journal of the American Society for Information Science and Technology 62(4), 776–788 (2011)
8. Engeström, Y.: Learning by Expanding: An Activity-Theoretical Approach to Developmental Research. Orienta-Konsultit, Helsinki (1987)
9. Beetham, H.: Review: developing e-learning models for the JISC practitioner communities: a report for the JISC e-pedagogy programme (2004)
10. Che, P.-C., Lin, H.-Y., Jang, H.-C., Lien, Y.-N., Tsai, T.-C.: A Study of English Mobile Learning Applications at National Chengchi University. International Journal of Distance Education Technologies (IJDET) 7(4), 38–60 (2009)
11. Kuutti, K.: Activity theory as a potential framework for human-computer interaction research, Context and consciousness: activity theory and human-computer interaction, pp. 17–44. MIT press, Cambridge (1996)
12. Chen, H., Zhou, X., Man, H., Wu, Y., Ahmed, A.U., Jin, Q.: A Framework of Organic Streams: Integrating Dynamically Diversified Contents into Ubiquitous Personal Study. In: ATC-UIC 2010, Xi'an, China (2010)
13. Chen, H., Jin, Q.: Ubiquitous Personal Study: A Framework for Supporting Information Access and Sharing. Personal and Ubiquitous Computing (ACM/Springer) 13(7), 539–548 (2010)

An Ontology Based E-Learning System Using Antipatterns

Dimitrios Settas and Antonio Cerone

United Nations University, International Institute for Software Technology,
Macau, SAR, China
{settdimi,antonio}@iist.unu.edu

Abstract. Antipatterns are mechanisms that describe how to arrive at a good (refactored) solution from a fallacious solution that has negative consequences. These mechanisms are used in a variety of computer science topics and although their integration in teaching and computer science curriculum has been proposed, the development of an e-learning system using antipatterns, still remains an open issue. Previous work has proposed the use of WebProtege, a Web-based environment that allows collaborative editing as well as annotation and voting of both components and changes of the antipattern ontology. This ontology has been implemented as the knowledge base of SPARSE, an intelligent system that uses semantic web tools and techniques in order to detect the antipatterns that exist in a software project. In this paper, we leverage this semantic web technology and the formalism of ontology in order to propose a peer-production based e-learning system for the electronically supported learning of antipatterns. We illustrate how this Web-based system can transfer antipattern knowledge using an e-learning scenario as an example.

1 Introduction

An antipattern is a new form of pattern that has two solutions. The first is a problematic solution with negative consequences and the other is a refactored solution, which describes how to change the antipattern into a healthy solution [8]. This healthy solution has an improved structure that provides more benefits than the original solution and refactors the system toward minimized consequences. Antipatterns have been recently proposed as a knowledge transfer mechanism in teaching software engineering and human-computer interaction [2, 7]. After comparing the effects of learning and teaching using design patterns and antipatterns, the authors concluded that negative advice doesnt help students much. Students find negative advice in the form of enhanced guidelines more confusing than when presented with positive advice in the same format. Negative advice does not aid students significantly in comprehending, recognizing and avoiding software development pitfalls. Rogers and Pheatt [10] have

H. Leung et al. (Eds.): ICWL 2011, LNCS 7048, pp. 243–252, 2011.

proposed an approach to overcome the aforementioned issues by using a catalog of student accessible antipatterns. This can be used as an adjunct to design patterns discussions in Software Engineering and Object Orientated design courses. As a result, antipattern concepts are couched in a positive fashion using examples to avoid the aforementioned negative concept problem. In this paper, we propose a Web-based e-learning system that consists of a dynamic repository of antipatterns that brings learners and instructors together in a collaborative environment using semantic Web tools and techniques. An important element of this e-learning system is it's peer production approach that allows learners to actively participate in creating the content for this system. This approach allows e-learning using antipatterns in a constructive manner by allowing learners to identify, edit and define new antipatterns.

Ontologies and Semantic Web techniques offer new perspectives on intelligent educational systems by supporting more adequate and accurate representations of learners, their learning goals, learning material and contexts of its use, as well as more efficient access and navigation through learning resources. However, ontology-based e-learning is still at an early stage of gestation not only due to the problems regarding the technology of ontologies but mainly due to the nature of e-learning itself. E-learning is not just concerned with providing access to learning resources using a repository of learning resources, such as presenting a catalogue of antipatterns, but is also concerned with supporting features such as collaboration, between learners and between learners and instructors [1]. According to Dicheva et. al [6], an e-learning community will succeed if the participating members perceive some value in their participation. The authors highlighted the importance of providing a pool of up-to-date teaching materials made available to community members through sharing and collaboration in order to provide value and motivation for sustainability. The e-learning system proposed in this paper adds more value and motivation for learning using antipatterns by providing a dynamic Web-based environment to collaboratively identify, define and construct new antipatterns.

In this paper, WebProtege ontology editor is proposed as an ontology based e-learning framework to allow learners, instructors and other users to collaborate using the web-based version of the antipattern ontology. The ontology is used as the knowledge base of SPARSE, an intelligent system that can bring the learners attention to focus on antipatterns that are specifically suitable to a specific software project. Hence, learners and instructors will not only benefit from the collaborative editing of the ontology, but instructors will be able to follow a blended teaching practice by combining traditional teaching with a modern e-learning system. For example, instructors can provide examples of problematic scenarios of software projects using case studies and learners will then use the system to choose the relevant antipattern symptoms, detect the possible antipatterns using SPARSE and study how and why they are related. Instructors can also add e-learning content by defining new antipatterns. Learners can then edit the ontology knolwedge base and actively participate in enriching it with new antipattern knowledge in the form of new ontology components or discussions. Instructors can also benefit from the system by having access to an e-learning system that hosts antipattern learners and an organized catalogue of antipatterns that allows learners to collaborate in understanding antipatterns without requiring them to memorize antipatterns.

This paper discusses the benefits of using SPARSE and the web-based antipattern ontology to both learners and instructors to share antipattern information, discussions and collaborate in ontology enrichment. The paper consists of 5 sections, which are organized as follows: Section 2 describes the background, the related work and the literature review used in our research. Section 3 presents the application of the Web-based collaborative ontology to e-learning. Section 4 presents an e-learning scenario using this semantic Web technology. Finally, in Section 5, the findings are summarized, future work is proposed and conclusions are drawn.

2   Background and Related Work

The most common mistake made with design patterns is the application of a particular design pattern in the wrong context or setting. Antipatterns redefine the concept of design patterns in a new form that attempts to resolve this problem by providing detailed templates [4, 8] that state the causes, symptoms and consequences of an antipattern. Studying failures and learning from mistakes is a far more suitable approach for software development practices that rely on learning that comes from experience, such as project management.

In previous work, SPARSE has been implemented as a stand alone ontology-based intelligent system that can detect the antipatterns that exist in a software project. There are three underlying technologies involved in SPARSE: (a) ontologies, through the use of the OWL ontology language, (b) Description Logic (DL) reasoners, through the use of the Pellet DL reasoner and (c) production rule engines, through the use of the CLIPS production rule engine. In this paper, we propose the use of a single Web-based e-learning system that brings together SPARSE with the Web-based collaborative editing of the antipattern ontology. The goal of this exploration is to allow learners to effectively contribute and share new antipatterns in a central web-based OWL ontology file that contains an up to date antipattern catalogue for a specific course or project. The system is able to define different privileges for different user roles (i.e. instructors and learners). The ability to communicate and collaborate while editing or creating an antipattern, will ultimately motivate learners to use the proposed e-learning system. Users are able to reach consensus and agree on ontology changes with other learners. Instructors can then participate by approving or disapproving these changes.

Boskovic et al. [3] have developed PatternGuru, an educational system for learning software patterns.The basic idea of PatternGuru is to provide learning of software patterns in collaborative manner and to present them as an integral part of software development. The tool is developed by extending ArgoUML, an open source project, so it can be used for both software engineering and education. Intelligent systems have been widely used in many different settings including a teaching environment to support a cognitive simulation project in an undergraduate introductory AI course [9].

The relevant literature contains a plethora of ontology-based e-learning systems. Cheung [5] proposed an Ontology-based Framework for Personalized Adaptive Learning (OPAL) framework for students to learn basic Java programming with adaptive features according to their learning preference and learning performance. Tan et al. [11] investigated ontology-based approaches for representing information semantics in E-learning systems. Wang et al. [13] presented the ontology-based description of a learning object. Learning Object is a central notion of the majority of current researches to Web-based education, and many institutions devote themselves to research the standardization of learning object.

Dicheva et al. [6] proposed a framework for rapid collaborative development and sharing of learning resources for emerging disciplines, which is built on a set of intuitions shared by a wide range of academics: that knowledge should be open to use and reuse; that collaboration should be easier; that people should get credit and kudos for contributing to education research; that there should be a way for instructors to publicly acknowledge reuse of open content; and that the ability of authors and instructors to readily and dynamically access and update learning material is especially important in rapidly changing fields.

Despite the extensive body literature on ontology-based e-learning systems and intelligent systems used in teaching, as far as the authors are aware, the research summarized in this paper represents the first implementation of an e-learning system using a collaboratively developed ontological knowledge base in combination with an intelligent system for the transfer of antipattern knowledge.

3   Using the Web-Based Collaborative Antipattern Ontology in E-Learning

The WebProtege [12] ontology editor is an important step towards achieving collaboration in an e-learning system using the formalism of ontology. Using the WebProtege antipattern ontology installation, learners can create new instances of antipatterns, causes, symptoms and consequences in order to define new antipatterns and their attributes. Furthermore, learners can familiaze themselves with antipatterns by browsing or editing existing antipatterns while instructors can add new teaching material by including further attributes within existing antipatterns or removing and editing existing antipattern attributes.

The proposed e-learning system can broadcast up-to-date ontology changes and data to all ontology instances. Using synchronous access to the shared antipattern ontology, when a change is made in a stand alone installation of Protege that is connected to the WebProtege server, the change is immediately seen by all online learners as well. This ensures that all learners and instructors are provided with up-to-date ontology data. Ultimately, this will provide value and motivation for sustainability. Furthermore, depending on the level of the learner, user access can be controlled to specific parts of the ontology. Access control allows instructors or learners of the ontology to restrict access to certain parts of the ontology. It is possible to allow certain learners/instructors only to propose a change through discussion but not make the actual change. During ontology development, it is also important for assesment purposes for instructors to identify which learners make a change or votes for a change and which other learners vote in favor of or against it. Learners can make proposal for changes, review and approve changes of other learners with a voting mechanism. A learner or instructor can create a new proposal for a change in the ontology. Other users can then vote whether they agree or disagree with this proposal. The search function of Collaborative Protege allows an instructor or learner to find all changes made by a specific learner or browse the latest changes through discussions.

An important charactestic that provides some value in the participation of learners is the documentation and management of discussions and annotations during ontology development. Antipattern learners might not always have the same opinion on a particular antipattern, attribute or property. In this case, a discussion needs to be made in order to reach consensus. For this reason, Webprotege incorporates discussions and notes during ontology development. Other advantages of this functionality is that learners are able to understand why a change was made, track changes and consider alternatives. Furthermore, the ontology concepts, instances or roles being discussed can be easily examined since these discussions are being carried out during ontology development. Users of the system can communicate with other antipattern learners/instructors using chat and discussions. Since many users can connect to the same server, they can communicate using chat and carry out discussions in threads. Finally, instructors can provide their own constructive feedback to learner's additions and discussions and can carry out their own additions to the ontology. The following section demonstrates how this ontology acts as the knowledge of a the proposed Web-based e-learning system.

4 An E-Learning Scenario

This section describes an example scenario of using the proposed Web-based e-learning system. The scenario assumes the deployment of the proposed e-learning system with a blended teaching practice during a postgraduate University course.

Figure 1 illustrates the proposed e-learning system. In this scenario, instructors deliver lectures and reading material to learners regarding case studies that describe problematic situations and problematic practices in software projects. Learners are asked to study the document and identify the symptoms of problematic scenarios or problematic practices that occured during the software project. Learners then access the proposed Web-based systems and choose the symptoms that they identified (Figure 2). This information can then be used from SPARSE in order to detect antipatterns based on the new antipattern, antipattern attributes (causes,symptoms and consequences) and properties. The result window displays two sets of antipattern. On the left hand side there are the related symptom-based antipatterns, which are antipatterns linked through their symptoms. Antipatterns that appear on the right hand side are related through causes or consequences. By clicking on an antipattern SPARSE displays the description and the refactored solution of the antipattern. By selecting the explanations option, SPARSE provides explanations to the learner on the reasons that a specific antipattern has been proposed. Figure 3 illustrates an example of the explanations that SPARSE provides on how a selected symptom is linked through causes and consequences of other antipatterns. Learners are then asked to use the antipattern ontology Webprotege installation in order to participate in the enrichment of the content of the e-learning system and allow instructors to assess them.

After choosing the antipattern ontology from the ontology menu, the learner signs in with the username and password that has been previously assigned by the Administrator. For the purposes of this paper, the OWL antipattern ontology contains data from 31 software project management antipatterns that exist on the Web. The learner can then choose to edit an existing antipattern or antipattern attribute, edit the description of an antipattern, remove the relationship between two antipattern attributes or create new ontology components. For example, after selecting the "Individuals" tab, the learner can select "Antipatterns" to create a new instance of an antipattern and can perform the same task for the "Cause", "Symptom" and "Consequence" classes. The learner can then create new property values for each new class invididual. For example, WebProtege can be used to define a "CauseToSymptom" relationship. This relationship indicates that a specific cause of an antipattern is related with a specific symptom of another antipattern. Before carrying out any task in the ontology, learners are encouraged and asked to create discussions regarding these changes. This can be done using the Webprotege technology that was described in the previous section. Instructors can then assess learners based on their contribution and the degree in which they collaborated with other learners. Instructors can also provide their feedback regarding proposed changes and paricipate in discussions and ontology enrichment. Using this peer-production model, there is almost no distinction made between the users of the system and the contributors of the knowledge.

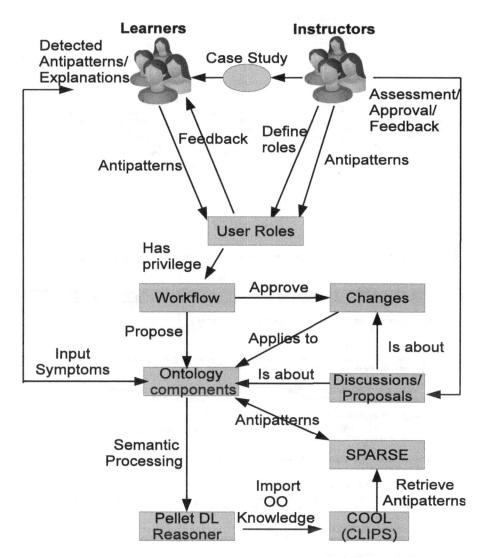

Fig. 1. The ontology based e-learning system using antipatterns

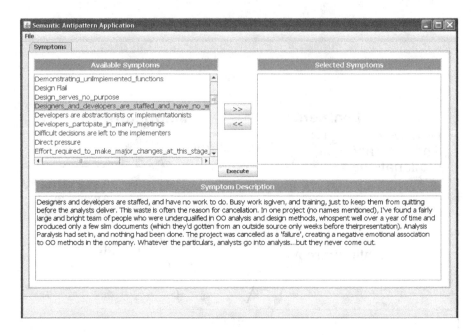

Fig. 2. Selecting a set of symptoms that exist in a software project using SPARSE

Fig. 3. The explanation window of SPARSE describing why an antipattern might be a relevant result

5   Conclusion

The proposed Web-based system, offers a modern peer-production based e-learning system that can support the transfer of the knowledge encoded in antipatterns. Providing an up-to-date knowledge base supported by collaborative editing with communication mechanisms is an essential requirement for any e-learning systems that aims to provide value to its users and motivation for sustainability. In this paper, the transfer of antipattern knowledge and the electronically supported learning of antipatterns is proposed using Webprotege, a web based ontology editor and SPARSE, an ontology based intelligent system. The combination of both tools offers an extensible e-learning system that leverages semantic Web technology and can be used by both learners and instructors in any e-learning scenario that uses antipatterns.

Ultimately, the strong social aspect and peer production capabilities of the system will provide sufficient motivation for the adoption of the system and the platform will evolve by taking account different kinds of antipatterns on various computer science topics and by forming a worldwide community of antipattern e-learning users. The release of the tool as an Open Source project aims to develop both SPARSE and Webprotege in a single Web-based application and future work is aimed in this direction.

SPARSE is currently available as a stand alone application and can be launched by executing the .jar file. Before using the tool, the associated OWL ontology should then be imported from the File menu. Users can download SPARSE together with the OWL antipattern ontology from the Web or participate in the open source project.

References

[1] Barker, P.: Developing teaching webs: "advantages, problems and pitfalls". In: Proceedings of the World Conference on Educational Multimedia, Hypermedia and Telecommunication Conference, pp. 89–94 (2000)

[2] Biljon, J.V., Kotzé, P., Renaud, K., McGee, M., Seffah, A.: The use of anti-patterns in human computer interaction: wise or ill-advised? In: Marsden, G., Kotzé, P., Adesina-Ojo, A. (eds.) Fulfilling the promise of ICT, SAICSIT (ACM Conference Proceedings Series), pp. 176–185 (2004)

[3] Bošković, M., Gašević, D., Devedžić, V.: Patternguru: An educational system for software patterns. In: Proceedings of the Fifth IEEE International Conference on Advanced Learning Technologies (ICALT 2005), pp. 650–654 (2005)

[4] Brown, W., McCormick, H., Thomas, S.: AntiPatterns in Project Management. Wiley Computer publishing (2000)

[5] Cheung, R., Wan, C., Cheng, C.: An Ontology-Based Framework for Personalized Adaptive Learning. In: Luo, X., Spaniol, M., Wang, L., Li, Q., Nejdl, W., Zhang, W. (eds.) ICWL 2010. LNCS, vol. 6483, pp. 52–61. Springer, Heidelberg (2010)

[6] Dicheva, D., Dichev, C., Zhu, Y.: Sharing open-content learning resources in emerging disciplines. In: Proceedings of the 14th International Conferenceon Artificial Intelligence in Education Workshop on Ontologies and Social Semantic Web for Intelligent Educational Systems (SWEL 2009), pp. 23–30 (2009)

[7] Kotzé, P., Renaud, K., van Biljona, J.: Don't do this - pitfalls in using anti-patterns in teaching human computer interaction principles. Computers and Education 50(3), 979–1008 (2008)

[8] Laplante, P., Neil, C.: Antipatterns: Identification, Refactoring and Management. Taylor & Francis (2006)

[9] Martincic, C., Metzler, D.P.: An expert system development environmentfor introductory ai course projects. The Journal of Computing Sciences in Colleges, The Proceedings of the Tenth Annual Consortium for Computing Sciences in Colleges Northeastern Conference (2005)

[10] Rogers, J., Pheatt, C.: Integrating antipatterns into the computer science curriculum. Journal of Computing Sciences in Colleges 24(5) (May 2009)

[11] Tan, W.-A., Yang, F., Tang, A., Lin, S., Zhang, X.: An E-learning System Engineering Ontology Model on the Semantic Web for Integration and Communication. In: Li, F., Zhao, J., Shih, T.K., Lau, R., Li, Q., McLeod, D. (eds.) ICWL 2008. LNCS, vol. 5145, pp. 446–456. Springer, Heidelberg (2008)

[12] Tudorache, T., Vendetti, J., Noy, F.N.: Web-protege: A lightweight owl ontology editor for the web. In: Proceedings of the Fourth Workshop in the The OWL: Experiences and Direction, OWLED (2008)

[13] Wang, X., Fang, F., Fan, L.: Ontology-Based Description of Learning Object. In: Li, F., Zhao, J., Shih, T.K., Lau, R., Li, Q., McLeod, D. (eds.) ICWL 2008. LNCS, vol. 5145, pp. 468–476. Springer, Heidelberg (2008)

Opportunities and Challenges of Formal Instructional Modeling for Web-Based Learning

Michael Derntl[1], Susanne Neumann[2], and Petra Oberhuemer[2]

[1] RWTH Aachen University, Information Systems & Databases, Aachen, Germany
derntl@dbis.rwth-aachen.de
[2] University of Vienna, Center for Teaching and Learning, Vienna, Austria
{susanne.neumann-heyer,petra.oberhuemer}@univie.ac.at

Abstract. In digital repositories around the globe there is an abundance of available resources like learning objects, learning designs, teaching methods, and assessments. Building web-based learning opportunities by exploiting these resources is a complex endeavor with controversial motivational underpinnings. It requires provision of support for accessing, using and packaging the resources with interoperable, usable and user-friendly tools and within a trustworthy environment. In this paper, we address the interoperability issue by implementing tool support for the process of designing learning opportunities based on existing educational resources in a tool called OpenGLM. We conducted a qualitative end-user evaluation based on an instructional design task. Addressing the motivational underpinnings, we identify a number of challenges and opportunities to adoption of formal instructional modeling: on the individual level the main challenge is the lack of motivation to share good-practice examples; on the institutional level the key to harness the opportunities lies in the provision of support measures and quality control.

1 Introduction

Educational policy tends to aim at increasing the quality and transparency of educational offerings and qualifications as well as the mobility of students and teachers; an example of this is the Bologna Declaration in Europe [1]. Higher education institutions increasingly face global competition as stated in the Trends 2010 report [2]. Policy change and competition do not only affect research related agendas, but have to be viewed also with regard to study program portfolios and organizational change to meet economy needs and enhance global attractiveness. Offerings of web-based learning which can be delivered and consumed independently of time and location add to the competitiveness of the global education market. In response to these challenges, higher education institutions need to elaborate institutional learning, teaching and assessment strategies that emphasize unique strengths and assets aiming to attract students and increase retention rates [3]. At some institutions, management recommend a set of defined and documented teaching practices as an integral part of quality assurance at the course, module or even at the curricular levels. Yet others develop new

H. Leung et al. (Eds.): ICWL 2011, LNCS 7048, pp. 253–262, 2011.

business models, such as shifting the provision of face-to-face teaching towards standardized and reusable self study units, or by offering/selling their courseware to remote campuses and institutions. Institutions that strive for program accreditation are among others confronted with the task of systematically describing course structures, assessment and teaching methods. Whatever measures are introduced to achieve strategic advantages, formal representations of teaching and learning models may be an appropriate instrument to enable documentation and comparability of courses and study programs, enhance presentation and transparency of pedagogical approaches, and make excellence in teaching visible as an institution's unique selling proposition.

The objective of this paper is to investigate the adoption of a formal, interoperable instructional modeling approach from the perspective of modeling tool users and from the perspective of institutional roll-out of such an approach. Adopting the framework defined in [4], the aim was to support and evaluate the following phases of instructional modeling (see also [5]):

1. Definition of intended *learning outcomes*. A learning outcome is a statement of what a learner knows, understands, and is able to do on completion of a learning opportunity [6].
2. Definition of *teaching and learning activities*, i.e. the development and reuse of teaching methods (e.g. lecture, problem-based learning) and learning designs. A learning design arranges teaching methods, assessment methods, content and tools towards learning outcome attainment (e.g. a PBL approach to teaching "Computational Chemistry").
3. Selection, reuse, and development of *learning content* and teaching materials.

As an infrastructure for embedding and supporting these phases in an interoperable tool environment, we chose the *Open ICOPER Content Space (OICS)* [5,7] to store artifacts produced and resources used during instances of these phases. The OICS is a federation of existing repositories that host educational resources; it provides services and APIs for federated search, publication, and retrieval of resources. An IMS Learning Design (LD) [8] authoring application called Open-GLM (Open Graphical Learning Modeler) was developed and connected to the OICS for facilitating access to and reuse of existing teaching methods, learning designs, and content during the instructional modeling phases described above. This paper focuses on the qualitative end-user evaluation of the instructional modeling use cases supported by this tool.

The paper is structured as follows. In the Section 2 the OpenGLM tool and its support of formal instructional modeling is presented. Section 3 presents the methodology and findings of a qualitative end-user evaluation of OpenGLM. Section 4 discusses the opportunities of institutional adoption of formal instructional modeling in the light of the findings, and Section 5 concludes the paper.

2   Open Graphical Learning Modeler (OpenGLM)

Open Graphical Learning Modeler (OpenGLM) is an open source Java desktop application which was built on the Reload editor [9] code base. It enables users to design IMS Learning Design (LD) compliant instructional models using a visual design metaphor, i.e. using visual symbols and drag/drop. As such it provides tool support for the instructional design (ID) process, in particular the analysis, design and development phases of the ADDIE model [10], which the most prominent process model for ID.

- Analysis: definition of goals and objectives, as well as learner roles and prerequisites;
- Design: definition of learning objectives, and alignment of and with teaching methods and assessment methods, as well as description of teaching and learning activities;
- Development: setup and development of specified technology, content and learning objects.

In addition to supporting the ID process, OpenGLM's strong point is that it is connected to the Open ICOPER Content Space (OICS), a large repository where users can download, enrich, and share ID artifacts in an *interoperable* way: all artifacts stored in the OICS have a custom LOM metadata record [11]. Additionaly many artifacts are stored there in an interoperable format, e.g. IEEE RCD [12]for learning outcomes, IMS LD [8] for learning designs and teaching methods, IMS QTI [13] for assessments. This contributes towards easier exchange of ID artifacts between involved systems and ID stages (e.g. between the design environment and the learning management system). Interoperability of tools and artifacts is also a strong requirement for institution-wide adoption of systems.

A screenshot of the OpenGLM main window including the modeling pane as well as a dialog window showing the search & import of existing learning designs is given in Fig. 1. The screenshot shows the user is searching for learning designs that have intended learning outcomes mentioning the keyword "write".

In terms of supporting the ID process and the interoperability of artifacts, the following features were implemented in OpenGLM. For all user interface design and development decisions, simplicity of use was the guiding principle.

Analysis: It allows the definition of intended learning outcomes and learner prerequisites. Properties of different learner and teacher roles can be specified in detail (e.g. in a group learning scenario a learner group may consist of 3-4 learners). The main advantage of OpenGLM in this phase is its connection with the OICS, which provides a large pool of existing learning outcome definitions and instructional models from various disciplines. Thus, users can build on previous work shared by their peers.

Design: It supports the visual modeling of learning and support activities (see the central modeling pane in Fig. 1) as well as the definition of different roles for learners and teachers and their assignment to activities. Teaching methods, learning designs and assessments are offered for reuse through a search and import feature connected to the OICS. It is possible to export the design as a ready-to-play IMS LD package. This is particularly relevant for web-based learning environments, since IMS LD was created to support the design and delivery of computer-managed, web-based learning activities.

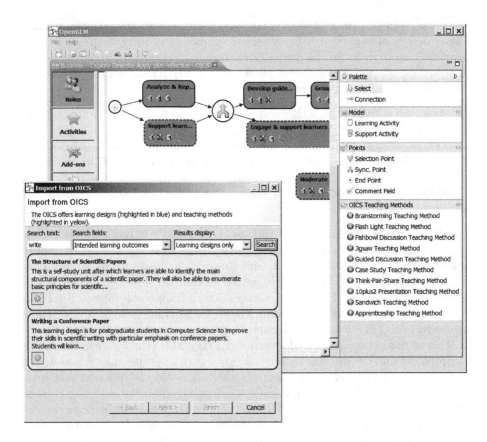

Fig. 1. Screenshot of OpenGLM main window with OICS import dialog on top

Development: It offers designers and developers features for assembling content packages and providing them with access to reuse of assets ranging from single learning objects to full web-based learning units. These features are offered directly within the OpenGLM tool.

3   End-User Evaluation

3.1   Methodology

The use and adoption of systems supporting the ID process have personal and institutional implications that are beyond issues of interoperability addressed by ID tools. To contribute to the understanding of these implications, a qualitative end-user evaluation of OpenGLM was conducted at two European institutions. Eleven participants participated in the evaluation. All participants are higher education teachers in technical subjects with no particular experience or interest in instructional design or with IMS LD. The evaluation proceeded as follows. First, the participant had to complete a prescribed ID task using OpenGLM.

The task covered the OpenGLM features and use cases related to the ID process and OICS. The task description was provided as a one-page handout to work with. To get feedback regarding the usability and learnability of the software, the instructions regarding the interaction with the software in the task were deliberately formulated differently from those typically found in handbooks or user guides: Users were instructed to perform tasks, but they were neither instructed nor assisted in how to achieve these in OpenGLM. A person was available for assistance in when a user got lost in the task. The overall task included 6 steps:

1. **Import:** To get started, users had to import an existing learning design from OICS by using the search and import feature. This feature offers keyword search combined with several options for filtering, e.g. looking for IMS LD packages addressing learning outcomes mentioning "geometry" in their title.
2. **Learning outcomes:** Users had to add intended learning outcomes to the learning design by creating new learning outcomes and by reusing learning outcome definitions available in the OICS.
3. **Teaching method:** To address the specified learning outcomes, the next step was to reuse one of the shared good-practice teaching methods offered by the OICS that address those outcomes. OpenGLM offers a quick and simple way of doing via drag and drop.
4. **Content:** Users had to search the OICS for relevant content and add the content to learning and/or teaching activities in their learning design. OpenGLM offers the option of searching for content in the OICS in all spots where IMS LD allows the attaching of resources to objects (e.g. to an environment as a learning object).
5. **Descriptive metadata:** To reflect the changes, users had to adapt the general metadata of the learning design, e.g. title and description, or licensing.
6. **Export & Sharing:** To share the created learning design with others, users finally had to export their learning design to the OICS. This action would make the learning design available for other users as an IMS LD package.

After the user had completed the task, an interviewer administered a structured interview consisting of open-ended questions related to different question strands: (*i*) Questions about the perception of the ID task and how it was supported by OpenGLM; (*ii*) Questions about expected organizational implications when implementing OpenGLM in the participant's organization and critical success factors for implementation and deployment of systems based on OpenGLM.

The interviews were summarized in text form by partners at the interviewing institutions. Essentially, each summary contained a synopsis of the responses of a participant to each of the interview questions. The summaries were analyzed for recurring themes and statements expressed by interviewees in regard to the two perspectives described above (personal and organizational).

3.2   Results and Recommendations

Support of Instructional Design Tasks. The users generally perceived smooth interaction with OpenGLM during their task. They reported that OpenGLM supported them well in completing the ID task steps described in the previous section. A number of issues were reported by participants during the interviews: Some of the users encountered problems with the terminology used in Open-GLM. One user did not know what is meant by the concept of "learning outcome." Based on the resulting misinterpretation this user encountered problems during the task step related to specifying intended learning outcomes (step 2 of the task). Another user also had problems with terminology used in teaching methods, thus complicating the reuse of teaching methods in OpenGLM. We recommend that institutions should implement the vocabulary commonly used by teachers at the institution and map this terminology to the vocabulary underlying institutional information systems.

One user had problems adding resources to the learning design (step 4 of the task). He tried to add resources based on their URL on the web. He figured that this would be possible in the "Add OICS resource" dialog. However, adding a web resource is part of the IMS LD specific functionality of OpenGLM and can thus be found in a different dialog. This is a usability issue and we recommend that instructional modeling software should adopt user interface metaphors that have meaning to teaching practitioners during the instructional modeling process. This requires user involvement during tool development and customization of the tool to institutional "customs".

One user got confused when uploading the learning design to OICS (last step of the task). It is possible to send the learning design as a new version or replacement of the original learning design imported during step 1 of the task. The user figured that changing the title of the learning design would already indicate the intent to have a new version. The source of this confusion lies in the separation of local OpenGLM and remote OICS versions of the learning design. Title and other descriptive informations are kept in the OICS metadata, so a title change does not necessarily imply a replacement of the whole learning design. This is also an issue where the technicalities underlying the implementation shine through to the user interface.

One user reported a problem during the teaching method drag & drop activity (step 3 of the task): It was not clear how to integrate the activities of the dragged-and-dropped teaching method into the learning design's existing activities. Since the perception of the modeling activity is mostly dependent on the modeling metaphor and the quality of its implementation, the modeling activity itself was excluded from evaluation.

Learning Design Tools in an Institutional Context. Apart from the technical difficulties reported above, users generally perceived OpenGLM as a useful and usable tool to create learning designs by reuse. However, they made several remarks in regard to the institutional implications of rolling out such a tool. The themes extracted from these remarks are summarized in the following.

Usability. The design process in the tool was majorly perceived as intuitive and easy to follow, even though some critical remarks about the complexity and arrangement of the user interface were made. Since OpenGLM is a prototypical implementation of interoperable instructional design support, more effort needs to be put in improving the user interaction if this tool were to be rolled out in an institution. We also recommend that instructional modeling tools should be oriented towards the steps that teachers and learning designers commonly perform during instructional modeling, rather than forcing them to learn a prescribed process.

Integration. Some of the participants were unsure whether what they were doing had any actual relevance to their life as a teacher. In most institutions teaching does not have a significant impact on the academic career, so time spent with planning and improving teaching is generally not considered as a wise investment. This could be changed, for instance, by using formal instructional models to identify teaching workload and student workload. Such a practice would strengthen the impact of effort spent on developing and using more meaningful and time-intensive teaching methods. To support teachers in adopting and accepting instructional modeling tools, institutions also need to make sure that the process of learning design implemented in the tool aligns smoothly with existing course planning procedures and steps teachers take during planning at the institution. So both the software and its institutional embedding in teaching processes need to integrate with exisiting procedures and systems.

Training. Almost all participants in the evaluation pointed to the fact that the introduction of such a tool at institutional level would require training and more comprehensive and sophisticated tool-internal help and tutorials. We thus recommend that institutions should offer training and support to teachers when adopting instructional modeling software.

Terminology. One notable aspect that was mentioned several times are the problems with terminology used by OICS and OpenGLM. To some users it was not clear what the terms learning outcome, teaching method, and other technical terms actually refer to. For institution-wide adoption it may thus be advisable to map the names of these and related concepts to terminology used within the institution.

Content Quality. Some statements address OpenGLM more in its role as an interface to a large federated repository of learning and teaching resources (OICS) than as an instructional modeling tool. Test participants were concerned about the quality and quantity of resources offered through the search functionality. Many participants suggested that the institution should provide a quality controlled repository to teachers . Moreover, the way users access OICS objects using OpenGLM's search functionality was considered sub-optimal by some users; they suggested the use of categories to facilitate search. Even with a large number of quality-controlled units of learning and teaching methods available in the repository, many users expressed concerns whether the information displayed in the tool would be sufficient to actually (re-)use the teaching methods. They expected more information like user ratings, comments, and information about obstacles, weaknesses, challenges, and how to apply the teaching method. It may thus be recommendable to complement the teaching methods and learning designs stored in the repository with material that provides the required additional information.

Sharing and Development. Several users were intrigued by the fact that tools like OpenGLM help teachers connect with each other based on their teaching; the tool is seen as an opportunity to enrich the repertoire of teaching activities through shared repositories. The tool was also seen as a vehicle to support teacher training and professional development measures at institutions. We recommend that instructional modeling should be used to support the documentation, sharing, and provision of innovative, quality controlled teaching practice among practitioners. Instructional models could in this spirit also be used for coordination and discourse on concepts and methods among teachers, teachers and students, and between institutional layers.

4   Discussion of Opportunities

The results of the end-user evaluation exhibit a mixed picture. On the one hand, the users liked designing and reflecting about their teaching strategies when adopting a formal modeling approach. They perceive added value through sharing of knowledge and artifacts during the design process. On the other hand, users encountered a number of issues related to the usability of the tool and to the implications the institutional roll-out of such a tool would have. To structure the discussion in a future-gazing way, we view the findings in the light of two propositions related to the opportunities generated by adoption of a formal instructional modeling approach:

Firstly, teachers and institutions should explore opportunities to make use of instructional modeling to enhance the quality of teaching and learning. Instructional modeling, and IMS LD in particular, has applications in higher education in facilitating the work of teachers, and the contextualization of that work in institution and curriculum. It enables common descriptions of instructional models to be developed and exchanged, opening up opportunities for innovative processes, which address some of the challenges which currently face education institutions as outlined in the introduction section. For instance, the need to become ever more accountable to funding agencies for the educational activities carried out, and for their quality, can be supported by describing instructional models in a way which can be analyzed across courses and programs. The use of formal instructional modeling enables specific and clear examples to be provided of pedagogic approaches which might otherwise be vaguely defined. These can for instance be used to support professional development and induction of new teachers, to document the pedagogic work carried out by teachers, and to share good practice. This is of particular importance when education institutions seek to maintain a consistent experience for cohorts which are distributed across a number of locations, which is very common for web-based learning providers.

Secondly, institutions should explore opportunities to make use of instructional modeling to support the management of institutional policies and processes. Institutional strategies often refer to pedagogic issues, e.g. when dictated by policy like the Bologna Process in Europe [1]. However it is difficult to obtain a shared understanding of what these strategies mean in practice, or to tie them to specific actions. The documentation of teaching practice in a formal way makes it possible to translate strategies into explicit exemplars which can be put into practice, and which can be reviewed by the members of the institution. The formal nature of the instructional model provides opportunities for integration with existing information technology processes. For example, the teaching method adopted will have implications for workload. These can be represented, and brought into the planning process, enabling teachers to negotiate their workload more effectively, and managers to keep track of budgets. Formal instructional models could also be used to impose a single centrally determined view of pedagogy, but other approaches are possible which can support a discourse on pedagogic concepts and methods. Interoperable instructional models can take an underlying model and create multiple representations which are appropriate for different stakeholders. Similarly, instructional modeling can be used to achieve an agreed abstracted model of the pedagogies being deployed. A strategy for teaching and learning which is exploited in these ways provides a focus for institutional identity which can even constitute a unique selling point.

5   Conclusion

This paper has tackled the adoption of formal instructional modeling from a personal end-user perspective and from a future-gazing institutional perspective. Key phases of the instructional design process were explained in the context of a standards-based, interoperable tool and resource environment. Tool support for this process was implemented in OpenGLM, an open-source instructional modeling tool that allows users to create IMS LD units of learning with visual modeling interactions. The tool was extended with features providing search, retrieval and publishing access to a large federated repository of sharable educational resources that offers learning designs, teaching methods, and content.

Formal instructional modeling in OpenGLM was subjected to an end-user evaluation with higher education teachers at two universities. The results indicate that formal instructional modeling is seen as having potential when strong institutional support is provided regarding the course design processes, sharing of instructional models, and software training. Users reported expected benefits in documenting and sharing teaching practice through instructional models.

Acknowledging the limitations of the presented findings, it is clear that the sample size in the evaluation is too small to draw general conclusions. Also, with OpenGLM being a tool that implements the authoring perspective of an interoperability specification like IMS LD, it is difficult—if not impossible—to clearly and objectively separate usability and adoption issues that are intrinsic to the specification from those issues that are rooted in a sub-optimal implementation of the specification. In any case, the voice of the users in the evaluation has indicated further research directions regarding the tool support in instructional modeling and its institutional adoption.

Unfortunately, most educational institutions currently do not follow the practice of documenting and sharing formal models of their teaching methods, courses, and instructional strategies. However, this paper advocates that institutions should adopt and support these practices to strengthen the impact of good practice in teaching and learning. Ignoring such opportunities from a management point-of-view may lead to inferior competitiveness in an increasingly globalized and standardized market of web-based education. The opportunity propositions for formal instructional modeling laid out in the discussion section above depend on the ability of formal instructional modeling to link between individuals, systems and institutions. It is therefore essential that the implementation of an instructional modeling based system is connected to the institutional practices, processes and policies.

Acknowledgments. This work was supported by European Commission funds in the projects ICOPER (ECP 2007 EDU 417007) and TEL-Map (FP7 257822). Thanks go to Philipp Prenner for OpenGLM development, Michael Totschnig for supporting OICS integration with OpenGLM, and to Anh Vu Nguyen-Ngoc and Denis Kozlov for organizing the evaluation sessions at University of Leicester and University of Jyväskylä, respectively.

References

1. European Commission: Bologna Declaration (1999), http://is.gd/bologna99
2. Sursock, A., Smidt, H.: Trends 2010: A decade of change in European Higher Education (2010), http://is.gd/trends2010
3. Johnson, M., Griffiths, D., Hanslott, Z.: Positioning Learning Design: Learner Experience and the challenges of transforming teaching practice. In: Open Workshop of TENCompetence - Rethinking Learning and Employment at a Time of Economic Uncertainty, Manchester, UK (2009)
4. Simon, B., Pulkkinen, M.: ICOPER Deliverable D7.3a: ICOPER Reference Model Specification Draft (2010), http://tinyurl.com/icoperd73a
5. Totschnig, M., Derntl, M., Gutiérrez, I., Najjar, J., Klemke, R., Klerkx, J., Duval, E., Müller, F.: Repository services for outcome-based learning. In: Proceedings of the 4th International Workshop on Search and Exchange of e-le@rning Materials 2010 (SE@M 2010). CEUR-WS, vol. 681, pp. 3–12 (2010)
6. European Commission: The European Qualifications Framework for Lifelong Learning (2008), http://is.gd/eqf2008
7. Totschnig, M.: ICOPER Deliverable D1.2: Open ICOPER Content Space Implementation of 2nd Generation of Open ICOPER Content Space including Integration Mini Case Studies (2010), http://tinyurl.com/icoperd12
8. IMS Global: IMS Learning Design specification (2003), http://www.imsglobal.org/learningdesign
9. Reload Learning Design Editor, http://www.reload.ac.uk/new/ldeditor.html
10. Dick, W., Carey, L.: The Systematic Design of Instruction, 4th edn. Haper Collins, New York (1996)
11. IEEE: Standard for Learning Object Metadata (2003), http://is.gd/ieeelom
12. IEEE: Standard for Learning Technology - Data Model for Reusable Competency Definitions (2008), http://is.gd/ieeercd
13. IMS Global: IMS Question & Test Interoperability Specification, http://www.imsglobal.org/question

Evaluating the Performance of a Diagnosis System in School Algebra

Naima El-Kechaï[1], Élisabeth Delozanne[1], Dominique Prévit[1],
Brigitte Grugeon[2], and Françoise Chenevotot[2]

[1] LIP6, UPMC-Sorbonne Universités, Paris, France
{Naima.El-Kechai,Elisabeth.Delozanne}@lip6.fr,
dominique.previt@ac-rennes.fr
[2] LDAR – Université Paris Diderot, Paris, France,
brigitte.grugeon@amiens.iufm.fr,
francoise.chenevotot@univ-paris-diderot.fr

Abstract. This paper deals with *PépiMep*, a diagnosis system in school algebra. Our proposal to evaluate the students' open-ended answers is based on a mixed theoretical and empirical approach. First, researchers in Math Education list different types of anticipated patterns of answers and the way to evaluate them. Then, this information is stored in an XML file used by the system to match a student's input with an anticipated answer. Third, as it is impossible to anticipate every student's answer, the system can improve: when an unknown form is detected, it is added to the XML file after expert inspection. Results from testing 360 students showed that, in comparison with human experts, *PépiMep* (1) was very effective in recognizing the different types of solutions when students' input was an algebraic expression (2) but was less effective when students entered a reasoned response expressed by a mix of algebraic expressions and natural language utterances.

Keywords: Assessment of open questions, Cognitive Diagnosis, School Algebra, System evaluation.

1 Introduction

Modeling a student's knowledge is known to be a difficult problem and much research was dedicated to investigate this matter. The *Pépite* project intends to diagnose students' difficulties in order to adapt the learning process [1-2]. Its objective is to design an intelligent aid that supports math teachers when they monitor learning in a classroom context, taking into account their students' cognitive diversity. This paper deals with diagnosing students' cognitive profiles in algebra. We assume that it is necessary to assess how students produce by themselves algebraic expressions. From our computational point of view, we focus especially on one of the key difficulties of such work: modeling the wide variety of types and levels of students' knowledge. We designed a system, called *PépiMep,* that automatically diagnoses students' answers, even when students express their answers in their own ways. *PépiMep* is used online in

H. Leung et al. (Eds.): ICWL 2011, LNCS 7048, pp. 263–272, 2011.

MathEnPoche (MeP), a web-based platform, developed by *Sésamath* [11], a community of mathematic teachers. This free platform is used by thousands of students and teachers in French speaking countries. In this paper, we examine the following specific research questions:

- Question 1: How to typify anticipated correct and incorrect solutions and how to specify the various different patterns of answers for each type of solutions?
- Question 2: How to ensure the quality of the automatic diagnosis, when it is impossible to anticipate every student's production?

To answer these questions, we propose a mixed theoretical and empirical approach. A trade-off was made so that the system would be generic enough to apply to many classes of algebraic problems, and specific enough to detect students' personal conceptions. Thus the main points in our proposal are (i) to anticipate most current students' approaches to solving one class of questions by detailed and accurate epistemological and empirical studies [3, 4 ,10], (ii) to design and implement a specific Computer Algebra system (CAS) called *Pépinière*, to deal with correct and incorrect algebraic rules [2] (iii) to generate a set of answer patterns representing each solution approach stored in an XML file, (iv) to design a system that can be improved by incrementally augmenting the anticipated answer pattern file when new patterns of answers are collected.

We begin with a brief review of the research on diagnosing students' difficulties, especially in mathematics, followed by an overview of the *Pépite* project. Then we present the diagnosis system *PépiDiag* and an evaluation of our proposal. We end with a discussion and plans for future research.

2   Background and Related Projects

Assessment and student modeling are a hot research topic in the e-learning and ITS (Intelligent Tutoring Systems) communities. The most popular approach for on-line assessments is based on tests involving closed questions that are especially tailored to provide evidence about targeted competencies or knowledge. The student's knowledge is described as a part of the reference competency model with the same structure, but with missing or incompletely mastered items. For instance, the evidence-based design used in ACED [5] relies on: a competency model; a task model to collect evidence on variables from the competency model (generally closed questions); a scoring model to interpret a student's answer (generally a score estimates whether it is correct or not); and a statistical model that aggregates scores across tasks to link observable variables (scores) to the competency model variables [5]. Many of these systems rely on a sound statistical grounding named Item Response Theory (IRT), and propose adaptive testing.

E-assessment aims to deliver a final evaluation or sometimes to provide feedback to students. In the *Pépite* project, the objective of the assessment is different: the diagnosis is the first step to monitor, in a classroom, learning paths adapted to different students' knowledge states and levels. As in evidence-based design, in the *Pépite* project, the diagnosis is based on three models; but they are different in many ways. The competency model includes both the referential competence and common misconceptions. The task model includes open-ended exercises. The analysis of each answer (called local diagnosis) is based on a multidimensional model expressed by a set of criteria (see section 3.2) and on using a CAS to match students' answers with patterns linked to the criteria. Then, heuristics based model aggregates the result of the local diagnosis to draw a student's cognitive profile.

A second approach aims at drawing a description of the student's knowledge including personal knowledge building and misconceptions. The *Pépite* project is a contribution in that direction. Some ITS analyze open answers when they are numerical or reduced to a simple algebraic expression (Algebra Tutor, ASSISTments [6], LeActiveMath [7]). Very few analyze the whole reasoning. From this point of view, closely related to our work are Diane [8] and Aplusix [9]. Diane is a diagnosis system to detect adequate or inadequate problem solving strategies for some arithmetic classes of problems at elementary school level. Diane analyses open-ended numerical calculations according to several criteria. However, for more complex domains such as Physics or Algebra, researchers had to use a standard CAS, or to develop one which is specific to the type of students" inputs and the intended diagnosis. For instance, Aplusix provides a fine grained analysis of students' use of algebraic rewriting rules. *Pépite* does not analyze so deep on the algebraic writing dimension, but assesses a broader panel of skills on other dimensions (see section 3.2). Its objective is to link formal algebraic processing with other students' conceptions related to the meaning of letters or the meaning of algebra. Thus, in the *Pépite* project, there are very different diagnosis tasks involving algebraic expressions but also geometric figures and calculation programs.

3   Project Design and Development

The objective of the *Pépite* project is that students develop or strengthen right conceptions, and question wrong or unsuitable ones that interfere with, and, sometimes, prevent learning [10]. The key point of the *Pépite* assessment approach is that students' answers to problems are not simply interpreted as errors or lack of skills but as indicators of incomplete, naive and often inaccurate conceptions that the students themselves have built. A fine analysis of the student's work is required to understand the coherence of their personal conceptions. Detecting these conceptions is a very complex task that requires special training and a lot of time without the help of automatic reasoning on the student's performance.

3.1   Project Overview

We developed such a cognitive diagnosis tool. Our research approach is a bottom-up approach informed by educational theory and field studies [3, 4, 11]. In previous work, we started from a paper and pencil diagnosis tool grounded in mathematical educational research and empirical studies. Then we automated it in a first prototype, also called *Pépite*, and tested it with dozens of teachers and hundreds of students in different school settings [1]. In more recent work, we implemented *PépiGen* that generalizes this first design to create a framework for authoring similar diagnosis tools, offering configurable parameters and options [2]. In 2010 and 2011, we implemented *PépiMep* to deploy the *Pépite* diagnosis tool on *MathEnPoche* (MeP) a web-based platform widely used by math teachers. Next sections deal with the design, implementation and evaluation of *PépiDiag* that carries out the automatic characterization of students' answers. The whole project relies heavily on the quality of the local diagnosis implemented in *PépiDiag* (Figure 1).

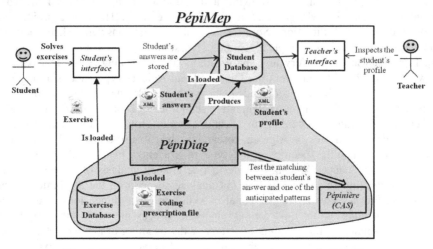

Fig. 1. The automatic diagnosis of a student's answer in *PépiMep*

3.2   The Diagnosis Process

In *Pépite,* as in other diagnosis tools [12], the diagnosis is a three stage process. In this paper we focus on the first stage. Next ones are more detailed in [1]. We just briefly introduce them to situate the work described here in the whole process.

First, for each student's answer to a diagnosis task, a *local diagnosis* provides two kinds of information: (i) a *type* that characterizes the answer in the context of the exercise and (ii) a *set of codes* referring to the different general evaluation *criteria* involved in the question. Types are specific to the exercise when codes apply to the whole set of exercises at this school level. Codes are used to situate the answer within the more general level of a multidimensional model of algebraic competence. In *Pépite*, the set of codes gives an interpretation of the student's answer according to a set of 36 *criteria* on 6 *assessment dimensions* (see Table 1 and table 2 for examples).

Second, *Pépite* builds a detailed report of the student's answers by collecting similar criteria across different exercises to have a higher-level view of the student's activity. At this stage, the diagnosis is expressed (i) by success rates on three *components of the algebraic competence* (usage of algebra, translation from one representation to another, algebraic calculation), and (ii) by the student's *strong points* and *weak points* in these three components. This level is called *personal features* of the student's cognitive profile.

Third, *Pépite* evaluates a level of competence in each component with the objective to situate a student in relation with the whole class. This third level is called the *stereotype* part of students' profiles. Stereotypes were introduced to support the personalization of learning paths in the context of a whole class management, and to facilitate the creation of student working groups. Figure 2 shows a cognitive profile built by *PépiMep*.

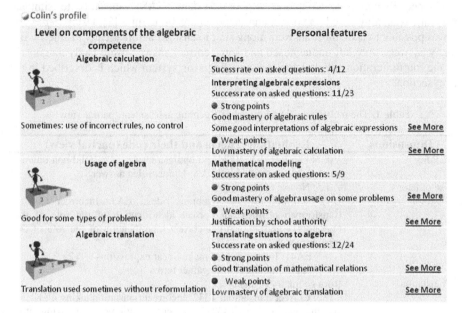

● **Description of the sub-group B** ⊞
Students practice algebraic calculation with low control, using sometimes incorrect rules.
They use a suitable algebraic approach to solve, at least, one type of problems.

Colin's profile

Level on components of the algebraic competence	Personal features	
Algebraic calculation	**Technics** Sucess rate on asked questions: 4/12	
	Interpreting algebraic expressions Success rate on asked questions: 11/23	
	● Strong points Good mastery of algebraic rules	
Sometimes: use of incorrect rules, no control	Some good interpretations of algebraic expressions	See More
	● Weak points Low mastery of algebraic calculation	See More
Usage of algebra	**Mathematical modeling** Success rate on asked questions: 5/9	
	● Strong points Good mastery of algebra usage on some problems	See More
Good for some types of problems	● Weak points Justification by school authority	See More
Algebraic translation	**Translating situations to algebra** Success rate on asked questions: 12/24	
	● Strong points Good translation of mathematical relations	See More
Translation used sometimes without reformulation	● Weak points Low mastery of algebraic translation	See More

Fig. 2. An overview of Colin's cognitive profile automatically built by *PépiMep*

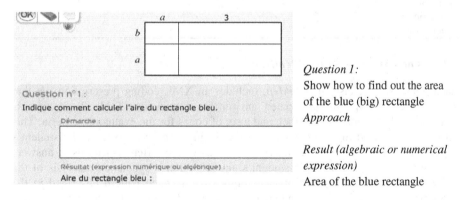

Question n°1 :
Indique comment calculer l'aire du rectangle bleu.
Démarche :

Résultat (expression numérique ou algébrique) :
Aire du rectangle bleu :

Question 1:
Show how to find out the area of the blue (big) rectangle
Approach

Result (algebraic or numerical expression)
Area of the blue rectangle

Fig. 3. The student's interface for exercise 3 in *PepiMep*

The following sections examine the iterative process to design and test *PépiDiag*, the system that implements the local diagnosis. For readability purposes, we illustrate our approach on a simple example where answers are expressed by one algebraic expression. Figure 3 shows the student interface of this exercise, called exercise 3. The first iteration began with an educational research project that defined a multidimensional model of competency and develop a paper and pencil diagnosis test with a very detailed analysis of anticipated students' solutions [4]. This test was filled by 600 students. The team used this corpus to refine the first analysis and to specify an electronic version of the test and a first prototype called *Pépite*. In the second iteration, we tested this first *Pépite* prototype in different school settings. In the third iteration we developed *Pépinière*, a Computer Algebra System (CAS) especially to simulate student's reasoning based on correct and incorrect algebraic rules [2]. Using *Pépinière*, it was possible to code most answers along six dimensions automatically (Table 1). But many answers were left undiagnosed and some correct answers were badly diagnosed. In the fourth iteration, we developed a new diagnosis system which is described in the next section.

Table 1. The multidimensional model of algebraic assessment (partial view)

Dimensions	Evaluation criteria and their code (partial view)
Validity	V0: No answer, V1: Valid and optimal answer ,V2: Valid non optimal answer, V3: Invalid answer, Vx: Unidentified answer
Use of letters	…L5: No use of letters…
Algebraic writing	EA1: Correct use of algebraic rules…,EA3: Incorrect use of transformation rules but correct identification of the role of the operators × and + , EA4: Incorrect identification of the role of the operators × and +
	EA41: Incorrect rules make linear expressions a²->2a
	EA42: Incorrect rules gather terms
Translation	from geometry to algebra …
	T132: Correct translation, T332: Incorrect translation taking into account relationships, T432: Incorrect translation without taking into account relationships, Tx: No interpretation
Type of Justification	…
Numerical calculation	…

3.3   The Diagnosis System *PépiDiag*

Each diagnosis exercise in *PépiMep,* includes an XML coding prescription file that describes every type of anticipated answer for a question (Table 2). A type is characterized by a number, a label, and a set of codes for the evaluation criteria. This information is used in the next stage of the diagnosis process to build the student's cognitive profile. It is also characterized by a list of the different patterns of answers used by the system to assess a student's answer. After a syntactical analysis of the student's algebraic answer, *PépiDiag* compares it to each pattern described in the coding prescription file. The comparison is made by *Pépinière* (the project CAS) that deals with operation commutability problems. When the student's answer matches a pattern, *PépiDiag* returns the type and the set of codes. They are stored in the student's log file along with the student's answers.

4   Evaluation

According to our research questions relating to the quality of the diagnosis, we state three criteria to evaluate this new PepiDiag: (i) no correct answer is badly diagnosed,

(ii) better no diagnosis than a wrong one, (iii) a minimal number of answers left undiagnosed. To assess the system validity, we set up a study with three experts. For each exercise of the test, we sorted the answers collected by types and by answers. Then, we asked the three experts to evaluate the automatic local diagnosis. We asked them to check, for both correct and incorrect answers, if they were: (i) diagnosed correctly, (ii) diagnosed incorrectly; (iii) undiagnosed. For undiagnosed ones, we asked them if they could complete the automatic diagnosis.

They found this task quite easy when working on a single exercise. They made very few interpretation mistakes and when they disagreed, they reached a consensus very quickly. So we were able to compare the system's diagnosis to the experts' consensual diagnosis even if, for some answers, they were puzzled and could not interpret them.

Table 2. Patterns of anticipated students' answers classified by type and code

Type	Label	Code	Patterns of equivalent expressions
1	Correct expression of the area as a product Length × Width	V1, T132	$(a + 3)\times(b + a)$
2	Correct expression of the area by adding the areas of the different rectangles	V2, T132	$ab+a^2+3b+3a$; $(a\times(a+b))+(3\times(a+b))$; $a(a+3)+b(a+3)$
3.1	Recognition of sub-figures with parentheses errors (e.g. a+3 × a+b)	V3, EA3, T332	$(a+3)\times b+a$; $a+3\times(b+a)$; $a+3\times b+a$; $a+3\times a+b$; $a+b\times a+3$
3.2	Recognition of sub-figures with gathering transformations	V3, EA42, T332	$(a+3)(ab)$; $(b+a)\times(3a)$; $a+3 \times ab$; $ab\times a+3$; $3a\times a+b$; $a+b\times 3a$
3.3	Recognition of sub-figures with linearization transformations a²->2a	V3, EA41, T332	$5a+ab+3b$; $ab+2a+3b+3a$
4	Confusion between area and perimeter	V3, T432	$(a+b)+(a+3)$; $(a+b+a+3)\times 2$
4.1	Transformations by gathering	V3, EA42, T432	$6a + 4b$; a^2+3b; $ab+3a$; $ab+4a$; $a(3+b)$; $2a+3b$; $2ab+3$
5	Translation by gathering the figure items	V3, EA42, T432	$a^2 b + 3\,ab$; $3a^2b$; $3a^2+3b$ $3a^2+3ab$; $a^2+ 4\,ab$; a^2+3ab $3ab$; $3+a^2+b$; $3+a^2b$; $a^2+ 7\,ab$
6	Confusion between the operators + and × (e.g. 3a × 3b × a2 × ba)	V3, EA4, T432	$3a \times 3b \times a^2 \times ba$; $ab+a^2\times3b+3a$ $(a^2+3a)\times(ba+3b)$; $ba\times b\times3+a^2+a\times3$
7.1	Partial Formulae	V3 T332	$a(b+a)$; $3a+3b$; $b(a+3)$; $ba+3b$ $3(b+a)$; $ab+a^2$; $a(a+3)$; a^2+3a
7.2	Wrong operations (division, cube)	V3 T432	$(a^23b):2$; $3b^2 + a^3 + 3a$ $(b + a)/(a + 3)$; $a+3\times b+a/2$
8	Numerical values	V3 L5, T432	(no use of letters)
9	No interpretation	Vx	

4.1   Results

The following tables report the results when comparing the *PépiDiag* diagnosis with the consensual experts' diagnosis on the working example. For this exercise, Table 3 shows that a quarter of the 360 students did not answer the question. On the whole, *PépiMep* diagnosed 82% of answers and failed to diagnose 18%. To assess the first quality criterion, we distinguish between the correct answers (149) and the incorrect ones (117).

Table 3. Numbers of answers automatically analyzed/unanalyzed by *PépiDiag* in the first testing of the diagnosis on exercise 3 with 360 students

Empty answers	Students' answers	**Automatic coding**		**Unanalyzed answers**
94/360 = 26%	266/360 = 74%	218/266 =82%		48/266= 18%
Correct answers analyzed by		Correct answers unanalyzed by		Correct answers
PépiDiag	Experts' agreement	*PépiDiag*	Human Experts	149
136/149=91%	136/136	13/149=9%	0	
Interface Problems				
Use of letters in place of operators		Mix of algebraic expressions and natural language		
5/13		8/13		

Correct Answers. Table 3 shows that out of the 149 correct answers collected, *PépiDiag* never diagnosed a correct answer as a wrong one. Only 13 correct answers (Table 5) for the following reasons: 5 students used letters "x" or "X" instead of the sign "×"; eg. (b+a)X(a+3);8 students mixed algebraic expressions and natural language, eg. "(a+b)(3+a)=area of the blue rectangle", "(a+b) times (3+a)".

Incorrect Answers. Table 4 shows that *PépiDiag* diagnosed 82 incorrect answers and experts fully agreed for 80 of them. For the two remaining answers ("b+a×a+3" and "3+a×a+b"), both system and experts assessed them as incorrect, but they were classified by experts as parentheses errors (type 3.1), while *Pépidiag* matched them with 3+a²+b (Translation by gathering the figure items, type 5). Indeed, *Pépinière* converted "a × a" into "a²".

Table 4. Incorrect answers in comparison with human experts

Incorrect answers analyzed by			Incorrect answers unanalyzed by		Total
PépiDiag	Experts' agreement	Pépinière Problems	*PépiDiag*	Experts	
82/117=70%	80/82	2/82	35/117=30%	24/35	117

Table 4 shows also that 35 incorrect answers were left undiagnosed by PepiDiag. Eleven answers were expressed using either letters in place of operators, or a mix of natural language and algebraic expressions; 24 answers were not anticipated in the coding prescription file. The three human experts could not typify them (eg. "3a+3b+a²+b²" or "a²×6×b²×b²").

4.2   Discussion

An important result of this study is that at no time *PépiDiag* was mistaken on correct answers. This meets the first quality criterion. For incorrect answers, the result of the comparison is also very good. There is a very small discrepancy. We are still studying if it is worth changing this feature of rewriting "a×a" as "a²" while avoiding to disrupt the rest of the analysis. For both correct and incorrect answers, to minimize undiagnosed answers, teachers and educational researchers suggested to constrain the interface to prevent students from typing letters other than those relating to the exercise. They advised that it was an acceptable trade-off between no constraint and a better automatic diagnosis of expressions that students could enter by themselves.

We tested with 30 students a new interface preventing students from inputting letters different from a et b (in the example). We did not notice any problems when students were solving the exercise. Three new patterns of answers were collected. They were added to the coding prescription XML file and then, no answers were left undiagnosed and there was a full agreement with the experts.

The study evaluated *PépiDiag* as a valid diagnosing tool to assess algebraic expressions, but it is not sure yet that is can assess a whole reasoning process. In [2] we reported how we dealt with analyzing a particular reasoning process. But the result on a large scale does not fully satisfy the three criteria at present, mostly when students mixed algebra and natural language. We are currently working on that question.

After testing the validity, we are working on evaluating the usefulness of this diagnosis system. This is a hard challenge, and, at the moment, we did not make any formal evaluation. In our opinion, a first sign of usefulness is that *Sésamath*, an important community of math teachers, asked for the *Pépite* diagnosis tool to be deployed on their web-based platform. Another sign is that in a validation cycle: it took between seven and ten hours for human experts to diagnose a whole class of 30 students with a whole test. The three experts found this task very tedious and they made many slips. They felt the need for an automatic system. Currently, educational researchers are using *PépiMep* to investigate students' misconceptions and to develop, with teachers, learning paths tailored to fit the *PépiMep* diagnosis.

5   Conclusion

In this paper, we presented the design of *PépiMep* and a study to evaluate its performance. We benefited from empirical and theoretical educational studies to design and implement *PépiDiag*, a system that automatically diagnoses the students' open-ended answers even when students enter their solution in their own ways. Anticipated patterns of correct and incorrect solutions are typified according to six evaluation dimensions based on detailed and accurate epistemological and empirical studies. *Pépinière*, a computer Algebra System (CAS), was designed in order to simulate a student's reasoning based on correct and incorrect algebraic rules. *PépiDiag*, which relies heavily on this CAS, can diagnose most students' inputs. We evaluate the performance of *PépiDiag* by testing 360 students. In this paper, we presented the results on a simple example where students have to express their reasoning by producing one algebraic expression. We described how we reify in a coding prescription file the way experts typified anticipated solutions. For each type of solutions, this file lists different patterns of answers that the system could match with a student's answer. We showed that the system could improve with usage when unknown answers occurred. Then we showed that *PépiDiag* was very efficient according to three quality criteria. Currently, we work on two directions. On the diagnosis side, we are improving and generalizing the analysis of students' reasoning. On the learning side, we are designing a software assistant to display learning tasks adapted to the students' cognitive profiles.

Acknowledgements. The *PepiMep* project is funded by the Region Ile de France. We thank Christian Vincent, Aso Darwesh, Josselin Allys and Arnaud Rommens for their contribution to implement *PépiMep* and Julia Pilet and math teachers from *Sésamath* for testing and suggestions. We acknowledge John Wisdom for correcting the correctness of English,

References

1. Delozanne, É., Vincent, C., Grugeon, B., Gélis, J.-M., Rogalski, J., Coulange, L.: From errors to stereotypes: Different levels of cognitive models in school algebra. In: E-Learn, Vancouver, pp. 262–269 (2005)
2. Delozanne, É., Prévit, D., Grugeon, B., Chenevotot, F.: Automatic Multi-Criteria Assessment of Open-Ended Questions: A Case Study in School Algebra. In: Woolf, B.P., Aïmeur, E., Nkambou, R., Lajoie, S. (eds.) ITS 2008. LNCS, vol. 5091, pp. 101–110. Springer, Heidelberg (2008)
3. Kieran, C.: Learning and teaching algebra at the middle school through college levels. In: Second Handbook of Research on Mathematics Teaching and Learning, pp. 707–762. Frank K. Lester (2007)
4. Grugeon, B.: Design and development of a multidimensional grid of analysis in algebra (in French). RDM Journal 17, 167–210 (1997)
5. Shute, V.J., Hansen, E.G., Almond, R.G.: You Can't Fatten A Hog by Weighing It–Or Can You? Evaluating an Assessment for Learning System Called ACED. IJAIED 18, 289–316 (2008)
6. Feng, M., Heffernan, N., Koedinger, K.: Addressing the assessment challenge with an online system that tutors as it assesses. UMUAI 19, 243–266 (2009)
7. Melis, E., Ullrich, C., Goguadze, G., Libbrecht, P.: Culturally Aware Mathematics Education Technology. In: The Handbook of Research in Culturally-Aware Information Technology: Perspectives and Models, Blanchard E. and Allard D, pp. 543–557 (2009)
8. Hakem, K., Sander, E., Labat, J.-M., Richard, J.-F.: DIANE, a diagnosis system for arithmetical problem solving. In: AIED, Amsterdam, pp. 258–265 (2005)
9. Nicaud, J.-F., Chaachoua, H., Bittar, M.: Automatic Calculation of Students' Conceptions in Elementary Algebra from Aplusix Log Files. In: Ikeda, M., Ashley, K.D., Chan, T.-W. (eds.) ITS 2006. LNCS, vol. 4053, pp. 433–442. Springer, Heidelberg (2006)
10. Artigue, M., Grugeon, B., Lenfant, A.: Teaching and Learning Algebra: approaching complexity through complementary perspectives. In: ICMI, Melbourne, pp. 21–32 (2001)
11. Sésamath (May 28, 2011), http://www.sesamath.net/
12. Delozanne, É., Le Calvez, F., Merceron, A., Labat, J.-M.: A Structured set of Design Patterns for Learners' Assessment. JILR 18, 309–333 (2007)

A Problem-Based Learning Approach
for Green Control and IT in a Master Program

Emmanuel Witrant[1] and Elvira Popescu[2]

[1] Grenoble Image Parole Signal Automatique (GIPSA-lab), Université Joseph
Fourier / CNRS, BP 46, 38 402 Saint Martin d'Hères, France
emmanuel.witrant@ujf-grenoble.fr
http://www.gipsa-lab.fr/~e.witrant/
[2] University of Craiova, Software Engineering Department, A.I.Cuza 13, 200585
Craiova, Romania
popescu_elvira@software.ucv.ro
http://software.ucv.ro/~epopescu/

Abstract. Students' interest for science and technology studies has been
decreasing during the last decade, to the profit of careers with more social impact or economic benefit. While the economic aspect is related to
industrial policies and out of reach for university curriculum designers,
problem-based learning (PBL) can be a solution to renew the students'
interest for science. This work presents an example of curriculum design
at the master level where the theoretical classes of systems, control and
information technologies (SCIT) are illustrated with PBL-oriented labs
and projects related to a topic with high social impact: environmental
sustainability. The focus of the paper is on practice and experience sharing; the general approach to motivate the need for SCIT in sustainable
and green development is presented, along with some specific projects
carried in the master program. The perspective of relying on Web 2.0
tools to improve communication and collaboration in the PBL framework
is also discussed.

1 Introduction

Young people's drive for scientific studies has decreased in the recent years,
leading to a shortage of engineers before the financial crisis that is expected to
propagate in the forthcoming years (cf. [4] and references therein). The conclusions proposed in [4] highlight the importance of raising the view of technology
from a daily commodity to a mean for fascinating scientific advances. Becker also
encourages university education to motivate less-gifted students with hands-on
applications rather than focusing on the extremely challenging nature of science.

It is interesting to note that, according to the European report [10], the young
people's attraction for science is still relatively high. Indeed, the presented study
shows that the news on science and technology raise 67% interest and that most
young people have a positive view about science (one third strongly agree that
science brings more benefits than harm). Furthermore, one-third strongly thinks

H. Leung et al. (Eds.): ICWL 2011, LNCS 7048, pp. 273–282, 2011.

that profit motives have too much importance on the potential science benefits. Such results reflect the potential involvement of young people into scientific curricula with clearly identified social and/or environmental benefits.

The inter-disciplinary approach provided by curricula in systems, control and information technologies (SCIT) allows for a large range of applications. The approach described in this work is focused on combining the SCIT analytical framework with green (or sustainable) development applications. This is achieved with a problem-based learning (PBL) approach to the theoretical SCIT topics, where the problems considered are the green applications. The Master program in SCIT[1] has been proposed at University Joseph Fourier (UJF, Grenoble, France) since 2008. International issues and the expected learning outcomes for this program are described in [23]. Several labs and projects have been set according to the green SCIT objectives. The motivation for the selected topics, the specific contributions of SCIT and the objectives given to the students are reported in this paper. An experience to motivate high-school students for such higher education is also described.

The paper is organized as follows: first, some theoretical aspects regarding problem-based learning are introduced in Sec. 2. Next, the practical application of PBL in the context of SCIT master courses is illustrated in Sec. 3; the PBL outcomes obtained by the master students serve also as motivational material to attract high school students toward the SCIT field, as described in Sec. 4. Finally, Sec. 5 summarizes the lessons learned from the implementation of PBL in the master curriculum, outlining both the achievements and the difficulties encountered; the perspective of introducing Web 2.0 tools to improve communication and collaboration in the PBL framework is also envisioned.

2   Theoretical Background - Problem Based Learning

According to [3], PBL represents "the learning that results from the process of working towards the understanding of a resolution of a problem". So the emphasis is not on the solution, as in the case of conventional problem solving strategies, but on the process leading to it [15]. The approach was first introduced in medical education at McMaster University in Canada about four decades ago and its use was extended to many other areas in the meantime [2]. PBL is an instructional model rooted in constructivist principles [18]: i) understanding is an individual construction and comes from our interactions with the environment; ii) learning is driven by cognitive conflict or puzzlement; iii) knowledge evolves through social negotiation. Accordingly, in PBL all learning activities are anchored to a larger task or problem, which must be authentic and reflect the complexity of the real-world environment in which students will eventually apply that knowledge. The teacher assumes the role of facilitator, supporting the learner in developing the metacognitive skills associated with the problem solving process, encouraging them to think both critically and creatively. The problem solving takes place

---

[1] http://physique-eea.ujf-grenoble.fr/intra/Formations/M2/EEATS/PSPI/

in collaborative groups, in which students' knowledge is tested and enriched with peer's alternative views [18].

According to [22], students follow several steps during the PBL: i) identify the problem; ii) explore pre-existing knowledge; iii) generate hypotheses and possible mechanisms; iv) identify learning issues; v) self study; vi) re-evaluation and application of new knowledge to the problem; vii) assessment and reflection on learning [15].

The efficiency of PBL was reported in various papers, in different areas of study [9,11,19]. This can be explained by the fact that PBL is based on four modern insights into learning: constructive, self-directed, collaborative, and contextual [11]. Nevertheless, there are also some researchers who take a more critical stand towards PBL [1,8], outlining various disadvantages: i) students may have gaps in their cognitive knowledge base and not demonstrate expert reasoning patterns; ii) PBL can be very costly; iii) PBL may have a robust positive effect on skills but a negative effect on knowledge [11]. Therefore, in our master program we decided to apply a blended approach, combining traditional lectures with PBL scenarios, thus aiming to take the best of both worlds.

The next section describes the practical application of PBL for Green SCIT, outlining the key topics and the actual problems that are proposed to the students. The objectives of the course were divided into milestones, which were transformed in self-contained problems [20]; each problem raises concepts and principles relevant to the content domain and at the same time is highly motivating to the students.

3 Problem-Based Learning for Green SCIT

3.1 Green IT, Systems and Control

The rising importance of IT and pervasive computing on everyday life renders the IT sector contribution to greenhouse gases a topic of major interest. Indeed, the emissions due to IT are projected to increase from 3 % of total global emissions (CO_2 equivalent) in 2009 to 6% by 2020. This figure shall be balanced by the potential use of IT to create a low carbon society, as this sector could lead to emissions reductions five times larger than its own contribution [21].

The analysis of systems and global control strategies typically provide a framework to monitor and optimize large-scale plants for a reduced consumption based on IT solutions. A significant contribution to sustainable development can thus be brought by educating systems and control engineers with a specific sensitivity for Green IT applications. While this field is particularly broad, specific topics can be selected to illustrate some key applications. They can be classified as: i) sustainable power generation; ii) efficient use of energy at the industrial level; iii) efficient use of energy at the domestic level; iv) anthropogenic impact on the environment.

Each of these topics is illustrated by an application where SCIT plays a major role and which motivates the students' involvement in the next subsections.

3.2 Sustainable Power Generation: Tokamaks Modeling and Control

Controlled thermonuclear fusion is a topic of prime interest as a source of sustainable energy, which could possibly compete with classical fission reactors in terms of efficiency and as a key process to produce energy. In the forthcoming years, the main challenge for the fusion community will be to develop experimental scenarios for the tokamak ITER[2] (International Thermonuclear Experimental Reactor, the largest fusion process ever built and with a first run planned for 2018). From the SCIT point of view, a tokamak is a complex process with multiple interconnected dynamics, several (possibly conflicting) control objectives, a large number of sensor signals to handle and challenging objectives in terms of real-time control.

While implementing the students' controller on a real tokamak would not be feasible, two PBL topics are proposed in the master program: the real-time modeling of a complex system and the optimization of a feedback source. For each lab, a technical document describing the main physical processes is provided to the students, along with an experimental data set[3]. As numerous concepts in this document relate to specific knowledge in fusion engineering, students have to complement their understanding with web resources or questions to the professor. The requested outcome is to provide an input/output description of each subsystem, identify the interconnections and the specific challenges addressed in an integrated approach. Once each student gained a sufficient level of understanding of the process, the class is divided in groups of two to work on specific topics. Collaborative work is emphasized in one lab, where each group has to design a *Simulink*® model for a specific subsystem. The groups have to interact in order to get the appropriate specification and format for the interconnection variables, the ultimate goal being to assemble the blocks designed by each team in a global *Simulink*® tokamak model, presented in Fig. 1(a).

3.3 Green Buildings and Networked Intelligent Systems

The concept of green (or sustainable) buildings implies the efficient use of energy and water resources to reduce the impact of the built environment on humans' health and natural environment. To fulfill this goal, intelligent buildings control is seen as a key solution that raises several research problems of immediate actuality, such as wireless automation and control of complex interconnected system. An interesting case study is provided by [7], where the potential energy savings obtained by a connected workspace product (fully relying on IT solutions) are estimated to be up to 44 %. Another case is related to the ventilation system, with potential significant improvements both in terms of user's comfort and energy savings.

---

[2] http://www.iter.org

[3] A collaboration with Tore Supra tokamak, operated by the Commissariat à l'Énergie Atomique - Institut de Recherche sur la Fusion Magnétique (CEA/IRFM at Saint Paul lez Durance, France), provides some real data set for teaching purposes.

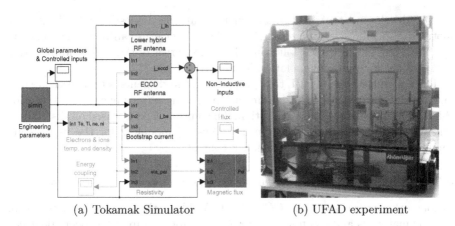

(a) Tokamak Simulator   (b) UFAD experiment

Fig. 1. Examples of PBL applications for green SCIT: sustainable power generation (tokamak) and intelligent buildings (UFAD)

The topics related to SCIT include protocol design for large-scale networking, wireless sensing and actuation capabilities, networks security, embedded control design and centralized energy optimization. More specific problems (e.g. associated with the ventilation problem) also necessitate control-oriented models and robust multiple-input multiple-output regulation strategies. A reduced-scale experiment, presented in Fig. 1(b), has been built at UJF to illustrate the main associated automation problems. Three different PBL projects are set along these lines.

The first project is focused on under floor air distribution (UFAD), which was highlighted as a particularly efficient solution in comparison with traditional ceiling-based ventilation systems [6]. Successive projects contributed to the design of the UJF experiment. The general tasks for the students are to propose simplified physical models for this system, identify the model parameters from the measurements and design some feedback regulation schemes.

The second project considers wireless sensor networks, with the real-time tuning and application protocol synthesis for a wireless controller PAN (Personal Area Network) based on the IEEE 802.15.4 MAC (Medium Access Control) layer. These protocols are set on ZigBee motes that contribute to the UFAD experiment by providing temperature measurements and actuating the fans.

The third project aims at producing green resources using the building architecture. People environment in cities is then improved thanks to an appropriate exploitation of the available space and resources to grow different kinds of plants in an energy-efficient way. Within this framework, a specific solution has been proposed by the *vegetalworkshop* team[4] to grow up plants on Grenoble library.

3.4 Domestic Energy Savings: the Heat Pump Automation

The heat pump extracts energy from the outside air to provide it for domestic heating. This process allows for significant energy savings and is thus a key issue

---

[4] http://www.vegetalworkshop.com

for the development of sustainable energies at the domestic level. This topic motivated specific scientific research. Modeling concerns can be tracked back to the beginning of the 1980's, following the energy crisis of the 1970's. More actual concerns are focused on simulation and control issues [13].

The aim of the related PBL task proposed to the students is to investigate new automation solutions for the minimization of heat pumps energy consumption thanks to real-time feedback operation. This automation is based on distributed sensing capabilities, networked sensors, physical modeling for the process automation design and real-time feedback control.

3.5 Anthropogenic Impact and the Ozone Depletion Problem

Among other trace gases, CH_3CCl_3 (1,1,1-Trichloroethane, used as a solvent for organic materials and as an aerosol propellant, for example) has been identified as responsible for the ozone layer depletion effect. Many applications have been identified as harmful for health in 1970 and CH_3CCl_3 was completely banned in 1996 by the Montreal protocol (when its ozone depleting effect was identified). Trace gas (small concentration in the atmosphere) measurements in interstitial air from polar firn (permeable snow in the top 50-100 m of the polar cores) allow to reconstruct their atmospheric concentration time trends over the last 50 to 100 years. This provides a unique way to reconstruct the recent anthropogenic impact on atmospheric composition (see e.g. [24] and references therein).

The PBL task proposed on this topic illustrates the importance of SCIT for the reconstruction of CH_3CCl_3 history based on a gas transport model, atmospheric scenario and firn measurements. The data set and a transport model are given to the students[5]. The conclusions of this lab illustrate the need of SCIT analysis tools to provide reliable information out of sparse measurements.

4 Motivating High School Students to Join Science

A one day visit for a class of high school students from Lycée Barthélemy-de-Laffemas (Valence, France) was proposed at UJF. Several activities were organized, such as doing a physics lab and visiting the experimental areas of research and education labs. A connection with the PBL projects presented above was done with short presentations from the master students to the high school visitors. Each group of master students was asked to prepare a twenty minutes talk with an experimental demonstration (when applicable), intended for a large audience.

The high school students were very enthusiastic about this experience, both for being included in a multi-cultural class (nine nationalities were composing the class, with non French-speaking students) and for the topics that were presented. This experience gave them a refined idea of the university life and of the possible achievements at the end of the curriculum. They were impressed by

---

[5] Provided by the Laboratoire de Glaciologie et Géophysique de l'Environnement (LGGE, Grenoble, France) and by GIPSA-lab, respectively.

the possible realizations of the master students and it increased their interest for long scientific studies. The master students also gave a positive feedback, as they felt directly involved in the science transmission task. They got into numerous informal discussions with the high school students concerning their PBL topics, personal curriculum and life as a student.

While the proposed framework cannot be extended to a large number of students, it allowed for specific interactions beyond the classical teacher/student relationships. The interest for scientific studies of the involved group of young people was clearly raised and such experience ought to be repeated in the forthcoming years.

5   Discussions and Conclusions

5.1   Lessons Learned

The green orientation of SCIT brought with the PBL approach was very successful to motivate the students to get involved into the class and to compensate for their natural hesitation to address complex and not necessarily well-defined problems. This was especially true for specific students with low to middle interest in the theoretical aspects who could thus compensate with outstanding reports. The diversity of the lab topics led to the success of different students on different topics, which was valuable both for the class motivation and for providing future references to potential employers. Indeed, a well structured report on an innovative topic was particularly efficient to trigger an employer's interest for some students.

While the students were able to get substantial results on the projects (running on one semester), the labs on advanced green topics (such as tokamaks) were difficult to adjust to the allocated time (two times three hours per lab on the average). Support from corrected homework and mid-lab reports helped to overcome this difficulty. On the other hand, team-working aspects and project management appeared as the major difficulties in the projects.

The choice of several specific topics in the green-SCIT field (especially with the building-related projects) generated stimulating discussions between the groups that did not necessarily occur with groups on different topics (a project on robotics was also proposed). The interest for green applications extended to other classes, where some students chose related topics on their own (such as the talk for the speech class). The presentation from master to high school students was a particularly rich experience to motivate master students to convey their findings and understanding to non-specialists in the field.

A difficulty observed with the proposed PBL approach was to channel the intra and inter groups communication, and to carry out the information over the years (the goal being that the students of each year build on the work achieved during the previous years). Hence, the need for providing improved communication and collaboration support, as envisioned in the following subsection.

5.2   Perspectives: Introducing Web 2.0 Support Tools

Since PBL relies on group work and collaborative generation of content (e.g., the deliverables teams have to hand in at various stages of the problem solving process), Web 2.0 tools may be seen as an appropriate support framework for communication and collaboration.

Web 2.0 is a term promoted by Tim O'Reilly [14], which designates a set of interactive and collaborative aspects of the Web seen as a platform (i.e., the applications are built on and for the Web, not for desktop). Web 2.0 brings a user-centered approach - designing applications whose content is generated by the users and therefore depend heavily on their contribution (e.g., YouTube, Flickr, Delicious). Consequently, Web 2.0 is also known as "participative Web": the user is not just content consumer but also content generator (often in a collaborative manner). Furthermore, Web 2.0 is also called "social Web": with the advent of social networks, it started offering support for users to interact, communicate and collaborate (e.g., Facebook, MySpace, Twitter). Recently, Web 2.0 tools (e.g., blog, wiki, social bookmarking systems, media sharing tools) have been introduced in educational contexts, with encouraging results with respect to student satisfaction, knowledge gain and/or learning efficiency [16]. This is motivated by the fact that the principles Web 2.0 is based on (user-centered, participative architecture, openness, interaction, social networks, collaboration) are in line with modern educational theories such as socio-constructivism.

In this context, it is only natural to rely on Web 2.0 tools for providing the collaborative framework for PBL. Indeed, several authors have emphasized the inherent alignment between PBL and Web 2.0 technologies and reported successful experimental results in Health Science education ([12], [5]), but also in Telematic Engineering education ([15]). We believe that the approach will prove successful also in Green SCIT studies and we aim to introduce it in our master program.

More specifically, the collaborative learning scenario that we envision involves the following Web 2.0 tools:

- A blog for communicating between team members, for discussing and analyzing the problem, for planning actions and sharing experiences. This could be supplemented by a microblogging tool (e.g., Twitter) for the exchange of shorter messages (with wider and immediate availability, as they can be sent and received also by SMS).
- A social bookmarking tool for finding online resources relevant for the problem at hand and sharing them with the team
- A wiki for gathering and organizing learning resources, for collaboratively constructing the solution as well as for co-writing the team deliverables.

Thus, the face-to-face lab sessions will be supplemented by asynchronous collaboration; students will be able to contribute from remote locations, at the time and the pace they choose. This flexibility is particularly important in case of master students, who often hold part-time jobs. Students' activities and progress will be recorded in the blog and wiki - thus the instructor will be able to continuously monitor students' problem solving steps, observe group dynamics and provide feedback and guidance when needed. Furthermore, the teacher has the opportunity to see not just the final deliverable, the end product of the collaboration, but the whole process of tackling the problem, enriching the assessment potential [5].

As far as the technical solution is concerned, there are several possible approaches: i) use stand-alone Web 2.0 tools on top of the course framework (as in [5]); ii) use a learning management system (LMS) with integrated Web 2.0 applications (e.g., Moodle as in [12] or .LRN as in [15]); iii) use a dedicated social learning environment, which integrates all the required Web 2.0 tools, together with additional support for both learners and teachers (e.g., eMUSE [17]). We are currently investigating the integration of the latter solution within the master program framework.

Acknowledgements. The research leading to these results has received funding from the European Union Seventh Framework Programme [FP7/2007-2013] under grant agreement n° 257462 HYCON2 Network of excellence. It was also supported by the European Commission and the American Department of Education with the ATLANTIS program DeSIRE[2] (Grant Agreement for EU-US Cooperation program in Higher Education and Vocational Training, Excellence in Mobility Projects; Agreement n° 2008-1773/001-001 CPT-USMOBI).

References

1. Albanese, M., Mitchell, S.: Problem-based learning: a review of literature on its outcomes and implementation issues. Academic Medicine 68, 52–81 (1993)
2. Barrett, T., Mac Labhrainn, I., Fallon, H.: Handbook of enquiry and problem based learning. CELT, Galway (2005)
3. Barrows, H., Tamblyn, R.: Problem-based learning: an approach to medical education. Springer, New York (1980)
4. Becker, F.: Why don't young people want to become engineers? Rational reasons for disappointing decisions. European Journal of Engineering Education 35(4), 349–366 (2010)
5. Buckley, C., William, A.: Web 2.0 technologies for problem-based and collaborative learning - a case study. In: Adult Learning in the Digital Age: Perspectives on Online Technologies and Outcomes, pp. 118–125. IGI Global (2009)
6. Center for the Built Environment: Design guide on underfloor air distribution (UFAD) systems. Tech. rep., ASHRAE (2002),
   http://www.cbe.berkeley.edu/RESEARCH/ufad_designguide.htm
7. Cisco: Office design case study: how Cisco achieved environmental sustainability in the connected workplace. Tech. rep., Cisco Systems, Inc. (2007)
8. Dochy, F., Segers, M., Van den Bossche, P., Gijbels, D.: Effects of problem-based learning: a meta-analysis. Learning and Instruction 13, 533–568 (2003)
9. Dolmans, D., De Grave, W., Wolfhagen, I., Van Der Vleuten, C.: Problem-based learning: future challenges for educational practice and research. Medical Education 39(7), 732–741 (2005)
10. EU: Young people and science: Analytical report. Flash Eurobarometer Series 239, European Commission, Brussels (2008)

11. Garcia-Robles, R., Diaz-del Rio, F., Vicente-Diaz, S., Linares-Barranco, A.: An eLearning standard approach for supporting PBL in Computer Engineering. IEEE Transactions on Education 52(3), 328–339 (2009)
12. Kaldoudi, E., Bamidis, P., Papaioakeim, M., Vargemezis, V.: Problem-based learning via Web 2.0 technologies. In: Proceedings of the 2008 21st IEEE International Symposium on Computer-Based Medical Systems, pp. 391–396 (2008)
13. Karlsson, F., Fahlén, P.: Capacity-controlled ground source heat pumps in hydronic heating systems. International Journal of Refrigeration 30, 221–229 (2007)
14. O'Reilly, T.: What is Web 2.0. Design patterns and business models for the next generation of software (2005), www.oreillynet.com/pub/a/oreilly/tim/news/2005/09/30/what-is-web-20.html
15. Pardo, A., Delgado Kloos, C.: Combining Web 2.0 technology and problem-based learning in a blended learning environment. International Journal of Continuing Engineering Education and Lifelong Learning 19(2/3), 222–231 (2009)
16. Popescu, E.: Students' acceptance of Web 2.0 technologies in Higher Education: findings from a survey in a Romanian university. In: Workshops on Database and Expert Systems Applications (DEXA), pp. 92–96 (2010)
17. Popescu, E., Cioiu, D.: eMUSE - Integrating Web 2.0 Tools in a Social Learning Environment. In: Leung, H., et al. (eds.) ICWL 2011. LNCS, vol. 7048, pp. 41–50. Springer, Heidelberg (2011)
18. Savery, J.R., Duffy, T.M.: An instructional model and its constructivist framework. Educational Technology 35, 31–38 (1995)
19. Schmidt, H.G., Vermeulen, L., Van Der Molen, H.T.: Longterm effects of problem-based learning: a comparison of competencies acquired by graduates of a problem-based and a conventional medical school. Medical Education 40(6), 562–567 (2006)
20. Stevenson, D., Parham, J.: Problem-based and case-based methods in computer science. The Creative College Teaching Journal 3, 53–66 (2006)
21. The Climate Group: Smart 2020: Enabling the low carbon economy in the information age. Tech. rep., Global eSustainability Initiative (GeSI) (2008), http://www.smart2020.org/_assets/files/02_Smart2020Report.pdf
22. Walsh, A.: The tutor in problem based learning: a novice's guide. McMaster University Health Sciences, Hamilton, ON (2005)
23. Witrant, E., Thiriet, J.M., Retière, N.: Establishing a Systems & ICT master program in the international framework. Journal Sur Lénseignement Des Sciences Et Technologies De línformation Et Des Systèmes 10(1), 1005 (2011)
24. WMO: Scientific assessment of ozone depletion: 2010, Global ozone research and monitoring project, Report No.52. World Meteorological Organization, Geneva (2011)

Development of Web-Based Remote Laboratory for Education and Research on RF Engineering

Wonshil Kang and Hyunchul Ku

Electronic Engineering, Konkuk University
1-Hwayang-dong, Kwangjin-gu, Seoul, Korea
{newwon,hcku}@konkuk.ac.kr

Abstract. This paper presents the design of a remote laboratory platform using web-based technologies for radio frequency (RF), microwave measurements and their analysis. The developed RF remote laboratory system is easy to operate using web-based graphical user interfaces in controlling the test equipments and displaying the test results. The various measurement and analysis engines for RF devices, circuits, and systems are developed using graphical language, LabView. The remote RF laboratory system with the developed user interfaces and engines is used in education and research on RF engineering. The developed system can increase efficiency of education and research on RF engineering cost-effectively by providing similar environment with an actual laboratory using web-based technologies.

Keywords: Remote laboratory, radio frequency (RF), microwave, web-based.

1 Introduction

Web-based laboratory has advantages regarding time, space, maintenance, and cost. The user can conduct experiment from a remote location at a convenient time. The number of measurement equipments can be also reduced by using scheduling and time sharing techniques for multiple remote users (students and engineers). Although the hands-on laboratory experimentation is important for the students majoring electrical engineering (EE) to gain experience and knowledge for the electrical circuit and system, the remote laboratory can also provide an environment similar to real experiments on a remote location. The effectiveness of using a remote laboratory is much different from that of using only simulation [1-3]. An e-learning class with a remote laboratory can provide effective learning by providing combination of theoretical lectures with laboratory works. Recently, several remote laboratories have been developed using web and internet technologies [1-10]. The iLAB project at Massachusetts Institute of Technology (MIT) [4], the Netlab project [5,6], and European Remote Radio Laboratory (ERRL) project [7,8] are examples. In Korea, System Semiconductor Promotion Center in Electronics and Telecommunications Research Institute (ETRI) has developed a remote lab, which is Electronics & Telecommunications Remote Laboratory (ETReLa) [9].

With the rapid growth of wireless communication industries, it is necessary to provide more experimental experiences to the students and engineers in a radio

H. Leung et al. (Eds.): ICWL 2011, LNCS 7048, pp. 283–288, 2011.

frequency (RF) engineering field. However, RF instruments such as an RF signal generator (SG), a network analyzer (NA), a vector signal analyzer (VSA), and a spectrum analyzer (SA) are expensive, and they are hard to use easily. The remote RF laboratory based on the web and internet technologies can be cost-effective, easy, and safe method providing a real RF laboratory experience [7-10]. In [10], the requirements for developing a remote RF laboratory as perspectives of educators in EE departments at the university or technical colleges are studied. The results show that educators have interest in more sophisticated RF measurement environment.

We have developed an ETReLa platform, and are extending the platform to provide RF measurement and analysis for education and research on RF engineering. In this paper, web-based graphical user interfaces are developed to control the test equipments and show the test results. In addition, several RF analysis engines are developed using graphical language. In section II, the ETReLa system is introduced. In section III, we describe the development of graphical interfaces and RF engines for remote RF laboratory with examples.

2   Electronics and Telecommunications Remote Laboratory

The ETReLa was developed by the ETRI-affiliated System Semiconductor Industry Promotion Center in 2008. The users (students and engineers) can access this system at http://etri.iptime.org. The developed platform includes the followings.

- Web-based graphical user interfaces for controlling each measurement equipment and showing the test results
- A real-time video streaming for observing real test, and controlling position & focus of the camera
- On-line booking and scheduling program
- Educational contents for the students and engineers
- Analysis engines for the measured results

The overall configuration of remote laboratory platform and its real environments are shown in Fig. 1. Instruments are connected to web server by using the parallel General Purpose Interface Bus (GPIB) and LAN cables. By adding the educational contents and RF analysis engines, the ETReLa supports universities and small businesses for their research and development.

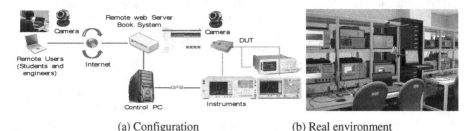

(a) Configuration   (b) Real environment

Fig. 1. Configuration and real environment of the ETReLa

The LabView and PHP programming language are used for system development. The LabView software has developed by National Instrument (NI) and based on Graphics language (G-language) [11]. By adding some blocks and connecting wires, users can simply code their program architecture. The finished source code could be re-used for other codes and saved as Virtual Instrument (VI) type. Supporting many utility drivers for various instruments, LabView has many advantages such as ease of use for beginners and intuitively handling the collected data.

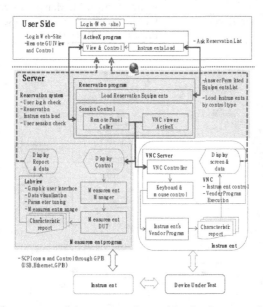

Fig. 2. The structure of the server and user sides for the remote laboratory

The structure of server and its interface are described in Fig. 2. The server checks the user's reservation program which is based on PHP language when the remote user's PC is connected the ETReLa at the first time. Through the Active X program which is on the web server book system, the remote users can get their permission to use instruments in ETReLa. The remote user PC controls the instruments to acquire measured data and send remote users acquired data. The web server operates in two modes. One of the modes is based on LabView software. Another is based on VNC which uses the inherency engine of instruments.

3   Development of the Remote RF Laboratory

The objects of remote laboratory for RF measurement and analysis are summarized in Table. 1. The remote laboratory can support measurement for RF device, circuits, and system with the listed experiments in Table 1. The hardware configuration for the remote RF laboratory is shown in Fig. 3 (a). The platform structure, interconnection, and test procedure of the remote RF laboratory is shown in Fig 3 (b). The platform is programmed using G-language, LabView.

Table 1. Objects of Remote Laboratory for RF Engineering

	DUT	List of Experiments
RF Device	Transmission Line, Diode, R/L/C, Transistor	S-parameter, I-V, f_t, f_{max}, K-factor, Phase delay, Power
RF Circuit	Power Amplifier Resonator, Filter, Combiner, Antenna	S-parameter, Power, Efficiency, ErrorVector Magnitude (EVM), Adjacent Channel Power Ratio (ACPR), Inter-Modulation Distortion(IMD), AM/AM, AM/PM, Memory Effects
RF System	Transmitter, Receiver	EVM, ACPR, Signal to Noise Ratio(SNR), Bit Error Ratio (BER), Power

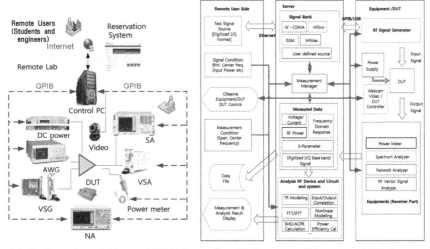

(a) Configuration of the remote RF lab   (b) Structure of the remote RF lab

Fig. 3. The configuration and structure of the developed remote RF laboratory

To enable RF measurement and analysis in the platform, RF engines are also developed with G-language. An example for ACPR measurement is demonstrated in Fig. 4. These RF engines are used to analyze transmitter or received signal performance of RF circuits and systems.

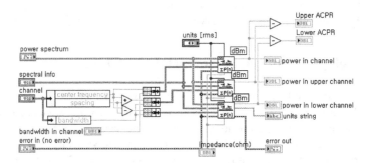

Fig. 4. An RF engine (ACPR measurement and analysis) programmed by G-language

The developed RF engines are used in remote RF laboratory. The web-based graphical interfaces are developed to provide user friendly laboratory environment. Fig. 5 shows an example of measurement of RF device using the developed web-based remote RF laboratory. In (a), a device under test (DUT), a RF transistor, is shown. The DUT is located in server side, and the remote user can observe real test using real-time video streaming. The figure in (b) is user interface that is shown on the remote user's screen. The figure in (c) is developed RF engine to measure I-V characteristics of transistors. The RF engine is programmed in sever computer. The measured results in (d) are shown in remote user's screen. The developed RF laboratory is also used to test RF circuit and system.

(a) DUT (Transistor) and test environment

(b) Remote user's interface

(C) RF engine for I-V curve measurement

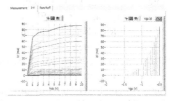

(D) Test results on the remote user's screen

Fig. 5. Remote RF experiment example (RF device case)

4   Conclusions

This paper described the development of a remote laboratory platform in the field of RF engineering. The previously developed remote laboratory, ETReLa, was extended. The graphical interfaces and RF engines for measurement and analysis of RF device, circuit, and system, have been developed using G-language. The developed graphical interfaces and RF engines were implemented on the ETReLa platform, and several demonstrations have been included. The developed remote RF laboratory is currently used on the education and research on RF engineering. We expect that the use of the developed system will improve the restricted RF experimental infrastructure in the universities and the small businesses, and give the more chances of RF experiments to students and engineers.

Acknowledgement. This work was supported by the National Research Foundation of Korea (NRF) grant funded by the Korea government (MEST) (No. 2011-0003299).

References

1. Asumadu, J.A., Tanner, R., Fitzmaurice, J., Kelly, M., Ogunleye, H., Belter, J., Kor, S.C.: A Web-Based Electrical and Electronics Remote Wiring and Measurement Laboratory (RwmLAB) Instrument. IEEE Trans. on Instrumentation and measurement 54(1), 38–44 (2005)
2. Gustavsson, I., Zackrisson, J., Akesson, H., Hakansson, L., Claesson, I., Lago, T.: Remote Operation and control of Traditional Laboratory Equipment. Journal of Online Engineering 2(1) (2006)
3. Kara, A., Aydin, E., Ozbek, M.E., Cagiltay, N.: Design and development of a remote and virtual environment for experimental training in Electrical and Electronics Engineering. In: 9th International Conference on Information Technology Based Higher Education and Training (ITHET), pp. 194–200 (2010)
4. Harware, J., et al.: The iLab shared architecture: a web services infrastructure to build communities of internet accessible laboratories. Proceedings of the IEEE 96(6), 931–950 (2008)
5. Machotka, J., Nedic, Z.: Online remote laboratory (NetLab). In: Proc. 5th UICEE Annual Conference on Engineering Education, Chennai, India, pp. 179–183 (2002)
6. Nedic, Z., Machotka, J., Nafalski, A.: Remote laboratory NetLab for effective interaction with real equipment over the internet. In: HIS 2008, Krakow, Poland, pp. 25–27 (May 2008)
7. Kara, A., Aydin, E.U., Oktem, R., Cagiltay, N.: A Remote Laboratory for Training in Radio Communications: ERRL. In: IEEE 18th International Symposium on Personal, Indoor and Mobile Radio Communications, PIMRC 2007, pp. 1–5 (2007)
8. Aydin, C.C., Turkmen, G., Ozyurt, E., Aydin, E.U., Cagiltay, N.E., Ozbek, M.E., Alparslan, N.C., Kara, A.: Distance laboratory applications ERRL: A study on radio communication in electronic field. In: 11th International Conference on Optimization of Electrical and Electronic Equipment, pp. 157–162 (2008)
9. Kang, W., Jo, H., Ku, H., Kim, Y.: Electronics & Telecommunications Remote Laboratory for RF Transmitter and Power Amplifier Characterization. In: 2010 Asia-Pacific Microwave Conference Proceedings (APMC), pp. 1444–1447 (2010)
10. Cagiltay, N.E., Aydin, E., Oktem, R., Kara, A., Alexandru, M., Reiner, B.: Requirements for remote RF laboratory applications: An educators' perspective. IEEE Trans. on Education 52(1), 75–81 (2009)
11. Egarievwe, S.U., Okobiah, O.K., Ajiboye, A.O., Fowler, L.A., Thorne, S.K., Collins, W.E.: Internet Application of LabVIEW in Computer Based Learning. European Journal of Open and Distance Learning (2000)

Educational Justifications for the Design of the ISCARE Computer Based Competition Assessment Tool

Manuel Fernández Molina, Pedro J. Muñoz-Merino,
Mario Muñoz-Organero, and Carlos Delgado Kloos

Universidad Carlos III de Madrid, Department of Telematic Engineering,
Avda de la Universidad, 30, E-28911 Leganés (Madrid), Spain
manuferna@gmail.com, {pedmume,munozm,cdk}@it.uc3m.es

Abstract. Students learn more and better when different educational theories are applied successfully in practice. We believe that competition among students can make the learning process much more enjoyable and motivating if the educational competition experience is conveniently designed, and other educational theories are combined with competition properly. In this paper, we analyze the main design decisions of a computer based competition assessment tool (named ISCARE, Information System for Competition during pRoblem solving in Education) that have educational implications, connecting these decisions with the correspondent educational justification.

Keywords: adaptive learning, assessment, competition, motivation.

1 Introduction

There is not a consensus about if competition in education should be encouraged or repressed and this is a debate from years ago. We believe that the benefits or damages of competition depend on how the competition is applied, in line with [1].

We designed and implemented the ISCARE system. Our starting point was to try to adapt the Swiss-system of competition (widely used e.g. in chess) for education. Moreover, a proper combination of already known educational theories and aspects can make a better learning tool, such as the following list:

- The need of structured hierarchical relationships between different contents and activities based on defined objectives [2].
- The importance of motivation in education. This is an evidence that was introduced by Thorndike [3] (the effects of rewards and penalties) and Skinner [4].
- Cognitive theories. The adaptation of contents and activities to students goes in this direction. One of the first works in learning adaptation is in [5].
- Problem Based Learning (PBL). PBL has been proved as a successful strategy (e.g. [6]) as a part of an active learning philosophy by doing activities.
- Evaluation. The evaluation of contents or students is needed to improve the materials, activities, or to generate a convenient feedback for students.
- Interoperability. Several educational resources can be reused if they follow standards (e.g. IMS-QTI for questions, http://www.imsglobal.org/question).

H. Leung et al. (Eds.): ICWL 2011, LNCS 7048, pp. 289–294, 2011.

2   Related Work

There are different systems that generate exercises that students must solve as an active learning experience (e.g. ASSISTment [7], Andes [8] or the hinting extension [9] for XTutor). In addition, there are other systems that generate exercises [10] using the IMS-QTI specification to enable interoperability and reusability. ISCARE also provides exercises that students must solve and although the problem solving possibilities are not so big, however, ISCARE implements the competition process that is not present in the commented systems.

There are also several competition systems in education that use questions such as Joyce [11] which is based on a board table where to move forward depends on the students' success or failure to the questions, or QUEST [12] that proposes challenges that students must solve and they are rewarded depending on the time they last in answering the questions or a collaborative. The ISCARE system differs with respect to these existing competitive tools for education. One of the most important differences is the application of a modified version of the Swiss-system for organizing the competition. In addition, other differences rely on the combination of different educational principles.

3   Overview of the System

ISCARE has two different profiles: teachers and students. Teachers can manage tournaments while students can participate in tournaments and request for it. Each tournament has a number of rounds. For each round, the system calculates the pairings (2 participants per pairing) depending on configured criteria (e.g. trying to pair students with similar knowledge level). Students compete one against another, answering a set of questions in a limit of time. The problems to show for each pairing are different and selected by the system. This selection can be based on the students' knowledge level. There is a student scoring for each match. Students can see and answer the different questions as well as their opponent scoring evolution in the match through a screen similar to the presented in fig.1.

Each student can obtain a maximum of 2 points in each round for the general tournament scoring. 1 point depends on the students' performance on the resolution of problems without taking into account the comparison with his/her opponent, while another 1 point depends on the comparison with his/her opponent. Another different concept is the maximum round points during exercise solving in a match that is greater than 2 (and can be different for each pairing), which is later used for the general tournament scoring. Fig. 1 shows the round points in a moment for a match competition. In this case, the maximum is 7 points for this round and pairing.

A final tournament ranking is presented, as well as the ranking after each round for every student. There is also a general students' ranking that includes all the different tournaments, and a summary of statistic data about each problem.

A complete description of the ISCARE system can be found in [13].

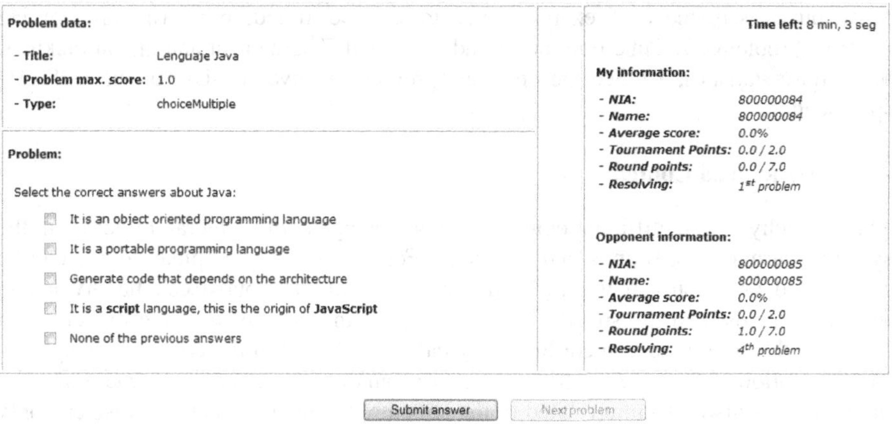

Problem data:		Time left: 8 min, 3 seg
- **Title:**	Lenguaje Java	
- **Problem max. score:**	1.0	**My information:**
- **Type:**	choiceMultiple	- *NIA:* 800000084

Problem:

Select the correct answers about Java:

- ☐ It is an object oriented programming language
- ☐ It is a portable programming language
- ☐ Generate code that depends on the architecture
- ☐ It is a **script** language, this is the origin of **JavaScript**
- ☐ None of the previous answers

My information:
- *NIA:* 800000084
- *Name:* 800000084
- *Average score:* 0.0%
- *Tournament Points:* 0.0 / 2.0
- *Round points:* 0.0 / 7.0
- *Resolving:* 1st problem

Opponent information:
- *NIA:* 800000085
- *Name:* 800000085
- *Average score:* 0.0%
- *Tournament Points:* 0.0 / 2.0
- *Round points:* 1.0 / 7.0
- *Resolving:* 4th problem

[Submit answer]   [Next problem]

Fig. 1. Competition screen for a student in ISCARE when solving exercises

4   Educational Theories vs. System Features

Table 1 shows some systems features (in columns) and their relationships with the educational aspects (in rows). The relationship is represented with an 'X'. If a box is empty, then there is not a relationship between this system feature and the correspondent educational aspect. The level of relationship has been set by the authors in the design phase. The different educational aspects and its relationship with these selected tool features are explained in each subsection.

Table 1. Relationship between some ISCARE features and the educational issues

Educational issues / System features	1	2	3	4	5	6	7	8	9	10	11
Structured contents	X	X			X						
Motivation I: Rewards						X		X			
Motivation II: Penalties						X		X			
Motivation III: Comparison with Peers			X			X	X	X		X	
Motivation IV: Close to the Achievement				X	X		X			X	
Enjoyment			X				X	X		X	
Problem Based Learning (PBL)		X									
Close to Students' knowledge level					X						
Evaluation of Students		X				X	X	X			
Evaluation of Exercises		X				X	X		X		
Interoperability											X
Reusability											X

The different column numbers of the educational aspects have the following meaning: 1.-Different tournaments and rounds, 2.-Different exercises to solve in each round, 3.-Compete with a peer each round, 4.-Adaptive assignment of pairings for each round,

5.-Adaptive assignment of exercises per match and round, 6.-Scoring system per different problems, 7.-Time limit per round, 8.-Round, Tournament and global rankings, 9.-Exercise statistics, 10.-See the opponent progress on live, 11.-Use of the IMS-QTI specification.

4.1 Structured Contents

The hierarchy among different contents can be managed with 3 hierarchy levels in the system: tournaments, rounds and exercises. For example, a complete course can be represented as a tournament, the different topics of the course can be divided in different rounds, and the specific topic concepts can be covered in the exercises. In this way, the structured content hierarchy can be reflected in the competition system. The adaptation of exercises so that an exercise can only be selected in some rounds by the system, is also a feature related to the structured contents, so an exercise can only be shown if their contents are related to the ones of the specific round.

4.2 Motivation and Enjoyment

The different motivation sources have been divided in these groups:

- Rewards. Students are rewarded immediately with round points for each correct problem resolution and each student can see the rewards through fig. 1. In addition, there are continuous students' rankings for rounds, tournaments, and global, in which students can increase their assigned points if they performed well. One out of the two tournament points of a round is only devoted to the students' performance on the questions but not on the comparison with the assigned opponent. These rewards can be seen as external and can have an effect on intrinsic motivation as reported in [14] although the connection of these specific rewards with [14] should be further studied.

- Penalties. In a similar way, if a student answers incorrectly, the student is penalized immediately in his/her round scoring, and the different rankings allow students to score fewer points if they performed badly.

- Comparison with peers. Students can compare in each round with its opponent, seeing both scorings. This comparison is reinforced as it is done on live, seeing the opponent and the own evolution of the scoring until the time limit, so the desire to defeat the opponent can be increased with this display window. Furthermore, when the round finishes, students can compare with its round opponent for the final round result and obtain 1 out of the 2 points depending of that comparison. In addition, there is also a comparison of all the students for all the rounds with the different rankings, which also motivates students to know their relative positions in the rankings.

- Close to achievement. As ISCARE can adapt the pairings to pair students with a similar number of points (so with a similar students' knowledge), then each pairing match can be balanced and students can feel that they are close to win against their opponents. This increases the feeling of being close to achievement and reinforces the motivation as students know they have possibilities to win. In a similar way, ISCARE can adapt the exercises for each pairing depending on the students' knowledge level, which makes students to feel they are close to solve these exercises and obtain the points for correct resolution. In addition the continuous display window with the time left and the opponent evolution of his/her points during the match, makes possible the continuous comparison with his/her opponent to know how close is to win.

Moreover, ISCARE makes students to enjoy the experience. The competition among peers, the display window of their opponents' performance and the time left, or the final updating of the round results and tournament rating, makes ISCARE to have many analogous features to present games that make students to enjoy.

4.3   Problem Based Learning and Close to Students' Knowledge Level

The different exercises that students must solve in each round is a way of problem based learning, as part of the active learning philosophy, in which students learn with an active intervention instead of being only receptors of information.

The exercises for a round can be configured with a percentage that is selected randomly and another percentage that is selected so that the exercises' level have to be close to the students' knowledge level (based on the students' tournament points until that moment). This is according to the cognitive theory that students can increase their knowledge based on their previous concepts, so if the exercises are adapted so that their level has to be close to the students' knowledge, then students can increase their knowledge better. Different students' pairings have different assigned exercises so that these specific pairing exercises adapt to the specific students' knowledge.

4.4   Evaluation, Interoperability and Reusability

The important facet of the evaluation, which is included in many different educational theories, is reflected in ISCARE. As each student obtains a different scoring on an exercise depending on the students' performance over a limit of time, then students can be evaluated based on their scorings on the different exercises, and this has a reflection on the different round, tournament and global rankings. Moreover, the different exercises can be evaluated through the global statistic screens depending on the different students' interactions with these exercises.

Reusability and interoperability are guaranteed as ISCARE follows the IMS-QTI specification. Therefore, ISCARE can receive and import exercises from other systems or the Web, and ISCARE can export exercises to be used in other systems. A part of IMS-QTI was selected that includes a specific instance of multiple choice, multiple response and fill in the blank exercises (e.g. the IMS-QTI support for hints is not included in ISCARE). Some IMS-QTI patterns have been defined, so that an exercise designer can follow one of these patterns to compose new questions that are understandable by the system.

5   Conclusions

This work presents the connections of different educational theories and aspects with some of the system features of the ISCARE competitive system for education, and the impact of these system features from the educational perspective is shown. In this way, the motivation, enjoyment, problem based learning, cognitive theories, adaptation, evaluations (of students and exercises), interoperability or reusability are present in the system with different features.

Acknowledgments. Work partially funded by the Learn3 project TIN2008-05163/TSI within the Spanish "Plan Nacional de I+D+I", and the Madrid regional community projects S2009/TIC-1650 and CCG10-UC3M/TIC-4992.

References

1. Ediger, M.: Cooperative Learning versus Competition: Which Is Better? Journal of Instructional Psychology, 204–300 (1996)
2. Gagne, R.: The conditions of learning. Holt, Rinehart and Winston, New York (1965)
3. Thorndike, E.: Education: A First Book. Macmilla (1912)
4. Skinner, B.: Teaching Machines. Science 128(3330), 969–977 (1958)
5. Pask, G.: Artificial Organisms. General Systems Yearbook 4, 151 (1959)
6. Sendag, S., Odabasi, H.F.: Effects of an on-line problem based learning course on content knowledge acquisition and critical thinking skills. Computers & Education 53(1), 132–141 (2009)
7. Feng, M., Heffernan, N.T., Koedinger, K.R.: Predicting State Test Scores Better with Intelligent Tutoring Systems: Developing Metrics to Measure Assistance Required. In: Ikeda, M., Ashley, K.D., Chan, T.-W. (eds.) ITS 2006. LNCS, vol. 4053, pp. 31–40. Springer, Heidelberg (2006)
8. VanLeghn, K., Lynch, C., Shulze, J.A., Shapiro, J.A., Shelby, R., Taylor, L., Treacy, D., Weinstein, A., Wintersgill, M.: The Andes Physics Tutoring System: Five Years of Evaluations. In: Artificial Intelligence in Education Conferrence, pp. 678–685 (2005)
9. Muñoz-Merino, P.J., Delgado Kloos, C.: A software player for providing hints in problem based learning according to a new specification. Computer Applications in Engineering Education 17(3), 272–284 (2009)
10. Martínez-Ortiz, I., Moreno-Ger, P., Sierra, J.-L., Manjón, B.F.: <e-QTI>: A Reusable Assessment Engine. In: Liu, W., Li, Q., Lau, R. (eds.) ICWL 2006. LNCS, vol. 4181, pp. 134–145. Springer, Heidelberg (2006)
11. Chang, L., Yang, J., Yu, F.: Development and evaluation of multiple competitive activities in a synchronous quiz game system. Innovations in Education & Training International 40(1), 16–26 (2003)
12. Regueras, L.M., Verdu, E., Munoz, M.F., Perez, M.A., de Castro, J.P., Verdu, M.J.: Effects of Competitive E-Learning Tools on Higher Education Students: A Case Study. IEEE Transactions on Education 52(2), 279–285 (2009)
13. Muñoz-Merino, P.J., Fernández Molina, M., Muñoz-Organero, M., Delgado Kloos, C.: An Adaptive and Innovative Question-driven Competition-based Intelligent Tutoring System for Learning. Submitted to Expert System with Applications Journal (2011)
14. Deci, E.L.: Effects of externally mediated rewards on intrinsic motivation. Journal of Personality and Social Psychology 18, 105–115 (1971)

Automated Lecture Template Generation
in CORDRA-Based Learning Object Repository

Neil Y. Yen[1], Timothy K. Shih[2], Qun Jin[1], and Li-Chieh Lin[3]

[1] Dept. of Human Informatics & Cognitive Sciences, Waseda University, Japan
neil219@gmail.com, jin@waseda.jp
[2] Dept. of Computer Science & Information Engineering, National Central University, Taiwan
timothykshih@gmail.com
[3] Digital Education Institute, Institute for Information Industry, Taiwan
lichieh@iii.org.tw

Abstract. Sharing resources and information on Internet has become an important activity for education. The MINE Registry, a branch of distributed repository, inherited the architecture of CORDRA has been developed for storing and sharing Learning Objects. Following the usage experiences, especially those being utilized to generate the lecture, the interaction structure is defined to clarify the relationships among Learning Objects. The methods to social network analysis are applied to quantify the implicit correlations and to evaluate the interdependency. In addition, an intelligent mining algorithm is proposed to explore the developed interaction structure and automatically generates lecture templates corresponding to the query criteria. The concentration of this study is to facilitate the complex and time-consuming process of creating lectures through a simple search mechanism. The implemented system has demonstrated the preliminary results and the feasibility are also revealed by the evaluation results.

Keywords: Lecture Template, Intelligent Mining Algorithm, Searching, Ranking, Knowledge Network.

1 Introduction

Although SCORM and CORDRA have provided preliminary solutions for searching and reusing LOs, a few fundamental issues are still left unsolved. Two major challenges are involved: (1) Time-Consuming Lecture Generation Process: A huge numbers of queries have to be sent by instructors to obtain useful LOs. Although built-in search service can serve the initial situation, the cost of time in selecting related LOs is still necessary. (2) Uncertain Reuse Scenario of LO: Though the alteration histories can be tracked and quantified, the use of this information has yet been addressed. In other words, the past experiences, especially in generating lectures, cannot be referred or applied to current scenario.

To cope with the situations, contributions of this study involve (1) the LONET (Learning Object Network), as an extension of Reusability Tree, is constructed to

H. Leung et al. (Eds.): ICWL 2011, LNCS 7048, pp. 295–304, 2011.

clarify the vague reuse scenario in the past, and to summarize collaborative intelligence through past interactive usage experiences. Once LOs are revised and reused for other specific objectives, relations among them can be graphed and can be quantified through their newly added interdependency, and (2) as a practical contribution, an interactive search method is proposed to gather possible organization paths for lecture generation in accordance with the past usage experience in the LONET. The obtained lectures are based on input query and can be revised up on instructors' immediate feedbacks. If there are newly added connections, they will be added to the LONET for further usage.

The organization of this paper is given as follows. Related works will be discussed in Section 2. The construction of LONET along with the metrics to interactive search process will be addressed in Section 3. The evaluation and experiment on this work will be given in Section 4. The implementation will be given in Section 5, and we will conclude this work and address the possible future work in Section 6.

2   Related Work

Research into Social Network Analysis has revealed a promising approach to clarify the complex interactions among participants (e.g. human and/or object) by quantifying potential interactive processes to an interconnected relation graph or network. It not only makes easier to clarify interpersonal information, but furthermore enables domain researchers to discover those indirect relationships by mining information associated to common intersections [1]. In this study, we concentrate on the mining algorithm to achieve social-like structure discovery. SNA (Social Network Analysis) emphasizes on mining the exchange of resources among participants ranging from individual to organizations. The methods to search social networks can be categorized into (1) Path-Oriented, and (2) Efficiency-Oriented. The first one emphasizes on discovering shortest and complete paths to connect different nodes. The second one pays more attention on improving the overall search efficiency to reduce the possible time cost. For example, Kleinberg [2] proved that a simple greedy strategy could achieve shortest path length, in $O((ln\ N)^2)$, in a scalable range (i.e., hierarchically nested groups) by converting the structure into specific dimensions of space vector. To make improvement, NeuroGrid [3] utilized Routing Tables generated by past query histories to achieve intelligent route selection. As another instance, SSON (Semantic Social Overlay Networks) [4] made use of response frequencies to obtain nodes that might respond to the requests, and utilize the LRU (Least Recently Used) to remove the redundant connections.

Research works have pointed out the trends of Social Network development, which mainly emphasize on how implicit information, such as neighborhood selection, associated to specific nodes is obtained within a specific network environment. This concept has also been applied in the scope of distance learning for learners to obtain appropriate models to follow. As to instructors' aspects, difficulties to lecture creation are one of the issues that discourage the popularity of distance learning. In this work, we adopt the concept of Social Network to construct the social structure, based on Reusability Tree of the MINE Registry, of LOs to clarify usage experiences of social knowledge, and to utilize the relationship between LOs to achieve intelligent lecture generation in a systematic way.

3   Learning Object Network (LONET)

3.1   Construction of LONET

Learning Object Network (LONET) is derived from the concept of Social Network. It is used to clarify the relationships between LOs, especially those used for assembling lectures for specific objectives, and is constructed by the possible alterations recorded by Reusability Tree. With the relations from alteration history, inherited from Reusability Tree, the LONET is defined as a weighted digraph expressed by

$$G_{LONET} = (V, E, W)$$

where $V = \{v_1, v_2, \dots, v_n\}$ represents the set of nodes (i.e., LOs) used for a specific lecture generation, $E = \{e_{ij} | if\ correlation\ exists\ between\ v_i\ and\ v_j\}$ represents the link between two nodes; and the element w_{ij} belongs to W and stands for the weight (or strength) of the links between vertex v_i and vertex v_j. Its value, ranged from -1 to 1, decides the direction between v_i and v_j. The value of w_{ij} will be determined by the direction of link(s) connecting v_i and v_j.

The possible correlation (or interdependency) that forms the link(s) between nodes can be categorized into three major types, (1) **Prerequisite Correlation:** This relation is a mandatory dependency. That is, some LOs have to be utilized before accessing the LO with perquisite attributes. If not, it will be considered as an invalid access. For instance, the LO "Linked List" shall be taught before LO "Tree" while performing a lecture "Data Structure." (2) **Inheritance Correlation:** This relation is a weak dependency. That is, it is optional. It indicates a specific concept, usually a core concept that can be applied to other LOs for further usage. For instance, the LO introducing "Sorting" is related to the LO introducing "Sorting in Tree." (3) **Reference Correlation:** This relation does not possess dependency. That is, it can exist independently. It is the same as an Inheritance Relation as an optional item. For example, it can be regarded as LOs that contained several videos or figures for describing the LO introduced "Tree."

In general, nearly all of the correlations can be obtained from the past usage experiences. However, it is still insufficient to determine the "Prerequisite Correlation". For instance, there may exist lots of possibility if there is a direction from v_i to v_j. Thus, in LONET construction, the LOM-based metadata is adopted to determine predefined correlation (i.e., Prerequisite), and the Reusability Tree is used to track for rests. To quantify the weight of links, two major factors (Correlation Type and Usage Frequency) are concerned. The first is the correlation properties of LOs and the second is the actual frequency of usages to specific links. Through requirements, w_{ij} can be quantified by

$$w_{ij} = \frac{\sum \left(C(e_{ij}) \cdot (1 + H_{coe}) \right)}{m} \tag{1}$$

where $C(e_{ij}) = \{C_1 | C_2\}$, and

$C_1 =$ 1, if Prerequisite exists between v_i and v_j
     $= -1$, if Prerequisite exists between v_i and v_j
     $=$ 0, otherwise
$C_2 =$ $F(e_{ij})$ if other correlation exists between v_i and v_j

The frequency of usage in LONET shall be interpreted as the patterns, from v_i to v_j, adopted to generate lectures. Considering the Revised Hebbian Rule [5], the weight of links shall be raised if they are triggered in accordance with existing patterns. On the contrary, it shall be reduced if the pattern is changed (i.e., only one of them is triggered). This approach is applied dynamically to adjust the weight of link and to highlight the patterns often used. Thus, in Eq. (1), the additional weight, considering frequency of usage, is added to w_{ij} by H_{coe} which can be expressed as

$$H_{coe} = \varphi \sum \overrightarrow{e_{ij}} \overrightarrow{e_{ij}}^T \tag{2}$$

where $\varphi = \{z | -1 \leq z \leq 1, z \neq 0\}$

The link between v_i and v_j will be converted to vector $\overrightarrow{e_{ij}}$, and its length will increase with the frequency of usage. In order to avoid the extreme value, the vector $\overrightarrow{e_{ij}}$ will be projected onto a virtual coordinate space to obtain additional increment or reduction to w_{ij} under normalization. That is, the obtained value will be relative to every other node connected to the datum node. An equilibrium coefficient φ is set in accordance with the directional relation (or usage direction) between nodes. Its value will be within -1 and 1, but will not be equal to 0 since the existing pattern identifies that there is at least one link between nodes. In LONET, the value of H_{coe} can also be regarded as the credibility of specific patterns.

3.2   Metrics to LONET Analysis

The *degree centrality* identifies the links, incoming and outgoing, which a specific node v_i may have within LONET. It can be quantified through Eq. (3). Its value reflects the importance of nodes within LONET. That is, it explains why a node is needed by other nodes or needs other nodes to support its existence. From the perspective of lecture generation, the path can be produced through the connection of links, which identify the possible sequence of construction of specific objectives associated to nodes.

$$DegCent(v_i) = \frac{InDeg(v_i) + OutDeg(v_i)}{2} \tag{3}$$

For a single node v_i, its degree centrality will be the average of every incoming links, $InDeg(v_i)$, and outgoing links, $OutDeg(v_i)$. Note that the degree centrality of a specific node v_i will not be 0 since every node was generated for specific objective(s), so that it must have at least one incoming or outgoing link. The metrics for obtaining degree of incoming and outgoing will be discussed as follows.

In LONET, the number of incoming links indicates the popularity (or degree of attention) a node has. From the perspective of lecture generation, the node with many incoming links can be regarded as a component often used for specific objectives. The PageRank algorithm is adopted to be the basis for quantifying the incoming links. In addition, the time-series issue [6] is also concerned to be a factor that highlights the importance during different timescales. The formula can be simplified as in Eq. (4).

$$InDeg(v_i) = \delta \frac{\sum T(v_{ji}) R_{in}(Ts, v_{ji})}{R_{in}(v_{ji})} \tag{4}$$

where $R_{in}(Ts, v_{ij})$ represents the incoming links to node v_i v_i in a selected timescale (Ts). The least measurement unit for Ts is assumed to be one day, but can be adjusted by an administrator or instructor. The variable δ (default value is 1) is used to balance the final outcome value if the extreme value happens. The variable $T(v_{ij})$ indicates the additional weight that shall be assigned to incoming links to node v_i. We revised the Tilt-Time Window Model [7] to calculate the weight for specific timescale by Eq. (5).

$$T(v_{ij})_l = \frac{D_{n-l+1}}{\sum D_l} \tag{5}$$

The $T(v_{ij})_l$ indicates the weight of every other node v_j to node v_i in a specific timescale D_l. And n is the number of units that we separate the total length of time for obtaining different weight of link from v_j to v_i.

Similarly, for nodes used to generate lectures, they are bound to have outgoing links in accordance with the definition in the IMS Simple Sequencing. The exception can only happen in the starting node, which may have lots of outgoing links and no incoming link. For the end nodes, the types of missing links are opposite. The outgoing link, from v_i to v_j, can be calculated through Eq. (6).

$$OutDeg(v_i) = \delta \frac{\sum T(v_{ij}) R_{out}(Ts, v_{ij})}{R_{out}(v_{ij})} \tag{6}$$

3.3   Lecture Generation from LONET

A Lecture Path can be considered as the possible re-composition of LOs used to generate lectures for specific objectives. The lecture path is produced according to possible sequences within LONET. Each node is considered as a center in a lecture web, and can be used to determine the direction to lecture path generation in accordance with its implicit properties. This iterative retrieval process will be kept in a temporary array to achieve continuous path. In addition, the shortest path is not the primary purpose to assemble the lecture, but the frequency of usage from users is what we have concerned instead. The higher frequency of usage represents higher credibility, and can also be served as the countable reference for lecture path generation. Thus, common user experiences are used. The generation of lecture path can be categorized into following steps.

Step 1: In the beginning, the attribute array, will be generated by converting the query from user in accordance with its corresponding metadata description. Then, to return the top-N items, $V_{ent}[v_m]$, the matched objects in LONET will be ranked, from high to low, on the basis of their relative similarity. The process is shown below.

Step 2: The Swarm algorithm [8] will be revised to be the basis for visiting every node that has connections with node v_m in V_{ent}. The nodes with a shorter path, with less nodes between v_m and $v_{(m,j)}$, and a higher OutDegree will be the priority obtained. The main reason is that the node with a higher OutDegree identifies that more nodes can be accessed. In other words, the node offers more choices for the system to select. Thus, we set up a rule that if the visited node $v_{(m,j)}$ has a higher OutDegree value, a shorter distance than v_m will replace the original one. And a new entry node array $V_{ent}'[v_m']$ will be generated. The process is shown below.

Input: ranked search results V_{ent}
Output: entry array of candidate node array V_{ent}'

1: reset V_{ent} by neighbor node of v_m with higher OutDegree
   1.1 for each node $v_{(m,j)}$ in V_{ent}, find nearest node v_n
       if $(InDeg(v_{(m,j)}^l) < InDeg(v_m)$ AND
       $OutDeg(v_{(m,j)}^l) > OutDeg(v_m))$
       $v_m \leftarrow v_m' = v_{(m,j)}^l$
   1.2 reorder the V_{ent}' based on $OutDeg(v_m')$

Step 3: The returned entry array, $V_{ent}'[v_m']$, will be converted to a two-dimension vector space, $P_{cdt}[v_x][v_y]$, where v_x represents the entry nodes from v_m' and v_y indicates the possible path to v_x as shown in Figure 2. The circle with light-color represents the possible position of entry node where the others are default to *null* for expansion. The following algorithm is applied.

Input: revised candidate node array V_{ent}'
Output: initialized vector space for lecture generation

1: initialize path array P_{cdt}
2: initialize the direct edge e_{xy} of each node v_x in P_{cdt}
   $v_{(x,j)} \leftarrow v_{(m,j)}'$
   $v_{(y,j)} \leftarrow null$

Step 4: The nodes used to generate the lecture path are supposed to have correlations with specific sequence. But it is difficult for us to know if the entry node, the first node to generate the lecture, can be determined by a user's query. What we can do is to obtain an appropriate entry node, with a high OutDegree, in accordance with the user's query. As to the entry node, it may locate at any order in the path. Hence, the proposed metrics, the weight of edge between two connected nodes and Degree Centrality, are utilized to determine the possible direction of path for those correlations that do not belong to "Prerequisite." The possible directions can be tracked backward or forward. As stated in previous section, the correlations can be categorized into four types, and there is only one mandatory interdependency (the other three are optional). That is, the correlations except "Prerequisite" will not affect the generation rule of lecture path. Thus, we only consider the edge with Prerequisite correlation. If such kind of correlation exists, it will be added to the path without calculating the Degree Centrality, and the following direction will be determined. The detail algorithm is listed below.

Input: revised candidate node array V_{ent}'
Output: filled path array P_{cdt}

1 : for each v_x
      let its tolerable threshold κ for candidate neighbor
      nodes selection with direction dir
2 : for $\forall\ v_i \in V$ that has not been visited
      for k-th neighbor nodes $v_{(x,j)}^k$, $k = \{0,1, \dots, n\}$
        if $v_{(x,j)}^k \notin P_{cdt}$
          calculate highest weight $\left|w_{(x,j)i}\right|$ from $v_{(x,j)}$ to v_i
        else compute the mining direction (forward or backward)
3 : Return P_{cdt}

Step 5: To avoid duplications (i.e., two same nodes appear in a same path), the mechanism named "Duplicated Nodes Removal" has been utilized to make cross-comparison to all the nodes within $P_{cdt}[v_x][v_y]$. If duplication exists, the node being added later will be removed directly, and the process will go back to the previous one to look for alternative nodes. If there is no existence of duplicated node, the produced candidate array $P_{cdt}[v_x][v_y]$ will be converted to a list of single paths that will be the result responded to a user's query. Then decisions can be made by users to make further modifications. The detail algorithm is shown below.

4   System Evaluation

Our repository system, the MINE Registry, has stored around 22,000 LOs in the past few years. Most of the learning objects were collected from open access training programs, such as Open University, UK and ADL (Advanced Distributed Learning), USA, and from the local universities. In the beginning, the TREC [9] was adopted to evaluate the overall search performance in MINE Registry. The general metrics, Precision-Recall Testing, for estimating the performance are applied. In addition, the Non-Interpolated Precision [10] is also applied to calculate the precision of retrieved LO within a ranked result. The variable r_j is the sum of queries sent to system, the $LO_j(i)$ is the order of retrieved LO in a list, and the i is the order of query. In this research, the cut-off coefficient for nIAP was set to 10 by default.

P'= number of relevant LOs retrieved / number of LOs retrieved
R'= number of relevant LOs retrieved / number of relevant LOs

$$nIAP = \frac{\Sigma \dfrac{i}{LO_j(i)}}{r_j}$$

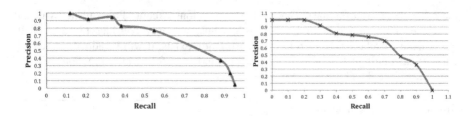

Fig. 1. P-R Curve for (a) Raw Data and (b) Non-Interpolated Data

Two kinds of data were examined. The Raw Data, Fig.1(a), represents for the results of common LOs in the MINE Registry while the Non-Interpolated Data, Fig.1(b), is for the ranked results. Through the results above, the Precision-Recall curve for both Raw Data and Non-Interpolated Data are as shown below.

As to lecture path review, we follow the same method to conduct another experiment to evaluate the accuracy of the selected nodes in lecture path generation. The selected nodes to generate lecture path were utilized to compare with the ones we obtained in candidate array. This relation is used to generate a Precision-Recall curve. We involved two P-R curves in the previous experiment as the based line, which will be compared with the one generated according to the proposed interactive search mechanism. In Fig.2, the curve with circle dots on it is the result while using interactive search. The linear dashed line goes across these three curves is the average trend. It is obvious that there is no prominent part in this curve through comparison with the baselines. But, by and large, the proposed search method can reach the average accuracy.

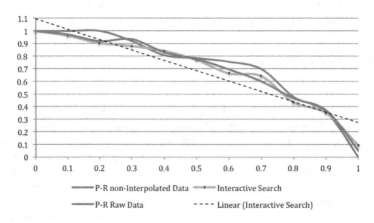

Fig. 2. P-R Curve for of Selected Nodes in Lecture Paths

5   Implementation

A concrete example is given while accessing our repository. Most LOs were collected from online training programs, such as Open University and MIT OpenCourseWare, and have been reused for generating lectures corresponding to specific topics. In this example, we make a query by using a combination of keywords, "photoshop + intro + example." The results, shown in Fig.3, are ranked and the detail information, such as similarity and diversity, that assists instructors in realizing the degree of derivation are also shown next to each result.

Fig. 3. Search Results in Reusability Tree

We assume instructor selects the first result. The detailed information includes the metadata description, its original content, and the possible lecture path for related objective. The layout can be shown in Fig.4.

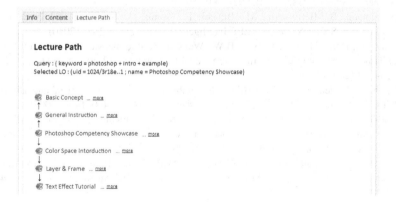

Fig. 4. The Lecture Path based on Selected LOs

Once the instructor clicked the "Lecture Path" button in the upper menu, the possible composition lecture path is generated. Instructor can take this as a template, and make further modification by clicking the "more" button.

6 Conclusion

The major contributions of this paper can be summarized as follows. Firstly, based on concepts from social network, we proposed LONET (Learning Object Network). Based on the Hebbian Rule, we added weights to commonly used links among LOs. Moreover, inspired by the Swarm Intelligence algorithm, two algorithms were proposed and developed to generate candidate paths and allow users to reorganize preference paths. By using the prerequisite relation among LOs, as well as the attributes from these LOs, candidate paths can be generated. The generated paths are templates, which can be reorganized by the users themselves, and can be stored back to the repository for further reference and reuse. The implemented system has demonstrated the high usability and user satisfaction. We believe that the proposed mechanism can make LOs in a repository more reusable, by providing an automatic mechanism to reduce the load of lecture creation.

References

1. Tolsdorf, C.C.: Social Networks, Support, and Coping: An Exploratory Study. Family Process 15(4), 407–417 (1976)
2. Kleinberg, J.: Navigation in a small world. Nature 406 (2000)
3. Joseph, S.: NeuroGrid: Semantically Routing Queries in Peer-to-Peer Networks. In: International Workshop on Peer-to-Peer Computing, pp. 202–214 (2002)
4. Lin, S., Chalupsky, H.: Discovering and Explaining Abnormal Nodes in Semantic Graphs. IEEE Transactions on Knowledge and Data Engineering 20(8), 1039–1052 (2008)
5. Stent, G.S.: A Physiological Mechanism for Hebb's Postulate of Learning. National Academic Science, USA 70(4), 997–1001 (1973)
6. Bringmann, B., Berlingerio, M., Bonchi, F., Gionis, A.: Learning and Predicting the Evolution of Social Networks. IEEE Intelligent Systems 25(4), 2–35 (2010)
7. Chen, Y., Dong, G., Han, J., Wah, B.W., Wang, J.: Multidimensional Regression Analysis of Time-Series Data Streams. In: International Conference on Very Large Data Bases, pp. 323–324 (2002)
8. Chen, Y.P., Peng, W.C., Jian, M.C.: Recombination and Dynamic Linkage Discovery. IEEE Transactions on Systems, Man, and Cybernetics 37(6), 1460–1470 (2007)
9. Buckley, C., Voorhees, E.M.: Retrieval Evaluation with Incomplete Information. In: The 27th Annual International Conference on Research and Development in Information Retrieval, pp. 25–32. ACM Press, New York (2004)
10. Jarvelin, K., Kekalainen, J.: IR Evaluation Methods for Retrieving Highly Relevant Documents. In: The 23rd ACM International Conference Information Retrieval, pp. 41–48 (2000)

Combining Collaborative Filtering and Sequential Pattern Mining for Recommendation in E-Learning Environment

Yi Li[1,2,3], Zhendong Niu[1,2,3], Wei Chen[1,2,3], and Wenshi Zhang[1,2,3]

[1] The School of Computer Science, Beijing Institute of Technology, Beijing, 100081, China
[2] The Software Laboratory, Beijing Institute of Technology, Beijing, 100081, China
[3] Beijing Lab of Intelligent Information Technology, Beijing, 100081, China
{liyi,zniu,wchen,zws871109}@bit.edu.cn

Abstract. In this paper, we describe a Web log mining approach to recommend learning items for each active learner based on the learner's historical learning track. The proposed method is composed of three parts: discovering content-related item sets by Collaborative Filtering (CF), applying the item sets to Sequential Pattern Mining (SPM) and generating sequential pattern recommendations to learners. Different from other recommendation strategies which use CF or SPM separately, this paper combines the two algorithms together and makes some optimizations to adapt them for E-learning environments. Experiments are conducted for the evaluation of the proposed approach and the results show good performance of it.

Keywords: recommendation, E-learning, collaborative filtering, sequential pattern.

1 Introduction

The aim of recommender systems in Web 2.0 environment is to provide useful recommendations such as items or products for users. Suggestions for books on Amazon, or movies on Netflix, are examples of real-world recommender systems [1]. As the rapid growth of E-learning applications on the Web, more and more learning resources are accumulated. Finding suitable learning resources for individual learners becomes a challenge. This has made resource recommendation in E-learning environment an important direction of research [2].

CF is regarded as one of important and useful algorithms in recommender system. [3-4]. CF in E-learning environment is supposed to predict learning items for a learner based on the preferences of a group of learners that are considered similar to him/her. CF has many forms [5]: (a) Looking for users who share the same rating patterns with the active user and then use the ratings from those like-minded users to calculate a prediction for the active user; [5-6] (b) Finding out similar items preferred by users and use the ratings from these similar items to compute a prediction for the active user [7].

H. Leung et al. (Eds.): ICWL 2011, LNCS 7048, pp. 305–313, 2011.

SPM, which is commonly used for sequence mining, extracts sequential patterns which appear more frequently than a user-specified minimum support while maintaining items in occurance order. Many sequential pattern mining algorithms, such as Generalized Sequential Pattern (GSP) [8], Prefix Span [9-10], SPADE [11] and SPAM [12], have been proposed.

E-learning recommender system has particular issues: (a) Learning items can be classified into groups by their preferences, popularities and content relevances; (b) Learning items should be learned by sort of sequential orders. While CF uses a database of preferences for learning items by learners to predict additional items a new learner might like and SPM focuses on the occurrence order among the learning items. Thus, it's important to raise a new method, which is combined with CF and SPM, does not only focus on the items' content-relevance but also take the strong orderly sequence into account.

In this paper, a combined algorithm that contains two approaches is proposed: (a) Finding out items that are similar to other items the user has liked; (b) Using the results from CF to generate the strong ordered sequential patterns by SPM. We have made some adaptations to the combined algorithm to make it suitable for the E-learning system. One is to add damping function into computing the values of rate of each item by each user. The other one is to improve the scalability of the CF algorithm. Experiments are also conducted to find out the optimal values of parameters for the combined algorithm and compare these three algorithms' recommendation qualities.

The rest of paper is organized as following. Section 2 introduces the recommendation model using the combined algorithms. Section 3 depicts the adjustments of the combined algorithms adapted for the E-learning environment. In section 4, experiments are conducted for the evaluation of the combined algorithm. Finally, conclusion and future work are presented.

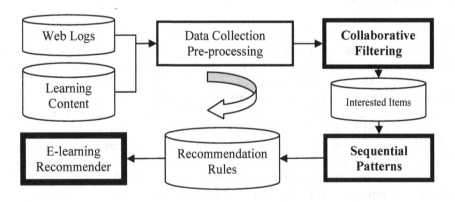

Fig. 1. Recommendation model

2   Recommendation Model

The Recommendation Model in the E-learning environment is depicted in Fig. 1, which shows the data analysis process that integrates the CF Algorithm and the SPM Algorithm.

Collaborative Filtering is supposed to predict the utility of items for a particular user based on the items previously rated by other users [13]. The relations between items are relatively more static and allow us to precompute the potential items for each user. **Sequential Patterns** can be defined as the process of discovering all sub-sequences that appear frequently on a given sequence database and have minimal support threshold. The support label is useful and efficient in pruning candidate items and discovering frequent sequential patterns.

3   The Combined Algorithms Used in E-Learning Environment

The combined algorithms are supposed to recommend a list of learning items, which are both predicted and strongly ordered, to the learners. We use item-item based CF algorithm and then generate the list of learning items through SPM algorithm.

3.1   Finding Out Predicted Items by Collaborative Filtering

In a typical E-learning environment, each learner u corresponds to a list of items Iu. An item $i \in I_u$ represents that i has been learned by the learner u before. A rating score of a learning item corresponds to the rating given to the item i by learner u. Ratings are represented using a user-item rating matrix as shown in Fig. 2 (a). The next approaches can be generalized by the algorithm in the following steps:

1. Computing similarities between each two items. The most commonly used measurement of similarity is Adjusted Cosine Similarity. The similarity between items i and j is calculated as follows:

$$sim(i, j) = \frac{\sum (R_{u,i} - \overline{R}_u)(R_{u,j} - \overline{R}_u)}{\sqrt{\sum (R_{u,i} - \overline{R}_u)^2} \sqrt{\sum (R_{u,j} - \overline{R}_u)^2}} \quad (1)$$

where $R_{u,i}$ is the rating given to I_i by user u, $\overline{R}$ is the mean rating of all the ratings provided by u. An item similarity matrix is generated as shown in Fig. 2 (b).

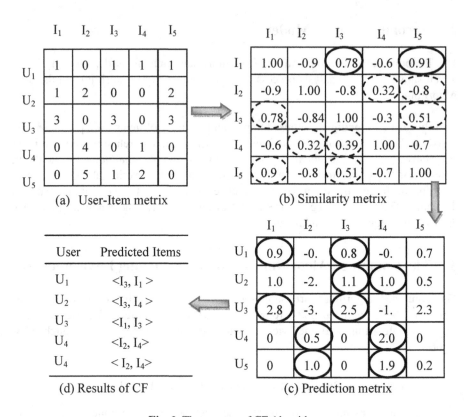

(a) User-Item metrix

(b) Similarity metrix

(c) Prediction metrix

(d) Results of CF

User	Predicted Items
U_1	$<I_3, I_1>$
U_2	$<I_3, I_4>$
U_3	$<I_1, I_3>$
U_4	$<I_2, I_4>$
U_4	$<I_2, I_4>$

Fig. 2. The process of CF Algorithm

2. Selecting other k items which have highest similarities with the current item. Those items form the similar item sets of the current item.
3. Computing predictions on an item i for a learner u by computing the sum of the ratings. The prediction for each user u correlated with each item i is represented as follows:

$$P_{u,i} = \frac{\sum_{t \in N}(sim(i,t) * R_{u,t})}{\sum_{t \in N}(\|sim(i,t)\|)} \tag{2}$$

where N represents the item i's similar item sets, and $R_{u,t}$ is the rating given to item t by learner u. The prediction matrix generated in this step is shown in Fig. 2 (c).

Fig. 2 (d) summaries the preferred items of each learner acquired from the prediction matrix. For example, as shown in the prediction matrix, I_3 and I_4 have the biggest prediction value for U_2. Therefore, I_3 and I_4 will be recommended for U_2.

3.2 Adaptive Optimization for CF in E-Learning Environment

We have further made two adaptations for the item-based CF approach for the E-learning environment.

Computing Rate Values. In E-learning environment, the previous rate values of items given by users could not really reflect the current user-item rate value. Thus, a damping function is introduced that decrease the influence of ratings made a long time ago, shown as follows:

$$Weight(t) = \frac{2}{1 + e^{-(t-t_0)}} \tag{3}$$

where t_0 represents the current time of visiting. More weight is assigned to ratings that are given more recently. The maximal weight is 1. We take the weight into account when using (1) to compute the similarities between each two items.

Decreasing Space Complexity. Because the item-item based similarities are static, we can precompute the predicted items offline. Through saves time, the method still requires $O(n^2)$ space for n items. Thus we develop two methods to decrease space complexity. First, in an E-learning Environment, the items which have smaller similarities play fewer roles in the prediction results. Therefore, for each item i we confine the number of similar items as k, where $k \ll n$. The corresponding change of algorithm in computing similarities is retrieving the k most similar items corresponding to the target item i. In this way, the space complexity can be reduced greatly. For instance, the set of I_1's similar items (except for I_1) with their degressive rating values are $\{I_3, I_5, I_4, I_2\}$, but only the first 2 items, such as I_3 and I_5 in the set can make sense in computing the predictions for users.

The second method focuses on delimiting the current active learner session. Since the active user session is to extract from the Web Log file, we identify only the records representing the last W visited items which can be closely associated with the current items. For example, let W be a fixed size, then if the active user visited the items with W=4 is $\{I_1, I_2, I_3, I_4\}$, and the item "I_5" is visited by the user recently, thus the visiting slide becomes to $\{I_2, I_3, I_4, I_5\}$. In short, only the latest four visited items will affect the recommendation result.

3.3 Discovering Sequential Pattern

After processing the algorithm of CF, the k most similar items related with a certain item i for each user u are retrieved. However, those k similar items are only ranked by their similarities with i, rather than by general learning order.

The main procedures of Generalized Sequential Pattern (GSP) can be described as follows:

- **Initial pass:** determines the support of each item. At the end of the initial pass, the algorithm acquires the frequent 1-sequence, which contains only one item.
- **Candidate-items generation:** generates new potential patterns. From the set of all the frequent $k-1$ $(k > 1)$ sequences, the algorithm generates new k-sequence candidates.
- **Pruning:** prune away the candidate sequences whose support is less than the minimal support.

After applying the result sets from CF to GSP, the sequential patterns for each learner are presented in Table 1. We can see that the recommendation track for U2 is to first adopt I3 and then I4, because the support of subsequence of <I3, I4> is 40%, larger than the minimum value of 25%.

Table 1. Sequential Pattern Items (min-support=25%)

User	Sequential Pattern
U1	$<I_3, I_1>$
U2	$\mathbf{<I_3, I_4>}$
U3	$<I_3, I_1>$
U4	$<I_2, I_4>$
U5	$< I_2, I_4>$

4   Experiments and Results

4.1   Experiment Setup

The Dataset. The expriment data are collected from our E-learning website[1] and used to test performances of CF, SPM and the combined algorithm. A total of 24 students are invited to evaluate the recommendation result. Before they begin their learning activities, they need to rate their interesting items. These rates are used as benchmark in evaluating the quality of the combined algorithm. Table 2 lists the detailed summary of courses and log records in the E-learning System.

Evaluation Metrics. We use the Recommendation Error Metrics (REM) to evaluate how effective the recommendation engine is. REM is computed by first summing up recommendation-errors of each user-item pairs and then computing the average. The lower the REM, the more accurate the algorithm is.

Table 2. Summary of Learning Courses

Summary / Learning Topics	Courses	Log Records
Maths	10	123
Psychology	10	231
Music	10	121
Programming	10	127
Human	10	121
Magic	10	150
Total	60	873

---

[1] http://evaluate.guoshi.com/publishg/

4.2 Experimental Results

In this section, we present our experiment results of applying CF, SPM and the combined algorithm to generate recommendation. Before evaluating the quality of recommendations, we firstly focus on the sensitivity of some parameters such as the size of similar items and value of min-support.

Sensitivity of Similar Size. The size of similar items plays an important role in recommendation quality. We implement an experiment of various numbers of similarity sizes and compute REM. The results are presented in Fig. 3. We observe from the figure that REM decreases when we increase the similar size. But when the size varied from 7 to 10, the curve does not drop much. Considering the fact that the bigger the similar size is, the more space complexity it is, we choose size = 6 as an optimal value for next experiments.

Sensitivity of Minial Support. To determine the sensitivity of min support, we carry out another experiment where the value of min support varies from 0.01 to 0.09 in an increment of 0.1. The experiment results are presented in Fig. 3. From the figure, we can see that the value of min support can influence the quality of recommendation much. REM decreases while the min support increases from 0.1 to 0.15, after the point 0.15 REM increases as the min support increases from 0.15 to 0.2. Hence, we choose support = 0.15 as min support as optimal choice for the next experiments.

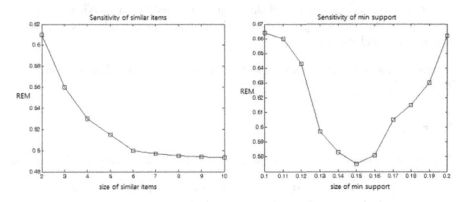

Fig. 3. Sensitivity of the parameter of similar size and min support

Quality Experiments. After obtaining the optimal values of the parameters, we compare CF algorithm, SPM algorithm and combined algorithm. The results of the comparison of recommendation quality of the three algorithms are presented in Fig. 4. We observe that the combined algorithm performs better than the two other algorithms at all the values of similar size (min-support = 0.15) and all the values of min-support (similar items = 6).

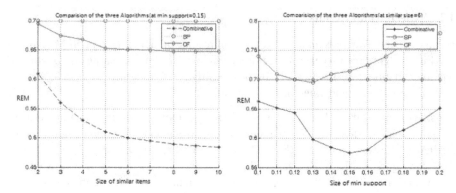

Fig. 4. Comparison of recommendation quality of the three algorithms

5   Conclusion and Future Work

In this paper, we propose a resource recommendation algorithm in an E-learning environment which combines collaborative filtering and sequential pattern mining together. Adaptations are made for the approach to be suitable for the E-learning environment. The results from experiment show that the combined algorithm provides best recommendation results compared with others.

Our subsequent research includes some personalization services such as adjustation module according to the learner's feedback. So the solutions discovered are both useful and practical.

Acknowledgements. This work is supported by the 111 project of Beijing Institute of Technology.

References

1. Prem, M., Vikas, S.: Recommender System, Encyclopedia of Machine Learning, pp. 1–9 (2010)
2. Manouselis, N., Drachsler, H., Vuorikari, R., Hummel, H., Koper, R.: Recommender Systems in Technology Enhanced Learning, pp. 1–31 (2011)
3. Adomavicius, G., Tuzhilin, A.: Toward the next generation of recommender systems: a survey of the state-of-the-art and possible extensions. IEEE Transactions on Knowledge and Data Engineering 17(6), 734–749 (2005)
4. Herlocker, J.L., Konstan, J.A., Riedl, J.T., Terveen, L.G.: Evaluating collaborative filtering recommender systems. ACM Transactions on Information Systems 22(1), 5–53 (2004)
5. Collaborative Filtering, http://en.wikipedia.org/wiki/Collaborativefiltering
6. Kong, F., Sun, X., Ye, S.: A comparison of several algorithms for collaborative filtering in startup stage. In: Proceedings of the IEEE Networking, Sensing and Control, pp. 25–28 (March 2005)
7. Ingoo, H., Kyong, J.O., Tae, H.R.: The collaborative filtering recommendation based on SOM cluster-indexing CBR. Expert Systems with Applications 25, 413–423 (2003)

8. Hirate, Y., Yamana, H.: Generalized Sequential Pattern Mining with Item Intervals. Journal of Computers 1(3), 51–60 (2006)

9. Pei, J., Han, J., Mortazavi-Asl, B., Pinto, H., Chen, Q., Dayal, U., Hsu, M.-C.: PrefixSpan: Mining Sequential Patterns Efficiently by Prefix-Projected Pattern Growth. In: Proc. of IEEE ICDE 2001, pp. 215–224 (2001)

10. Pei, J., Han, J., Mortazavi-Asl, B., Wang, J., Pinto, H., Chen, Q., Dayal, U., Hsu, M.-C.: Mining Sequential Patterns by Pattern-Growth: The PrefixSpan Approach. Trans. of IEEE Trans. on Knowledge and Data Engineering 16(10), 1–17 (2004)

11. Zaki, M.: An Efficient Algorithm for Mining Frequent Sequences. Machine Learning 40, 31–60 (2000)

12. Ayres, J., Gehrke, J., Yiu, T., Flannick, J.: Sequential Pattern Mining using Bitmap Representation. In: Proc. Of ACM SIGKDD 2002, pp. 429–435 (2002)

13. Adomavicius, G., Tuzhilin, A.: Toward the Next Generation of Recommender Systems: A Survey of the State-of-the-Art and Possible Extensions, pp. 734–739 (2005)

Supporting Resource-Based Learning on the Web Using Automatically Extracted Large-Scale Taxonomies from Multiple Wikipedia Versions

Renato Domínguez García, Philipp Scholl, and Christoph Rensing

Multimedia Communications Lab - Technische Universität Darmstadt
64283 Darmstadt - Germany
{renato,scholl,rensing}@kom.tu-darmstadt.de
http://www.kom.tu-darmstadt.de

Abstract. CROKODIL is a platform for the support of collaborative resource-based learning with Web resources. It enables the building of learning communities in which learners annotate their relevant resources using tags. In this paper, we propose the use of automatically generated large-scale taxonomies in different languages to cope with two challenges in CROKODIL: The multilingualism of the resources, i.e. web resources are in different languages and the connectivity of the semantic network, i.e. learners do not tag resources on the same topic with identical tags. More specifically, we describe a set of features that can be used for detecting hyponymy relations from the category system of Wikipedia.

Keywords: Resource-based Learning, Hyponymy Detection, Wikipedia Mining, TEL Recommender.

1 Introduction

Learning is becoming a lifelong process due to changing working environments and decreased life-span of knowledge. Learners are responsible for their own learning processes and can decide what, when, where and how they want to learn. Self-directed learning using learning resources is called *Resource–based Learning*. In Resource-based Learning on the web, one challenge for learners is to find relevant web resources. However, in learning settings, where a community exists, there is a high probability that relevant resources were already found.

Recommender systems can be helpful in order to find these resources. However, the domain of Technology Enhanced Learning (TEL) has special requirements. For example, in TEL there are different audiences in different stages of achieved expertise needing different types of learning materials: Novices need resources giving a broad overview of the learning domain, whereas experts need resources having a very narrow scope. Further, the different levels of knowledge are reflected by the used terminology. A taxonomy of topics may be helpful to

H. Leung et al. (Eds.): ICWL 2011, LNCS 7048, pp. 314–319, 2011.

recognize general and specific topics and provide support of learners in knowledge acquisition. This goal should be achieved by deriving a taxonomy of topics using a machine learning approach with a set of features from the category system of Wikipedia. The Wikipedia category system provides pairs of related concepts whose semantic relation is unspecified [9]. Our set of features is used to differentiate between *is-a* (taxonomic) and *not-is-a* (all other kind) relations. In section 2, we describe our application scenario. Related work is presented in section 3. In section 4, we describe our proposed approach. The results of our evaluation using different languages are presented in section 5. Finally, we draw conclusions in section 6.

2   Our Application Scenario

The scenario we address with this work is self-directed, collaborative, resource-based learning on the web using a platform called CROKODIL [1]. It supports learners in acquiring knowledge based on web resources and combines functionalities for the management of resources with functionalities of social networks. Users can save web resources within CROKODIL and annotate them by assigning tags. Specifically, the concept of semantic tagging [1] is applied, where a tag is associated with its semantic meaning by the selection of a tag type from a predetermined set.

We focus on the use of taxonomies as the basis for recommender systems for tags and resources in CROKODIL: (1) Tag recommendation mechanisms ease the process of finding good tags for a resource, but also consolidating the tag vocabulary. In figure 1 this is shown by the recommendation of the related tags "vehicle" and "limousine", where user A tags some resources with "car", which is a hypernym of "limousine" and a hyponym of "vehicle". (2) Recommendation of general or specific resources of a topic: Learners need different types of resources in different stages of expertise. Novices need more general resources giving a broad overview of the topic, whereas experts need more specific information as they want to deepen their knowledge. This is shown in figure 1 as we recommend user A a resource about "vehicles" or "limousine" depending on the expert level of the user.

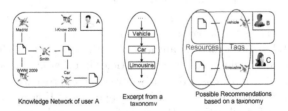

Knowledge Network of user A   Excerpt from a taxonomy   Possible Recommendations based on a taxonomy

Fig. 1. Recommendations based on a Taxonomy

We identified domain-independency, actuality and multilingualism as relevant requirements for a taxonomy to support learners. Wikipedia satisfies all these requirements: It offers more than 3'000.000 of articles (English version), more than 1000 new articles per day and Wikipedia versions for 281 languages. In the last years approaches have been mostly developed especially to work on English Wikipedia. They provide good results and large coverage, but also incomplete socio-cultural knowledge for different languages. Socio-cultural knowledge is knowledge of cultural, regional or local relevance or importance. For instance, there is no article about the resistance of the German anti-nuclear movement to the "Castor-Transport" in the English Wikipedia. In E-Learning scenarios, socio-cultural knowledge is crucial, for example, in school scenarios where students are doing homework about a regional topic. In this paper, we present a method for a language-independent recognition of hyponymy relations in Wikipedia towards taxonomy acquisition. This method can be applied to a single Wikipedia version in order to acquire large-scale taxonomies with socio-cultural knowledge. We can cope with the multilingualism of the resources in CROKODIL by using large-scale taxonomies in different languages depending on the languages used by the learners.

3   Related Work

In the last decade multiple projects have been developed to derive multilingual knowledge bases. Some of them develop manually created multilingual ontologies. An extensive overview can be found on the Web page of the Global Word-Net association[1]. However, many of the projects are still in progress, have been abandoned or are not freely available. Further, manually created knowledge bases often do not contain terminology of very specific domains and emerging topics (e.g. "iPad"), because new concepts have to be added to the ontology by a group of experts. Other approaches derive the semantic information automatically from Wikipedia. Wikipedia consists of articles that describe a specific concept. Articles are often linked to other languages using so called *interlanguage links* and belong to categories that group articles in related topics. Further, articles commonly link to other related articles by *wikilinks*.

Most of the approaches based on Wikipedia are difficult to apply in other languages as they rely additionally on external corpora (e.g. [9]) or on other knowledge bases (e.g. [10]). For a more extensive explanation of these approaches, see [5]. There are only few approaches being applied to languages other than English ([3] and [11]). However, the authors of both papers state that they could not fully use the original approach as the articles in other languages do not have the same coverage as in English. Recently developed approaches use the interlanguage links [7] to derive multilingual knowledge bases. However, interlanguage links do not exist for all articles. Because of this, Navigli et al. [6] construct a multilingual ontology using an automatic translation system and a language corpus to get translations for non-existing interlingual links. However, socio-cultural knowledge is not incorporated as the core of the approach is still the English

---

[1] http://www.globalwordnet.org/ - retrieved 01.06.2011.

Wikipedia. In contrast to this approach, MENTA [4] weights the taxonomic information contained in 127 different Wikipedia versions and applies heuristics to decide if entities in different languages belong together or not. This approach seems to be very promising, but it contains a lot of irrelevant information for CROKODIL. For example, it contains information in many foreign languages that are not used in CROKODIL.

Our goal is the development of an approach for taxonomy acquisition that work on multiple languages without major changes to the algorithm. Our approach only uses Wikipedia for this task, instead of using additional corpora or human effort. Using language-specific resources does not only hinder portability to other languages but also in some cases affects the quality and completeness of information within the knowledge base and makes the approach dependent on third parties.

4 Language-Independent Acquisition of Hierarchical Relations

In the following we present the different features we use to recognize *is-a* relations from Wikipedia. The proposed method uses a set of 14 features. We differentiate between three different feature types: Syntactic, Structural and Article-based feature types.

Syntactic features use string matching of syntactic components. `position-OfHeadFeature` uses the fact that the lexical head of two category names is a very effective method for labeling *is-a* links [9]. This feature is defined as follows:

$$
f_3(c_1, c_2) = \begin{cases} 2 & \text{if lexical head of } c_2 \text{ is at the end of } c_1 \\ 1 & \text{if lexical head of } c_2 \text{ is in the middle of } c_1 \\ 0 & \text{if lexical head of } c_2 \text{ is at the beginning of } c_1 \\ -1 & \text{else, i.e. no occurrence} \end{cases}
$$

`cooccurrenceOfWordsFeature` represents cooccurrences of words in both category names.

Structural Features exploit the structure of the category and the wikilink system. `coocurrenceFeature` returns `true` for pairs of categories which have at least one article in common [9]. `c1c2IncommingLinksFeature` and `c1c2Outgo-ingLinksFeature` count the number of articles in c_1, which have at least one (incoming or outgoing) link to any article in c_2. Their goal is to measure the strength of the relation between both categories [2]. `c1NumberOfSubcategoriesFeature`, `c1NumberOfSupercategoriesFeature`, `c2NumberOfSubcategoriesFeature` and `c2NumberOfSupercategoriesFeature` just count the number of sub- and super-categories of c_1 and c_2. Finally, `CommonWikilinksFeature` counts the number of common wikilinks between c_1 and c_2.

Article-based Features are applied to the Wikipedia articles and their content. The first sentence of an article has a special meaning for taxonomic applications as it usually contains a definition of the concept described in the article [8].

This fact is used by `definitionSentenceFeature` to recognize *is-a* relations not in the whole article, but in the first sentence. This means that if an article a belongs to a category c_1 with both having the same label, then we search for occurrences of the lexical head of c_2 in a in the first sentence of the article. If the check is positive, then this feature returns `true`. An advantage of this method is that a language-dependent search of patterns is not needed, and thus it can be applied in different languages. Further, the feature `c2Inc1Feature` counts the number of occurrences of the lexical head of c_2 in the rest of the article of c_1. `c1ArticleFeature` and `c2ArticleFeature` match c_1 and c_2 to Wikipedia articles. If c_2 can be matched to an article then we assume that this category is an existing concept, otherwise it may be a category used to structure the categories in Wikipedia.

5   Evaluation

We evaluated our approach in four different languages: three European languages (English, German and Spanish) and one language with non-latin characters (Arabic). We used a manually labelled corpus for each language to obtain results by extracting the features for each category pair and then classify the pairs automatically. Our corpus consists of 1000 randomly selected Wikipedia articles and categories. The selected Wikipedia pages were labelled manually with the relevant relations (*is-a* and *not-is-a*). For our evaluation we choose decision trees as a classifier. All classification results were subject of ten-fold cross validation. Table 1 gives an overview of our results. It shows correctly and incorrectly classified instances. On average, 82.6 % of the labelled links are labelled correctly and 17.5 % are labelled incorrectly.

Table 1. Summarized results of our approach by languages

Language	English	Spanish	German	Arabic
Correctly classified instances	3539 (81.4 %)	1841 (84.7 %)	1968 (81.8 %)	2255 (82.3 %)
Incorrectly classified instances	806 (18.6 %)	333 (15.3 %)	437 (18.2 %)	484 (17.7 %)
Total number of instances	4345	2174	2405	2739

For Precision, we obtained average results of 76.1 % and Recall was 73.2 % for *is-a* relations and for *not-is-a* relations Precision was 81.2% and Recall 87.8 %. The major source of misclassification are incorrectly classified *is-a* links. The reason is that a high number of *is-a* instances could not be matched by any feature. This led to a misclassification of these instances. One possibility to improve the results presented here is to use interlanguage links to integrate the results from different languages or to improve single features, e.g. `firstSentenceFeature` may be improved by not only matching the category name, but also synonyms contained in redirect pages.

6   Conclusion and Future Work

In this paper, we presented a scenario of resource-based learning using Web resources. We described our research prototype CROKODIL that aims to support self-directed learning and describe possible recommendations based on a taxonomy. We analyzed related work on the basis of the requirements of our scenario, identifying the need for language-independent extraction of hierarchical relations from Wikipedia in order to build a large-scale, up-to-date taxonomy in different languages. We described a robust language-independent approach which does not depend on other external sources of knowledge. Eventually, we evaluated the proposed features by measuring the accuracy of the classification of instances for each language. In future work, we plan the development of a recommendation system based on the extracted taxonomies. An open question is, whether and how learners benefit from the offering of general or more specific topics. Further, we see room for improvement of our language-independent approach: the use of semantic similarity of articles in order to recognize important links in articles and applying features over different languages are examples of proposed ideas in order to improve this approach.

Acknowledgments. This work was supported by funds from the German Federal Ministry of Education and Research under the mark 01 PF 08015 A and from the European Social Fund of the European Union (ESF). The responsibility for the contents of this publication lies with the authors.

References

1. Anjorin, M., Rensing, C., Bischoff, K., Bogner, C., Lehmann, L., Reger, A.L., Faltin, N., Steinacker, A., Lüdemann, A., Domínguez García, R.: CROKODIL - A Platform for Collaborative Resource-Based Learning. In: Kloos, C.D., Gillet, D., Crespo García, R.M., Wild, F., Wolpers, M. (eds.) EC-TEL 2011. LNCS, vol. 6964, pp. 29–42. Springer, Heidelberg (2011)
2. Chernov, S., et al.: Extracting Semantic Relationships between Wikipedia Categories. In: 1st Int. Workshop: SemWiki2006 - From Wiki to Semantic (2006)
3. Kassner, L., et al.: Acquiring a Taxonomy from the German Wikipedia. In: Proc. of the 6th Int. Conf. on Language Resources and Eval. (2008)
4. de Melo, G., Weikum, G.: MENTA: Inducing multilingual taxonomies from Wikipedia. In: Prof. of the 19th Int. Conf. on Inf. and Knowledge Manag. (2010)
5. Mendelyan, O., et al.: Mining meaning from Wikipedia. International Journal of Human-Computer Studies 67(9), 716–754 (2009)
6. Navigli, R., Ponzetto, S.P.: BabelNet: Building a very large multilingual semantic network. In: Proc. of the 48th Annual Meeting of the ACL 2010 (2010)
7. Nastase, V., et al.: WikiNet: A very large scale multi-lingual concept network. In: Proc. of the LREC 2010 (2010)
8. Nguyen, D.P.T., et al.: Subtree Mining for Relation Extraction from Wikipedia. In: Proceedings of HLT-NAACL, pp. 125–128 (2007)
9. Ponzetto, S.P., Strube, M.: Deriving a large scale taxonomy from Wikipedia. In: Proc. of the Second Conference on Empirical Methods in NLP, pp. 117–124 (2007)
10. Wu, F., Weld, D.S.: Open Information Extraction using Wikipedia. In: Proc. of the 48th Annual Meeting of the Association for Computational Linguistics (2010)
11. Yamada, L., et al.: Hypernym discovery based on distrib. sim. and hierarch. struct. In: Proc. of the 2009 Conf. on Empirical Methods in Natural Language (2009)

Association Link Network:
An Incremental Web Resources Link Model
for Learning Resources Management

Hongming Zhu, Xiangfeng Luo, Zheng Xu, and Jun Zhang

School of Computing Engineering and Science, Shanghai University,
Shanghai 200072, P.R. China
{zhm19870119,luoxf,xuzheng,zhangjun_haha}@shu.edu.cn

Abstract. Association Link Network (ALN) is proposed to establish association relations among Web resources, aiming at extending the hyperlink-based Web to an association-rich network and effectively supporting Web intelligence activities, such as Web-based learning. However, it is difficult to build the ALN one-off by direct computing since the huge number and quickly increasing learning resources on the Web. Thus, how to rapidly and accurately acquire the association relations between the new coming and existing learning resources has become a challenge in the incrementally building process of ALN. In this paper, a new algorithm is developed for incrementally updating ALN to cater for the dynamic management of learning resources increasing with time.

Keywords: Association Link Network, Web-based Learning, Incrementally Updating.

1   Introduction

The management of hyperlink-based learning resources lacks of semantics between the linked learning resources and makes user difficult to find his/her needed resources on the Web. For this issue, an effective solution is building a semantic overlay to link the learning resources with semantics, which will provides an easy and rapid management process for learning resources.

The Semantic Web [1],[2] extends the network of hyperlinked human-readable Web pages by inserting machine-readable metadata about pages and how they are related to each other, enabling automated agents to access the Web more intelligently and perform tasks on behalf of users. However, there is a fatal flaw that it cannot automatically extract semantic relations from Web resources.

Association Link Network (ALN) [3],[4], a kind of semantic link networks [5], is proposed by Luo and Xu et al. to extend the hyperlink network to an association-rich network by establishing association relations among various Web resources. Later, an incrementally building algorithm for ALN has been proposed by Xu, et al [6]. However, the authors only discuss two different strategies of finding candidate resources, while the incrementally updating cycle and the weight threshold of association relations between resources have not taken into considerations.

H. Leung et al. (Eds.): ICWL 2011, LNCS 7048, pp. 320–326, 2011.

Overall, the challenges of incrementally building ALN are as follows.

(1) How to efficiently and exactly update the association rules. Given an existing ALN, the naive way of extracting association rules is to compute the whole set of existing Web resources with the new coming Web resources, which is a difficult task since the huge number of existing resources.
(2) How to ascertain two thresholds: the threshold of association relation weight between resources and the updating cycle of incrementally updating ALN.

The rest of this paper is organized as follows. A detail discussion about the incrementally updating algorithm for building ALN is given in Section 2. Some strategies for the proposed algorithm are given in Section 3. Experimental results are discussed in Section 4. Finally, conclusions are given.

2　Incremental Updating of Association Link Network

We define the topics in an ALN as a data set $D=\{t_1,t_2,......,t_n\}$, where n means the number of topics in D and t_i is composed of keywords and association rules [4]. Thus, ALN can be defined as follows,

$$ALN = \begin{Bmatrix} aw_{11} & \cdots & aw_{1n} \\ \vdots & \ddots & \vdots \\ aw_{m1} & \cdots & aw_{nn} \end{Bmatrix} \tag{1}$$

where aw_{ij} denotes the association weight between topic t_i and topic t_j.

The index of one topic can be easily got from the matrix of ALN so that it simplifies the process of incrementally constructing ALN. We define the words in D as a set $W = \{w_1,w_2,...w_m\}$, where m means the number of words in W. Thus, keywords of topics in D used in our algorithm can also be defined as a following matrix,

$$KW(X) = \begin{Bmatrix} tkw_{11} & \cdots & tkw_{1n} \\ \vdots & \ddots & \vdots \\ tkw_{m1} & \cdots & tkw_{mn} \end{Bmatrix} \tag{2}$$

where X represents a set of topics, $tkw_{ij}=1$ means topic t_j has keyword w_i while $tkw_{ij}=0$ indicates that the topic t_j doesn't contain keyword w_i.

2.1　Incrementally Updating of Association Rules

On the basis of the traditional way of building ALN, the main challenges are focused on how to and what time to incrementally updating association rules. Association rules reflect meaningful association relations between keywords. For a given dataset D with a large number of topics and a new coming dataset d with a small number of topics, to update association rules, a native way is to extract association rules in $D \cup d$ again. Obviously, it is unadvisable that it must cost much time in this way.

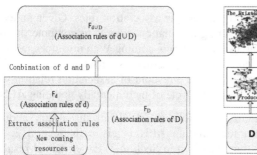
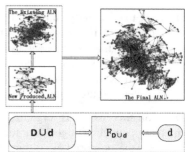

Fig. 1. An illustration of incrementally updating association rules

Fig. 2. An illustration of incrementally building ALN

In this paper, D is the set of topics denoted by ids; F_D is the set of association rules in D; a set of new coming topics denotes as d; F_d is the set of association rules of d; $F_{d\square D}$ is the set of association rules of $d\cup D$. As shown in Fig.1, for a given threshold α of association relations and a new coming set of topics d, we can know that

$$F_d\cup_D \in F_D\cup F_d \tag{3}$$

Thus, we can use $F_D\cup F_d$ to substitute for the association rules of dataset $D\cup d$.

2.2 Incrementally Updating of ALN in the Topic Level

According to the discussions above, the whole algorithm can be described as follows and illustrated by Fig.2.

Input:	D is the set of resources describe in ids; F_D is the set of association rules of D; an association weight threshold α; a new coming resources set d in a new updating cycle T;
Output:	All pairs of resources $<x, y>$, where $x \in D \cup d$, $y \in d$, $w(x, y) \geqq \alpha$ and $x<y$;

1 $S \leftarrow \Phi$;
2 $KW(d \cup D) \leftarrow KW(D) \cup \{\text{extract keywords of resources in d}\}$;
3 $Fd \cup D \leftarrow FD \cup \{\text{extract association rules of d}\}$;
4 for each $x \in D \cup d$ do
5   $A \leftarrow$ get the set of keywords of resource x from $KW(d \cup D)$;
6   for each $y \in d$ do
7   if $x \geqq y$
8   continue;
9     $B \leftarrow$ get the set of keywords of resource y from $KW(d \cup D)$;
10    $Support(x \rightarrow y) \leftarrow 0$;
11   for each $k1 \in A$ do
12   for each $k2 \in B$ do
13   if $k1 == k2$ or $k1 \rightarrow k2$ is not in $F d \cup D$;

14	continue;
15	Support(x→y)←Support(x→y)+1;
16	Support(x→y)←Support(x→y)/Size(F d $\cup$ D);
17	if Support(x→y) $\geqq$ α
18	put (x,y, Support(x→y)) in S;
19 return S;	

3 Updating Strategies

Actually, when our algorithm is put into practice, there exist two problems described as follows.

(1) The size of dataset d is closely related to updating cycle, short updating cycle will lead to small size of d.
(2) When using $F_D \cup F_d$ to substitute for $F_{d\square D}$, some noises may be brought in the set of association rules.

3.1 Instant Strategy

It is very important for Web-based learning that the users need to know the newest learning resources or information in time. Thus, instant updating strategy is introduced into our algorithm.

Herein, instant updating means that updating cycle should be fixed as short as possible so that there will be nearly no delay of information users wanted. We can use the number of topics to indicate the updating cycle. As a matter of fact, we will start the instant updating strategy as long as a new topic comes. That is to say, we choose one topic as the updating cycle of instant updating strategy in our algorithm.

Instant updating strategy ensures the newest learning resource can be added into ALN as soon as possible.

3.2 Global Strategy

The main idea of global updating strategy can be described as follows: d_i is a dataset of new coming resources in the instant updating cycle i, thus, the new coming resources in a global updating cycle can be described as follows,

$$d=d_1 \cup d_2 \cup d_3 \cup \ldots \cup d_k, \tag{4}$$

where k indicates that there are k instant updating cycles contained in a global updating cycle.

From the above discussion, we can easily infer that if k is bigger; the size of d is also bigger. Therefore, we need to know how to fix the global updating cycle (i.e, the number of topics d contains) so as to ensure the precision of the discovery of users' interesting resources for users' queries.

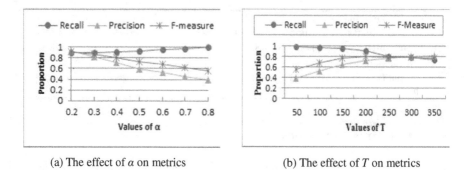

(a) The effect of α on metrics   (b) The effect of T on metrics

Fig. 3. Experiment results of our method

4   Experimental Evaluations

In this section, we carry out experiments on a real dataset (about 1000 Web hot topics containing 300000 Webpages totally) to evaluate our algorithm by comparing it with traditional method of building ALN in topic level.

4.1   Experimental Setting

To evaluate our algorithm of incrementally building ALN in topic level, the metrics [7], Precision, Recall and F-measure are employed.

4.2   Experiment Results

In our algorithm, there is a parameter α which indicates the lowest weight of association relations between two association topics, the "weak" relationships will be pruned if the weight is smaller than α. We evaluate different values of α on Precision, Recall and F-measure to find a best value of α for the following experiments.

In our measurement of α, we acquire the average Precision, Recall and F-measure by compute that of each certain topic. Fig. 3(a) shows the effect of α on Precision, Recall and F-measure. According to Fig. 3(a), we find that as α increases, Recall increases while the Precision and F-measure decrease. Logically, the highest value of F-measure is obtained when $\alpha=0.2$ so that we can set $\alpha=0.2$ for the best value of α. However, if the value α is too small, there are a large number of relationships, whose weights are larger than α (but the relationship is still actually "weak"). Therefore, we chose $\alpha=0.4$ to be the best value of α at which level the Precision, Recall and F-measure are still in a high level.

After setting the value of α, the parameter T in incrementally updating algorithm should be tested then. Because a long updating cycle results in a big size of d, we can use the number of topics in d to denote the updating cycle T in our algorithm. Similar to the setting of α, we test several values of T to evaluate the effect of T on Precision,

Recall and F-measure for setting a best value of T. As Fig. 3(b) shows, F-measure fetch the highest value at the point T = 200. So, we set T=200 as the best value of T, which is set as the global updating cycle in our algorithm.

When α and T are set respectively, the incremental updating of ALN in topic level can be carried out then. Because that there are limited topics (less than T) in each updating cycle, the time consumption of each updating cycle must be satisfactory or acceptable.

In conclusion, after a proper setting of α and T (e.g. α=0.4 and T=200), our new algorithm implements incrementally building ALN with an acceptable time consumption and without much losing on precision and recall. In another word, the incremental mechanism of our proposed algorithm achieves better performance for incrementally building ALN in topic level.

5   Conclusions

In this paper, a new algorithm for incrementally building ALN is developed for management the learning resources in the Web. The experimental results show that our algorithm maintains a high accuracy and low time consumption. The main contributions of this paper are as follows:

(1) An algorithm for incrementally building ALN is developed to manage the learning resources, which largely reduces the time consumption of the discovery of users' interesting resources.

(2) Instant updating strategy has been proposed for ensuring the newest learning resource to be added into ALN as soon as possible. Global updating strategy has been proposed for ensuring the precision of the discovery of users' interesting resources. Based on these two strategies, users could quickly get what they want in his/her learning process on the Web.

Acknowledgments. Research work is partly supported by the key basic research program of Shanghai under grant no. 09JC1406200, by the National Science Foundation of China under grant nos. 91024012, 61071110, and 90612010, Students Science Foundation of Shanghai University (grants SHUCX111001), and by the Shanghai Leading Academic Discipline Project under grant no. J50103.

References

1. Berners-Lee, T., Hendler, J., Lassila, O.: The semantic web - a new form of web content that is meaningful to computers will unleash a revolution of new possibilities. Scientific American 284, 34–43 (2001)
2. Schwartz, D.G.: From open IS semantics to the Semantic Web: the road ahead. IEEE Intell.Syst. 18, 52 (2003)
3. Luo, X.F., Xu, Z., Yu, J., Liu, F.: Discovery of associated topics for the intelligent browsing. In: Pro. 1st IEEE Int. Conf. Ubi-Media Computing and Workshops, pp. 119–331 (2008)

4. Luo, X.F., Xu, Z., Yu, J., Chen, X.: Building Association Link Network for Semantic Link on Web Resources. IEEE Transactions on Automation Science and Engineering 8, 482–494 (2011)
5. Zhuge, H.: Autonomous semantic link network model for the Knowledge Grid. Concurrency and Computation: Practice and Experience 7, 1065–1085 (2007)
6. Xu, Z., Luo, X.F., Lu, W.J.: Association Link Network: An Incremental Semantic Data Model on Organizing Web Resources. In: 15th International Conference on Parallel and Distributed Systems, pp. 793–798 (2009)
7. Hasegawa, T., Sekine, S., Grishman, R.: Discovering Relations among Named Entities from Large Corpora. In: Proceeding of ACL 2004 (2004)

Recommendation in E-Learning Social Networks

Pierpaolo Di Bitonto, Teresa Roselli, and Veronica Rossano

Department of Informatics, University of Bari "Aldo Moro"
Via Orabona, 4 - 70125 Bari, Italy
{dibitonto,roselli,rossano}@di.uniba.it

Abstract. In the past years learning has evolved from face-to-face to computer-supported learning, and we are now entering yet a new phase. The (r)evolution that yielded the knowledge transforming the Web 1.0 into Web 2.0 is now coming to e-learning contexts. Social media are the technologies most widely used to share educational contents, to find colleagues, discussion groups, and so on. But while in the Web 1.0 the most "time-spending" activity was to find suitable learning content, in the Web 2.0 era the search process is focused on different types of resources. This paper proposes a recommendation method that, by using a clustering algorithm, is able to support users during the selection steps. The recommendation is based on the tags defined by the network learners and the items to be recommended include not only contents but also social connections that could enrich the user's learning process.

Keywords: Social network, recommendation systems, clustering algorithm.

1   Introduction

In the last few years, the web has undergone a radical change that has allowed users to become producers (prosumers [1]) of the contents delivered. In this new scenario, the interactions among users are defining new participation models that are contributing to offer a knowledge creation open process. As stated in [2], Knowledge Management and Learning Management can be viewed as two sides of the same coin, so the multidimensional (r)evolution that is involving the knowledge creation process is also affecting learning processes. These are going from a top-down to a bottom-up model [2], leading to a paradigm shift of social interaction from a knowledge-push to a knowledge-pull model, where users are at the heart of the knowledge creation/learning process [3]. The current research trend is addressing the question whether the Web 2.0 could be used effectively in educational environments. In particular, much study has focused on how the social media can transform the effectiveness of social relationships into learning effectiveness [4, 5, 6]. The main drawbacks in using social media in educational contexts are the information overflow on the web [5] and the fact that the entertainment traits may take priority over the educational objectives. The main characteristic of social software, in fact, is to allow users to share as much media, news, links, contacts, and so on, as they wish. The more resources and users there are in the network, the more important the network. Thus, in order to promote the successful use of social software in educational

H. Leung et al. (Eds.): ICWL 2011, LNCS 7048, pp. 327–332, 2011.
© Springer-Verlag Berlin Heidelberg 2011

contexts it is necessary to use the computational intelligence to personalize the delivery of resources and services, as already occurs in knowledge management. This point of view is the basis of the current trend of research, which aims at bringing together the findings in knowledge management and in e-learning in order to better support the use of social media in users' knowledge creation processes. The most common fields investigated by researchers in both areas are recommender systems and the cluster theory in order to support the user in the selection process. In this context some solutions have been proposed. In [7] the authors underline that the design of an e-learning recommender system is quite different from that of a recommender system for other domains. In the e-learning context, in fact, a recommender system has to improve the educational provision in order to abbreviate the time spent to find suitable resources for the user's learning style and/or objectives. In [8] a novel social network mining scheme is presented, aimed at recommending appropriate learning partners to the individual learner. Since social interactions often affect the effectiveness of the learning activities, the authors explore the active and interactive relationships among learners and propose a recommender technique serving to enhance the performance of the individual in cooperative e-learning settings. In [9], a multi-agent mechanism is used to manage and organize learners and groups. Unlike the first approach, this uses clustering algorithms to group learners according to their preferences and learning behavior. Semantic web techniques have also been used to group people in a learning social network [10]; in this case an extension of the most popular FOAF (Friend of a Friend) [11] ontology has been proposed, adapting it to the learning context. The solution adopted in this research is the definition to join a recommendation method with a clustering algorithm in order to recommend both didactic resources and learner groups, and to facilitate the learning process. The selection of items (contents, users, groups) to be recommended is based on the tags defined by other network learners. The tags are grouped in clusters using a clustering algorithm, then the recommendation method measures the proximity of each item to the clusters and according to this measure it builds the list of recommended items. The two main differences between our research and previous works are: the clustering and recommendation processes are based on tag clouds assigned by users to all the resources in the social e-learning network, and both processes are general enough to be used with all kinds of resources, i.e. information/contents, users and discussion groups. The paper is structured as follows: section 2 describes the main features of the implemented social e-learning network; section 3 presents the recommender technique and the clustering algorithm integrated in the social e-learning network; finally, some conclusions are outlined.

2   The Social E-Learning Network

The basic idea is to improve the involvement skills of the LMS by means of the sharing and enhancement of both the knowledge and the experiences of all the social network participants. It is for this reason that in designing the social e-learning network a "selfish" approach has been used. Rather than working on the whole connection in the network, the social network is focused on a local viewpoint, describing only individual dynamics. In particular, the social network is customized to the single user's needs, modeling only those connections that may be fruitful from the individual point of view, and depicting only nodes that are not more than two steps distant from it at most. The aim of this modeling is to analyze the social dynamics of the single user, in order to discover the role played in the social network by the set of her/his relationships. Another basic idea underlying our approach is the group of interest, which is a step beyond the egocentric network because it establishes an interaction among users who are not friends but who can link up with each other through the membership. This is the basic idea of the common social network, but in this context it has been further developed in order to allow each single social network user to engage in knowledge sharing even with people that s/he does not directly know.

Fig. 1. The user's dashboard shows the Group, People and the LO recommender widgets

Starting from these two abstract concepts (an egocentric network and groups) the recommendation model has been implemented. It aims to suggest new learning activities, users, and discussion groups according to the user's learning and knowledge needs. The social e-learning network has been implemented using Elgg [12], an open source social network engine. Elgg has supplied all the basic functionalities of a social network: blog, forum, chat, dashboard, friendship, sharing content, evaluation of contents, tagging, and so forth. Unlike a generic social network, a social e-learning network should, like any learning environment, provide a LO management component. The functionalities offered allow the didactic resources to be inserted, described and sought. In order to facilitate resource sharing and seeking they are described using both metadata and tags. As regards the metadata, a set of specifications named EXM E-teaching eXperience Metadata) [13] has been used in order to facilitate sharing of both the didactic resources and learning/teaching experiences. Therefore, these metadata allow the social e-learning network users to search for LOs starting from their didactic content, but also from the contexts in which they were used, thus refining the level of sharing. At the same time, the tags are used by the recommender module in order to suggest the didactic resources best suited to the user's needs (server push), and are used during the structured search process (made using the structured metadata) to list the results in order according to the user's interests (client pull). The recommender module has been designed to be general enough to be applied to any type of items available in the social e-learning network. It makes recommendations according to the tag clouds: LOs, discussion groups and social connections. Fig. 1 shows the user's dashboard where the three recommendation widgets contain the suggestions of the three different types of items.

3   Recommendation Module

The recommendation method implemented is content-based. Unlike what usually happens, in the content-based method a clustering technique has been used to define similarities among items described using users' tags. Thus, the recommendation technique consists of two different steps: the neighborhood estimation and the prediction of the user's likely interests. The precondition for the recommender technique is that the tag similarity matrix should be calculated to define the semantic distance among tags of the user's preferences. Let us consider: $R_i < t_1, t_2, \ldots t_n >$ the tag list describing the resource R_i (where t_j is the j-th tag chosen by the user sharing the resource); $U_k < (w(t_1), w(t_2), \ldots, w(t_n)) >$ the list that describes user k 's interest in the tags t_j. The function $w(t_i)$ represents the level of user's interest in the tag t_j. All the tags used to describe the resources in the social network are represented using a matrix where the columns list the resources and the rows contain the tags. For example, if in the system we had n tags and m resources, the matrix M will contain for each couple (i,j) $M_{i,j}$ is 0 if t_i has not been implied for the resource R_j, 1 otherwise.

For the neighborhood estimation the Shared Near Neighbor (SNN) clustering algorithm was chosen. In this algorithm the similarity between two points is "confirmed" by their common (shared) near neighbors [14]. The SNN is based on the density of points in a defined area. This means that for each point of a cluster, the neighborhood of a specific radius should contain a minimum number of points, that is the density of an area should exceed a defined threshold. The SNN algorithm needs three input parameters:

- K, that is the number of the neighboring points;
- ε, that is the radius that defines the area of the point in which the neighbourhood can be founded (ε-neighborhood)
- Minpts is the minimum number of points (neighbours) that should be in the ε-neighborhood in order to consider the point a core-point of the cluster.

Using this similarity measure, the density of each point can be calculated as the number of near nodes that have a higher or equal level of similarity to a density threshold. The highest density points, named core-points, are defined according to the Minpts value. SNN, by basing the similarity among nodes on the number of nearest common nodes, makes it possible to map clusters of tags that are strictly linked. The strategy used to make the prediction of the items best suited to the user's preferences is shown in Fig. 2. It considers the proximity of the user to the defined cluster and at the same time the proximity of the resource to this same cluster. Thus, if the user and the resource share the same cluster the resource may be recommended to the user. The proximity of both the user and the resource is the Euclidean distance between the tags that describe each of them and the core-point of the cluster. The defined technique has some main advantages: the lack of coupling between the user and the recommended item reduces the cold-start problem, a typical issue in a content-based method. Moreover, it makes the recommender strategy general enough to be applied to any type of resource, such as friendships, or discussion groups. Another strong point of the defined technique is that it allows implicit relationships among tags to be discovered. In this way the recommendation process is able to suggest a greater number of resources, sometimes of unexpected type, than those suggested only by comparing the item vectors, U (the and R, in the typical collaborative approach.

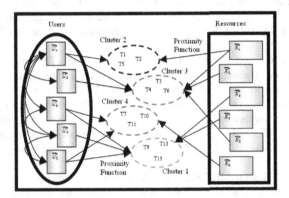

Fig. 2. Prediction of the user's likely interests

4   Conclusions

We are witnessing a multidimensional revolution from a top-down to a bottom-up model where the knowledge and learning coming from community members who create and share resources are making learning processes more open and dynamic. A social e-learning network does not replace a LMS, that is a system in which learning takes place in a formal way whereby the student receives the material created by the teacher, but is an environment where the benefits of informal learning can be enjoyed, and more active learner participation is allowed. The democratic structure of the social networks allows the constraints of the LMS to be overcome, thanks to offering users the chance to contribute to the knowledge and experience creation process, regardless of their role in the learning process. In any case, the social network promotes the role of users and groups to that of resources that can convey new knowledge, improving the time spent on finding the right resource. For this reason the research work proposes a solution that combines an advanced search engine which uses specialized metadata to describe learning contexts, with a recommender method which is able to suggest resources (contents, users, discussion groups) using clusters of tags associated to them. Currently, an experimentation of the proposed e-learning social network is ongoing, aimed at supporting knowledge and experience sharing among the families of type 1 diabetes patients.

Acknowledgments. This work was supported by Regione Puglia under grant Distributed Production as Innovative System (DIPIS) - PS092. We would like to thank our student, Antonio Barile, who allows the idea described in this paper to be implemented in his master thesis degree.

References

1. Giurgiu, L., Bârsan, G.: The prosumer – core and consequence of the web 2.0 era. Revista de Informatica Sociala V(9) (June 2008)
2. Chatti, M.A., Jarke, M., Frosch-Wilke, D.: The future of e-learning: a shift to knowledge networking and social software. Int. J. Knowledge and Learning 3(4/5), 404–420 (2007)
3. Naeve, A.: The human semantic web – shifting from knowledge push to knowledge pull. International Journal of Semantic Web and Information Systems (IJSWIS) 1(3), 1–30 (2005)
4. Tian, S.W., Yu, A.Y., Vogel, D., Chi-Wai Kwok, R.: The impact of online social networking on learning: a social integration perspective. International Journal of Networking and Virtual Organisations 8(3/4), 264–280 (2011)
5. Frosch-Wilke, D., Amine Chatti, M., Jarke, M.: The future of e-learning: a shift to knowledge networking and social software. Int. J. Knowledge and Learning 3(4/5) (2007)
6. Cho, H., Gay, G., Davidson, B., Ingraffea, A.: Social networks, communication styles, and learning performance in a CSCL community. Computers and Education 49(2), 309–329 (2007)
7. Drachsler, H., Hummel, H.G.K., Koper, R.: Personal recommender systems for learners in lifelong learning networks: the requirements, techniques and model. Int. J. Learning Technology 3(4), 404–423 (2008)
8. Chen, C.-M., Hong, C.-M., Chang, C.-C.: Mining interactive social network for recommending appropriate learning partners in a Web-based cooperative learning environment. In: IEEE Conference on Cybernetics and Intelligent Systems, pp. 642–647. IEEE Press (2008)
9. Yang, F., Han, P., Shen, R.-M., Kraemer, B.J., Fan, X.: Cooperative Learning in Self-Organizing E-Learner Communities Based on a Multi-Agents Mechanism. In: Gedeon, T(T.) D., Fung, L.C.C. (eds.) AI 2003. LNCS (LNAI), vol. 2903, pp. 490–500. Springer, Heidelberg (2003)
10. Ounnas, A., Liccardi, I., Davis, H.C., Millard, D., White, S.A.: Towards a semantic modeling of learners for social networks. In: SW-EL, Workshop at the AH 2006, Dublin, Ireland, pp. 1–6 (2006)
11. Friend-of-a-Friend project, http://www.foaf-project.org/
12. ELGG, Social Network Engine Open Source, http://www.elgg.org/
13. Roselli, T., Rossano, V.: Describing learning scenarios to share teaching experiences. In: Int. Conference on Information Technology Based Higher Education and Training (ITHET), July 10-13, pp. 180–186. IEEE Computer Society Press, Sydney (2006)
14. Ertoz, L., Steinback, M., Kumar, V.: Finding Clusters of Different Sizes, Shapes, and Density in Noisy, High Dimensional Data. In: Second SIAM International Conference on Data Mining, San Francisco, CA, USA (2003)

Author Index